LEICESTER

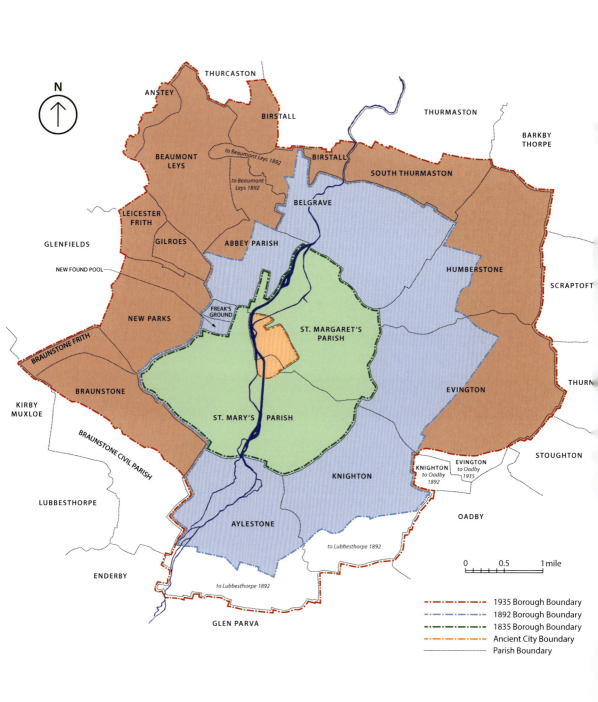

N

THURCASTON

ANSTEY

BIRSTALL

BEAUMONT LEYS

BIRSTALL

THURMASTON

BARKBY THORPE

to Beaumont Leys 1892

to Beaumont Leys 1892

SOUTH THURMASTON

BELGRAVE

LEICESTER FRITH

GLENFIELDS

GILROES

ABBEY PARISH

HUMBERSTONE

SCRAPTOFT

NEW FOUND POOL

FREAK'S GROUND

ST. MARGARET'S PARISH

NEW PARKS

BRAUNSTONE FRITH

EVINGTON

THURN

BRAUNSTONE

KIRBY MUXLOE

ST. MARY'S   PARISH

BRAUNSTONE CIVIL PARISH

LUBBESTHORPE

KNIGHTON

KNIGHTON to Oadby 1892

EVINGTON to Oadby 1935

STOUGHTON

OADBY

AYLESTONE

to Lubbesthorpe 1892

ENDERBY

to Lubbesthorpe 1892

GLEN PARVA

0   0.5   1 mile

— ·· — ·· —   1935 Borough Boundary
— ·· — ·· —   1892 Borough Boundary
— ·· — ·· —   1835 Borough Boundary
— ·· — ·· —   Ancient City Boundary
· · · · · · ·   Parish Boundary

Leicester:
A Modern History

RICHARD RODGER
AND REBECCA MADGIN
EDITORS

Leicester: A Modern History

Copyright © individual contributors, 2016

First edition

Published by
Carnegie Publishing Ltd
Chatsworth Road,
Lancaster LA1 4SL
www.carnegiepublishing.com

British Library Cataloguing-in-Publication data
A catalogue record for this book is available from the British Library

ISBN 978-1-85936-231-0 *hardback*
ISBN 978-1-85936-224-2 *softback*

Designed, typeset and originated by Carnegie Publishing
Print managed and manufactured by Jellyfish Solutions

Contents

Part II Reinventing Leicester

Foreword

by Sir Peter Soulsby, Leicester City Mayor

I AM delighted to welcome this book that explores the diverse and broad History of Leicester over the last 200 years. It is an important contribution to our understanding of the cultural fabric of the city. It brings the place in which we live into sharper focus. It explains the legacy of the past and how that inheritance informs who we are as individuals and as a city. From the Roman walls to Richard III – from its industrial growth to its re-invention as a multi-cultural and diverse centre – Leicester's layers of history provide much to inspire us for the future.

Richard Rodger, Rebecca Madgin and their contributors have lived and worked in the city for many years. Their research combined with their detailed knowledge of the city reveals to us a vibrant city that is both comfortable with challenges, and responsive to them. The authors explore the radical, independent and confident culture of an industrial city, and the efforts of civic and religious leaders, clubs and societies, businesses and institutions to put Leicester on the map.

The book particularly charts the changes that the city underwent during the nineteenth and twentieth centuries. It considers how these social, cultural, economic and political transformations re-shaped the look and feel of Leicester. Through the generations Leicester has enjoyed the vibrancy of new customs and cultures as immigrants from dozens of different countries have settled in the city, making it one of the most diverse in Europe. In doing so, the city has changed and adapted and added further layers to its proud history. The book brings these changes together and challenges us to ask what Leicester means to us today and what is the identity of a city built on plurality. Above all the book demonstrates that Leicester is a quietly confident city built on firm historical foundations that Leicester citizens of the twenty-first century can feel proud of.

Acknowledgements

PATIENCE, it is said, is a virtue. So our contributors must be very virtuous. Each has been extremely patient while this book has been in preparation, and they deserve a particular word of editorial thanks for their forbearance. Each contributor has brought out their special knowledge of the City of Leicester and generously provided valuable insights into the particularity and elusive identity of Leicester. We know it is better for their efforts, and for the extensive research that underpins their contributions.

This book has a strong connection with the Centre for Urban History at the University of Leicester both through the authors themselves and also through the many former Masters and Doctoral students. Among them are Helen Clements, Margaret Damant, Peter Jones, Denise McHugh, Ned Newitt, John Smith, Liz Tacey, and Neil Wood who though they do not appear in the list of authors have contributed important research that has found its way indirectly into the pages of this book. Sally Harthshorne's ability to track down obscure references to little-known historical events proved invaluable. That community of graduate students is gratefully acknowledged for the research environment to which they contributed.

To colleagues and friends based in Leicester who have helped to develop the book we would also like to extend our thanks. Sarah Levitt, Sophie Noon, Nisha Popat, Anne Provan and Jenny Timothy proved that the city's history and heritage has a bright future, and members of the Leicester City Mayor's Heritage Partnership provided different insights in to the management and protection of Leicester's built heritage. Thanks are due to Richard Courtney for helping to 'Build Shared Heritages', the first of a number of Arts and Humanities Research Council and Heritage Lottery Fund projects that helped to open up new vistas on Leicester's history.

One person who has contributed to several chapters is Colin Hyde. His wonderful images enrich the book and he has generously shared his encyclopaedic knowledge of Leicester buildings and sites. Colin's tireless energy as oral history guru for so many in the city and county is matched by his long-standing commitment to the East Midlands Oral History Archive (EMOHA). Malcolm Noble's diligence, care and precise eye for detail in clarifying images were also invaluable during the latter stages of the book.

Special thanks are also due to the archivists at the Record Office for Leicester, Leicestershire and Rutland (ROLLR), and in particular to Adam

Goodwin for his ever-willing assistance, and also to Simon Dixon in the Special Collections of Leicester University Library for facilitating access to the resources held there in conjunction with the JISC-funded Manufacturing Pasts project. At a late stage in the process, and another reason to thank contributors for their patience, was the generous access we obtained to the photographic collections of Leicester City Council. To Aboobakar Rashid particularly, and to Sally Coleman we are indebted for finding, scanning and sending images. This was facilitated by the City Mayor, Sir Peter Soulsby, whose enthusiasm for the publication, and Leicester's history generally, was unwavering, built as it is on a recognition of the relevance of the past for the future of the city.

Through the combined efforts of these individuals to provide illustrative material, as well as those of Anna Goddard and Alistair Hodge at Carnegie Publishing, the price of the book is more affordable. That was always our intention and to them all we are most grateful, as we are for the generous contribution towards publication costs from the Marc Fitch Fund, and from the University of Edinburgh. Readers are much in their debt. Finally, the lively engagement of local history groups within the city has been a source of consistent stimulation and enjoyment. Their interest in the city's history has enriched the process of discovering the many facets of Leicester's past revealed in this book. With them, and others, the future of Leicester's history is in safe hands.

Richard Rodger and Rebecca Madgin
July 2016

About the authors

Laura Balderstone completed her Ph.D. (2010) with a study of suburbanisation and associational activity in post-war Leicester. She studied at the Centre for Urban History, and then was Research Associate for the 'Mapping Memory' project in Liverpool which explored the changing nature of the waterfront community after 1950, using oral history, museum objects and visual sources to create an interactive website and documentary film. Her current research interests include associational life, suburbanisation and community engagement in twentieth century Britain, and in 2013 she was appointed as Lecturer in Modern British History at the University of Liverpool.

Siobhan Begley is an honorary research fellow of the Centre for Urban History and a tutor at the Vaughan Centre for Lifelong Learning at the University of Leicester. She completed a Ph.D. at the University of Leicester. Her particular interests are associational life, civic celebration and the local social calendar in the urban environment during the late nineteenth and early twentieth centuries. Siobhan Begley is also the author of a history of Leicester entitled *The Story of Leicester* (2013).

Shane Ewen is Senior Lecturer in Social and Cultural History at Leeds Beckett University. He is the author of *Fighting Fires: Creating the British Fire Service, 1800–1978* (2010) and of numerous journal articles on aspects of urban governance and urban disaster reform. Shane Ewen is a co-editor of *Urban History*, and author of *What is Urban History?* He has spent several years in Leicester completing his MA, Ph.D. and ESRC postdoctoral fellowship at the Centre for Urban History.

Lucy Faire is an Honorary Fellow in the Centre for Urban History and a Lecturer in Humanities and Arts in the Vaughan Centre for Lifelong Learning, (both University of Leicester). Her main research interest is home and family life in the twentieth century. Her central approach is to examine how people interacted with their environment and with each other, and to analyse people's subjective views of this experience. She is also interested in the history of leisure and is currently researching people's experiences of, and behaviour in, Nottingham and Leicester's city centres in the mid-twentieth century. She has co-authored *The Place of the Audience: Cultural Geographies of Film Consumption* (2003) and was co-editor of *Research Methods for History* (2012).

Simon Gunn is Professor of Urban History at the University of Leicester, and co-editor of the Cambridge University Press journal, *Urban History*. His books include *History and Cultural Theory* (2006) and co-author of *The Peculiarities of Modernity in Imperial Britain* (2011). He is the author of a series of recent articles on planning and industrial decline in post–1945 Britain and the impact of mass automobility on everyday life. With Susan Townsend he is running a Leverhulme-funded project on motor cities in Britain and Japan, *c.*1955–73.

Joanna Herbert is an oral historian whose research has focused on low paid migrant workers in London and the South Asian Diaspora, including the experiences of Ugandan Asians. She held an ESRC postdoctoral fellowship at the Centre for Urban History, Leicester, and then a Leverhulme Early Career Fellowship in Geography at Queen Mary, University of London where she also a Research Fellow. She was awarded the Oral History Association Book Award (2009) for *Negotiating Boundaries in the City: Migration, Ethnicity and Gender in Britain.*

Colin Hyde is a researcher and outreach officer at the East Midlands Oral History Archive at the Centre for Urban History, University of Leicester, and has been recording oral histories in Leicestershire for the past 25 years. His local history books include *Walnut Street: Past, Present and Future* (1994) and *TH Wathes and Co Ltd: A Hundred Years of Service* (2004). Other publications include journal articles, websites, videos, and educational materials covering a wide range of subjects. Recent work has looked at both migration into Leicester and the city's industrial past.

Rebecca Madgin is Senior Lecturer in Urban Development and Management at the University of Glasgow. Her research interests include the economic and emotional values of the historic built environment. This interest developed while an MA and Ph.D. student at the University of Leicester, and as a Lecturer at the Centre for Urban History, Leicester. She has conducted in-depth research on the city, working with local community organisations and creative industries, as well as with Leicester City Council.

James Moore recently returned to Leicester University as Lecturer in Modern British History after a spell in the 1990s attached to the Centre for Urban History, a period in London as Deputy Director of the Centre for Metropolitan History, and a lectureship at the British University in Egypt. His main interests are in the area of urban history and the political culture of Britain and her empire, specifically on popular politics and urban governance, heritage and cultural institutions – topics on which he has published widely.

David Nash is Professor of History at Oxford Brookes University. His early work was on aspects or secularism and nonconformity in the Victorian urban environment with particular relevance to the city of Leicester. He was co-editor of *Leicester in the 20th Century* and has moved on to write widely on aspects of religious history in Britain in the nineteenth and twentieth centuries – most notably blasphemy in national and international contexts. He has recently written a history of religious narratives in twentieth-century Britain and is now working on a book on secular narratives over the same period.

Richard Rodger co-edited *Leicester in the 20th Century* (1993), wrote a prize-winning book, *The Transformation of Edinburgh* (2001), and recently co-authored another work on Edinburgh entitled *Insanitary City* (2013). He retains strong links with Leicester where he was Professor and Director of the Centre for Urban History, Director of the East Midlands Oral History Archive. He is Professor of Economic and Social History at Edinburgh University and was elected a Fellow of the Academy of Social Sciences in 2004.

Julie Rugg is a Senior Research Fellow in Social Policy and Social Work at the University of York. Her research interests include the history of burial and policy relating to the management of death in the UK and Europe from the 18th century to the present day. Recent publications include *Churchyard and Cemetery: Tradition and Modernity in Rural North Yorkshire* (2013).

Dieter Schott is Professor for Modern History at the TU Darmstadt, Germany, and was previously Professor for the History of Urban Planning at the Centre for Urban History, Leicester (2000–04). His fields of research are 19th and 20th century urban and environmental history, and he is particularly interested in the history of rivers in relation to cities. His latest book is a survey of European urbanization from the Middle Ages to the 20th century, *Die europaeische Urbanisierung 1000–2000* (2014). He is chairman of the German Society for Urban History (GSU) and principal editor of the urban history journal *Informationen zur modernen Stadtgeschichte*.

Stephen Wagg graduated from Leicester University in 1970 and received his doctorate from the University of Surrey in 2004. He is currently a professor in the Carnegie Faculty of Leeds Beckett University. He writes regularly on the politics of sport, of childhood and of popular culture. His latest books are all co-edited: *Sounds and the City: Music, Place and Globalization* (2014); *Thatcher's Grandchildren? Politics and Childhood in the Twenty-First Century* (2014); and *An Introduction to Leisure Studies: Principles and Practice* (2014).

John Welshman was educated at the Universities of York and Oxford, and is Senior Lecturer in the Department of History at Lancaster University. He spent the period 1993–96 attached to the Centre for Urban History, Leicester, where he worked on the Wellcome Trust project 'Public Health in Twentieth-century Leicester'. His research interests are in the history of public policy in twentieth-century Britain on which he has published widely. His most recent book is *Underclass: A History of the Excluded Since 1880* (2013).

Preface

R EADERS might ask: why produce a book about the social history of Leicester?' Apart from the obvious answer – there has been a great deal of research and writing in the last twenty years since the Council-sponsored book *Leicester in the Twentieth Century* was published – the reality is that the identity of Leicester remains something of a mystery. Compared to other British cities, deeply researched publications on Leicester are still few in number, and some of the research that has been undertaken is hidden away in unpublished theses and scholarly journals not easily accessed by the public. So a stocktaking is overdue.

So the question remains: what sort of place is Leicester and how has it evolved? For researchers and the Leicester public alike, conveying the character of the city is not the easiest task. Many cities are closely identified with striking images, often iconic buildings. Internationally the Empire State building and the clustered Manhattan skyline is synonymous with New York; the Eiffel Tower, Brandenburg Gate, Tower Bridge, and Guggenheim, with Paris, Berlin, London and Bilbao, and Sydney Opera House with … Sydney, of course. Nearer to home, Birmingham's Bull Ring and York cathedral are synonymous with those places. As a recent bus shelter advert in Edinburgh proclaimed superimposed on an image of the Castle: 'You wouldn't visit New York without visiting the Empire State Building.' Which is as if to say: "if you miss this building [Edinburgh Castle] you haven't visited the city and you can't talk about it without visiting its most prominent icon." Smaller towns practise the same. A casual survey of postcards on sale in Chester, Ripon, Carlisle or Norwich, or indeed almost any town, confirms a focus on a distinctive ancient building or street promoted as the identifier of place. Such postcard images are compressions of space and time and serve only to lodge places in the public consciousness. Google provides the contemporary instrument for the same purpose. However, though such visual constructions of place may satisfy visitors, they are shallow representations of place as residents know them since images cannot capture the dynamics of social relations and community structures that for residents are the realities of place.

While the Clock Tower, Town Hall Square, New Walk, Lutyens war memorial, Turkey Café and the Market Place are identifiable physical features for Leicester residents, and provide fine postcard images in the process, the attachment to places within the city is more subtle, complex and longstanding. While Leicester residents could probably put most of these places on a map, their spatial reference framework is much more local, more intimately connected to their neighbourhood, with mental maps constructed around daily patterns and sensory experiences – the trek to the school playground, the winter wind in the bus shelter, the buskers in the (now defunct) underpass, mindless musak in the supermarket or GP's waiting room, the strident voice of a Leicester market trader or Big Issue vendor, the post-Christmas returns queue, the buzz amongst the crowd leaving the King Power Stadium or Welford Road, or on the last bus back after a night out. These sights and sounds and smells of the city in the twenty-first century are products of cumulative layers of history. We are where we are in Leicester as a result of developments in the past, and understanding them aids us in understanding the present, and influences the way we approach the future. What we choose in the future to preserve of the past is defined by what we understand about the historical journey of Leicester and its inhabitants.

Leicester: A Modern History is in two parts with a dividing line around World War II. Both parts are introduced by a survey essay (chapters 1 and 8). These surveys provide a context for the individual chapters in which authors describe and analyse particular historical aspects of Leicester that contribute to layers of meaning that make the city the place it is now. *Leicester: A Modern History* explores the social, economic and cultural forces that have shaped the city. It does so in two interconnected ways. Some chapters consider long run changes in the city by reviewing developments in politics and institutions, rituals and ceremonies, immigration, class relations, environmental conditions, and employment patterns. Arguably every other British city has been affected by similar influences, but it is the ways these elements have developed and been combined in differing permutations that gives Leicester its distinctive identity. These longitudinal studies are intersected by more focused chapters that provide in-depth understanding of moments in time that reveal particular characteristics of the city – the Leicester pageant; cemeteries and dealing with death; the music scene in the 1950s; the town planning vision for post-war Leicester of Konrad Smigelski; the Liberty Building and the loss of an iconic building in the 1990s; and local club memberships in the era of the TV and suburban sprawl. Each chapter is illustrated to provide a visual version of the developments discussed and to give a sense of spatial change that takes account of how the textures of Leicester have changed as represented in the mass, density, materials and colours of the built environment.

So the book seeks to unravel the historical journey – a journey from about 1800 – that has contributed to the complex layers of meaning and experience that have created this recognisable twenty-first-century Leicester. Part of that identity is defined, as it is for many groups and even individuals, in an oppositional way: Leicester is *Not* Nottingham, and is *Not* to be confused with its near neighbours and sporting arch-rivals, Derby and Coventry. Knowing what it is *Not* may contribute to an identity crisis for Leicester since there is no visible or single identifier that conveys place to locals or visitors. Perhaps the act of electing a mayor in 2011, a preference simultaneously rejected by several English boroughs, indicates the independence of Leicester and a preference for self-determination, confident that the reinvention of the city has in the past been possible through radical and secular values, and independent business flair.

Leicester's motto, *Semper Eadem* – 'always the same' – implies an unchanging character. *Leicester: A Modern History* shows just that: Leicester has always been the same – constant, but constantly adapting.

PART I

Understanding Leicester

Leicester Pharus Map, 1911.

Reproduced by kind permission of the National Library of Scotland Map Collection.

1

Understanding Leicester:
independent, radical, tolerant

O N 28 May 1889, the Leicester Mayor, Edward Wood submitted a proposal to the Town Council. He sought, and obtained, approval to petition the 'Queen's Most Excellent Majesty' to grant city status to Leicester. The petition proudly stated Leicester's credentials. It was 'one of the most ancient of our municipalities', and had long-standing powers granted by royal charter and an uninterrupted line of mayors since 1208. Mayor Wood was careful to refer to the fact that from AD 679 Leicester had had a succession of bishops – a cathedral was one criterion for city status – and, though there had been an interruption of a thousand years, a bishop had recently been reinstated in Leicester. Wood did not spare Queen Victoria and her advisers a local history lesson. He continued with references to the Leicester associations with royalty, noted that parliaments had been held in Leicester in the fifteenth century, and concluded with a summary of the recent prosperity and growth of the borough. The petitioners concluded that they and the inhabitants of Leicester were 'desirous of securing the revival of the ancient title' and asked the Queen to 'confer the title and dignity of "city" upon the Borough of Leicester.'[1] In less than a month the 'carefully considered' reply was received. The petition was refused; those of Leeds and Sheffield were approved. It was a further thirty years before Leicester was accorded the status of 'city' in 1919.[2]

The confidence with which the Mayor presented the Leicester case was not unjustified. Since about 1850 an impressive level of infrastructural development by the Council marked out Leicester as progressively 'modern' and aware of the benefits of high-quality services to both business and residents – values that were not conspicuous before 1836 when a corrupt oligarchy controlled local government in Leicester.[3] Nowhere was this more evident than in the moral and cultural environment of the city. For instance, the adaptation of a school building on New Walk (1849) provided Leicester with one of the first municipal museums in Britain, later described as architecturally 'dignified' (1.2).[4] A public lecture hall,

1.1 Edward Wood (1839–1917), boot and shoe factor; councillor 1880, chair of the Gas and Water committees; Mayor on four occasions (1888, 1895, 1901, 1906); Freedom of the Borough in 1892; knighted 1906.

Artist: Walter William Ouless. *Source*: Leicester City Council.

Art School and gallery were added to the museum, though this early cultural quarter then became something of an architectural mongrel. A Council resolution to build a Free Library in 1862 became a reality in 1871 with the opening of another renovated building, New Hall in Wellington Street, and branch libraries took the civic mission to the very fringes of the city.[5] Indeed, the trust deeds of the Garendon branch library, accepted by the Mayor at the opening ceremony in 1883, captured the confidence of the municipal mission in a tablet that was always to remain in the building with the inscription:

1.2 Museum and Art Gallery, New Walk. Built 1836 as a nonconformist school, adapted 1849 as a museum.

Source: Colin Hyde.

> This building, with fittings and 1,550 volumes of books was presented by Mr Councillor Israel Hart to the Mayor and Corporation of Leicester on the 27th June, 1883, to be held in trust for the inhabitants, to be used as a free library and reading room.

1.3 Israel Hart (1835–1911), wholesale clothing manufacturer, elected 1874; Mayor 1884, 1885, 1886, 1893 concerned with social conditions of Leicester inhabitants.

Source: Leicester City Council.

New public buildings appeared not just in the fashionable central area around New Walk but throughout the city, and were indicative of that developing civic consciousness which the Mayor conveyed to the Queen in 1889. Best known, of course, was the distinctive Queen Anne style Town Hall (1.4; 1.13) completed in 1876, but this was just one of several substantial municipal building projects in the 1870s and 1880s: the Borough Lunatic Asylum (The Towers, Gypsy Lane 1869) (1.5); cattle market and abattoirs (opened 1872) (1.6); public baths at Bath Lane (1876) and Vestry Street (1891); isolation hospital (1872) at Freake's Ground, north of Beatrice Road; and a refuse destructor near Charnwood Street (1889). Each in their own way addressed public health concerns shared by Leicester residents since death rates and infant mortality levels were well above the national average in mid-century. Civic investment in these amenities contributed to the reduction in mortality in the city, and, as declared on the tablet in the Garendon library, demonstrated concern for common good.

More by accident than intent, however, the Corporation created something of a green belt around the south of the city. It certainly was not conceived as an environmental policy. The combined impact of the first municipal cemetery[6] (for both Church of England and nonconformist burials, 1850) at Welford Road, Victoria Park (the racecourse until 1882, 69 acres), Freemen's Common (85 acres), and Welford Road recreation ground (now Mandela Park, 11 acres), together with the County Asylum (now the University) (1.8) and new County Cricket and Filbert Street football grounds, together with the flood plain of the River Soar, produced a green girdle around the south of the city that remains a durable geographical feature and leisure amenity (1.10). To the north, it was Queen Victoria's representative, the Prince of Wales, on his way to Bradgate to visit the Earl of Stamford who formally opened Abbey Park to the public in a ceremony in May 1882.[7] Further east, Spinney Hills Park was purchased from the estate of C.S. Burnaby in 1885 to provide a lung for that part of the borough (1.9).[8]

The Corporation also intervened in the markets for both gas and water. Unlike many towns and cities, the Leicester Gas Works (established 1821) remained in private hands for over half a century and distributed generous dividends every year, despite a reduction of 77% in the price of gas between 1824 and 1877. Only when the company sought to acquire over 18 acres of public land and double its capital to expand capacity did the Corporation move to acquire the Gas Works. This was achieved in 1879, at a cost of over

1.4 Town Hall 1873–76, with pigeons. The crest is a cinquefoil and on the top of the Queen Anne style gable, is a wyvern (a winged dragon), both confirmed in 1619 as associated with Leicester. The red Lancastrian lion was added in 1926 on either side of Elizabeth I's motto, *semper eadem*, Architect: F.J. Hames.
Source: Colin Hyde.

1.5 Borough Asylum (the Towers) 1869, final cost £50,000; designed capacity 274 but over 1,200 in the 1940s. Architect: Edward Loney Stephens, borough surveyor.
Source: Colin Hyde.

1.6 Cattle Market (1871) detail of pig's head. Architect: J.B. Everard.
Source: Colin Hyde.

1.7 Victoria Park racecourse, 1874.

Painter Edward Benjamin Herberte. *Source*: Leicester City Council.

£476,000, equivalent to almost £40 million in 2016 prices. Shortly after, and with demand increasing appreciably, the Corporation moved quickly first to expand gas production and then to erect chemical works covering 3.5 acres adjoining the Aylestone Road Gas Works to deal with the substantial volume of ammonia sulphate and tar by-products produced each week.[9]

If by national standards the Corporation was slow to manage gas production it was more in line with other boroughs in its attempts to secure water supplies. Since there was no piped water before 1850 and the river received household sewage and industrial effluent, then pumped water from polluted wells provided the main source of water. Infant mortality, a sensitive indicator of poverty and general ill-health, was higher in Leicester than in 95% of the parishes in England and Wales; the death rate was 30/1,000 in 1840, compared to the English average of 22/1,000; in 1859, contaminated water caused diarrhoea responsible for one death in every nine in Leicester.[10] The borough water supply was a matter of notoriety nationally. Land for reservoirs at Thornton (1853: watershed of 2,850 acres) and Cropston (1866: watershed 4,400 acres) were early acquisitions in a nineteenth-century version of a private finance initiative in which the Corporation was a minority shareholder in a private company, the Leicester Waterworks Company. Eventually, in 1879, Leicester Corporation assumed overall control of water supplies in a capital restructuring arrangement

1.8 Leicestershire County Asylum, 1837 (now University of Leicester, administration building). Architects: Wallett (County asylum superintendent) and William Parsons; wings added by Parsons and Dain, 1848–49.
Source: Colin Hyde.

1.9 Spinney Hill Park (1886).
Source: Colin Hyde.

1.10 Green girdle of land to south of Leicester.
Source: National Library of Scotland, Thornley's Pharus map and street guide of Leicester (*c*.1911).

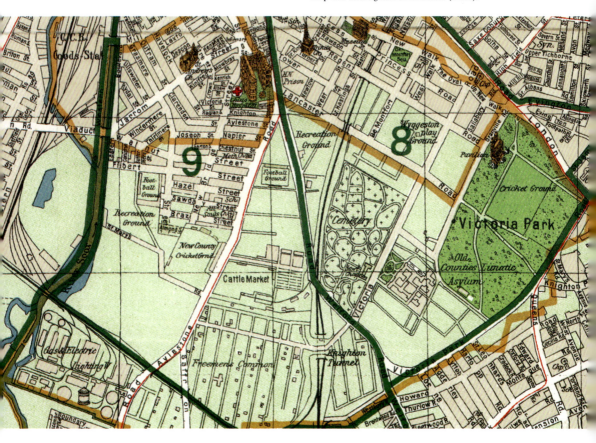

similar to that for the Gas Works. So by 1874 the death rate of the borough had dropped to 23.3/1,000, the lowest of all manufacturing towns in England, and by 1909 had fallen further to 14.6/1,000. It was another cause for civic pride and contributed to the confident plea to the Queen for city status in 1889. 'The Leicester method', as it became known, relied on a combination of plentiful clean water supplies, an aggressive hygiene campaign by the anti-vaccination lobby, and a recognition that, in the absence of day nurseries as recommended by the Medical Officer of Health, by substituting female factory work for domestic employment rising household incomes had a positive effect on children's health.

Water supply was one problem; waste water disposal was another. Distinguished civil engineers – Thomas Wicksteed, Robert Stephenson, Sir Joseph Bazalgette, and Thomas Hawksley among them – were engaged to formulate proposals for Leicester. Wicksteed's plan to dry off liquid waste to produce 10,000 tons of manure annually and to sell it as fertiliser at a net profit of £1 per ton proved unduly optimistic, and so a programme of main and subsidiary sewer construction was pursued in the late 1870s and early 1880s, followed by proposals for Beaumont Leys Sewage Farm and Pumping Station in 1887.[11] These infrastructural improvements, combined with a Flood Prevention Scheme to build storm culverts and widen and deepen the river were masterminded by the Borough Surveyor, Joseph Gordon, and fundamentally altered the environmental condition of Leicester in the last quarter of the nineteenth century. Given its low-lying location, a fifth of Leicester dwellings were routinely subjected to flooding when rainwater run-off could not be absorbed by ground increasingly paved and tarred. The River Soar and its tributary streams burst their banks as a consequence.[12] Successful water management significantly reduced flooding and thus facilitated the introduction of water closets and the retreat of the 'Rochdale' pail closet system of disposal by which human waste was carted through the town centre. As The Times explained, Gordon's 'great engineering ability' and 'ceaseless energy' meant 'his extensive operations greatly reduced the death rate' of Leicester.[13]

To the buildings and civil engineering projects designed to manage public amenities the Corporation added a web of new and improved streets. The list was extensive (Table 1.1) and involved complex negotiations with property owners. For example, the scheme to widen Gallowtree Gate and continue it into Rutland Street involved just over half an acre and £33,500 in compensation to demolish 35 houses and numerous shops. These planned improvements to traffic circulation and access required complicated negotiations with eleven property owners, six of whom had their compensation claims decided by a special jury. In the 1880s alone there were over twenty separate street improvement schemes, and the Corporation paid over £30,000 compensation for the 6 acres of houses and lands acquired. In so doing city centre access to the enlarged market area was improved, and new and widened bridges aided traffic flow on many of the radial roads to the commercial centre.[14] By 1894, the public buildings, building land, house property, and ornamental grounds owned by the Corporation amounted to almost 100 acres, with Victoria Park, Welford Road recreation ground, and cemeteries adding a further 432 acres to the municipal real estate.

Table 1.1 New and improved thoroughfares, 1880–95

New streets	New roads	Street improvements
De Montfort Street	Park Road	Cart's lane
Napier Street	Victoria Road widened	Castle Street
Chestnut Street	Hinckley Road widened	The Hollow
Walnut Street	Lancaster Road	Bath Lane
Princess Street extension	Abbey Park Road	Dunn's Lane
Pocklington's Walk	Mere Road	Bond Street
Grey Friars Street	Corporation Road	High Street
Filbert Street	Western Boulevard	St Nicholas Steet
Hazel Street	East Park Road	Northgate Street
Granville Street		Holy Bones
Salisbury Road		Newarke Street
Cross Walk		Loseby Lane
Jarrom Street extension		Northampton Street
Cattle market (2 streets)		Humberstone Road
Slater Street extension		Fosse Road
St Augustine Street		Bishop Street
Clarendon Street extension		Bowling Green Street
Grasmere Street		Horsefair Street
Ullswater Street		Granby Street
Rydal Street		
Thirlmere Street		
Widermere Street		
Buttermere Street		
Coniston Avenue		
Horsefair/Gallowtree link to Market Place		

Source: J. Storey, Historical Sketch (Leicester, 1894), 6–12.

These initiatives provided transport links that proved sufficient to allow subsequent tram and early motor transport to access the city centre, and only in the 1950s was a new vision for mobility around and within Leicester considered necessary.[15] To these capital projects significant management responsibilities were added and after 1871, when the town council devolved authority for street lighting to its Watch Committee, public administration mushroomed with the assumption of a variety of public protection services which included regulating hackney carriages and tramway cars,

Leicester: a modern history

supervising cabmen's shelters, managing the public mortuary, licensing theatres, enforcing fire safety regulations governing the storage of petroleum and explosives, and regulating the use of bicycles.[16]

Though local improvement acts authorised the levy of a few extra pennies in the £ on local taxes (Rates) this rarely contributed much to the financing of the new amenities. The halfpenny addition to Rates for the Library produced only £450 – enough only to employ a librarian and some modest clerical help. The reality was that most developments were funded by a combination of subventions from general borough revenue, operational profits on public utilities, occasional bridging loans from the Local Government Board in London and, more frequently, by issuing municipal bonds to finance the capital costs of civic projects secured against the guarantee of future local tax revenues in the borough.

In the fifteen years prior to Mayor Wood's pleading letter to Queen Victoria to award city status to Leicester, the population increased by 62%. By contrast the taxable value of property increased by approximately 162% – an indication of how the entire population, property owners and tenants, were faced with higher rates of local taxation to finance improvements (1.11). This direct charge on the population pales when compared to the rising levels of debt burden heaped upon future generations of Leicester inhabitants. The debt on the sanitary account alone, for example, rose from £79,000 in 1874 to over £800,000 in 1889 – a ten-fold increase – and was nearer to £1.5 million (twenty times the level of 1874) when gas and electricity loans were taken into consideration. Despite this apparent insolvency, council officials were relaxed about their exposure to debt on the grounds that the operating profits on the gas, electricity and water activities were sufficient to pay both the interest and the capital over the thirty-year period of the loans.[17]

1.11 Local Taxation in Leicester 1845–1914 (rate in the £).

Source: based on M. Elliott, *Victorian Leicester*, 159.

On bank holiday Monday, 7 August 1876, the Council met in the Old Guildhall for a final meeting there (1.12). Before proceeding to the newly completed Town Hall they passed a resolution:

> That having for between three and four centuries conducted the Public affairs of this ancient Borough in this Guildhall, the Municipal Council finds that the growth and prosperity of Leicester demand better accommodation for the transaction of business in the Town.

'Growth and prosperity', already apparent in 1876, provided confidence in the municipal mission; subsequently, the flood control measures were considered 'a monument of the courage and enterprise of the Council of Leicester' and 'a work of great magnitude and character outside the ordinary duties of Local Government'. Little wonder that in 1889 Mayor Edward Wood was confident of the Leicester claim for 'city status' in his letter to Queen Victoria.

1.12 Guildhall Courtyard.
Painter: George W. Moore Henton, 1882.
Source: Leicester City Council.

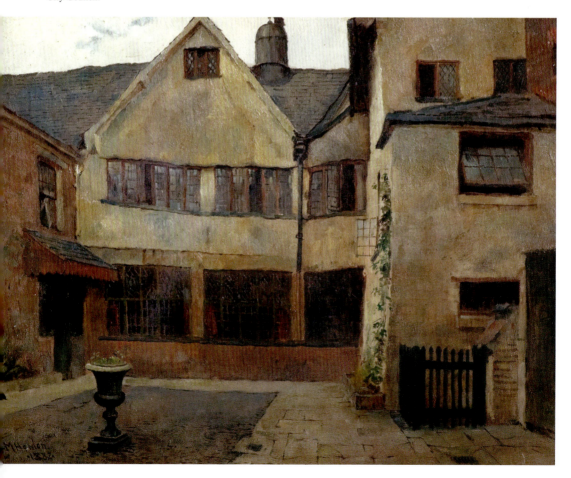

1.13 Leicester Town Hall, completed 1876 shows a scale and character that reflects a Town Council sufficiently confident to reject the designs of the long-standing editor of *The Builder*, George Godwin, an architect with a national reputation.
Architect: F.J. Hames. *Source*: Colin Hyde.

Growth and prosperity

No doubt some of the confidence in its pursuit of city status stemmed from Leicester becoming, briefly, the largest borough in the East Midlands. Ranked 25th in Great Britain in 1861 with a population of 68,000, and below Nottingham (20th), Leicester was ranked 18th in 1871 with 95,000 people and surpassed Nottingham (21st) to become, briefly, the premier East Midlands borough.[18] Population growth was both a result and a cause of prosperity, reflecting, as it did, the ability of individuals to find work in Leicester's dominant industry – hosiery. This industry included socks and stockings, gloves, cravats, braces, and shirts, and in 1801 employed almost half the population of the borough. Structural changes in the hosiery industry, including the development of a wide frame and specialist branches such as glove manufacturing, fuelled a migration of low-waged framework knitters and agricultural workers from rural Leicestershire parishes where

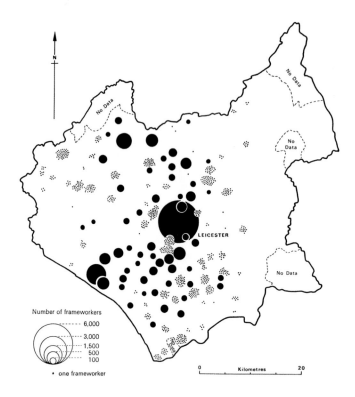

1.14 Distribution of hosiery workers in Leicestershire, 1851.

The dispersion of hosiery workers was greater than among shoemakers, where already by mid-century Leicester dominated the county.

Number of frameworkers

- 6,000
- 3,000
- 1,500
- 500
- 100
- one frameworker

0   Kilometres   20

1.15 Distribution of shoemakers in Leicestershire, 1851

Source: P.R Mounfield, 'The foundations of the modern industrial pattern, in N. Pye (ed.), *Leicester and its Region* (Leicester 1972), 367, 369.

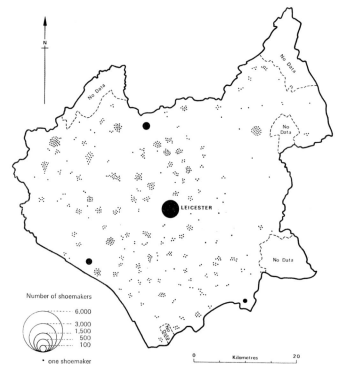

Number of shoemakers

- 6,000
- 3,000
- 1,500
- 500
- 100
- one shoemaker

0   Kilometres   20

they provided the workforce for expanding factory-based production from mid-century (1.14).[19] Only in the 1890s was the migratory pattern arrested when manufacturers began to build factories in the villages.

The position of Leicester in the hierarchy of English urban places was boosted further from mid-century by the expansion of the boot and shoe industry (1.15). Whereas until the 1850s leather uppers were cut and closed in a workshop or small factory, the shoe making and finishing was undertaken by out-workers, often in those villages on the fringes of the city where framework knitters were under-employed. The transition from a handicraft shoe-making activity to a modern British wholesale manufacturing footwear industry owed much to hand-riveting the sole to the shoe upper and insole. This was first developed by Thomas Crick in the 1830s, adapted in their Highcross Street premises by his son, John Thorne Crick, and patented in 1853 for large-scale steam-powered manufacturing.[20] Between 1853 and 1867 Crick's turnover increased by 2,750%, and the number of boot and shoe factories in Leicester increased from 4 to 70 in the same period, and to 117 by 1870. As result, Leicester superseded Northampton as the footwear metropolis of Britain. Famous names such as Stead and Simpson, and Olivers, were founded in this formative phase, and the buoyancy of footwear manufacturing was apparent in Crick and Son's workforce: it expanded from 34 workers in 1851 to more than 1,000 by 1867. Outworking came into the factory. So many footwear factories were built between 1861 and 1891 that a century later 60% of the firms in the footwear industry did so from premises constructed in this late-Victorian period. As Spencer's *New Guide to Leicester* noted in 1868: 'The prosperity of the town has never diminished since the adoption of the [footwear] industry. Prior to it, the only staple trade, the manufacture of hosiery, was at its very lowest ebb.'[21]

That 'prosperity' owed much to complementary products developed in conjunction with the hosiery and footwear industries. Gussets to fit shoes snugly around the ankles using fine threads of vulcanised rubber were developed in the 1850s, with production peaking in the 1870s.[22] John Biggs, a glove manufacturer, applied for and received a patent for making elastic-wristed gloves and within four years had 330 frames manufacturing them. Whereas in 1846 only Biggs and Caleb Bedells had been manufacturing elastic web, by 1861 there were twenty firms. Using woven latex garters, corsets and suspenders provided an alternative for many firms when elastic webbing for shoes suffered a downturn in fashion in the last quarter of the nineteenth century. Where local blacksmiths and frame-smiths had once built machines for the hosiery and shoe trades, in the age of steam it was boilermakers and iron- and brass-founders that forged a recognisable engineering sector with over 7,000 male workers by 1900. Leicester's engineering firms prospered into the twentieth century, boosted by rising demand, wartime orders, and inter-war trends for automatic and semi-automatic production methods in the twin strengths of the footwear and hosiery industries. Leicester was dominated by industry, and dominated the region in hosiery, footwear, and specialist mechanical engineering.

It was manufacturing innovation coupled with modest capital requirements and leasing arrangements for equipment that contributed to the industrial success of Leicester in the second half of the nineteenth century (1.16; 1.17). Corts' apprentices founded small engineering works in the 1840s; Pegg's company supplied equipment to dyeworks; Goodwin, Barsby and Parker produced machinery for quarries; Richards' Phoenix foundry specialised in heavy castings for several railway companies; the Gimson family firm of millwrights on Welford Road built the Vulcan Works beside the Midland Railway; Gent's clocks can still occasionally be seen in the city; Taylor Taylor & Hobson manufactured lenses and optical instruments and morphed into photographic equipment suppliers used in World War I for aerial reconnaissance; Pearson & Bennion made specialist boot and shoe machinery at their Union Works in Belgrave Road for the American-owned consortium which was re-badged as the British United Shoe Machinery Company. The annual Post Office directories of the period confirm the number and variety of engineering enterprises that supported and complemented the industrial structure of the borough and this pattern continued into second half of the twentieth century when a fifth of the male workforce still obtained their pay from a broadly defined engineering sector (see figures 1.16 and 1.17).

Industrial successes in the mid-nineteenth century were underpinned by transport and infrastructural developments. As a hub, Leicester fulfilled

1.16, 1.17 The century-long dominance of manufacturing in Leicester is captured in these census data for 1861–1951.

Source: D. Reeder and R. Rodger, 'Industrialisation and the city economy', in M.J. Daunton (ed.), *Cambridge Urban History of Britain*, vol. 3 (Cambridge 2000), 553–92.

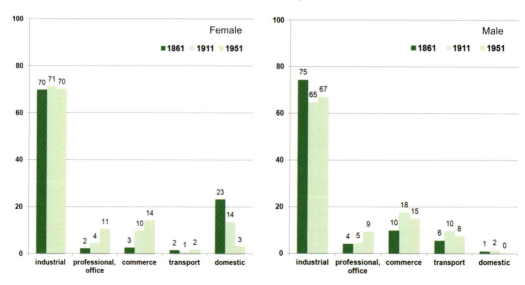

| Leicester: a modern history

1.18 Campbell Street Station. Though the Leicester and Swannington Railway had a terminus at West Bridge from 1832, the Midland Counties Railway station at Campbell Street was the first station in Leicester, built in 1840. The reorientation of the entrance to London Road in its current form was completed in 1894.

Source: Record Office for Leicester, Leicestershire and Rutland, DE3736 Box 6, Campbell Street Station.

important administrative and judicial roles as a central place within its county area, and acted as a transport hub for several radiating turnpike roads, for the Union Canal linking Leicester to London, and for a developing railway network.[23] Geographically, then, Leicester was well placed to exploit the age of steam when, in 1828, just three years after the opening of the Stockton and Darlington Railway, a consortium of Leicestershire colliery interests had tabled a proposal to connect Leicester to the abundant coalfields in the north of the county. An Act was obtained in 1830; the skills of the railway engineer Robert Stephenson were secured; and the line opened in 1833 from the West Bridge in Leicester to Swannington. The price of coal dropped immediately by 60%, and 'this greatly encouraged the extension of mechanical power in the town's industry. The number of steam engines at work more than doubled in the 1830s.'[24] Stephenson claimed that he had saved Leicester £50,000 per year since the coal, bricks and stone transported increased from 11,000 to 203,000 tons in the ten years after 1832. Such external linkages were advantageous to Leicester, but the

1.19 The
expansion
of Leicester
showing the
main railway
lines.

Source: R.H.
Evans, 'Leicester
and Leicestershire
1835–1971' in N.
Pye (ed.), *Leicester
and its Region*
(Leicester, 1972),
293.

Medieval walled area and probably Roman

Up to the Industrial Revolution c. 1820

First industrial spread, nineteenth century and up to 1914

Second industrial spread, twentieth century up to 1939

circulation of goods and people within the modestly sized borough of 68,000
were arguably just as important to business efficiency, as was the modest
physical extent and gentle gradients of the central districts where industry
was still located.

Instrumental in a different way was the Leicester Trade Protection
Society (LTPS), an early version of a credit rating agency, which from the
1850s verified the creditworthiness of businesses from its premises in New
Street after 1872.[25] It was an important financial intermediary for small
firms in an age when rapid urbanisation and frequent bankruptcies caused
businesses to be anxious about their customers' ability to pay. It was also
intended to combat the commercial fraudsters such as the 'Towzery Gang'
and 'Lottery Tribes' who as migrant traders established business premises,

ordered stock on credit and then fled overnight. Between 1870 and 1900 the LTPS received about 60–90 written requests daily and about 80–100 verbal enquiries about the status of firms.[26] One business, Archibald Turner & Co., elastic and India rubber goods manufacturers at Bow Bridge Works on King Richard's Road, directed 41 queries to the LTPS between 1891 and 1897. One of their customers, Bailey & Co., Glastonbury, was considered 'very safe' for £100 credit as they had been 'trading for 30 years'. For a modest subscription, the TPS evened out fluctuations in the cash flow of their members by functioning as a debt collection agency and pursuing their debtors through actions in the County Court. To minimise the impact of bad debts beyond the borough boundaries, information about firms was passed to TPS branches developed throughout the UK and eventually a federated organisation, the Association of Trade Protection Societies, functioned from its Leicester headquarters for this purpose.

Expansion

With successive decennial population increases in the 1860s, 1870s and 1880s averaging 37% Leicester became a Victorian boomtown. From Warwickshire, Staffordshire and Northamptonshire a migration of considerable proportions swelled the workforce and the percentage of the Leicestershire born population in the borough declined consequently from 80% to almost 70% by 1900. The influx of migrants to Leicester was evident from the age structure in 1881 when women aged 15–29 swelled those age cohorts disproportionately and disrupted the normal pattern exacted by death.

Perhaps what defined Leicester more than anything, however, was the complementary nature of employment in the borough. In 1881, six out of ten workers in hosiery were women; seven out of ten workers in the shoe trade were men. This was highly significant. In terms of household income Leicester families were heavily insulated against bouts of unemployment. Though not exempt from trade cycles, hosiery and footwear as consumption-based industries were less prone to the periodic and sometimes prolonged depressions and 'lumpy' investment patterns that were characteristic of capital goods industries. Making-do, hand-me-downs, and mending clothes and shoes could only achieve so much for growing family members. Across Britain middle-class demand for fashionable footwear and clothing provided Leicester workers in these segments of the market with steady employment. Though the contribution to Leicester employment from textiles and shoe making declined to some extent before the First World War, this was a reflection of a healthy diversification of employment prospects for men in transport, distribution, commercial, and professional work, as well as in the army of clerks and inspectors associated with extended town council responsibilities in environmental and community health, and municipal trading in

1.20 Faire Brothers factory, Rutland Street.

Source: Colin Hyde.

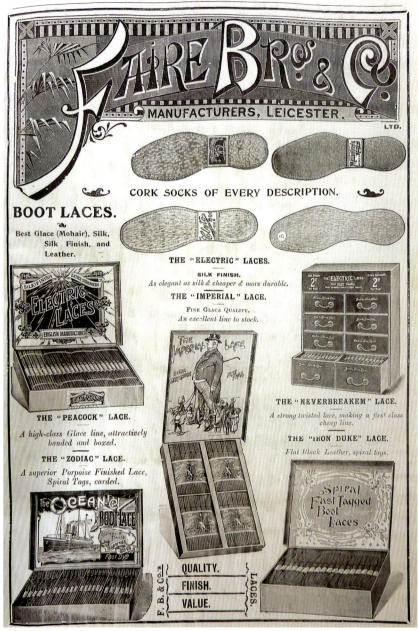

1.21 Faire Bros. and Co. products from the *Boot and Shoe Trades Journal*, 30 June 1905, 557.

gas, water, electricity generation, and transport. For Leicester women, the late-Victorian decline in low-paid domestic work was less marked than in other towns and cities, and the expansion in commerce, transport and local government before World War I represented an improvement in their employment prospects.

1.22 Transitions: from workshop to factory: Welford Road Court 1840s.

Source: Colin Hyde.

1.23 Transitions: from workshop to factory: Freeman, Hardy, Wills, Wimbledon Street

Source: Record Office for Leicester, Leicestershire and Rutland, DE3736 Box 31, Wimbledon Street.

No less significant for Leicester was the so-called 'participation' rate for women – the proportion of women of working age who were active in the labour force. Of Leicester women aged 13–64 in 1911, 54% were described as 'occupied' in work. This compared favourably with other Midlands boroughs and with the average for England where female participation rates were only about two-thirds that of Leicester.[27] For the 14–24 female age-group, the Leicester workforce participation hovered around the 90% mark before 1914 so that the world of work was an almost universal experience for young women. But what was particularly noteworthy, too, was that employment beyond marriage was common among Leicester women: 27% of married women remained in paid work after their wedding vows, and 35% of widows worked following their husband's death. How far this exceptional involvement in the labour force for women of all ages and marital status contributed to women's independence and self-esteem is difficult to assess, but what is clear is that even though their wage rates were only a third, or at most half, that of their men folk their contribution to the household budget was vital, lifting the family out of poverty and facilitating improvements in its health and wealth.[28] When it came to inheritance and

1.24 Pex Socks, hosiery factory, originally Whitmore's Factory built *c*.1844.

Source: Record Office for Leicester, Leicestershire and Rutland, DE3736 Box 31, West Bridge, Folder 1, General Views.

the transmission of wealth, women were responsible for about 30% of all wills written in Leicester in the period 1858 to 1900 and this compared favourably to their sisters in Birmingham, Stockport, and London.[29] In short, women's legacies though often modest provided fixed incomes from annuities and rents, and so made an important stabilising contribution to the local economy.

The structure of the Leicester economy and its associated patterns of consumption played an important role in the physical character and expansion of Leicester. While the Victorian skyline had its share of chimneys it was not dominated by the bulky form of cotton mills or blast furnaces; business organisation in Leicester relied more on medium-sized family firms and less on the large-scale factories and multi-plant mergers that became increasingly common in British industry between 1870 and World War I.[30] In this respect Leicester's manufacturing base had more in common with Birmingham than Sheffield.[31] Complementarity of work and wages for men and women in the footwear and hosiery industries, supported by a vibrant engineering sector, steadied household incomes and provided an ability to pay rent without undue fear of bouts of unemployment or short time. In turn, the performance of manufacturing sector – there were 187

1.25 N. Corah and Sons, St Margaret's Works, moved in 1865 to a 4 acre site (off what is now Burley's Way) from former premises in Granby Street and, before that, Union Street (1824). The firm employed over 1,000 workers before World War I and was latterly an important supplier to Marks and Spencer's.

Source: reproduced by permission of the Centre for English Local History, Leicester University, Leic/B/LEI/17/P4.

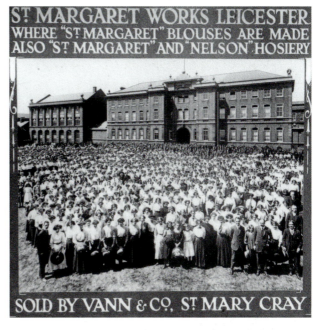

1.26 Densely packed Victorian streets survive to the present (1988).

Source: Leicester City Council.

1.27 Spencer's map (1857) showing how the municipal area expanded following municipal reform in 1836.

Source: Record Office for Leicester, Leicestershire and Rutland.

LEICESTER in 1857
Based on Spencer's Map

SCALE OF YARDS
0 100 200 400 600

KEY

A All Saints Open
B The Crescent
C Pocklington's Walk
1 Independent Chapel
2 The Great Meeting
3 Baptist Chapel
4   "
5 Newton's Charity School
6 National School
7 British School
8 Collegiate School
9 East Gates
10 Haymarket
11 St Margaret's Church

12 All Saints' Church
13 St Nicholas' Church
14 Ch. of St Mary de Castro
15 St Martin's Church
16 St George's Church
17 St Johns Church
18 Trinity Church
19 Museum
20 County Gaol
21 Infirmary
22 Union Workhouse
23 Trinity Hospital
24 Town Hall
25 Borough Gaol

Old municipal boundary – – – –
New municipal boundary ——————
established in 1836

bootmakers, 163 boot and shoe manufacturers and 105 hosiery manufacturers in 1914 – underpinned purchasing power and provided a cushion for a host of industrial suppliers, retailers and services.

Using the quantity and quality of nineteenth-century Leicester housing as indicators then the patterns of work and wages were translated into housing of a generally high standard of accommodation. The population doubled between 1851 and 1881, and doubled again to 1911 when it reached just over 227,000. Yet Leicester builders kept pace with this burgeoning demand. Over 38,000 houses were completed between 1851 and 1911, a quadrupling of the housing stock, and thus the average household size on the eve of World War I (4.5 persons) was slightly lower than in 1851 (4.7 persons).[32] This meant that home life was more congenial for Leicester citizens because the number of persons per room was 20% below the average of the larger English boroughs. The extent and durability of this pre-1914 housing stock can be assessed from the fact that 35% of the habitable housing in Leicester in 2011 was built before 1914 compared to the national average of just 25%.[33]

Quadrupling the number of houses in sixty years inevitably and irrevocably changed Leicester. Colour, style, density, and texture gave a uniformity to Victorian housing and is still evident today in a warm red

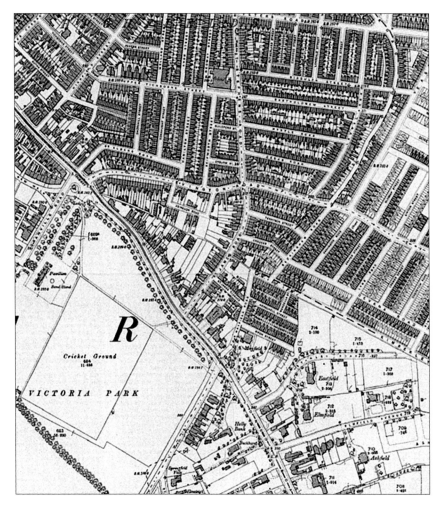

1.28 Generous detached villa plot sizes around London Road. These contrasted with the high density terraced houses in Highfields.

Source: Ordnance Survey, 1904.

brick terraced form scattered across the city. Spencer's map of 1857 (1.27) showed the limited spatial extent of the borough; later maps illustrate the grid-like geometry introduced by streets of terraced houses increasingly subjected from the 1870s to building regulations, the discipline of municipal sewer and gas pipe connections, and the practical economics of the building industry (1.28). The break-out began with middle-class migrations from downtown streets such as Granby, Market, Belvoir, Wellington, Lansdowne, Claremont, and Albion Streets to Highfields, Belgrave Road and Braunstone Gate in the 1860s. Just as the death rate for the borough achieved notoriety in the 1870s as the worst in the country – even above that of Bombay[34] – the suburbanising process accelerated to the southern suburbs straddling London Road. The term 'park', as in Victoria and Clarendon Park, was really a synonym for an exclusive middle-class area and it typified the social and residential segregation that was gathering pace in the last quarter of the nineteenth century. With its Arts and Crafts features, and elaborate tile, wood and ceramic materials, the Stoneygate area and later Manor Road development remain among the most attractive of English residential suburbs of the late-Victorian and Edwardian ages.

For Leicester citizens with less disposable income – machinists, dressmakers, bookbinders, butchers, shoe finishers, stonemasons, clerks – it was the availability of land to the west of the River Soar from the

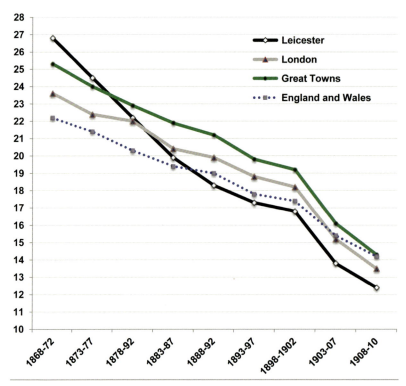

1.29 Death rates in Leicester compared to large English boroughs, 1868–1910.

Note: The data refer to crude death rates – that is, unadjusted for the age composition of the population. From 1870 English and Welsh towns only were included in the 'Great Towns' grouping.

Source: J.T. Biggs, *Leicester: Sanitation versus Vaccination* (London, 1912).

1860s that transformed the housing market (1.30). The key events were the estate sales of Danett's Hall (1861) and Westcotes manor hall (1886) which resulted in extensive housing developments on dozens of streets along and between Narborough and Fosse Roads. With the sale and subdivision of the Duke of Rutland's Aylestone manor in 1869 a different suburbanising process was underway: village-based industrial development accompanied by housing development. The decline and break-up of peripheral gentry estates at Belgrave, Knighton, Humberstone, Braunstone and Evington was also accompanied by spurts of industrial expansion and housebuilding, and were soon the target of Leicester's greater aggrandisement as it sought, successfully in 1892, to annex these parishes and their taxable value.[35] Landownership was a central factor to the expansion of North Evington and Spinney Hills where the architect Arthur Wakerley mopped up parcels of available land after 1885 and developed a network of geometric streets for mixed residential and industrial purposes.[36] There was, then, an element of chance in the suburbanising process as land became available almost coincidentally through death or a decision to sell up when confronted by the advancing frontier of urbanisation. The unavailability of sites also influenced physical expansion, as at Newfoundpool where early preservationists successfully opposed the Midland Railway Company and forced it to re-locate the proposed station that endangered both the Roman Jewry wall and the medieval castle, and to build 300 houses as compensation for the demolition involved.[37]

The suburban break-out on the Cradock estate to the south is instructive (1.31; 1.32). These 120 acres were sold in 1877 by Edward Hartopp Cradock of Knighton Hall to two Leicester manufacturers, Alfred Donnisthorpe and Charles Smith, and a solicitor, Samuel Stone. Their strategy was to lay out roads and plots and then sell them on to private buyers or their agents – builders, architects, or the Freehold Land Society – and this contributed to the diversity of the suburb, as did the slow uptake of plots since a quarter of the former Cradock estate remained grassland twenty years later at the turn of the century. The transition from field pattern to street pattern is shown in figures 1.29 and 1.30.

The visual coherence of terraced housing that resulted from population growth and rising real household incomes was supplied, perhaps paradoxically, by a building industry that was highly fragmented and dominated by small-scale firms. Some 70% of all housebuilding plans approved involved the construction of five or fewer houses. These practical and pragmatic builders followed tried and tested designs for terraced houses. Larger firms might use a few architect-designed templates when building 200–300 houses, as in the case of Orson Wright at Knighton Fields. Elsewhere, among the middle classes, bespoke designs were obtained from local Leicester 'starchitects' with developing national reputations. Ernest Gimson – 'an architect of more than local importance'[38] – Joseph Goddard, Stockdale Harrison, Shirley

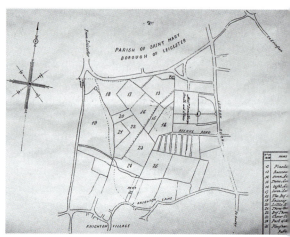

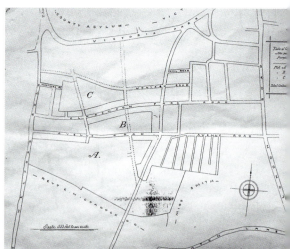

1.30 Building out west: the sale and development of Danett's Hall was well underway in 1877, but little else had changed in Newfoundpool and West Cotes Hall, or the estates of West Leigh and Wyggeston Hospital.

Source: private copy.

1.31, 1.32 The Cradock estate and the development of Clarendon Park showing the layout of the fields and the plots that were eventually turned into streets.

Source: private copy.

Harrison, Samuel Perkins Pick, Isaac Barradale, J.B. Everard, Edward Burgess and Alfred Henry Paget provided distinctive plans not just for middle-class houses but for banks, commercial and industrial premises, and a variety of public buildings in Leicester.[39] Together with expert decorative lead and plasterwork by such experts as George Bankart, high-quality craftsmanship in glass and ceramics, and Arts and Crafts inspired furniture by Ernest Gimson the interior quality of buildings, whether residential, commercial, industrial, or ecclesiastical, enjoyed stunning levels of design excellence. Such was the reputation of Leicester's built environment that when Humberstone Garden Suburb was mooted as the location for Anchor Boot and Shoe Company's cooperative housing it was to the internationally renowned planners of Letchworth, Raymond Unwin and Barry Parker, that they turned in 1907 (1.33; 1.34).

Joseph Goddard, though described as a architectural 'Goth' was more of an apostle given his enthusiasm after 1870 for terracotta elaboration in his buildings.[40] Like many English towns and cities the phoenix, wyvern, and assortment of clay animals and birds were mounted on buildings, together with terracotta tiles pargeted or fixed to roofs at angles that defied gravity. Glazed tiles provided new reflective effects and different combinations and designs of red, buff and blue bricks on the most modest of homes introduced polychromatic patterns to the built environment (1.35). With the reorganisation of town centre space in the last third of the nineteenth century the buildings that lined new and improved thoroughfares introduced new concepts of decoration and design by using cast iron, glass, and tiles in imaginative and expressive ways. The existence of a number of specialist

1.33, 1.34 Humberstone Garden Suburb. Between 1908 and 1914 the Anchor Boot and Shoe Co-operative Society, whose works were in Asfordby Street, built 94 gabled cottages to form a self-contained community with a play area for children, church, shop and community hall, as well as a bowling green, tennis courts, skittles, and cricket pitch. Pictured: Keyham Lane homes and the centenary gates 1902–2002.
Source: Richard Rodger.

1.35 Tiles and terracotta, glass, plaster and wood. All provided visual variety for late Victorian Leicester housing.

Source: Colin Hyde, Richard Rodger.

Regent Road, 1871.

Lansdowne House, 1872.

Prince's Road East, 1875.

St Saviour's Road.

Granville House, 1876.

Salisbury Road, 1878.

Upper Tichborne Street, 1876.

Alexandra Road, 1879.

Regent Road, 1880.

Ratcliffe Road, 1885.

London Road, 1890.

Springfield Road, 1894.

Springfield Road, 1894.

Sykesfield Avenue, 1902.

producers such as the Hathern Station Brick & Terra Cotta Company (established 1874), and Stanley Brothers of Nuneaton contributed significantly to the terracotta revival of late-Victorian Leicester and fundamentally altered the colour and complexity of the built environment of central and suburban areas from the 1870s.

Street names are by no means confined to local connections as a glance at any Yellow Pages will confirm. In Leicester, streets grouped by the names of authors and poets at Knighton Fields, biblical connections on one side of Narborough Road and ancient tribes of Britons, Celts, and Gauls in the street names opposite; there are Scottish places and golfing greats on either side of Troon Way, and Lake District place-names adjoining Eastern Boulevard. Most towns and cities have something similar; after all, to the speculative builder with several streets to complete it was convenient to use a series of names – Edinburgh has it 'flower colonies' and Liverpool its 'Cunard' streets. Perhaps Britain was lucky to avoid 'A' and 'B' street, First Street, Second Street, and so on. What does go unremarked, though, are the names and meanings embedded in terracotta and cement on the façades of terraced houses. These are saturated with meanings. In a sample of over 1,300 plaques spanning 1870 to 1913 from different parts of Leicester, the façades proudly identify homes as Rose, Ivy, Fernleigh, and Palm Cottage. Botanical references abound, as do personal names – Clare, Oscar, Ebenezer and Sebastian to name just a few. Terraced houses, mainly, leech meaning from the names of prominent people – Wesley, Dreyfus, Gordon, Cromwell, Byron, Rhodes, Nelson, Marconi, Wellington, as well as pairings such Grace and Darling, Livingstone and Stanley – and national, though not local, politicians, including Burghley, Gladstone, Salisbury, Balfour, Beaconsfield, and Cadogan. Predictably, the monarchy is represented and

1.36 a–d Tyrell Street. Grace Darling and the rescue of sailors near the Longstone Lighthouse, Bamburgh in 1838.

Source: M. Péro.

Leicester: a modern history

1.37, 1.38 Bleak Houses, 38–40 Derwent Street; and Perseverance Houses, 27–29 Buller Road.

Source: M. Péro.

historical events, mostly battles, are recalled, the most common of which are Mafeking and Waterloo, though Saratoga and the lesser known Varna (1444) also figure. Emotional, even sentimental, feelings are inscribed on the façade: Perseverance, Home Again Cottages, Naivete. Bleak Houses, and Day Dawn Villa among them. This sense of belonging, or not, brings a more personalised dimension to the home, and familiarity might also be expected of the most numerous category of plaques – geographical references. Overall, the gazetteer of place-names on terraced houses shows a wide geographical reference frame with 40% of the international references having an East or South African connection, and Italian links most numerous among European places. These international references represented about a quarter of the geographical category, and collectively plaques plastered to the external walls of terraced houses in Leicester demonstrate a contemporary awareness of late nineteenth-century geo-political events.

1.39 Diamond Jubilee plaque, 1897. Spa Place.

Source: Richard Rodger.

1.40 Mafeking, 45–47 Paget Road.

Source: M. Péro.

Values and ideals

After electoral reforms in 1835 and for most of the century, Leicester was a Liberal town. Or, more accurately, it was a loose alliance of liberal-minded individuals where a mixture of civic conscience and private imagination promoted public-spirited initiatives. By 1881 a manufacturing and merchant class of men accounted for about 60% of councillors and represented a considerable overlap between the social and political elites. Indeed, they sought public office 'as a means of expressing their social status'.[41] Alfred Henry Paget, for example, was from an established Leicester Liberal family, and a London architecture graduate apprenticed to the Goddard firm. He was a councillor for Leicester's East St Mary's ward, served on the Council's Museum Committee, was a magistrate, and a long-serving Treasurer. Paget was 'unwearied' in the service of the Unitarian Great Meeting, President of the Literary and Philosophical Society in 1887–88, and a founder member and Secretary of the Leicester Kyrle Society, established in 1881 to 'bring the influence of natural and artistic beauty within the reach of the poor' by means of internal decoration, paintings, flowers, gardens, open spaces for recreation, concerts and entertainment.[42] Men such as Paget had real personal wealth and a third of the senior councillors in the last quarter of the century left over £50,000 in their wills, equivalent to about £4 million in 2013 prices.[43] These business leaders had the financial means to take time out from their family enterprises and devote it to public causes, including council business and the governance of charities, voluntary organisations and cultural interests. However, as the scale and complexity of business developed in the last decades of the nineteenth century, and foreign competition became noticeably more intense, this caste of civic leaders began to retreat from political life so that from almost two-thirds of councillors in 1881 the presence of businessmen fell to barely half in 1901 and contracted further by 1931 to only one-third.[44] It was a trend councils experienced elsewhere, for instance, in Edinburgh, where the decline almost exactly replicated the timing and extent in Leicester.[45] As the pressures of business life escalated and the complexity of municipal administration advanced, so rise of the expert in the form of the salaried municipal expert was enshrined in the persons of the borough engineer, surveyor, medical officer of health, and an army of inspectorates with their battery of degrees and diplomas. The business of the council no longer valued the counsel of business.

A parallel explanation for the retreat of business leadership was also apparent. Until the mid-1880s a high degree of political stability and consensus prevailed, with leadership in the council chamber provided by business. But at the very moment that Leicester's manufacturing and associated population expansion seemed to ooze confidence, the businessmen of the borough began to focus increasingly on their principal interest

– business. The dual threat of foreign competition and tariff barriers was cause for concern among hosiery manufacturers from the 1870s and footwear firms from the 1890s. Employers' responses varied. Production was restructured: steam-powered factories and mechanisation resulted in de-skilling and the substitution of female for male workers, and young for old workers. Employees responded where they could by expanding cooperative production, defensively preserving the gender-based division of labour, and electing a more outspoken breed of trade union officials. The

1.41 'Orlando pursuing Fata Morgana'.

Painter: George Frederic Watts (painted 1846–48). *Source*: Leicester Arts and Museums Service.

dynamic was changing. Though the boot and shoe lock–out of 1895 signalled a victory for employers, it was the high–water mark of liberalism locally since the ensuing recession and its impact on unemployment and poverty ignited a phase of rising support for the Leicester Labour Representation Committee. Eventually a Lib–Lab pact was thrashed out, designed to exclude Conservatives, and Ramsay MacDonald was elected as MP for Leicester in 1906 in the context of a landslide Liberal victory in the national polls (see chapter 3). In periods of retrenchment work and workplace had a bearing on political radicalisation since Liberals demonstrated their limited ability to adjust to changing class relations to benefit an emerging labour presence in the borough. If the nineteenth century was an era of Liberal hegemony in Leicester the twentieth century was Labour's.

For much of the nineteenth century personal wealth made it possible for manufacturing men and merchants in Leicester to participate in political life and actively shape municipal policy and provision. It was a heady mixture of civic conscience and private imagination that promoted public-spirited initiatives. Private donations were generous. Bequests from Charles Clifton and Henry Rice, together with collections gifted by the dissolved Mechanics Institute, enabled the Library to open with over 9,000 titles; William Billings, solicitor, donated £5,000 to buy paintings; George Frederick Watts R.A. presented his canvas 'Orlando pursuing Fata Morgana' to the Art Gallery in 1888 (1.41). The Museum benefited from the collection of British and foreign mammals gifted (1869) in the legacy of Henry Bickley, from a bequest of 74 cases of British birds, and from the private collection of the Leicester Literary and Philosophical Society. Civil society was an important contributor to the civic mission.

1.42 Winston Churchill's invitation to visit Secular Hall and Institute, 1903.

Source: Sir Winston Church Archive Trust.

The pattern of patronage and public spiritedness functioned to the benefit of Leicester citizens generally. Prominent citizens gave their time generously and variously, yet features inherent in the socio-economic structure contributed to a streak of independence too: abundant work for men and women; the durability of traditional outwork methods; a high degree of autonomy for workers; significantly improved living standards; track record of early nineteenth-century political radicalism; a vibrant artisan culture, including a trade union presence. These varied independent strands contributed to the particular characteristics of Leicester. They were reinforced by systems of belief that produced a distinctively radical culture and ranged from unitarianism, to secularism, to cremation – in 1902 Leicester was the seventh borough to introduce a municipal crematorium (see chapter 6).

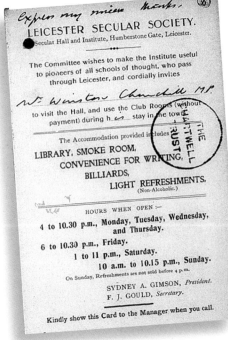

Express my [ ] thanks. ㉟

LEICESTER SECULAR SOCIETY.
Secular Hall and Institute, Humberstone Gate, Leicester.

The Committee wishes to make the Institute useful to pioneers of all schools of thought, who pass through Leicester, and cordially invites

Mr. Winston Churchill MP.

to visit the Hall, and use the Club Rooms (without payment) during his stay in the town.

The Accommodation provided includes

LIBRARY, SMOKE ROOM,
CONVENIENCE FOR WRITING,
BILLIARDS,
LIGHT REFRESHMENTS,
(Non-Alcoholic.)

HOURS WHEN OPEN :—

4 to 10.30 p.m., **Monday, Tuesday, Wednesday, and Thursday.**

6 to 10.30 p.m., **Friday.**

1 to 11 p.m., **Saturday.**

10 a.m. to 10.15 p.m., **Sunday.**

On Sunday, Refreshments are not sold before 4 p.m.

SYDNEY A. GIMSON, *President.*
F. J. GOULD, *Secretary.*

Kindly show this Card to the Manager when you call.

To return to Alfred Henry Paget: he was a Unitarian. Like many others in Leicester he rejected the Christian doctrine of the Holy Trinity, namely, the teaching that God the Father, God the Son, and God the Holy Spirit constituted three separate entities. In this respect he embraced the radical spirit of Leicester. This independent streak was also evident in the Secular Society whose central belief held that human fellowship was superior to conventional religious principles as an organising moral force. Founded in 1851 and with its headquarters at the Secular Hall (completed 1881) in Humberstone Gate, Leicester's Secular Society was, and is, the oldest in the world. By foregrounding rationalism and free speech, challenging religious privilege, working for justice and fairness, and promoting virtues such as kindness, loyalty and fairness, Secularists emphasised the importance of moral codes of behaviour and championed them in opposition to the dominant Christian ideology of the time.[46] Sunday observance, for example, was challenged in the 'cricket wars' during the summer of 1885 when Secularists played on the Pasture in defence of their right to use public recreation space for just such a purpose – on Sundays! This was typical of 'freethinkers'; their 'revolt against priestly pretensions' and search for 'a happier social environment' was their highly contentious justification for adding the bust of Jesus alongside those of Voltaire, Paine, Socrates and Owen to the façade of Secular Hall (see chapter 2).[47] Indeed, the programme of speakers at Secular Hall between 1881 and 1900 read like a 'Who's Who' of socialist and radical thinkers with a strong feminist presence. They included women's activists and suffragettes Annie Besant and Dr Alice Vickery, Robert Owen's daughter Rosamunde Dale Owen, Mary Kingsley, Charles Kingsley's niece; Social Democratic Federation members H.M. Hyndland and William Morris; socialists Charles Bradlaugh, and Harriet Law; secularist Charles Watts; several church reformers such as the Rev. C.W. Stubbs, and G.W. Foote, a convicted blasphemist, and artists and authors including George Bernard Shaw, Arthur Ransome and W.W. Collins. With these and other noteworthy speakers Leicester, and Leicester Secularists in particular, were hard-wired into progressive movements and their national champions.[48] Perhaps most instructive regarding the character and identity of Leicester was the balance of 64 places of worship: the Church of England had 16 places; nonconformists had 48.[49] No wonder Leicester was described as 'the bastion of non-conformity'.[50]

Re-calibrating the city

In 1845, the Unitarian congregation of the Great Meeting Chapel on East Bond Street, Leicester, sought to establish a Domestic Mission. They required a missionary to work among the town's poor. The surgeon Thomas Paget knew of the Rev. Joseph Dare's social work in Hinckley and appointed him to the post at a salary of £75 per annum. Had Leicester Unitarians

1.43 Sunday morning class, 1902 in Vaughan College.

1.44 Vaughan College, Great Central Street.

Source: both Record Office for Leicester, Leicestershire and Rutland, DE3736, Box 12, Great Central Street.

wanted a 'mission statement' it would no doubt have been derived from Dr Joseph Tuckerman, known as the 'father of American social work', who deplored 'the increasingly materialistic nature of society, particularly the uncaring attitudes it bred'.[51] Visitation was at the core of the Leicester Domestic Mission work – often Dare made 80 home visits each day – and there were parallel programmes of educational instruction, excursions, hobbies, sports, and nutritional and nursing advice funded by subscriptions from prominent Unitarians.[52] Anglicans, too, saw the merit of instruction for parishioners, and so the innovative vicar of St Martin's, David Vaughan, set up a reading room in Union Street in 1862 which became the Working Men's College in Great Central Street. It admitted women in 1880, and spearheaded the Workers' Education Association classes before in 1929 it became part of the Adult Education Department of Leicester University.[53]

Compassion and duty transcended class and sect to produce voluntary efforts and municipal policies. This was particularly so in relation to public health and even though death rates had fallen 34% between 1875 and 1900 to 18/1,000, deaths of children under five still accounted for 44% of all deaths. Mainly it was epidemic diseases – measles, scarlet fever, diphtheria, and infant diarrhoea – that were responsible for the deaths, and so in addition to improving the housing condition of the city guidance was also given to young mothers. A twin-pronged approach was adopted: an assault on the physical environment in which children lived; and sustained efforts to dispel the ignorance of young mothers.

Pressure for 'domestic nursing' was recognised in Leicester when the forerunner of district nursing, the Institution of Trained Nurses for the Town and County of Leicester (INTL) was formed in 1866, with five districts created two years later.[54] The continued presence of hosiery industry in congested homes meant workers were particularly susceptible to tuberculosis. Fresh air and sunlight were at the heart of district nursing.[55] Female sanitary inspectors were appointed in 1895, renamed 'Health Visitors' in 1906, and they advised mothers on infant feeding and the prevention of infection. This emphasis on the infant was then reinforced with three developments benefiting school-age children that positioned Leicester ahead of the rest of the country: firstly, a School Medical Service in 1905, three years before national legislation; secondly, a Municipal Milk Depot in 1906 on Belgrave Road that distributed dried evaporated cow's milk and provided guidance on the number (and times) of feeds for babies of varying ages; and thirdly, nine 'Schools for Mothers' opened by a voluntary organisation, the Leicester Health Society, between 1909 and 1915 offering home visits, instruction in childcare, and infant welfare clinics in each district of the borough.[56] By 1940 the School Medical Service had developed centralised specialist clinics – dental, ENT, orthopaedic, and ophthalmic – which the school medical officer described as 'money well spent … improving the health of the rising generation'.[57]

1.45 Temporary War Memorial: Town Hall Square.

Source: Record Office for Leicester, Leicestershire and Rutland, DE3736, Box 29, Town Hall Square, Folder 5, War Memorials.

World War I – 'the war to end all wars' – achieved neither that end, nor did the peace do much to improve well-being on the home front. The National Debt had risen tenfold during wartime and the determination to reduce it after 1919 and to 'return to normalcy' resulted in aggressive deflationary policies. To realign the pound, to 'return to gold' at the pre-war exchange rate of £1=$4.86, required a squeeze on costs to make British products competitive internationally; prices and wages needed to be reduced by 10% according to John Maynard Keynes' assessment in *The Economic*

1.46 'Wolsey Girls', leaving the Corn Exchange after a meeting about the Bedaux dispute. January 1932. Work stoppages in protest against job grading, time and motion studies, and wage incentives were most common in the textile industry in the years 1926–39. Wolsey's workforce supported the Trade Union Congress' determination to fight Charles Bedaux's 'scientific management' principles 'to a standstill'.
Source: Record Office for Leicester, Leicestershire and Rutland, DE3736, Box 21, Market Place, Folder 2.

Consequences of Mr Churchill, the Chancellor of the Exchequer. As part of that strategy, and in a rather modern vein, social services expenditure was cut by almost 12% in 1922–23. This 'Geddes Axe', named after the chairman of the Committee on National Expenditure, imposed swingeing cuts on housing, education, and health and set the tone for central government relations with local authorities throughout the 1920s, and for abrasive labour relations ultimately leading to the General Strike in 1926 (1.46).

The newly minted City of Leicester was pitched immediately into difficult financial conditions that ensured a public–private partnership was essential for the maintenance of social services and housing. For example, the council-operated Westcotes Maternity Home charged a weekly rate of £2 – beyond the means of most women. Public charity and private philanthropy continued to be major contributors to health care throughout the inter-war period. The Charity Organisation Society, Wycliffe Society for the Blind (1.47), Leicester Guild of the Crippled, and Leicester and County Mission for the Deaf and Dumb thus retained pivotal specialist roles while the city's public health department broadened its range of activities considerably. The city assumed responsibility under the Local Government Act, 1929, for the General Hospital, and in addition to the School Medical Services and child welfare programmes, city-wide initiatives included birth control advice,

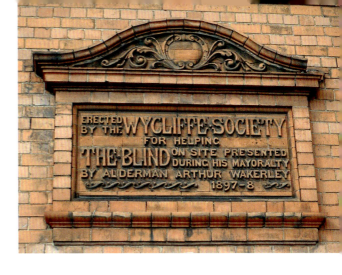

1.47 The Wycliffe Society for Helping the Blind. Founded in 1893 by Edwin Crew and Charles Harris in North Evington including a hospital and cottage homes. The first such charity was the Leicester Association for Promoting the General Welfare of the Blind (1858) founded by Robert Mackley with workshops in High Street. Architect: Arthur Wakerley.

Source: Colin Hyde.

maternity services, occupational therapy, cancer care, and a wide range of clinics administered by the increasingly stretched public health department.[58]

Public expenditure considerations affected post-war housing provision too. Lloyd George's election pledge of 'Homes fit for heroes' was not the beginning of council housing; Leicester, as elsewhere, had built three–storey blocks housing forty-two households in 1900. Indeed, the election slogan was no doubt sincere, but the reality was that post–war police and miners' strikes persuaded the Cabinet to counteract the risk of social unrest with a programme of Treasury subsidised public housing. Locally there was considerable support for the idea with the ILP holding the balance of power in the council chamber and influential secularist and Fabian councillors F.J. Gould and Herbert Hallam embracing the concept of planned communities with enthusiasm. Hallam observed 'that in St Margaret's [ward] children died three times as fast as the children of Spinney Hill ward'. The Leicester Tenants' Protection League, like their Clydeside comrades, protested against the unpatriotic action of local landlords in raising rents during wartime and were also in favour of social housing. Enthusiasm was one thing; delivery another. Ministry officials in London and regional representatives in Nottingham accused Leicester councillors in 1923 of poor performance in the provision of new housing. The criticisms were justified: Leicester was 20% below the average number of houses built per head of population compared to English boroughs generally.[59]

To a degree both parties were at fault. The Housing Committee found that the Ministry either delayed approval for their plans or sought alternatives, often repeatedly sending these back for revisions. The Ministry reduced subsidies in 1921, reintroduced them in 1923, changed the terms in 1924, and introduced bureaucratic steps requiring proof that local builders could not deliver the required units. Under the terms of the 1919 and 1923 subsidies Leicester built 1,384 houses costing £1.1 million, and though the largest project was at Coleman Road (1.48) and took some years to complete, there were 21 other construction sites. Managerial overheads and site supervision were problematic and the *Mercury* campaigned vigorously

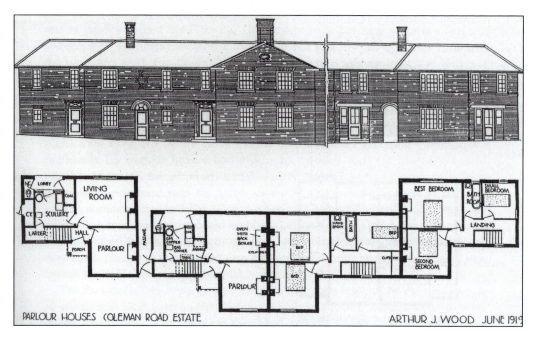

PARLOUR HOUSES COLEMAN ROAD ESTATE   ARTHUR J. WOOD JUNE 1919

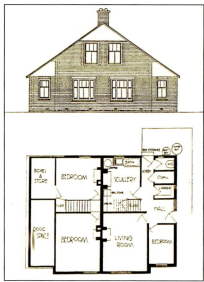

1.48 Coleman Road: 'Homes for Heroes'.
Source: Richard Rodger.

1.49 'Wakerley' houses: a distinctively Leicester council housing design, 1922.
Source: Richard Rodger.

for alternative materials – 'concrete stands the test of time' – and against council mis-management. What did emerge in these years were the 'Wakerley' houses – a distinctively Leicester design which pruned costs to conform to Ministry requirements and proved extremely popular and durable in the Leicester townscape.[60] By contrast, the Sheffield firm of Henry Boot and Co. built 2,000 brick and concrete houses between 1924 and 1927 on Saffron Lane estate and though amenities within the houses proved attractive, the lack of neighbourhood amenities produced a sense of isolation, and the term 'chinatown' was used to described the poor finish of the cracked roughcast exteriors. Long before many residents had moved in to Saffron Lane the city purchased 1,200 acres from the Winstanley family at Braunstone and J.S. Fyfe, the city's assistant architect, then designed the street layout for 2,500 houses built between 1927 and 1931 using a design with garden suburb elements that stressed wide verges, open spaces, curved streets and low densities.

1.50 Arthur Wakerley (1862–1941), architect. President, Leicester Society of Architects, and of Leicester Liberal Association. Councillor (1886) and youngest mayor (1897), aged 35. Wesleyan lay preacher. Planned and built North Evington, Turkey café, synagogue (Highfield Street), and Wycliffe homes (see 1.47).

Source: Leicester City Council.

1.51 Belgrave Gate slum clearance. Photographed from the rear of nos 183 to 193 on 26 January 1930.

Source: Record Office for Leicester, Leicestershire and Rutland, DE3736, Box 3, Belgrave Gate, Folder 1, Street Scenes.

This intensive period of council house construction peaked in 1927 and was replaced by a national campaign, partly financed by the Treasury, to demolish sub-standard housing defined as overcrowded as well as deficient in WCs and running water. Leicester embraced the initiative enthusiastically submitting almost 100 areas and 2,400 city centre houses for demolition. Two large new housing projects, Northfields (1935–39) and North Braunstone (1936–39) provided 2,800 homes for the families displaced. The effects of demolitions on kinship, credit networks, and on work, schooling and worship were disruptive, and these estates faced serious difficulties in establishing themselves and a sense of community. Overall, by 1939, 12% of the housing stock was publicly owned, and 35% of all new housing was provided by the city council – a little above the English average.

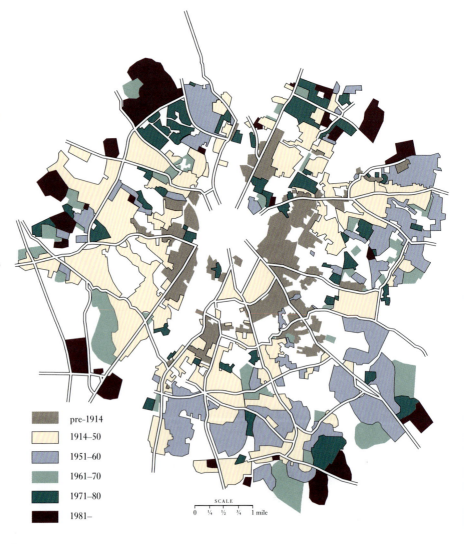

1.52 Historical development of housing in Leicester.

Source:
After R. Rodger, 'The built environment', in D. Nash and D. Reeder (eds), *Leicester in the Twentieth Century*, 33.

pre-1914

1914–50

1951–60

1961–70

1971–80

1981–

SCALE

0   ¼   ½   ¾   1 mile

The other 65% of new housing, of course, was provided by private housebuilders and swathes of semi-detached houses appealed to an expanding social class of middle class as mortgage rates plummeted from a plateau of 6% in the 1920s to just over 4% in 1936. With building costs also falling until the mid-1930s house ownership came within the grasp of a much wider income group. With white-collar pay averaging about £5 per week in 1936, and mortgages and rates accounting for about 15% of this, there was scope to fit out the new homes with furniture and soft furnishing, a wireless, electrical goods, and in some cases even to buy a car, the prices of which were falling for most of the 1930s. The suburban landscape was transformed. Semi-detached houses colonised the vectors between the radial roads. For example, between Scraptoft Lane and Uppingham Road and 'only five minutes' walk from the tram terminus and frequent buses from Humberstone Gate', Sherriff & Co., self-proclaimed as 'Leicester's leading house builder', constructed 575 houses 'of varied and distinctive design'.

The result of inter-war housing developments was radically to revise the social geography of Leicester. Workplace, social relations and networks in the nineteenth century had largely confined a class of factory hands and workshop employees to the central districts, ringed in a conventional pattern by middle-class suburbs. By the 1930s it was the wage-earners and labourers most affected by economic depression that had leap-frogged the Victorian suburbs and thereby encircled the middle classes through the development of peripheral council housing estates segregated by defined zones of middle-class semi-detached suburban settlement.

Social capital

The spatial revolution that was represented by new public sector housebuilding and slum clearances in the 1920s and 1930s dislocated communities, as did a programme of demolition in the 1954 to 1975 years. The accumulated knowledge, survival techniques, the ability to navigate a life course in the city were tossed aside in the wreckage of communities displaced and relocated to the margins of the city. Established interactions and relationships counted for little in the process of building new homes, and the fact that shops, community centres, GP practices, pubs, libraries and sports grounds were not generally factored into the new developments captures the low priority that were accorded to them and to community.

Social capital refers to 'connections among individuals – social networks and the norms of reciprocity and trustworthiness that arise from them'. Lacking that, society is weaker, vulnerable. The civic dimension is thus at its most powerful when embedded in reciprocal social relations.[61] Before 1914, church and chapel provided strong bonds of belonging. Workplace and neighbourhood, school and street, clubs and societies provided further elements of reciprocal social capital, and individuals were stronger for these

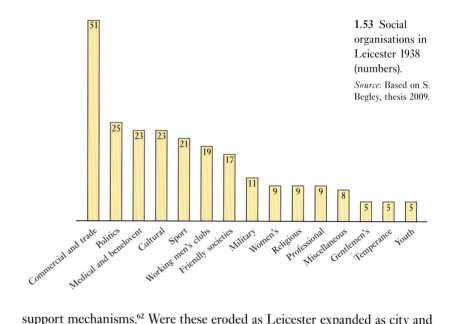

1.53 Social organisations in Leicester 1938 (numbers).

Source: Based on S. Begley, thesis 2009.

1.54 Scouts from the 11th Leicester St Peter's and St Hilda's Troup, 1920s.

Source: postcard.

support mechanisms.[62] Were these eroded as Leicester expanded as city and as spatial patterns changed? Certainly there is considerable evidence to show continued sociability in Leicester during the inter-war period. In addition to the annual Pageant (see chapter 7) there were over 270 clubs, societies, and organisations active in Leicester in 1938 and there is no convincing evidence that these were in decline in before World War II (1.53). Indeed, there is reason to believe that many informal and neighbourhood-based activities as well as sports clubs and hobbies never figure in listings, and that federated city-wide organisations like the scouts and guides, and chapters of freemasons, and ward level political activity are rarely identified (1.54).

Despite these data limitations, the evidence is of continuity in a highly visible level of social interaction in early twentieth century Leicester. In the

1930s work-based organisations such as Transport & Electricity Department Recreation Club; Midland Red Sports and Social Institute; British United Shoe Machinery Co. Institute (1.55); Highfields Railwayworkers' Social Club & Institute were vigorous and organised dances, drama performances, whist drives, and often a bar. In addition, the 'Works Teams' for football and cricket, and a women's hockey team were a common feature in local leagues and simultaneously provided visibility for the factory that only faltered in the 1970s as firms went out of business. Working Men's Clubs – at least nineteen of them in 1938 – were scattered around the city and also provided social activities and a neighbourhood focus. For instance, WMCs existed for the Aylestone, Belgrave, Clarence Street, Gypsy Lane, Belgrave, King Richard III Road, Newfoundpool, North Evington, and the Spinney Hills areas. Though there were also WMCs for the Coleman Road and Saffron Lane areas, these newly developed districts of Leicester were certainly under-represented in terms of community-based organisations.

At a ward level, too, social and political activity was combined by, for example, the Aylestone and District Unionist Club; Belgrave Liberal Club and Institute; Latimer Ward Conservative Institute; Leicester Trade Union Labour Club and Institute Ltd, which, in addition to door-stepping electioneering, raised funds and operated premises from which a number of social activities were organised. In a religious context St Patrick's Roman Catholic Club, the YMCA and YWCA, and the Christian Alliance of Women and Girls

1.55 British United Shoe apprentices 1927.
Source: by courtesy of British United History Group.

fused spiritual, charitable and social activities, and the Leicester branch of the Soroptomists Club, founded in 1921, encouraged working, business and professional women to improve the lives of women and girls in local communities. This showed a more direct form of engagement in contrast to the earlier Belmont House Society group of educated women from exclusive suburbs who, in addition to their shared reading interests, also undertook a variety of philanthropic works. Of course there were organisations such as the Leicester Women's Luncheon Club, Leicester Ladies' Swimming Club, Carisbrooke Lawn Tennis Club, Literary and Philosophical Society, and Clarendon Park Operatic Society which through their interests and subscriptions tended to elitism, but for every one of those there was a variety of allotment societies, medical and benevolent societies, the Leicester Children's Aid Association, British Legion and Old Comrades Association for the 'Tigers', Guards, and Territorials, and the Leicester Social Council for the Unemployed, each of which cut across lines of class distinction.

Voluntary associations throughout the period 1870 to 1939 increased in density and variety, and contributed to the organised social life of the town and the management of local public affairs. In so doing, social cohesion and civic identity – the reciprocity of associated with social capital – were mutually reinforced and the distinctive identity of Leicester forged. Part of that reciprocity was an increased input from the town council in the inter-war years; housing provision and health clinics were just two such areas of increased municipal management during the inter-war years. Policing was another. The remit of the Leicester Watch Committee, the council-appointed body responsible for policing, was divided among 21 sub-committees between 1918 and 1939. Their duties expanded exponentially to include the inspection of fire safety in cinemas and the safe storage of celluloid, chemicals and other flammable materials; enforcement of factory and workshop legislation under the Factories Act, 1901, including factory fire escapes; Sunday entertainment; and included licensing duties relating to pawnbrokers, metal dealers, street collections and public advertisements, as well as the use of the steam whistles and hooters that defined the rhythms of the factory day. Workplaces and public places required tighter police management as congestion and complexity posed increased risks to the public. Policing the street had always been a key role, but this became considerably more important both with rising levels of car ownership – registrations increased fivefold between 1923 and 1938 – and a succession of Road Traffic Acts. These prompted the formation of a police motor transport and a patrol department, vital for effective traffic management and another technological development, the introduction in 1931 of a city-wide police box system designed to improve communications between the emergency services and members of the public. Here, then, was social capital in action: in an increasingly complex world a degree of trust was invested in the police in return for improved management of public safety. Watching – watching out for the public – had another consequence: a rising volume of administrative circulars, policy recommendations, and standard operating procedures generated by Whitehall, city hall, and the fire and police service themselves. The Watch Committee was not unique in this respect; the workload of all town council committees was becoming more cumbersome as technical details and operational matters became more complex.[63] As one contemporary authority commented:

> A council … may direct policy and decide principles, but is an impossible body to give judgement on the multifarious problems falling to the lot of local government authorities to solve in these days. It has neither the time nor the knowledge.[64]

Public–private partnerships, as they would now be called, flourished in the educational arena, and specifically in relation to technical education. Leicester was a town of many small fortunes where leading businessmen, through successive generations, remained prominent as political and social leaders and contributed to charitable activities and civic bequests.[65] Even before the business endowments that contributed to the foundation of Leicester University College in 1927 there had been a long-standing interest from industrialists in the development of technical education.[66] This emerged from the Art College into design classes at Wyggeston School in the 1880s and then into the Technical and Art School (now the Hawthorn Building, De Montfort University) opened by Mayor Edward Wood in 1896. The popularity of the City and Guilds of London Institute qualifications after 1878, the introduction of National Certificates and Diplomas (forerunners of the HNC and HND qualifications) in 1921–22, and the development locally of many courses on accounting, typing, commercial and secretarial practice required extensions to the Technical and Art School in 1909 and 1927. Nor was schooling for the majority of children overlooked. Educational provision for them received a major investment from the Leicester School Board which built nine new schools between 1870 and 1880 and a further sixteen between 1880 and 1913. Instruction was prudently provided at about £9 per pupil per year – well below the national average – and with an eye on league tables, numeracy and literacy were at very high levels with exam pass rates over 90% in the 1890s.[67] This human investment was a foundation for the reinvention of industrial Leicester.

1.56 Municipal and Technical and Art School 1896.

Source: Richard Rodger.

One reason for the interest in design and technical drawing was that by 1911 hosiery and footwear industries were already under commercial pressure with male employment down one-fifth on the levels of 1861. It was light engineering that provided the industrial diversification that was Leicester's insurance premium in the difficult market conditions of the inter-war years. The city's exposure to the risk of unemployment was reduced by developments in light engineering including tool-making and drilling equipment (Jones and Shipman); mechanical engineering (Bentley) for footwear and knitwear; metal working and structural engineering (Wadkins); razor blades (Gillette – their first British plant was in Leicester); typewriters (Imperial Typewriters' main base was also in Leicester); thread manufacture (British Thread Mills Ltd); textile dyes (Oram); optical and photographic equipment (Taylor Hobson), and a variety of firms producing office and food-processing equipment. Heavy engineering played its part, too, with the firms of Pochin, Gimson, Frederick Parker, and Richard's Engineering making machinery for specialist firms producing cranes, lifting equipment, diesel engines, and pumps. As a result of knowledge-based research and development engineering accounted for 18% of the Leicester workforce in 1939, rising to 22% in 1951. Unconsciously, Leicester's industrial structure was diversified between the wars with engineering eclipsing combined hosiery and footwear by 1951 as the main sector of male employment. While this 'high-tech' emphasis created new jobs and added value to the local economy in engineering it simultaneously displaced semi-skilled workers so that the inter-war jobless total in Leicester hovered around 10,000. Despite this, the inter-war years were by no means as harsh a period for Leicester citizens as for those in British cities where there was a dominant industrial sector or employer – as in Sheffield, Middlesbrough or Belfast. There were still 250 hosiery and 200 boot and shoe manufacturers in the city in 1936 when the Statistical Bureau of the League of Nations confidently adjudged that Leicester was the 'second most prosperous city in Europe' – Lille was the first – though this may also have had much to do with levels of continental hyperinflation, reparations and economic depression in European cities.[68]

Local government work reflected this greater participation in everyday lives and was one of the growth areas of employment between 1920 and 1950.[69] Embossed on notepaper, street furniture, buildings and vehicles, Leicester City Council's 'fingerprints' were all over areas of expanding responsibility – education, housing, health, policing – and this raised the profile of the city as a whole. Clubs, too, prefixed their activity with 'Leicester' – not just high visibility Leicester City Football Club and Leicester 'Tigers' Rugby Club – but a wide range of other activities (see Appendix). Frequently these were federations of local interests such as manufacturers, workers, professional associations, immigrants, girl guides, faith groups, cultural interests and support organisations and each time this foregrounded 'Leicester', raising identity, and a consciousness of that identity, in the process both locally and beyond.

The results of public and private actions, and of voluntary and charitable initiatives were profound. Spencer's map of 1857 shows a tightly bounded built-up area. Wharf Street and the Three Gates areas were densely packed on an essentially ancient street pattern. If it were possible to resurrect someone from the 1860s and bring them back to life in the 1930s they would have immense difficulty in navigating their way around Leicester. Even where the street pattern persisted, the buildings, mental markers, the sites of personal memories and sociability, had changed. The boundaries of the built-up area were different, and the role of the City Council was unrecognisable. The bustling borough had indeed become a city.

Appendix 1   Selected organisations with a Leicester-wide focus, 1938

Leicester Association of Baptist and Union Churches
Leicester Boot Manufacturers' Association
Leicester Bridge Club
Leicester Catholic Club
Leicester Charity Organisation Society
Leicester Children's Aid Association
Leicester City Permanent Allotment Society
Leicester Co-operative Society
Leicester Constitutional Club
Leicester Devon and Cornwall Society

Leicester Diocesan Moral Welfare Association
Leicester District Nursing Association
Leicester Film Society
Leicester French Circle
Leicester Girl Guides
Leicester Guild of the Crippled
Leicester Labour Party
Leicester Lancastrian Society
Leicester Magic Circle
Leicester Master Printers' Association
Leicester Old Coldstreamers' Association
Leicester Permanent Building Society
Leicester Property Owners' and Ratepayers'
Association
Leicester Round Table
Leicester Scottish Dance Society
Leicester Socialist Society
Leicester Society of Chartered Accountants
Leicester Table Tennis Association
Leicester Temperance and General Permanent
Building Society
Leicester Territorials
Leicester Trade Union Labour Club and Institute
Ltd
Leicester Volunteer Old Comrades' Association
Leicester Water Bed Association
Leicester Women's Luncheon Club

Leicester Bond Street Friendly Society
Leicester Bowling Club
Leicester Caledonian Society
Leicester Central Conservative Association
Leicester Chess Club
Leicester City Football Club
Leicester Civic Society
Leicester Commercial Travellers' Association
Leicester County Nursing Association
Leicester Diocesan Church of England Temperance
Society
Leicester District Boy Scouts Association
Leicester Drama Society
Leicester First Permanent Money Association
Leicester Fruit and Potato Merchants' Association
Leicester Girls' Social Guild
Leicester House Agents' Association
Leicester Ladies' Swimming Club
Leicester Liberal Associations
Leicester Master Painters' Association
Leicester Medical Society
Leicester Peace Council
Leicester Private Fire Brigade Association
Leicester Railwaymen's Club and Institute

Leicester Rugby Club
Leicester Social Council for Unemployed
Leicester Society for Psychical Research
Leicester Symphony Orchestra
Leicester Teachers' Association
Leicester Temperance Society

Leicester Textile Society
Leicester United Friendly Societies Medical
Association
Leicester Walking Club
Leicester Welsh Society

Source: based on S. Begley, 'Voluntary associations and the civic ideal',
Leicester University Ph.D. thesis, 2009.

Appendix 2 Sectoral employment in Leicester, 1861–1951

		1861	1911 *Males*	1951	1861	1911 *Females*	1951
	Total occupied and unoccupied	31,766	83,426	134,723	36,290	98,584	150,458
		%	%	%	%	%	%
	Engaged in occupations	67	67	76	42	47	43
I	General or local government	1	2	5	0	0	2
II	Defence of the country	1	0	0	0	0	0
III	Professional occupations	3	3	4	2	4	9
IV	Domestic service	1	2	0	23	14	3
V	Commercial occupations	2	7	2	0	3	2
VI	Conveyance of men, goods	6	10	7	2	1	2
VII	Agriculture, farms, woods	4	1	0	1	0	0
VIII	Fishing	0	0	0	0	0	0
IX	Mine and quarry workers	1	0	0	0	0	0
X	Engineering, manufacture	7	10	22	0	1	7
XI	Precious metals, jewels	0	1	1	0	0	1
XII	Building and construction	8	7	8	1	0	0
XIII	Wood, furniture, decoration	3	2	2	1	0	0
XIV	Brick, cement, pottery, china, glass	1	0	0	0	0	0
XV	Chemicals, explosives, oil	1	2	3	0	0	2
XVI	Skins, leather, saddles	1	1	1	0	0	0
XVII	Printers, lithographers	1	3	3	0	3	3
XVIII	Textile manufacturers	10	8	10	15	33	32
XIX	Tailors, shoemakers, dress	32	25	10	48	30	17
XX	Food, tobacco, drink, lodging	4	3	3	3	4	7
XXI	Gas, water, electricity, sanitation	0	2	2	0	0	0
XXII	Other, general, undefined.	6	3	1	1	0	1
XXIII	Dealers	8	11	13	2	7	13
		100	100	100	100	100	100

Source: Census of England 1851, 1911 and 1951.

2

Leicester: metropolis of dissent

L EICESTER has more or less always been a nonconformist city in almost
every sense of this word. It has always had an uneasy relationship
with centralised forms of authority and has been comfortable, and even
positively happy, with its staunchly provincial outlook and character. This
has sometimes meant that it has provided a relatively secure home for ideas
and attitudes that are not orthodox or mainstream. This has certainly been
important in the area of religion where the city of Leicester became an
enclave of the religiously unorthodox and the dissenting.

The city arguably gave notice of this in its unswerving support for
the parliamentary cause during the Civil War – a decision that could at
specific moments have cost the local community quite dearly. Nonetheless
Leicester became a noted puritan stronghold which influenced not simply
religious worship but also wider morality. Drinking on the Sabbath and
gambling in taverns were prohibited, with legal action taken against those
who were caught indulging in these practices.[1] The parliamentary cause
was the natural home of many 'sectaries' and 'independents' who rejected
the doctrines and authority of the Church of England. These individuals
flourished in the religious toleration that was a feature of Cromwell's
Commonwealth between 1650 and 1660. The Act of Uniformity (1662)
which swiftly followed the Restoration was intended to bring a return to
orthodoxy by insisting upon undiluted Anglican doctrines and conformity.
This was intended to drive out unorthodox religious views and those
who believed them. In this it was successful as many independents and
Presbyterians left their parsonages in Leicester and its surrounding districts.
In the end it did little to prevent many independent, Baptists and dissenting
congregations from establishing themselves, albeit secretly, throughout the
county. Indeed, as one congregation's official history notes this was the
occasion upon which all who suffered under the Act of Uniformity became
united as nonconformists. Although things eased after the Declaration
of Indulgence in 1672 dissenting congregations were still hampered by
restrictions and an ongoing absence of resources.

Many individuals who entered these congregations were tradesmen
and artisans and Leicestershire's nineteenth-century religious dissenting
geography was complete when Methodism began to gain a foothold in the
mining areas to the west of the county. This should be contrasted with the

rural Anglican character of the east of the county shading into Rutland. Between the two of these was the town of Leicester which was the centre of a variety of shades of dissent and was to become home to more of these as the century progressed. At the end of the eighteenth century the most numerous nonconformist group in Leicester were the Baptists who met in two congregations of note in Friar Lane and Harvey Lane.

In the early years of the nineteenth century the most prominent centre of dissenting religion in the town was the chapel in East Bond Street which was known as the Great Meeting. This had been founded in 1708 by the collaboration of Presbyterians and Independents – groups who had been part of the dissenting tradition inherited from the Civil War, although at this earlier period they were in fierce opposition to one another. Both groups were determined to realise and implement the self-government of their congregation. This allowed the chapel and its members to pursue unorthodox theology and the character of the services and those presiding over them steadfastly reflected this.

2.1, 2.2 Great Meeting Unitarian Chapel, East Bond Street, founded 1708 as a 'meeting house for protestant dissenters.' The first seven mayors of the borough were all Unitarians.
Source: Colin Hyde.

Within the Great Meeting the Presbyterianism inherited from the seventeenth century gradually gave way to a more open toleration of diverging theological viewpoints under Dr Joseph Priestley. Within the first years of the nineteenth century a new theological position was adopted within the Great Meeting known as Unitarianism. This was, for the time, a somewhat extreme theological position which ostensibly denied the divinity of Christ, instead seeing him as an inspired and motivated, but wholly human teacher. Unitarian belief rejected the concept of the divine and was a theological position that was as controversial among other nonconformists as it was among the Anglican establishment. Opposition from this quarter was particularly significant since Unitarianism also denied the truth of the Trinity, that God, the Holy Spirit and Jesus were one and thus divine. The Trinity was an essential part of the Anglican Church's Thirty Nine Articles,

the catechism of the Church of England that was still used as a test of fitness for office and respectability. Thus the doctrines espoused in the Leicester Great Meeting were placed on the extreme theological edge. The paradox was that this theological position attracted many of the well-to-do elements of Leicester society, although this may have been due to the fact that the traditional gentry structures which normally supported Anglicanism had always been quite weak in Leicester and the surrounding county.[2]

Unitarianism also claimed to be an intellectual position that took an inquisitive approach not simply to religion but also to the wider natural universe. This attempt to understand the universe also inspired local individuals such as Richard Philips who was an advocate of the ideas of the deist Thomas Paine. This had been a philosophical position which had gradually developed from the seventeenth century onwards. It basically rejected the doctrines and institutions of organised religion and instead concentrated upon the idea that there was merely a divine presence which had created the universe to regulate itself. This interest in the material nature of the universe meant that inquiry and exploration were as fundamental as other aspects of belief, ensuring many ideas were propounded through the radical newspapers such as the *Leicester Herald* founded and managed by Richard Philips. Such ideas were also the staple of the lecturing platform, and of a reading room and literary society also founded by Philips. The views of deists blended radical religion with radical politics. Those who merely believed in a creator without giving power to established religion and religious hierarchies debated the nature of the universe. In doing so they made discoveries about man and the natural world and found themselves discussing electricity and democracy as pieces of knowledge that would transform the world. These deist views and the focus they gave to the contemporary world were to have a lasting impact upon the religious landscape of Leicester.

The nineteenth-century nonconformist conscience in Leicester

At the end of the eighteenth century dissenters were still excluded from public office and the outbreak of the French Revolution drew attention to this, prompting a petition to the Leicester Corporation demanding the protection of dissenters' rights alongside other citizens', but also requesting 'any civil honours or emoluments which are accessible to other subjects, without any regard to their religious opinions or practices'.[3] The corporation replied with the suggestion that dissenting views were contrary to the interests of the state and that dissenters enjoying such offices would use them shamelessly to advance the cause of their own party! This view was to be startlingly turned on its head in the period after the great parliamentary Reform Act of 1832. This had reformed parliament and redrew the representational

2.3 Robert Hall (1764–1831), Baptist clergyman, outstanding preacher, advocated freedom of Press, influenced by French Revolution, challenged corrupt government.
Source: Richard Rodger.

map of England. Its local counterpart, which sought to reform local government came in the shape of the Municipal Corporations Reform Act 1835, swept away centuries of customary and archaic governing practices. In Leicester the passing of this Act brought an end to Tory establishment dominance of the Leicester Corporation and finally opened it up to wider representation.

With the dissolution of the old, corrupt, corporation Leicester came to be dominated by a Whig political presence that manifested itself in strong and confident local government in the hands of leading nonconformists. From this the city also became a centre for many social and political causes associated with dissent. Harvey Lane Baptist church produced notable figures in the wider history of noncon-formity, such as William Carey who is credited with the establishment of foreign missionary work, and the charismatic Robert Hall who reputedly attracted audiences from all over England when he preached.[4]

In 1834 the city welcomed the great advocate of church disestab-lishment, Edward Miall, who came from Ware in Berkshire to take up a ministry presiding over the Bond Street Chapel. Miall found himself among like-minded nonconformists such as J.P. Mursell who claimed that dissent had become relaxed and unconfrontational in the wake of the repeal of the Test and Corporation Act, 1828, and the Birth and Marriage Registration Act, 1837. The first of these restricted membership of governing corporations to Anglicans who could satisfy the 'test' of being a communicant of the Church of England. The second provided for legal marriage and registration of births beyond the confines of the established Anglican Church. Both had been long-held grievances about office holding and legitimate access to the rights enjoyed by members of the established church. Miall and Mursell longed to rediscover dissent's confrontational and radical past and between them they argued that destruction of the monopoly enjoyed by the established church was a fundamental duty. It was seen to offend both justice and individual freedom of conscience and in their work they ensured that 'from the pulpits, the platforms, the press of the town and country, in ordination sermons, and newspaper articles they put forth their views of the principles of Dissenters; and with a degree of effect that soon gave to Leicester a "new reputation".'[5]

Disestablishment was a key dissenting cause which challenged the subsidies (tithes) paid by dissenters for the upkeep of the established Anglican Church, educational and other privileges. Its status as the established church also allowed its representation in the House of Lords which implied that parliament would always protect its privileged position despite growing evidence that it was no longer the national Church. Miall, however, was prepared to take forms of direct action in defence of members of his co-religionists who were prepared to protest about the iniquities of the prevailing system. In 1840 a member of his congregation William Baines, and twenty-six others, refused to pay his tithe declaring that he recognised no authority other than scripture. When he was jailed this led to the formation of the Leicester Voluntary Church Society. At its first meeting Edward Miall rose to speak with words that were echoed in the pages of the dissenting newspaper *The Nonconformist* and really convey the vehemence of the nonconformists' political motivation:

'I appeal,' he says 'to the honest, the thinking, the manly Dissenter of this Kingdom. What have you gained by your silence and inactivity? Not peace. For every Petty Officer of the State Church, emboldened by your apathy, ventures forth to insult you. Not a more kindly consideration of your claims, for no questions are treated by the Legislature with such haughty and supercilious derision as questions affecting the interests of religious liberty. All parties agree in neglecting and oppressing you. No consideration is paid to your feelings. It is not deemed important to preserve ordinary decency in reference to your affairs. You are laughed at, you are despised, you are most gratuitously kicked by men of every political creed, by men of every order, by men in power and men out of power, by the poor curate whose parish is his kingdom, and by the lordly bishop who utters oracles from the bench. If peace then be your object this is not the way to gain it. If you are seeking respect, you are utterly beside the mark.'[6]

The case against Baines and his imprisonment was reported in *The Nonconformist* until his release in June 1841. This incident was instrumental in persuading Edward Miall to resign his ministry and henceforth to devote himself to the political cause of disestablishment (2.4). He did this first through journalism and later as an MP for Rochdale (1852–57) and Bradford (1860–74) and promoted the continuity of political dissenting principles and attitudes forged in Leicester since the seventeenth century. All of these developments within the public sphere were responsible for marking

2.4 Edward Miall (1809–81) politician, journalist, and Congregational minister of Bond Street Church (1834–40), raised capital for *The Nonconformist* (1841); active in Anti-Corn Law League, and Chartism; published *The British Churches in Relation to the British People* (1849); took over John Bright's Rochdale seat in 1852.

Source: Vanity Fair, 1871.

Leicester out as a major centre of dissenting sentiment, politics and practice during the first half of the nineteenth century.

The Unitarian Great Meeting and its congregation was able to celebrate early nineteenth-century nonconformist dominance in Leicester in some style. It contributed the first seven mayors to preside over the reformed corporation, earning the building the soubriquet 'The Mayor's Nest'. These included important individuals such as Thomas Paget, John Biggs and William Biggs. One especial feature of Unitarian belief was an irrepressibly strong mission to improve the living and social conditions of mankind. In other localities individuals such as Mrs Gaskell in Manchester, author of the great social novel of the 1840s, *Mary Barton*, Harriet Martineau and Joseph Priestley involved themselves in charitable works providing essential assistance to the destitute. However, they also saw it as an important part of the mission to record and catalogue the plight of the poor so that others capable of providing assistance were informed.[7] In Leicester this prompted the foundation of the Leicester Domestic Mission in 1845.[8] This can be seen as a response to the range of demographic, social and economic strains that beset the Leicester of the first half of the nineteenth century. During this period the population of the city doubled, bringing with it a significant range of social problems.

Nonconformist philanthropy: learning about the modern city

The Domestic Mission was funded by private subscription and many prominent local figures from families such as the Pagets, the Coltmans, the Gimsons and the Whetstones contributed to this fund. Its first full-time missionary was Joseph Dare who held office from 1845 until the year before it ceased operation in 1877 and he seems to have been the linchpin around which all work of the mission turned. Dare left a series of yearly reports

2.5 Rev. Joseph Dare (1800–83), moved to Hinckley where he was secretary of the Widows and Orphans Society; appointed as missionary to work among the urban poor for the Unitarian Great Meeting chapel, 1845–76.

Source: reproduced from B. Haynes, *Working-class Life in Victorian Leicester: The Joseph Dare Reports* (Leicester Museums, Arts and Records Service, 1991).

which were a significant and detailed picture of the mission's operations and these give an important insight into the charity work inspired by the nonconformist conscience and what it sought to achieve. Unlike many of the other charitable organisations that aimed at tackling a single identified evil, such as the Temperance Society, the work of the Unitarian Domestic Mission in Leicester tackled an array of urban problems. This was characterised as the urge to 'relieve emergency, to comfort the sick and dying, to awaken self energy, self-reformation, and faith in the goodness of our Father in heaven, to instruct those especially who have been neglected and improve as much as may be their physical and social condition.'[9] Dare saw this as both a public and religious duty that he backed up with a regime of regular visits to houses within poor neighbourhoods. These he approached in a spirit of goodwill and a genuine desire to offer help and comfort, remaining opposed to the use of this as an opportunity for religious missionary work. This emphasis upon personal choice and conviction was also another manifestation of the nonconformist conscience that would regularly break the surface in Leicester.

Dare noted that a significant number of Leicester's problems were caused by the structural issues associated with the city's cyclical trade fluctuations. Hosiery was notorious for having only episodic and patchy seasonal demand for its products, which meant a considerable number of workers found themselves in only partial employment. Dare noted how working-class self-help often did what it could to alleviate matters but also argued that laissez-faire economics were substantially to blame for this, alongside the dreadful cost advantages that outwork still maintained in the city and its surrounding villages. The mission began to take a holistic view of the Leicester working classes and the problems they faced. Thus Dare's reports, year by year, would be culled from his observations about the contemporary character of the population at any particular moment and the problems they were facing. He would note the endemic problems associated with poor housing and the destitution that beset the city during acute and frequent slumps in trade. In connection with these he would regularly catalogue the efforts of private agencies to alleviate what suffering and poverty they could, and would note the effectiveness of the mission's own efforts in this area. The prevalence of diseases such as smallpox and measles also exercised Dare considerably, and these began to be seen as a further aggravation of the city's distressed condition.

Like many from a nonconformist background Dare ostensibly believed to a degree in a version of the Victorian doctrine of self-help. This he implemented within the Domestic Mission through a wide range of different and sophisticated educational opportunities for boys, girls and adults. Education played a specific role in encouraging self-reliance, through confidence and the acquisition of knowledge, which would be used positively to enable individuals to survive and better themselves. This attitude also explains Dare's frequent expression of pleasure when he observed occasions when the working classes were able to take advantage of brief periods of prosperity to invest in savings banks or other indicators of growing respectability. Dare's own approach to the doctrine of self-help allowed for the dispensing of charity only in dire need, and only with the intention of allowing and persuading individuals to get back upon their feet again. His reports contain evidence that he was discerning enough to be able to identify genuine need and what he considered to be destitution produced solely by bad habits, intoxication or criminal tendencies. However, the overall picture we can see from Dare's reports indicates that he could discern genuine need so often and so regularly that he almost came to argue that episodic charity work was merely a method of applying temporary sticking plaster to society's on-going and chronic social problems. Eventually Dare saw that lasting structural solutions were necessary to alleviate such persistent and acute social and economic problems. In particular he argued that the industrial structure of the city needed to change to factory-based employment which was more regular, better remunerated and more flexible in its response to economic turmoil.[10] Dare's work, and that of the Unitarian Domestic Mission, provided an important dialogue about social problems and represented a demonstration of the limitations of traditional, religiously inspired charitable works. These were motivated by both religious zeal and social conscience, but were superseded by more comprehensive state-inspired attempts to alleviate suffering. While Dare applied temporary forms of relief he observed that social problems were interlinked and needed tackling to prevent their causes rather than to ameliorate their effects.

The mid–nineteenth century: consolidation and complacency

The Baptists' presence in Leicester also developed during the first third of the nineteenth century. They were also responsible for constructing a number of new chapels in Leicester during the nineteenth century following on from the initial premises in Friar Lane, and Harvey Lane. Perhaps the most notable of these was the Charles Street Chapel which was erected in 1830. But most spectacular, arguably, was the Belvoir Street Chapel designed by Joseph Hansom and opened in 1845, ostensibly as a fitting backdrop for the preaching of J.P. Mursell, and the typically circular design was given the soubriquet of the 'Pork Pie chapel'.[11] Other manifestations of the nonconformist agenda also made their mark on the landscape of Leicester. In 1849 the public cemetery at Welford Road was opened and this broke the monopoly of the established church on the place and manner of burial. Joseph Dare noted that the cemetery would ensure that the established church could no longer refuse the burial service to nonconformists, unbelievers or the unbaptised.[12]

However, the importance of this series of fillips to nonconformist aspirations was damaged by the findings of the 1851 religious census. In truth this was a considerable shock to all religious denominations since it effectively, if crudely, suggested that only half the population attended a place of religious worship. One major finding from this exercise, pertinent to Leicester, was that the level of religious provision, defined as places of worship and seats within them, had scarcely kept pace with the great surge in the city's population. On the census day in 1851 Anglican congregations in Leicester totalled 8,165, while the total for the Baptists (both Particular and General sects) totalled 6,098. The combined congregations for the Methodist sects (Wesleyan, Primitive and other groupings) totalled 4,601 while Congregationalists and Calvinists combined totalled 3,427. While these figures suggest that Anglicanism remained the single largest religious group in Leicester the combined strength of the nonconformist groupings were over a third bigger than this.[13] We can deduce from this that when nonconformity acted together in concerted campaigns, and in the name of Liberalism, it was potent and powerful. But if it fragmented or became divided then its power would obviously diminish quickly.

The years after 1851 saw all religious denominations within the city respond in something of a frenzy, often channelled into the building of places of worship. In 1851 the Anglican Church had 9 churches, the last of which, St George's, opened in 1827.[14] By 1882 when the *Leicester Daily Post* undertook a survey similar to the 1851 Religious Census this had grown to a somewhat staggering 24. Whilst it should be noted that not all of these were purpose-built premises rendered in brick and stone – some were hastily constructed mission huts – this nonetheless represented a concerted response to the perceived problem of deficient religious facilities, provision of which would also be tackled in other ways. Baptist chapels had more than doubled their provision during this period, as had Congregational and those of the various species of Methodism. However, closer analysis suggests that, in many respects, in the latter half of the nineteenth century nonconformity began to falter in Leicester. Whilst the efforts of the Anglican Church to out-build the nonconformist sects was not itself a problem, there is evidence that it was more successful in filling its churches. Several purpose-built nonconformist chapels folded within a few years of their completion, with the Primitive Methodists appearing to be most susceptible to this calamity.[15] The later history of these organisations in Leicester, as nationally, was characterised by merger and the formation of 'circuits' with a mother church overseeing a number of satellites. In Leicester the mother churches were Bishop Street, Humberstone Road and King Richard's Road.[16]

There was also evidence that the Anglican Church, or at least some sections of it, was proving more adept at maintaining the commitment of their congregations and particularly their working-class ones. In the 1882 survey it was evident that the nonconformist groupings were manifestly less able to fill their churches and seats within them since these premises could scarcely keep pace with the social changes that occurred more rapidly within the urban environment. Meanwhile, for the Anglican establishment, the chance to build churches anew in greater numbers than nonconformists meant that these could be located in response to need and to target forgotten areas, or those that had recently developed as a result of inward migration and population growth.

2.6 St Andrew's (1860–62), Jarrom Street. Architect G.G. Scott.
Source: Colin Hyde.

| Leicester: a modern history

2.7 St Mark's church, detail (1869–72), Belgrave Gate. Architect Ewan Christian.
Source: Colin Hyde.

2.8 St Paul's (1870–71), Kirkby Road. Architects Ordish and Traylen.
Source: Colin Hyde.

2.9 Gott ist überall (God is everywhere), even on the façade of Aylestone Road terraced housing.
Source: Richard Rodger.

Several of these churches, such as St Mark's, St Andrew's and St Paul's further extended their appeal by installing tractarian, high church ritualist ministers who concentrated upon dispensing the sacrament rather than preaching and scripture which had been the mainstay of nonconformity.[17] These churches were also skilled at providing for a wider sense of mission among working-class congregations and enabled a wider number of clubs and organisations to flourish within the community. Their ritualist ministers proved popular among working-class parishioners, as they also did in other cities, notably London. Indeed it has been suggested that this was part of a much wider trend of diminishing working-class attachment to broad nonconformity. This attachment had been something of a social and political alliance forged around the great challenges to the establishment in the first half of the nineteenth century. The inspiration for dissent provided motivation for a number of working-class individuals to involve themselves in radical politics and to support the issues of self-help and disestablishment. The issue of representation, tithes and other abuses of power were also tailor-made to bring these two groupings, at least partly, together during the middle part of the century in a loose confederation. This situation had been confirmed by a noted willingness of the Leicester nonconformist elite to harness the power of working-class political sentiment.

Nonconformist Liberalism and the working classes: a progressive alliance?

Leicester's MP at the start of the second half of the century, the Unitarian and Radical John Biggs, who held the seat between 1856 and 1862, was an enthusiastic advocate of electoral reform in the form of an extension to the franchise. On his retirement in 1862, his replacement Peter Alfred Taylor, exemplified how nonconformity and radical politics could frequently come together, blending old and new. Taylor was a descendent of the Courtauld family, themselves Huguenots and refugees from religious persecution. Taylor was himself a Unitarian and also joined in radical politics at an early age. His inspiration came from meeting the Italian Guiseppe Mazzini in 1845. Mazzini was responsible for turning revolutionary republicanism and the quest for Italian unification into a genuinely popular movement and was an individual who personified the internationalist liberal desire to escape from despotism. For Taylor this contributed to a lifelong interest in international causes, an important strand of mid- and late nineteenth-century Liberalism. Taylor became a noted radical Liberal and was a vice-president of the Reform League. He was also one of the most prominent parliamentary advocates of republicanism in England and argued the case for this throughout the 1870s, the decade in which the monarchy attracted most criticism. Taylor was also involved closely in some of the more other radical liberal issues such as church disestablishment and the campaign to remove especially punitive game laws.[18] Taylor's radical Liberalism was itself a product of the radical involvement of the town in Chartism, the dissolution of which allowed Liberalism to absorb these tendencies. Local and national issues also came together and were influenced by other ideas that influenced aspects of the Liberal conscience. This was evident in the Leicester Anti-Vaccination agitation of the 1880s when opposition was marshalled in the form of a reaction against state coercion and the denial of rights to the individual.[19]

This radical understanding between working-class aspirations and nonconformity had also inspired working men to seek representation through the Liberal party to represent a form of progressive alliance. This was perhaps best embodied by the formation of the Leicester Democratic Association soon after the passing of the Electoral Reform Act, 1867. Daniel Merrick, an important local trade unionist, had formed the association and the links to mainstream Liberalism are emphasised by its support for Liberal candidates in the School Board elections after 1870. This quasi Lib-Lab alliance had been evident religiously and socially in the nonconformist congregations in the early half of the nineteenth century. Gradually these congregations became sparser as a result of social changes. Mainstream nonconformity was partially outflanked by the appeal of ritualism within the newly built Anglican churches and also by Anglican evangelicalism that in Leicester boasted some gifted individuals such as the charismatic Canon David Vaughan. Adult education was Vaughan's particular cause and he was responsible for the establishment of the highly successful Vaughan Working Men's College. This branch of Anglicanism was also seen as responsible for the recruitment of some influential sections of genteel nonconformity away from their dissenting origins.[20]

What this points to is a gradual dwindling of strength in traditional forms of dissenting nonconformity. Some genteel members were deserting precisely as its appeal among working-class members was also in a state of decline. It became increasingly less radical in its outlook and middle class in its composition. Its zeal had been simultaneously stolen by Anglican ritualism and the new attractions of the fringe forms of nonconformity and street corner evangelism which were a product of the religious revival culture of the last years of the nineteenth century. The traditional nonconformist denominations were arguably out of touch with the social and political world of which they had once been an intrinsic part. Bill Lancaster, in particular, noted that the power and forcefulness of the nonconformity of the first half of the nineteenth century under Miall, Mursell and Hall contrasted starkly with the attitude and comparative absence of nonconformity from the public sphere in the second half of the century.[21]

In some respects it is possible to see this 'rot' setting in comparatively early. It was still possible to see some of the great original dissenting causes momentarily still exciting public interest in the latter part of the nineteenth century. In 1870 the Liberation Society, the national descendent of Miall's original Leicester Voluntary Church Society, staged a conference in Leicester's Temperance Hall. This was called to reinforce the campaign for disestablishment, prompted by Miall's recent introduction of a reform measure into parliament. Various speakers commented on topics pertinent to this measure: Rev. A. Mackennal on 'Are establishments favourable to religion?' and Rev. E. Franks on 'Disestablishment: Ought it to be confined to Ireland?'. But even here, at this high point in national agitation – in one of nonconformity's most treasured causes – it was clear that all was no longer well within the Leicester nonconformist community or its leadership. When the Rev. C.C. Coe rose on 11 November to speak on the issue of 'The Connection Between Church and State Prejudicial to Both' his opening oration quickly turned to lamenting the faded, and failed, prominence of Leicester's militant nonconformity:

> But when I reflect that the best of causes deserves, if it does not always require, the best of advocates, I cannot but regret that some of the old and well-tried friends of Nonconformity of whom Dissenting Leicester may well be proud, and others whose eloquence

and debating power would have been of the greatest service to us, do not occupy a more conspicuous position in relation to the present movement.[22]

However, Mackenna also noted that there were reasons why the fire may have gone out of nonconformity's political identity when at the end of his lecture he addressed the young nonconformists of Leicester to note how all their practical grievances had 'nearly all been taken away', he continued,

> With the spirit of 'watchful jealousy' imposed as a necessity upon your fathers, you will scarcely be able, happily you will not need, to sympathise. The younger Churchmen with whom you may associate will also be largely free from the equally 'watchful' suspicion which characterised political Churchmanship less than a generation back … out of justice has come peace; few now would seek to re-impose the yoke under which your fathers groaned.

Leicester and Secularism

The second half of the century in Leicester witnessed the rise of an aspect of nonconformity for which the city was to become unique, and which arguably helped to set the seal upon the decline of conventional nonconformity and its attachment to mainstream Liberalism. Motivated by a real disdain for the establishment, not unrelated to mainstream nonconformity, Leicester became the centre of the most vibrant, lasting and successful secular society in Britain.[23] This secularist presence in Leicester was one notable and unusual product of the period after 1850 and it had its roots in some earlier radical developments on both the national and local scene. One individual on the national scene who was an heir to the eighteenth-century deist legacy was the social and economic reformer Robert Owen. His ideas about communitarianism, co-operation and economic reform had a significant impact on many localities and specific industries throughout the 1830s and 1840s. Of particular impact in Leicester were his ideas about social organisation without the evil of Christianity. These appeared in Leicester through the guise of Owen's own Social Missionaries who regularly visited Leicester as part of their work on a Midlands 'circuit'. One of these missionaries was George Jacob Holyoake who was also in effect the founder of the Co-operative movement in Britain. These missionaries preached what was construed as a godless and infidel message but it was also tinged with millenarian radicalism. Holyoake was perturbed by the simple association with infidelity and became heavily involved in protecting unbelievers from prosecution and the disdain of a society permeated with Christian belief and practices.

The words of these missionaries had an impact upon one of Leicester's many successful mid-century entrepreneurs. Josiah Gimson had been closely involved in Branch 26 of the Owenite Rational Society and was further influenced by the ideas of Holyoake. After Owenism collapsed at the end of the 1840s, Holyoake gravitated to a position that would protect unbelievers and freethinkers from the dislike and hatred of Christian groups. This moved away from openly challenging Christianity and instead suggested that knowing about the existence of God and his works was not so much wrong as impossible. This did not obviously suggest unbelief but rather a species of doubt based upon the deist and Unitarian ideas which had populated Leicester in the earlier years of the century. Holyoake saw this as a position that would protect unbelievers trying to survive in unfavourable circumstances among communities of Christians intractably opposed to the presence of infidels in their midst. By 1852 Holyoake called this intellectual and practical position 'Secularism' to denote an attitude that wanted peaceful co-existence with the religious portion of the urban community. This particular ideology attracted Leicester Owenites like Gimson and others, like William Henry Holyoak, who became initiators and stalwart members of

THE LEICESTER SECULAR HALL.

2.10 Secular Hall, Humberstone Gate (1881), the first Secular Society hall in the world. Secular societies were established as free-thinking rationalist bodies to provide working people with a positive alternative system to the Christian churches.

Architect Larner Sugden in a Free Flemish Renaissance style.
Source: Leicester Secular Society.

2.11 Busts of inspirational figures on the façade of the Secular Hall. *Left to right*: Socrates (d. 399 BC); Jesus (*c*.4 BC to *c*. AD 30–33); Voltaire (1694–1778); Thomas Paine (1737–1809); Robert Owen (1771–1858).

Source: Richard Rodger.

the first manifestation of Secularism in Leicester. Although there were false starts, the secularist presence in Leicester became established in the early years of the 1880s. This was because the now fully constituted Leicester Secular Society acquired its own distinctive and prominent Secular Hall in Humberstone Gate which remains today substantially as it was when it opened in 1881. The building arguably wore its ecumenical credentials on its sleeve with aspects of its construction mirroring its ideological borrowings from the past. The building was constructed of local material (Coalville brick), amid Arts and Crafts principles, but displayed its reverence for religious toleration by adopting Dutch architectural styles. This eventually led Nicolas Pevsner to describe the building as 'an unfortunate jumble of mostly Flemish motifs'.[24] More directly the building sported a number of busts on its fronting, sculpted by A.L. Vago which portrayed the great inspirational figures of modern thought; Socrates, Voltaire, Thomas Paine and Robert Owen. They were representative 'in a general way for wholesome criticism, for revolt against priestly pretensions, and for endeavours after a happier social environment'.[25] Controversy arose when Christians noted that one of these busts was a representation of the head of Jesus.

The Secular Society at Leicester flourished in its purpose-built hall after this auspicious start and provided a home for a variety of forms of radicalism until well into the twentieth century. The maintenance of this building was absolutely crucial to the survival of this society, and its ownership was concentrated within a well-organised trust structure presided over by the Gimson family who, over time, undertook to buy up the remaining shares in the property when they came on to the market. This preserved the hall, and the society, from dissolution and allowed it to survive where other such halls in many Yorkshire and Lancashire towns were lost to their local

2.12 Leicester Secular Society social and instructional programmes.

Source: Leicester Secular Society.

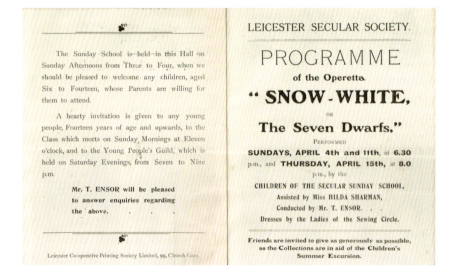

The Sunday School is held in this Hall on Sunday Afternoons from Three to Four, when we should be pleased to welcome any children, aged Six to Fourteen, whose Parents are willing for them to attend.

A hearty invitation is given to any young people, Fourteen years of age and upwards, to the Class which meets on Sunday Mornings at Eleven o'clock, and to the Young People's Guild, which is held on Saturday Evenings, from Seven to Nine p.m.

Mr. T. ENSOR will be pleased to answer enquiries regarding the above.

Leicester Co-operative Printing Society Limited, 99, Church Gate.

LEICESTER SECULAR SOCIETY.

PROGRAMME

of the Operetta

" SNOW - WHITE,

OR

The Seven Dwarfs."

PERFORMED

SUNDAYS, APRIL 4th and 11th, at 6.30 p.m., and THURSDAY, APRIL 15th, at 8.0 p.m., by the

CHILDREN OF THE SECULAR SUNDAY SCHOOL,

Assisted by Miss HILDA SHARMAN,

Conducted by Mr. T. ENSOR.

Dresses by the Ladies of the Sewing Circle.

Friends are invited to give as generously as possible, as the Collections are in aid of the Children's Summer Excursion.

Leicester: a modern history

secular societies. Thus the secularist presence in Leicester was historically important as the only vibrant and lasting presence of Secularism beyond the confines of the metropolitan movement. This was important since the London movement associated with Charles Bradlaugh was confrontational and campaigning. The movement in Leicester was arguably the antithesis of this since it emphasised a local almost 'congregational' life for its members.

The society in many ways replicated what was available at many of the nonconformist chapels and Anglican churches of the period. At various times cycling, sewing, skittles and extra-mural education classes were all staged at the Secular Hall in Humberstone Gate. However, the highlight of the society's activities were its Sunday 'services' at which a number of speakers from the Secularist movement and beyond appeared and offered their ideas to an interested and attentive audience. A particular feature of these 'services' or lectures was the opportunity for individuals to ask questions and to make salient points from the floor which were always well received. This was a deliberate attempt to put into action the ideology of John Stuart Mill who consistently argued for the maintenance of a free platform for all ideas that constituted an important service for the whole of society. All views popular or otherwise, orthodox or unorthodox, were to be discussed and consumed by the populace at large and, under the auspices of the Leicester Secular Society, to be spread far into the community of Leicester.

Whilst obviously the secular movement, and the Society at Leicester, were opposed to the power of religion within nineteenth-century society, it is valuable to see where they represent a part of nonconformity's history in Leicester. The adoption of Holyoake's idea of 'Secularism' – that the nature of God and a future life was totally unknown and unknowable – led the society at Leicester to effectively avoid confrontation with the town's Christian communities over a battle they would conceivably have lost. In this respect their decision to act as a congregation represented an attempt to protect their members and ideas from damaging internal arguments. However, their pursuit of knowledge, whether dispensed from their well-stocked lending library, or from their free and open platform, also addressed other aspects of nonconformity's past history. Those who dissented from established religion in the seventeenth century had done so following their own conscience based upon their own interpretation of the scriptures. These people had distrusted many, and most, forms of authority and regularly discussed their own ideas about the universe and the individual's place within it. In this respect what became known as the 'mechanick tradition', which had helped to create the Baptists and Independents of the Commonwealth and Restoration periods, had their descendants in the Leicester Secular Society. The veneration of the free platform where all and everything could be discussed further emphasised this. The aim was to empower individuals and to ensure the very latest ideas were tested against measures of viability and social utility.

While their connection to the 'mechanick tradition' provides an important link in time placing the Leicester Secular Society in its historical context, the society's history and its radicalism also represent a bridge between the militant nonconformity of the first two-thirds of the nineteenth century and the rise of socialism. Thus we might see elements of this producing an attitude that began to consider that alliances with Liberalism were somewhat out-dated and were not producing the political and social rights working men considered to be an implicit part of their own citizenship. Eventually it was no surprise to see the champions of separate working-class representation in Leicester emanate from the Leicester Secular Society.

However, to accomplish independent working-class representation Leicester needed to be filled with new radical ideas and political programmes. This changing message, which was moving beyond the early century's progressive dissent, can be observed in some of the ideas that came before the society. These regularly appeared on the society's platform where the Leicester Society represented, in many cases the most important provincial staging post of these ideas. Radicalism, and eventually Socialism appeared on the society's platform in many guises. Mid-century republicanism was represented by visitors such as George Standring, George Most, and Frederick Verinder, while more exotic forms of continental anarchism appeared on the platform in the guise of Stepnyak-Kravchinsky and Peter Kropotkin. Later nineteenth-century individualism was also represented by Wordsworth Donisthorpe and Frederick Millar of the Liberty and Property Defence League.

However, by far the most important of the ideas that left a lasting impression on the Leicester Secular Society were those that stemmed from socialism. H.M. Hyndman spoke to the society in 1883 about the mechanisms and intrinsic failure of capitalist society. Probably of greater importance in both the society's and Leicester's history was the decision of William Morris in 1884 to give in Leicester the first provincial hearing of his extremely influential lecture 'Art and Socialism'. This galvanised Ernest Gimson, the younger brother of the society's president, Sydney, to devote himself henceforth to working toward an Arts and Crafts ideal. To achieve this he relocated to Sapperton in Gloucestershire. From his workshop there he built furniture and furnishings that expressed William Morris's desire to recapture the beauty and joy inherent in the careful artisan craft work of the past.[26] However, the Arts and Crafts ideal, and the seed spread by Morris, was not wholly removed from Leicester and the work of organisations like the Kyrle Society and the Dryad firm manufacturing Arts and Crafts inspired furnishings and material for recreational handicrafts still displayed a remnant of nonconformist zeal. This further expressed a desire to improve the immediacy of living conditions and educational attainment – one that Joseph Dare would perhaps have recognised and readily endorsed.[27]

A group of Fabian members, Annie Besant, Graham Wallas, George Bernard Shaw, William Clarke and Hubert Bland spoke eloquently in Leicester and reportedly made many converts to socialism from the Society. This was to eventually make itself felt in Leicester in the militant trade unionism in the thirty years after 1880 and which was also instrumental in breaking the alliance between working men and radical Liberalism within the city. Where once radical Liberals, operating from a nonconformist conscience, had been both factory owners and working men, their outlook and the political climate had changed by the 1880s. Nonconformist dissent, Liberalism and Radicalism were no longer as inextricably linked as they had once been. Indeed, when George Lansbury appeared upon the Secular Society platform his approach to socialism seemed to demonstrate that the early century Leicester nonconformity had already found a new home: socialism had largely stolen its thunder:

> He dwelt on the necessity for personal effort in improving social conditions; for devoting more thought to politics than to football; for lightening the household drudgery of women of the working classes; for creating a public opinion which would value the work of Mrs. Fry in prisons, or Father Damien among the lepers, and other such service for humanity, as more importance than the accumulation of profits.[28]

When the Leicester Secular Society took up the challenge that Lansbury had laid down it did so from a profoundly socialist perspective. When it employed the young radical ethicist Frederick James Gould as its 'pastor' in the early years of the twentieth century he embarked on a campaign of radical journalism and wrote scathing critiques of the contemporary condition of Edwardian Leicester. In recognition of the legacy of the nonconformist conscience Gould defended an individual who had refused to distribute coronation medals upon the accession of Edward VII. Yet when he stood in the political sphere he was a socialist candidate.[29] This

2.13 Frederick James Gould (1855–1938), educationist and pioneer ethicist; involved with secularists while teaching in London; moved to Leicester (1899), became secretary of the Secular Society, served on School Board (1900–02), and as a Labour councillor (1904–10).
Source: Leicester City Council.

closely coincided with a final dissolution of the Lib–Lab pact in the wake of the city's unemployment crisis of 1905. By the 1920s the Liberals on Leicester's City Council had come to see socialism as a clear and unequivocal threat preferring to enter into an alliance with the Conservative Party to prevent the Labour Party seizing power locally.

Conclusion

Thus Leicester was marked out as a leading city of nonconformity as a result of the confluence of a number of conditions which favoured its growth and development. It wrestled power from the anachronistic and moribund Tory elite and aimed to create a haven for radicalism and nonconformist tendencies where they could flourish and develop the confidence to make regular forays into national politics. Viewed from the outside it indeed looked, at times, like the archetypal metropolis of dissent – particularly when Miall's quest for disestablishment or the anti-vaccinationists could make Leicester's issues national issues. However, by comparison, the latter half of the century seemed to witness Leicester nonconformity's fall from its previous lofty heights. Urban and social change wrought attrition upon the previously prosperous nonconformist congregations of the city, while some of their most energetic members of all classes were no longer attracted to them. Old Liberal and radical causes lost their credibility, or were answered by significant social and legislative progress. However, this also happened alongside the arrival of more wide-ranging and deeper aspirations for economic and social change. Nevertheless, the nonconformist ideas of self-reliance, freedom of choice and conscience were able to find a natural home in some of the manifestations of socialism and radicalism within Leicester itself. Nonetheless those who were disappointed by noncon-formity's performance in Leicester in the years after 1860 remembered the past and sometimes desperately tried to invoke it. Those who had acquired and entertained high standards based these on how the Leicester of the previous generation had trail-blazed nonconformist principles upon the local and national stages. The importance of this in making Leicester the metropolis of dissent in the first half of the nineteenth century was almost inevitably an impossible act to follow.

3

'Red Leicester': a reputation for radicalism?

F OR much of the nineteenth and early twentieth century Leicester was synonymous with radical politics.[1] Until the First World War Leicester maintained a reputation for being a Liberal town – and a radical Liberal town at that. The 1886 Home Rule Crisis resulted in Joseph Chamberlain's Birmingham allying to the Conservative cause, leaving Leicester as the spiritual home of Liberalism in the Midlands and the region's safest Liberal constituency.[2] Leicester's brand of Liberalism was often a controversial one, fed by a tradition of independent working-class radicalism, vocal nonconformist churches, and a Leicester Secular Society that was effectively the organising body of the national secularist movement.[3] Few nineteenth-century Liberals could have ever imagined Leicester as anything other than a Liberal town and yet by 1914 the future Labour Prime Minister James Ramsay MacDonald had pushed the local Liberal establishment aside and helped establish a strong independent Labour movement in the city.

However, Leicester's political history is not one of the inevitable triumph of Labour.[4] Ironically, for a man now often seen as an opportunist and responsible for the 'great betrayal' of the Labour party in 1931, MacDonald's principled opposition to wartime policy led to him being rejected by his working-class constituency in 1918 and the local Labour party struggled to recover. The inter-war period was a time in which Leicester's reputation for political radicalism gradually broke down. Labour was often in disarray over personal and ideological issues. The Liberals were disoriented by the mutual hostility between Asquith and his successor as Prime Minister, Lloyd George. They were also divided between Progressives, who wished to promote a social reform agenda, and anti-Socialists, who advocated alliance with the Conservatives to prevent a Socialist government. The beneficiaries were the Conservatives, whose gradual progress at municipal level, coupled to a change to single member constituencies, suddenly gave the party a chance for a parliamentary breakthrough. In October 1924, the almost unthinkable happened – the Conservatives took two out of Leicester's three parliamentary seats. It was not until the national Labour landslide of 1945 that the Labour party's position was fully reasserted, with the gain of all three seats in the general election of that year. The reasons for these dramatic changes are complex and controversial. We will examine four key phases of Leicester's political development – the era of Victorian Liberal domination, the growth of independent Labour politics from the 1890s, the age of realignment in the 1920s and finally the rise of Conservatism after 1929, when 'red Leicester' looked increasingly blue.

To what extent, then, does Leicester deserve its reputation as a 'radical' city? Does this characterisation reflect the city's political outlook or is it a convenient myth propagated by those sympathetic to radical causes? Much, of course, depends on the period one chooses to study. There is little doubt that Leicester had a strong radical Liberal tradition dating back to the so-called Great Reform Act of 1832 and the Municipal Corporations Act of 1835. Leicester's first elected city council was notorious for its rejection of tradition and one of its first acts was to sell the mayor's mace, corporation glass and civic garments of the despised former Tory corporation.[5] During the early part of the century Leicester also became a major organising centre for parliamentary reform and Chartism. Formidable public speakers such as Thomas Cooper were able to build substantial support and the movement continued to be influential throughout the 1840s.[6] The strength of Chartism in Leicester no doubt contributed to subsequent radical progress in the town. During much of the period to 1865 the town effectively had a three party system, with Radical Liberals and the more 'moderate' Whig Liberals even operating as two separate parties at times.[7] Although the Liberal party operated largely as a united movement from 1868 onwards, the divisions between Radicals and Whigs were institutionalised by Leicester's two member parliamentary system – typically a Radical took one seat and a Whig the other.

Leicester Liberalism drew much of its traditional strength from local religious nonconformity. By the late nineteenth century it had firmly established its reputation as being the 'capital of dissent' – the leading

3.1 The Liberal Club, 6 Bishop Street, the party's headquarters in the heart of the city (built 1885–88; architect E. Burgess), with a central staircase leading to a reading room, smoking and billiard rooms and elegant dining room.

Source: Record Office for Leicester, Leicestershire and Rutland, DE3736, Box 3, Bishop Street.

nonconformist town in England. This nonconformist influence had a major impact on the character of local Liberalism.[8] As late as the 1880s the town's leading radical thinker, the Rev J. Page Hopps, was a nonconformist minister. Much of Leicester's Liberalism took on an uncompromising moralistic tone, influenced by the town's nonconformist leadership. The movement of civil disobedience in the second half of the nineteenth century to resist the compulsory vaccination legislation was led largely by nonconformist ministers of the town; they even organised mass demonstrations outside prisons where protestors were incarcerated.[9] The evils of gambling took on great significance in Liberal and nonconformist campaigns. The radical *Midland Free Press* refused to print any horse racing columns in its pages and the Liberal-controlled city council controversially 'blacked out' the racing and gambling pages of other papers in public libraries for fear they would encourage immorality.[10] These campaigns did not always attract public support. The practice of censoring newspapers caused such an outcry that the council was eventually forced to reverse its decision. Concern over excessive drinking was also a special concern of the local Liberal leadership. Liberal property developer Arthur Wakerley was sufficiently confident in the attractions of temperance that he banned the public houses from his newly constructed housing estates.[11] The moralistic tone of local Liberalism was supported strongly by many in Leicester's 'respectable' working class, but the continuing popularity of gambling and the public house suggested that its power to change working-class culture was somewhat limited. One Liberal mayor provoked substantial popular criticism after he condemned working men's drinking habits. Nonconformist values appealed to many 'respectable' sections of the working class but its reach was far from universal.[12]

The enduring nature of nonconformist influence in Leicester was partly a product of the relative insularity of the town compared to the larger urban centres. Economically Leicester was not especially diverse, particularly when compared to larger industrial cities such as Birmingham, Manchester and Leeds. The town's industrial middle class had close social connections, often focused on the Liberal club at Gallowtree Gate or the major nonconformist churches. The town had two main industries – hosiery, and boot and shoe – and was relatively late in developing large-scale factory production. There were few other large industries in the area and Leicester's economic base still depended to some degree on its role as a county town, serving the largely agricultural community in its immediate environs. Leicester's market, which dated back to the Middle Ages, continued to be the hub of the county's economic life and maintained that role well into the twentieth century. The relatively insular economic character of Leicester influenced patterns of immigration to the town. In the latter half of the nineteenth century Leicester had a claim to be the most prosperous town in the Midlands, and arguably one of the most prosperous in England. This naturally attracted a large number of immigrants from the surrounding countryside and other nearby towns. However, this trend seems to have had little influence on the ethnic and cultural structure of the working population. Leicester developed little in the way of large Irish and Jewish communities. To some degree, the relative isolation and small size of the town was a deterrent to international migrants of the nineteenth century. It was not until the twentieth century that Leicester developed into a genuinely multi-cultural city.

The 'Golden Age' of Leicester Liberalism, 1880–1893

Liberalism had established an apparently dominant position but electoral success concealed divisions. First, there was the 'traditional' division between self-styled radical and moderate sections. Second, there was an overlapping division between those who were passionate supporters of nonconformist concerns, such as temperance and anti-gambling campaigns, and 'anti-faddists' who felt single issue campaigning could be dangerous. Finally, by the 1880s, there were those who admired Joseph Chamberlain and the new social policies of 'New Radicalism' and the 'anti-Constructionists' – those who preferred more traditional Gladstonian approaches which emphasised individual self-help and questioned the degree to which the

state should intervene on social questions. The Liberal party's apparent electoral hegemony had been bought at the cost of institutionalising the 'moderate' and radical divisions in Liberal party ranks. Divisions dated back to the Leicester by-election of 1856 when the death of MP Richard Gardner prompted radical John Biggs to resign the borough mayoralty and come forward as a candidate against moderate Thomas Tertius Paget.[13] In response the moderate Liberals formed an unstable coalition with the Conservatives and it was not until 1865 that the two branches

3.2 John Biggs (1801–71), mayor (1840, 1847, 1856) MP (1856–62). Manufacturer and exporter of fancy hosiery and gloves, Factory Act reformer, and from 1826 vigorous supporter of local reform. With a fellow hosier described as 'the Cobden and Bright of the Midland counties'.

Source: Leicester City Council.

of the Liberal party were re-united.[14] Only by agreeing to what was in effect a permanent division of the borough's parliamentary representation between the moderate and radical sections of the party could a semblance of unity be effected. This compromise did not demand that both elements of the party adopt common policies, nor imply an acceptance of collective party discipline. As late as 1882 radical MP Peter Taylor continued to make outspoken attacks on Liberal government policy, particularly on Irish issues and Britain's imperial policy in Egypt.[15]

Yet in some respects Leicester Liberalism drew its strength from the fact it could attract support from a range of different economic classes and religious factions. Middle-class Liberalism expressed itself through a highly successful Liberal Club in Gallowtree Gate with 1,000 members, many of whom were actively involved in canvassing at election times and in ward organisation.[16] In 1876 Liberal leaders scrapped the old registration society and replaced it with a more 'popular' Liberal Association based on the 'Birmingham model', supposedly with the aim of developing a more inclusive and participatory system of party organisation.[17] Meanwhile Taylor continued to represent the largely working-class ex-Chartist tradition in Leicester that had its own local political clubs.[18] The staple trade of Leicester, the boot and shoe, was highly unionised and also provided an important plank of Liberal strength. Thomas Smith, the Liberal borough agent for much of the 1880s and 1890s, was the first general secretary of the National Union of Boot and Shoe Operatives with its impressive headquarters in St James Street built in 1903 for £6,000. Smith's union successors, George Sedgewick and William Inskip, were also active in the party and became Liberal town councillors.[19] The Conservatives, in contrast, struggled to make any impact on Leicester politics. In 1881 their major club was said to have barely 100 members, even though reports for public consumption claimed over 1,000.[20] Until the mid-1880s the party lacked any formal representative association for the town or county. In the borough the Conservative Club was the major decision-making body, while in the county the party was organised more informally, generally around prominent local gentry.[21]

In the 1880s it seemed that the greatest threat to Leicester Liberalism was not the Conservatives but internal factional disputes spilling over into the electoral arena. The resignation or retirement of a sitting MP was often the signal for the renewal of factional rivalries. That had been the case in 1856 and despite the institutionalised division of borough representation between the two major wings of Leicester Liberalism, difficulties were not completely eliminated by this compromise. By February 1884 Liberals were coming to realise they would again soon face the hard choice of selecting new parliamentary candidates. Since the 1880 general election Taylor had suffered almost continual poor health.[22] With Alexander McArthur, the representative of 'moderate' Leicester Liberals also incapacitated, after an

3.3 National Union of Boot and Shoe Operatives badge, *c*.1930.
Source: Stuart Williams.

3.4 Co-operative Boot and Shoe Manufacturing Equity Works, Western Road, 1886.
This was the last footwear firm in Leicester, and closed in 2009.
Source: Colin Hyde.

accident, it became clear that at least one new candidate would have to be found for the forthcoming general election.[23]

Any moves made by the association leadership to 'manage' the selection of a parliamentary candidate had to be made very carefully and balanced against demands for popular participation in the decision and the need to ensure the decisions gained legitimacy.[24] The Trades Council engaged in lengthy discussion about the possibility of bringing forward a labour candidate, but eventually ruled out the suggestion as impractical and decided instead to urge the Liberal Association to adopt Richard Chamberlain, Joseph Chamberlain's brother, as candidate.[25] Meanwhile the Liberal leadership favoured J. Allanson Picton who was described at official meetings as 'the coming man for Leicester'.[26] At the selection meeting of the Liberal Association general committee Picton was only narrowly successful, taking 99 votes to Chamberlain's 74. With such a large minority supporting Chamberlain, the final decision clearly had to be delayed and the committee adjourned to a further week of deliberations.[27]

Organised labour began to flex its muscles. Trade union circulars stressed Chamberlain's suitability for 'a radical and working class constituency'.[28] J.H. Woolley, from the Trades Council accused Picton's supporters of class prejudice and accused them of manipulating the selection process:

> I can quite understand the offended dignity of some of our pastors and masters on being asked to support the nominee of a lot of stockingers

Leicester: a modern history

and shoemakers, the residuum you know, and they seem to forget that they have built their comfortable mansions at Stoneygate out of the sweat of them.[29]

Ultimately the efforts of organised labour failed. During this controversy Richard Chamberlain was visiting Australia and brother Joseph was unwilling to call him back to what could have easily turned into an unpleasant selection contest – 'a mere competition, which would be undignified alike to Mr. Picton and Mr. R. Chamberlain'.[30] At the subsequent meeting of the Liberal general committee, opposition to Picton continued, although without an alternative candidate, the battle was lost.[31] Working-class organisations, such as the trades councils, could have presented a danger if allied to a significant dissident Liberal faction – but alone, with no candidate or independent resources, there was little prospect of a challenge to the traditional institutions Liberal party authority. The incident did, however, reveal the growing class tensions in Liberal ranks – a grim harbinger of future problems.

Despite the Conservatives' historical weakness in Leicester, the early 1880s did see some attempts by the party to widen their appeal to Leicester's working-class electorate. The first election held under conditions of household borough suffrage saw Lord John Manners help organise a Conservative working men's organisation, and this was followed by similar attempts in subsequent elections to build urban working-class support.[32] By May 1884 the Conservatives had secured a candidate from London, Captain Cruikshank, and were preparing to try to exploit the rather lukewarm enthusiasm for Picton's candidature.[33] Thomas Canner, chairman of the Working Men's Conservative Club, took a prominent part in Cruikshank's lecturing tours, with the club being used as a platform for promoting a 'classless' popular imperialism.[34] The club, only established in the summer of 1883, claimed to have over 500 members and quickly became a model for others in the district.[35] Despite these preparations, the Conservatives still seemed a little caught out by Taylor's resignation in June 1884, and Cruikshank, perhaps fearing he would have to foot the bill for an unsuccessful campaign, failed to materialise.[36] Efforts to secure an alternative candidate through the Carlton Club were equally unsuccessful and on the Carlton's advice the Conservatives decided not to contest Picton's return.[37]

This episode typified many aspects of Leicester's late Victorian political scene. The Conservative party was attempting to build a popular political base but progress was slow and it was difficult to attract candidates without significant financial resources or serious prospects of electoral success. The Trades Council operated within the Liberal coalition and, while it was frustrated about the attitude of many middle-class Liberals to popular radicalism, it too lacked the resources or institutional framework to disturb the status quo. Importantly, too, it also lacked any ideological motivation to do so. Most trade union leaders were ardent Liberals who felt that

Gladstonian Liberalism best reflected working-class interests. Indeed, it is probable that the 1886 Home Rule crisis strengthened the links between the local trade union movement and the Liberal party. Nationally, Liberal party propagandists depicted the departure of dissident Liberals into alliance with the Conservative as 'the revolt of the Whigs' – the abandonment of the party by old-fashioned, wealthy right-wingers. At one level this was a distortion as radical Joseph Chamberlain himself left the party over the issue. However, a disproportionate number of those leaving the party on the issue were from wealthier, landed families, allowing the Gladstonian majority that remained to claim that they were the true heirs to 'popular' Liberalism. Ironically, had radicals had their way in 1884, and selected Richard Chamberlain, brother of Joe, as their parliamentary candidate, the local party may have ended up much more divided and the Liberal Unionists may have obtained an important foothold in the East Midlands.[38] Instead, Leicester largely stayed with Gladstone and, as a consequence of Birmingham's defection to the Unionist cause, could thereafter lay claim to being the leading centre of Liberalism in the Midlands.

Part of the reason for the limited divisions over the Home Rule crisis in Leicester was the continuing importance of local issues in Leicester politics. At the beginning of the Home Rule crisis in spring 1886 Leicester Liberals were involved in a major campaign on the 'Vaccination question'. Leicester had a strong tradition of local opposition to the national legislation for the compulsory vaccination of children, with Leicester Liberals taking a leading role in the Anti-Compulsory Vaccination League (see also chapter 10). Their campaigns achieved considerable success. In 1878 of the 4,446 children born in Leicester, 3,730 were vaccinated. By 1884, although the number of births had increased to 4,849, the number vaccinated had dropped to 1,700.[39] Parents of children not vaccinated were liable to fines and imprisonment, but until the early 1880s the local enforcement authority, the Board of Guardians, had taken a non-confrontational approach.[40] On the Leicester Board, those in favour of compulsory vaccination – and prosecution of 'offenders' – were almost exclusively Conservatives, giving this extremely controversial issue a strong partisan dimension. When, in October 1883, 1,000 prosecutions were authorised on the casting vote of the Board chairman, a substantial campaign of resistance and civil disobedience followed.[41]

At the triennial board elections in 1886, the local radical press backed a campaign to unseat Conservative supporters of compulsory vaccination and the contest rapidly developed into a straight partisan battle between the two parties.[42] By March 1886, 25 people had been sent to prison, 101 parents had had their homes broken up under distress for unpaid fines, and over 2,500 people had been brought before the magistrates, according to Liberal calculations.[43] Each imprisonment became an opportunity to publicise the anti-compulsory vaccination cause and each release from prison a celebration of defiance against the Conservative guardians. At the

Leicester: a modern history

next election in April 1886 the old regime, with its compulsory vaccination majority, was turned into a Liberal majority of 23–13. In all 26 members of the new board opposed the 'compulsory clauses' of the Vaccination Acts.[44] Remarkably this particular controversy dominated the local political agenda for several months, uniting the factions of the Liberal party, and marginalising those who wished to debate Home Rule. Even as late as 1886 the political agendas of Leicester politicians could be very different to those at Westminster.

Both of Leicester's Liberal MPs remained relatively quiet on the Home Rule issue until eventually announcing that despite some misgivings they would support the Gladstonian position.[45] Few prominent members of the local Liberal party ventured into Liberal Unionism. Among the dissidents were four members of the well-known Faire family, from Knighton, and Harry Simpson Gee. These individuals headed the most famous boot manufacturing companies in the town – Smith, Faire and Company, and Stead and Simpson Limited.[46] Both the Faires and Simpson Gee represented the wealthiest and most strongly Anglican element in the local Liberal party – as did another leading dissident, Thomas Fielding Johnson, the well-known philanthropist. Their departure from Liberal ranks may have been prompted by fears that Gladstone was flirting with disestablishment of the Anglican Church. However, the Leicester Liberal Unionist group found it difficult to sustain themselves as an organised party. Significantly, Leicester's leading supporter of Joseph Chamberlain, Rev. J. Page Hopps, remained in the Gladstonian camp and became an enthusiastic advocate of Home Rule.

Some commentators interpreted the controversy in class-based terms. The failure of Leicester's Liberal Unionists to establish any base of support in working-class communities made them vulnerable to the charge that they were merely an upper-middle-class elite out of touch with more progressive times. One Gladstonian Liberal propagandist characterised them as merely 'a small knot of Stoneygate Liberals' – a reference to the wealthy suburbs of Clarendon Park, Stoneygate and Knighton where several leading Liberal Unionists resided.[47] Another attacked, 'Liberal manufacturers and Liberal goslings … being made the tools of Tory and Whig lords.'[48] When Leicester Liberal Unionists decided to contest the general election of 1886 in alliance with the Conservatives, their candidate Robert Bickersteth polled fewer votes than the Conservative candidate in 1885. Given the changed circumstances this was a disastrous result for the Liberal Unionists, destroying their claim to be a serious threat to the Gladstonian party. The departure of more right-wing figures from Liberal circles offered more opportunities for a new generation of radicals to promote new social agendas. At national level this was typified by the social reforms of the party's Newcastle Programme of 1891 and in Leicester by the proto-socialistic Progressive Municipal Programme, tentatively adopted by Leicester's Liberal town council group in 1896.[49]

BROOKFIELD,
LEICESTER.

April 4th, 1919,

DEAR MR. MAYOR,

I have been reading with much interest the report of the meeting for the consideration of the proposed University Scheme, of which you were Chairman.

As the proposition somewhat forces my hand, it may perhaps be well for me to state my wishes and intentions in the matter. I have long felt that the beautiful site of the Old Asylum must be secured for the benefit of the Borough of Leicester. War Office requirements prevented my taking any steps for a time, but on the Armistice being signed, the position changed, and I ventured to negotiate, with the kind assistance of the Chairman of the County Council, for the purchase of the whole property—not as a speculation, but in the interest of the Borough of Leicester.

I am happy to say terms have been agreed upon, and only await the convenience of the Military Authorities for completion, when I shall be ready to submit my scheme which will embrace, firstly, a site for the two Wyggeston Schools (Boys and Girls), in which I have been interested for many years, and also for the proposed University College, now under consideration.

This land, which adjoins the Victoria Park from North to South, will provide ample space for all the requirements of the three Institutions, which, in conjunction, might form an effective architectural group, and a

Peace Memorial worthy of our ancient Borough.

I am,

Faithfully yours,

J. Fielding Johnson

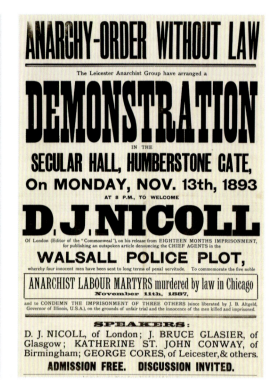

3.5 Thomas Fielding Johnson's letter to the Leicester mayor, 1919, proposing an arrangement to set up Leicester University College.

Source: University of Leicester Special Collections.

3.6 Anarchy: Order without Law 1893. Notice of a meeting to be held in the Secular Hall in support of free speech.

Source: University of Leicester Special Collections.

The long march of Labour, 1893–1914

Over the next two decades the main challenge to Liberal dominance in Leicester was to come from the political left rather than the right. In Leicester the class tensions evident in local politics of the 1880s were to have significant consequences over the subsequent two decades. In 1900 the Conservatives gained one of the two parliamentary seats, largely because of the intervention of an independent Labour candidate. This new independent labour movement drew support from a number of sources. Some of those associated with the new Independent Labour Party were former Liberals, a significant number came through the trade union movement, while others represented a new generation attracted to the novelty of Socialist ideas. The rise of an independent labour movement in Leicester can be dated to at least 1893, when a branch of the national Independent Labour Party began activity in Leicester. Some have chosen to take the party's origins back to a much earlier date. Lancaster has argued that independent labour traditions were rooted in earlier traditions of Liberal radicalism and an independently organised working class that was relatively free from the factory discipline seen in larger industrial cities such as Manchester.[50]

Table 3.1   Electoral fortunes of Labour (including Liberal/ Labour) parliamentary candidates in Leicester, 1894–1910

Election	Candidate	Result
1894 by-election (2 vacancies)	H. Broadhurst – Liberal / Labour	Elected (1st of 4) 33.8% vote share
1895 General Election	H. Broadhurst – Liberal / Labour J. Burgess – ILP	Elected (1st of 4) 33.6% vote share Defeated (4th of 4) 13.7% vote share
1900 General election	H. Broadhurst – Liberal / Labour J.R. MacDonald Labour	Elected (1st of 4) 32.3% of vote share Defeated (4th of 4) 13.0% vote share
1906 General election	H. Broadhurst – Liberal / Labour J.R. MacDonald Labour	Elected (1st of 3) 39.9% vote share Elected (2nd of 3) 39.8% vote share
1910 Jan General election	J.R. MacDonald	Elected (2nd of 4) 31.4% vote share
1910 Dec General election	J.R. MacDonald	Elected (2nd of 3) 38.5% vote share

Source; F. Craig, *British Parliamentary Election Results, 1885–1918* (Aldershot, 1989).

However, although there is evidence of organised working-class political activity before 1893, it is remarkable how much of this was dedicated to supporting causes close to those of the Liberal party. Despite serious provocation, the organised working-class's parliament, the Trades Council, backed Liberal parliamentary candidates and initially showed little interest in socialism. It was not until the great Liberal landslide election of 1906 that it was clear the electoral politics of Leicester's working class had changed and Liberals had to share the parliamentary representation of the city with a new political force, only loosely allied to their number. The two MPs elected for Leicester in 1906 personified the two rival elements of the late Victorian and Edwardian British Labour movement. Henry Broadhurst, member for Leicester since 1894, was a staunch supporter of Liberal-Labour politics, representing the tradition that had dominated the town's working-class allegiances for much of the late Victorian period. His nominal ally, James Ramsay MacDonald, represented a party, in the ILP, that had for more than a decade attempted to wrest 'Radical Leicester' away from Liberalism towards a socialist future. By 1906 the Leicester ILP had become an important player in Leicester politics. It had persuaded the local Trades Council to become one of the first to affiliate to the newly formed Labour party of 1900 and by 1912 the local party had as many as 800 paid-up members.[51]

Some have pointed to structural changes in the local economy, provoking rising class tensions, as a significant reason for this dramatic political development. Strikes and lock-outs in major industrial enterprises were a significant feature of this period and there were also long periods of high unemployment – particularly between 1904 and 1906. Clearly where communities faced an environment of growing industrial conflict, the prospects for the development of a strong local ILP were good.[52] Leicester's main industries were highly unionised, offering an institutional platform for the ILP and an organisational forum for Socialist ideas. During the early 1890s the major local trades, hosiery and boot manufacture, underwent significant structural changes, with moves to mechanisation and factory production, often leading to rising industrial tension.[53] However, even those who place great emphasis on the relationship between structural changes in the economy and the growth of support for independent labour politics are cautious about suggesting that the early ILP derived a broad base of support from these processes. Lancaster notes just how narrow the ILP following was in 1895 – 'essentially rooted in the skilled section of the two local major trades'.[54] Indeed, far from taking control of the Trades Council, by the winter of 1895 the council had resolved not to support labour candidates of any description in municipal elections.[55] It is therefore a matter of debate whether Labour's twentieth-century successes do indeed owe very much to the structural economic changes of the late nineteenth. Nor is there much evidence that the emergence of new trade unions, catering for unskilled workers, were neglected by the Liberals or captured by the ILP. Liberal trade unionist leaders such as William Inskip and the Trades Council were strong supporters of this 'new unionism' and assisted in the organisation of groups such as the Leicester corporation workers.[56]

Although the ILP gradually gained ground in the Trades Council there was often reluctance to provoke confrontation with a Liberal Association that seemed open to working-class influence. In 1894 George Banton, the socialist-leaning Trades Council president, intervened in a parliamentary selection dispute by arguing that the council should accept the decision of the Liberal party.[57] It was only the intervention of the national party leaders that saw the ILP bring forward a candidate – the well-known socialist journalist, Joseph Burgess, the editor of the *Workman's Times*.[58] Even then the Trades Council was reluctant to support the independent candidate, with 17 of the 38 trade council members attempting to block the move.[59] Eventually the Trades Council agreed to support a workman's ticket of Liberal Henry Broadhurst and Socialist Joseph Burgess for the two-member division. Despite the fact that the second Liberal candidate, employer Walter Hazell, proved to be something of an electoral liability, both Liberal candidates were elected with Burgess a significant distance behind. Many more voters had heeded the advice of the Liberal Association than the Trades Council.[60] This reopened further disputes in the Trades Council, with leading trade unionists becoming reluctant to endorse any candidates officially, even in municipal elections. It also enfeebled their wider campaigning activities. When, in 1895, the trade council president tried to persuade delegates to help organise a demonstration in support of the unemployed, the move was rejected on the grounds that it might once again open up partisan hostilities within the council.[61]

The ILP did make progress with unexpected municipal by-election victories, often benefiting from low turnouts and Liberal apathy; T.F. Richards' election in 1894 being a case in point.[62] The ILP also became adept at exploiting industrial relations questions, especially when employers failed to respect existing arbitration agreements. During a dispute in the boot trade the ILP brought out Israel Beck, a shoe riveter, in a municipal by-election to place the dispute at the forefront of the public mind. The result was a stunning victory for the ILP, with the Liberal candidate coming a very distant third behind the Conservative.[63] However, these minor triumphs did not translate into rapid progress at the general election, especially as the two Liberal candidates adopted increasing radical manifestos – even hinting at the possibility of land nationalisation. Joseph Burgess stood for election again in 1894. Following his second defeat in Leicester even Burgess had to acknowledge that the Liberal party contained many of socialistic views and that a major problem for the ILP was that many voters felt they were more likely to get socialistic legislation from the Liberal party than from waiting for the eventual success of the ILP.[64]

It was the Liberal party's decade out of office, between 1895 and 1905, and its continuing internal problems, that offered the Labour movement an opportunity to regroup and mobilise a wider trade union coalition behind the idea of independent labour representation. Gladstone's retirement, forced on him by his own cabinet in 1894, removed a major electoral asset from the party and created a series of leadership problems which were only finally resolved under the leadership of Sir Henry Campbell Bannerman.[65] Under the leadership of 'C.B.' the Liberal party enjoyed, in 1906, its greatest electoral triumph – a triumph assisted by its electoral alliance with Labour. It was an alliance that was brokered, in 1903, by James Ramsay MacDonald, with the Liberal party formally agreeing to stand aside in a series of seats in favour of candidates sponsored by the new Labour party, formed in 1900.

The secret negotiations behind the Lib/Lab pact have long been the subject of historical speculation. However, it seems that negotiations surrounded those towns that had enjoyed a significant independent labour or socialist presence prior to 1900 and which had trade councils sufficiently organised to support electoral campaigns. In many towns, including Leicester, the trades

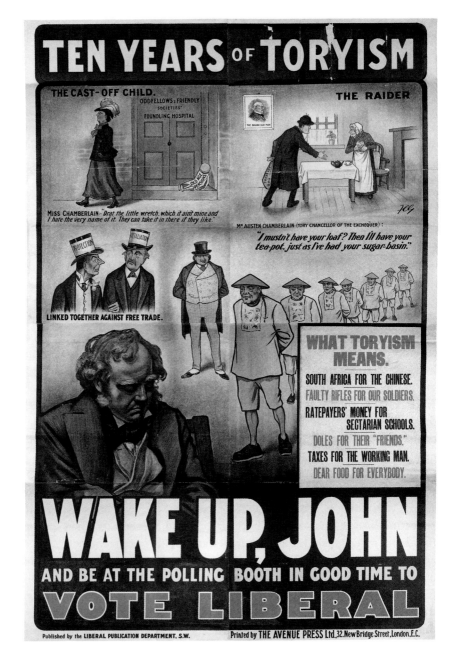

3.7 'Ten Years of Toryism: Liberal Party election poster, 1905.

Source: London School of Economics and Political Science. 0519–98.

councils became the new organising committee of the local Labour party. The gradual growth of ILP councillors in Leicester strengthened the case for the Liberal party to surrender one of its two parliamentary nominees to the new party. The result was that MacDonald, the Labour party's negotiator, benefited by securing the Labour nomination to the Leicester seat. However, the 'Progressive alliance' was not an altogether stable one and hostilities between the parties continued at municipal level. In January 1899 Sir Israel Hart, four times mayor of the city, left the aldermanic bench because of his opposition to the council's policy of growing municipalisation of services. This provoked a period of tension in Liberal ranks between Progressives and a 'moderate' wing that supported Hart. The internal battle reached a climax in February 1901 when Hart was forced to resign as president of Leicester Liberal Association. Hart responded by threatening to stand as a Liberal candidate in the subsequent parliamentary election against the Liberal/Labour joint ticket and only withdrew after failing to gain the necessarily internal support.[66]

However, this apparent triumph of the Progressives concealed further policy differences between those on the left of the Liberal party and Labour activists. This was nowhere more obvious than in elections for the Leicester Board of Guardians – the body that distributed poor relief. High unemployment in the early Edwardian period meant that levels of poor relief and its humane distribution became a key issue in local politics. In 1905 a group of unemployed Leicester workers marched to London on a 'hunger march' – an event similar to the famous Jarrow Crusade in 1936. Local socialists demanded a more generous poor relief policy and public works to relieve unemployment, while many Liberals took a more cautious approach, worried about the spiralling costs to poorer ratepayers. Labour's intervention in the 1904 Guardian election proved to be something of a watershed in local politics, revealing the fundamental differences that existed between the parties. One Liberal Guardian called Labour's intervention 'a kind of civil war', while another commented 'Labourites seem more concerned to persons who are really undeserving than to the unfortunate and struggling ratepayer'.[67] The Labour platform, however, was a popular one, boosting their own numbers but also splitting the Progressive vote and allowing the Conservatives renewed opportunities for success. At the 1907 election the Liberals lost seven seats – three to Labour and four, significantly, to the Conservatives. By March 1913 it was clear that three-party politics had arrived in Leicester, at least in local elections. The Board of Guardians election that year saw sixteen Liberals returned, while Labour and the Conservatives had fifteen each. A similar pattern could be seen on Leicester Town Council, which by 1913 was composed of eighteen elected Liberal members, fourteen Labour and sixteen Conservative.[68]

Conflict between Liberal and Labour activists at local level created major problems for MacDonald who had staked his electoral reputation on a national electoral alliance that would guarantee Labour a free run in many 'winnable' working-class constituencies. MacDonald's strategy for Labour's parliamentary expansion meant that he remained committed to an alliance with the Liberals. Indeed, he became more cautious in the face of a steady Conservative and Unionist recovery – the Labour party fielded just fifty-six candidates in the general election of December 1910, compared

3.8 Ramsay MacDonald (1866–1937), MP for Leicester 1908–18.

Source: Library of Congress, reproduced from G.G. Bain 29588 collection.

to seventy-eight in January. By-election results would seem to confirm that MacDonald's attempts to preserve the Lib/Lab pact and avoid three-cornered contests were well judged. Nationally, Labour's electoral position seemed weak. Between December 1910 and July 1914, Labour lost four seats in by-elections and finished at the bottom of the poll in all fourteen seats it contested.[69] The test for MacDonald came in June 1913 when the Liberal MP for Leicester resigned. Many local socialists were determined to bring forward a Labour candidate to fight the seat. MacDonald was implacably imposed, knowing that the chances of success in a three-cornered fight were small. Moreover, any Labour intervention would invite retaliation from the Liberals, which could have led MacDonald to lose his seat at a subsequent general election. Yet the local Labour party ignored MacDonald and sought approval for a candidate from the central party. The national executive committee overwhelmingly rejected Leicester's application, provoking uproar in local Labour circles. There was a serious split in the local party and ultimately the British Socialist party, and dissident ILP members promoted an unofficial candidate who polled just 2,580 votes.[70]

By the outbreak of war in 1914 Leicester politics had undergone some fundamental changes from the heyday of Liberal hegemony in the early 1880s. Labour and the Conservatives had made significant electoral progress on both the Board of Guardian and Leicester Town Council and the number of elected representatives on these bodies was shared almost evenly between the two parties. However, at parliamentary level the Lib/Lab pact remained strong and showed little sign of presenting the Conservatives with any opportunity to challenge Progressive dominance. The 1913 by-election demonstrated that unofficial Labour candidatures were unlikely to be successful given the Labour party's determination to protect the position of MacDonald. There was also significant evidence that Liberal policies on free trade, cheap food, old age pensions and national insurance were successful in maintaining a significant degree of working-class support for the Liberal party. These radical social policies were little different to those of MacDonald's Labour party – indeed some trade unions actually opposed parts of the national insurance legislation on the grounds that it was an unwarranted extension of state control over social policy. In Leicester, at least, the electoral understanding between MacDonald and the Liberals was still holding, even if there were signs it was dissolving elsewhere.

The First World War and the age of realignment, 1914–1931

Many historians naturally look on the First World War as a key turning point in British electoral history, marking the period when Labour emerged from its position as a junior partner of the Liberals to being a party of potential government. Measuring the impact of war is notoriously difficult,

3.9 War
Memorial,
Victoria Park,
1923. Architect:
Edwin Lutyens
(1869–1944).

Source: Record
Office for Leicester,
Leicestershire and
Rutland, DE3736,
Box 30, Victoria
Park War Memorial,
Folder 5.

not least because changes in the suffrage massively increased the electorate, giving the vote to all males and women over 30. Some historians point to the 'franchise factor' as the key to understanding the rise of Labour.[71] However, in Leicester, Labour's progress after 1918 was stuttering at best, despite the fact that the division of Leicester into three constituencies should have given them an in-built majority. Two of the new parliamentary divisions, Leicester East and Leicester West, were overwhelmingly working-class. Leicester West was dominated by Labour from 1918 to 1945, but Leicester East was a very volatile constituency which elected Liberal, Labour and Conservative members during this period. The division of the city into single-member constituencies served the Liberals little better. In theory they should have had an opportunity to take Leicester South – a mixed constituency that had traditionally been home to Leicester's Liberal elite. Yet, except for a brief interlude in 1923, it returned Conservative members throughout until the Labour landslide of 1945.

The inter-war period was one of dramatic electoral realignments and one in which electoral volatility increased significantly. Part of the explanation for this could be the blurring of party identities during decades when coalition governments almost became the norm.[72] In 1916 Lloyd George managed to persuade enough Liberals to unseat Prime Minister Asquith and form a wartime coalition with the Conservatives. This move was to cause bitterness for decades to come, especially when, in 1918, Lloyd George decided to fight the subsequent general election as a coalition and only issue coalition coupons to those supporting his followers. Around the county Liberals fought each other and party organisation, already damaged

'Red Leicester': a reputation for radicalism?

by war, fell apart. Yet in Leicester it was not only the Liberals who suffered from Lloyd George's tactics; Labour did too. MacDonald had long been a passionate opponent of militarism and had been a prominent opponent of the prosecution of the war. His comment that 'never did we arm our people and ask them to give their lives for less good cause than this' was constantly repeated by jingoistic political opponents and represented as unpatriotic even by Liberal newspapers such as the *Leicester Daily Mercury*.[73] For them it had been a 'war for national liberties and human rights'.[74] Even though decorated war heroes spoke in support of MacDonald at his public meetings, it made little difference.[75] Lloyd George's coalition gave their official ticket to J.F. Green, a National Democratic candidate, supported by the British Workers' League and assisted by Liberal and Conservative activists. Press hostility to MacDonald made it difficult for him to run an effective campaign and he eventually fell to a humiliating defeat, losing by 20,570 votes to 6,347. Labour candidates in the two other divisions suffered equally heavily defeats, despite the fact the party fielded two of its best-known local campaigners, Councillor F.F. Riley and veteran Alderman George Banton. The coalition arrangements meant that Leicester East was ceded to the Liberal Sir George Hewart, while Leicester South went to Conservative Thomas Blane. The Conservatives had established a significant foothold, boosting their local electoral credibility and demonstrating they could indeed record parliamentary victories in 'Red Leicester'.

The decision of Conservative backbenchers to throw off the leadership of Lloyd George marked the beginning of a three-year period of turmoil in British politics. It was a period that was saw the election of the first Labour government and its rapid collapse, the marginalisation of the Liberal party to third-party status and a series of Conservative and National governments. The Leicester Labour party regrouped after 1918 and, despite associations with 'unpatriotic' actions during the war, in 1922 recorded a remarkable by-election victory in Leicester East. Although the seat was narrowly lost at the following general election, the party did make a gain in Leicester West with, significantly, the Liberal candidate coming third behind the National Democrat.[76] In 1923 the party held Leicester West and regained Leicester East, following an aggressive campaign in which it made its policy of a capital levy on the wealthy a central feature of its platform.[77]

These successes, and the formation of the first Labour government, were instrumental in shaping local political alignments until 1945. The Liberal party had supported the formation of the first Labour government but soon became hostile to some of its more socialist policies. It was particularly hostile to Labour's 'Russian loans', a scheme whereby Britain supported loans to the Soviet regime, a regime that was already regarded as despotic by many Liberals. The Liberals were left in a difficult position. Their overall electoral position seemed increasingly weak. In 1923 they had won Leicester South in a straight fight with the Conservatives, but hopes of a significant revival were halted when Winston Churchill went down to a heavy defeat in Leicester West. They were now faced with campaigning against the party that they had helped put in power. In early October Lloyd George visited Leicester and issued a typically passionate denouncement of the extremism of the Labour party, Russian loans and the leadership of MacDonald.[78] Unfortunately these 'red scare' tactics seem to have done little other than helped drive voters to the Conservatives. In Leicester South Liberal MP Ronald Allen came third behind Labour, a remarkable result in an area formerly synonymous with Liberalism. The party could not even benefit from the general anti-Labour mood when given the opportunity of a straight fight; the Liberals failed to gain Leicester West with Labour actually polling more votes than the year before. Worst still was the fact that the Liberal party was now being depicted in the press as simply the junior partner in an Anti-Socialist movement. The Conservative *Leicester Mail* trumpeted Conservative and Liberal co-operation as representing 'The Real Party of Sane Progress'.[79] Persuading Liberals to join with the Conservatives in order to fight extremism had become a key party of Conservative strategy. 'Anti-Socialists must work loyally together in future if they are to dam back the tide of Socialism,' declared the advocates of this position.[80]

The Liberal party had been outmanoeuvred tactically, but might have recovered had it been able to recruit and retain populist local candidates determined to campaign between elections and assist local organisation. The Labour party benefited enormously from the work of activists such as Alderman George Banton whose determination to come back to fight Leicester East, despite several defeats, helped maintain the position of the party in that part of the city. The Liberals, however, seemed increasingly dependent on 'carpet-baggers' brought in to stand for election at short notice. M.A. Gerothwohl, Liberal candidate for Leicester West, was just such an example of this trend. Gerothwohl was a professor of Language and Literature with a distinguished literary career but was based in London and appears to have spent little time in Leicester during the campaign. This was a great contrast to Charles Waterhouse, the Conservative candidate in Leicester South – a 'working candidate in the truest sense' – who took care of local party organisation personally and recorded a landslide victory.[81] The intensity of party campaigning meant that more was expected of candidates than ever before – the attendance at an occasional public meeting and the issuing of an election address was no longer sufficient.

Yet alongside his 'professionalisation' of local politics some aspects of elections became increasingly trivialised both by politicians struggling to gain popular attention and a printed media competing desperately for circulation. The changing tone of press coverage in the fifty years from 1880 to 1930 was remarkable. Leicester's Liberal-dominated press of the late Victorian period was one that gave detailed, often verbatim, accounts of every major speech during the campaign, sober and analytical commentaries on policy

3.10 Liberal Party General Election Banner, 23 Oxford Street, 1929. The result produced two Labour MPs (Edward Frank Wise and Frederick Pethick-Lawrence for the East and West constituencies) and one MP for the Conservatives, Charles Waterhouse.
Source: Record Office for Leicester, Leicestershire and Rutland, DE3736, Box 25, Oxford Street.

issues, and frequently religious guidance on politics from local figures such the Rev. J. Page Hopps. By the 1930s Liberals could no longer rely on an influential Liberal press, or even a press offering a moral stance on major issues of the day. The *Leicester Mercury*, once the voice-piece of Progressivism, was no longer an unequivocally Liberal paper and showed little sympathy towards Labour causes. The *Leicester Mail* had grown in influence, articulating a strong anti-Socialist message at all available opportunities. The *Leicester Chronicle* had transformed itself into a popular illustrated newspaper with little political coverage, even during general election campaigns. By 1930 the tone of coverage had also fundamentally changed, with the press often emphasising political trivia over political substance. The enfranchisement of women on equal terms to men in 1929 brought a new body of younger women voters on to the electoral roll. However, there were few serious assessments of this change and instead local papers ran stories headed 'What the Flappers Thought of the Vote', with interviews with the said 'flappers' often reinforcing the stereotypical view that young women did not take politics seriously.[82] The irony, of course, was that the papers themselves were taking the elections less seriously. Leading features included comments on the types of motor cars driven by the major candidates and the eccentric ways in which individuals went to the polls – including one who went on a pram.[83] Even the *Leicester Mercury* could not resist running what amounted, in modern parlance, to a 'wives and girlfriends' feature, examining each of the candidates' partners, including their parentage, education and social life.[84]

The moral earnestness of Liberal and Labour campaigns against unemployment and intricate economic arguments may have sat uneasily with this change in tone of election coverage. Apart from the 'flapper vote' the 1929 general election was notable for Lloyd George's campaign against unemployment, drawing on the complex demand management economic

| Leicester: a modern history

theories of John Maynard Keynes. The *Liberal Yellow Book on Britain's Industrial Future* promised government intervention to tackle the problems of economic cycles and unemployment and provided the Liberal party with a platform for potential revival. However, nationally, the revival was not as extensive as hoped for and in Leicester the election results demonstrated that the Liberal party had been squeezed to the position of minor third party. In Leicester South, a seat they had won as recently as 1923, the party came third and barely took half the votes of the second place Labour candidate. In West and East they also came a distant third.[85]

National governments and 'Conservative Leicester', 1931–1939

The economic upheavals of the 1930s 'depression era' had profound political consequences for Leicester and well as for Britain. The decision of Ramsay MacDonald to form a National government in August 1931 further undermined the Liberal position. MacDonald's so-called 'great betrayal' split the Labour party but was disastrous for the Liberals. The right wing of the party supported the National government, leaving the radical wing to try to maintain an independent existence. In Leicester several prominent Liberals called on their supporters to vote Labour.[86] Some gave up the fight and joined Labour. M.T. Hibbart-Gilson, at one point the prospective Liberal candidate for South Leicester, joined the Labour party shortly before the 1931 election.[87] The Labour party, for its part, encouraged Liberal defections by emphasising its commitment to free trade, in contrast to the 'Nationals' who were flirting with trade protection and tariff reform.[88] Liberals who supported the National 'ticket' were rewarded with a free run against Labour stalwart F.W. Pethick-Lawrence in Leicester West. The result was a clean sweep for the National candidates – National Liberal E.H. Pickering took Leicester West, while National Conservatives took the remaining seats. In a bizarre turn of events the man who had done so much to promote socialist politics in Leicester, James Ramsay MacDonald, had helped to wipe out Leicester's Labour representation in parliament and give the Conservatives a local parliamentary majority for the first time.[89]

The election of a National Liberal MP for Leicester simply served to exacerbate the fragmentation of the Liberal party and conceal the rapid rate of its decline. Over the next few years the independent sections of the party regrouped, aided by E.H. Pickering's decision to leave the National coalition and support the opposition. However, this did little for Liberal fortunes in Leicester. The result of the 1935 general election revealed just how much the 'National Liberal' vote was really just a National – or perhaps a Conservative – vote. In West Leicester, the constituency Pickering had won as a National Liberal in 1931, the Liberal candidate came a poor third, almost losing his deposit, behind the successful National Labour candidate and the official Labour candidate. Both other constituencies remained in Conservative hands. For the Liberals the elections were uniformly disastrous. The party failed to field a candidate in its once great stronghold of South Leicester. In East Leicester its candidate made the headlines only for forfeiting his deposit.[90]

The stuttering performance of Labour and Liberal candidates in the inter-war years undermined Leicester's claim to be a bastion of political radicalism. Labour would have to wait until the national Labour landslide of 1945 to make a 'clean sweep' of Leicester seats and regain a position of local dominance, a dramatic turnaround that astonished the local media.[91] For the Liberals, 1945 simply marked a further stage of decline and it would be another sixty years before the party won another parliamentary seat in the city. Labour inter-war difficulties were partly a reflection of local conditions, partly the changing nature of the electorate and partly the success of the National government in promoting itself as a great patriotic cause at a time of national crisis. The division of Leicester into three parliamentary constituencies undermined the position of the Liberal party, but the creation of two distinctively working-class constituencies should have created a 'natural' Labour majority. However, the reality was somewhat different. The city's rejection of Ramsay MacDonald deprived the city of a potent national figure able to mobilise the Labour cause. Although a controversial figure in the Labour movement, much of the party's electoral growth in Leicester came under MacDonald's leadership, while the party's progress in the 1920s, after his departure, was stuttering at best. While some key Labour policies, such as the capital levy, appear to have been popular among the local working-class electorate, Labour seemed to find it difficult to translate this support into a strong local party organisation or lasting appeal. Labour also seemed to find it difficult to mobilise younger female workers – or the 'flapper vote' as it was often dubbed in the press. The unsuccessful Labour candidate for Leicester West in 1935 made an outspoken attack on 'the factory women' who, he felt, were 'a little bit, in a sense, too comfortable'.[92] While the depression affected Leicester like other Midlands towns, those in work often saw their real wages and living standards improve. Leicester's dependence on large amounts of female factory labour saw a significant number of working-class women enjoy relative prosperity and be less responsive to traditional working-class socialist messages. Moreover, the Labour party did little to encourage women candidates and made few specific appeals to the new female electorate.

Both Labour and Liberal candidates often commented on the failure of the expanded electorate to take politics seriously. While lively eve-of-poll meetings continued to be popular, there were signs that traditional public meetings and traditional oratory were in decline. The growth of commercial leisure meant that politics had to compete with a growing array of other attractions. In contrast to the days when spectator sport was frowned upon due to its associations with gambling, the inter-war newspapers dedicated far more columns to football, horse racing and cricket than they did to local politics. The popularity of the cinema also took away some younger audiences, so much so that some candidates, such as National Liberal MP Ernest Pickering, even took to addressing queues waiting outside cinemas.[93] The power of political celebrities was also on the wane, perhaps as a result of the stars of 'talkies' and other popular entertainment. Figures such as Lloyd George could still pull in a large audience, but there is little evidence that they made a significant electoral impact. Churchill's candidature in Leicester attracted much comment but insufficient votes to win him a seat. The nonconformist churches, once a key force for mobilising Liberal voters, adopted a less public role in election contests; by 1930 it would have been almost unthinkable for a religious leader such as Rev. J. Page Hopps to be openly campaigning for the party. With politics being gradually marginalised from the centre of public attention there was even greater stress on party organisation and the ability of parties to get reluctant electors to the poll. With most ordinary workers still working at least an eight-hour day, there was a small window of opportunity for voting on polling day. Many Labour activists believed that poor weather, particularly in the evening, was their great threat on election day. Unlike the Conservatives who could always command a large number of private motor cars, Labour always struggled to obtain sufficient conveyances. When Labour seats were lost by fewer than 100 votes, as they were in West Leicester in 1935, such apparently marginal factors could actually be crucial.[94]

The modern political legacy

Yet perhaps the most notable trend in politics during the period 1880 to 1945 was the gradual 'nationalisation' of local politics. In 1886, when the Home Rule crisis broke at Westminster, Leicester politicians took little interest. Most of the city's Liberal elite were much more engrossed in the compulsory vaccination question – a key local issue – than questions relating to the government of Ireland. However, from the Edwardian period national political issues, whether it be Free Trade in 1906, the House of Lords in 1910 or 'Homes fit for Heroes' in 1918, took an increasingly central role in Leicester's politics. The fragmentation of the Lib/Lab Progressive alliance gave the Conservatives the opportunity to establish themselves as the primary anti-Socialist party, but it was their ability to use coalition governments to articulate a message of national patriotism that made them such powerful opponents. This is one reason why so many Labour activists resented MacDonald – not only had be apparently abandoned his own party but he had adopted the same phoney patriotic language in order to sustain a coalition of convenience. In doing so he almost destroyed the party in Leicester that he had done so much to create, with the city failing to elect a independent Labour MP for the first time since 1906. His party, one that had begun as one pressing for working-class representation and socialist programmes, was in 1935 selecting candidates for Leicester with aristocratic backgrounds who had associations with right-wing political extremism. The Hon. Harold Nicholson, who won West Leicester for National Labour, was a friend of Oswald Mosley and had allegedly introduced Mosley to Mussolini.[95] While it seems unlikely that Nicholson maintained his close links with Mosley for very long thereafter, the episode reflects the political confusion and upheaval of the inter-war period.

The currents of radicalism in Leicester's urban politics remained strong, but it was a period of dramatic social change and political realignment. By 1918 most of the great middle-class Liberal families – the Wrights, Simpson Gees, Faires and Harts – had either left the party or had withdrawn from local politics. As in other regional centres, residual loyalty toward Liberal and nonconformist traditions sustained the party organisationally but in Leicester this did not translate into significant electoral success.[96] A significant number of electors, and some politicians, became disillusioned and abandoned traditional party allegiances, either as a result of the experience of the First World War, the failure of social reconstruction, the disappointments of the first Labour government or the 1929 crash. As voters switched sides, electoral volatility increased making local election results much less predictable. Like their respective national parties, Leicester's Liberal and Labour parties split, while the Conservatives re-defined themselves as an anti-Socialist 'patriotic' party. The 'onward march of Labour' had stalled and Leicester looked less like a city of radicalism than ever before. While the 1945 landslide election brought a new era of electoral success for Labour in Leicester, the city has never fully re-established its reputation for radicalism.

The success of the Conservative party in Leicester in the 1980s and the partial revival of the Liberals (and Liberal Democrats) since then suggests that the local electorate continues to be unpredictable and, perhaps, less tied to traditional party allegiances than before. The Liberal Democrats' shock 2004 parliamentary by-election victory in Leicester South showed a city still willing to use its vote to protest against unpopular government policies. While the Labour party has since re-established its electoral strength in Leicester, party members do not always follow the direction of party officials. Leicester South Labour Party's nomination of Jeremy Corbyn for party leader in 2015, in defiance of the views of its sitting Labour MP, suggests Leicester's tradition of independent-minded rebellion is not dead. If Leicester is a radical city, its radicalism is perhaps best seen in its historical unwillingness to accept the tutelage of any one party for any great deal of time and its enthusiasm for grass-roots revolt against established party leaderships.

Appendix

Parliamentary constituency results 1832–85

Election	First member	First party	Second member	Second party
1832	Edward Dawson	Liberal	Sir Henry Halford, Bt	Tory
1834				Conservative
1835	Thomas Frewen Turner	Conservative		
1836 by-election	Charles William Packe	Conservative		
1857			Viscount Curzon	Conservative
1867 by-election	Thomas Paget	Liberal Party		
1868	Albert Pell	Conservative		
1870 by-election			William Unwin Heygate	Conservative
1880			Thomas Paget	Liberal Party
1885	Redistribution of Seats Act: constituency abolished			

4

Watching the town: protecting Leicester from fire and crime, c.1870–1930

Between 1835 and 1967, the Watch Committee was the most prestigious municipal committee involved in the government of Leicester. It enjoyed a social, cultural and legal authority that, with few exceptions, was unparalleled within the administrative apparatus of urban local government. Initially established under the Municipal Corporations Act, 1835, the successive history of the Watch Committee, until its abolition under the Police Act, 1964, was intertwined with the broader structural and functional changes to urban local government in Leicester and across England and Wales. Its evolving powers reflected and refracted wider legal, financial and administrative changes to central–local relations. Moreover, as the first statutory committee established under the terms of the 1835 Act, the Watch Committee was a potent symbol of the enduring capacity of urban local governments to self-govern within, as it has been labelled 'the national world of local government'.[1] Any challenge to the authority and autonomy of the Watch Committee was a challenge to the tradition of local self-determination.

Although the Watch Committee was the fulcrum around which the management and delivery of public protection services such as policing and fire fighting pivoted, few historical studies have noted more than the regularity of meetings and devolution of 'day-to-day matters of discipline and deployment' to the Chief Constable, who was effectively the chief operating officer within the committee's formal proceedings.[2] More recently, the intermittent decline in the Watch Committee's control over operational policing has been traced, culminating in the transfer of police management from the borough watch committees to the county police authorities under the 1964 Act.[3] The demise of the Watch Committee is regarded as emblematic of a deeper, irrevocable shift in state power from the locality to the centre. As the exchequer assumed greater responsibility for the funding of public services, local conditions of service and administrative idiosyncrasies were superseded by fixed minimum standards and professional regulations.[4]

4.1 Leicester Guildhall, courtyard.

Source: Leicester City Council.

4.2 Leicester Town Hall.

Source: Colin Hyde.

Both buildings functioned as police offices and cells with Guildhall (built *c*.1343 for Corpus Christi guild) and occupied by Leicester Corporation from 1563 until the new Town Hall (built 1873–76) in Queen Anne style was completed. Architect: F.J. Hames.

Watching the town: protecting Leicester from fire and crime |

Leicester Watch Committee played an important administrative role in the governance of the town. Its by-laws, which were originally constituted in 1835 and expanded at various points during its administrative life cycle, helped order the town's social, economic and cultural activities. By the 1870s, the Watch Committee was the leading agency for public protection services, being responsible for the town's policing, fire protection and street lighting. Its leaders, who comprised a significant proportion of the town's social and economic elite, maintained strong economic and social interests as employers and ratepayers in guaranteeing a safe and ordered place. Through a case study of the rhythms of the Watch Committee meetings and its members, focusing on the alleged zenith of urban local government between the 1870s and 1930s, this chapter examines the evolving powers and relations that constituted municipal administration in a burgeoning industrial county town. Leicester Watch Committee operated within a professionalising policy community responsible for service delivery, which also involved input from the service providers themselves, increasingly represented in the public form of the Chief Constable and the Chief Fire Officer.

Structure and authority

Although the Watch Committee was statutorily constituted under the Municipal Corporations Act, 1835, it was its successor Act, passed in 1882, that stipulated specific criteria for membership of the full committee and its sub-committees. To minimise partisan interference, all watch committees consisted of the mayor and not more than one-third of a town council's elected members. Thus, the Watch Committee was one of only two standing committees prevented from co-opting unelected, and thereby unaccountable, members.[5] Paradoxically, though, it sat in secret and its proceedings did not require the legal approval of the full council, although it could not levy a rate without official sanction. Notwithstanding this limited control, the Watch Committee remained wedded to the cultural values of the municipal reformers, heeding the demands for greater public probity and transparency within the affairs of urban local government by producing annual estimates for public discussion and arranging for the auditing of its accounts.[6]

Although initially constituted to administer a borough's police force, the Watch Committee evolved in its status and powers throughout the nineteenth century, gradually assuming responsibility for the public protection of the town more generally.[7] It did so by adopting national statutes and local standing orders, a mix that ensured no two watch committees in England and Wales were alike in form and function.[8] For example, the Watch Committee commonly assumed responsibility for administering the fire brigade, invariably through a permanent fire brigade sub-committee, in order to share clerical and accounting resources with the police. Many towns, in the four decades following the 1835 Act, municipalised fire fighting as an extension to the beat constable's duties, establishing 'fire police' units within the police force. These consisted of a small group of men sworn in as constables whose duties were wholly devoted to fire protection, and assisted by a large body of police auxiliaries who provided logistical and organisational support during large fires. Leeds and Liverpool formed 'fire police' brigades in 1836, as did Leicester, which protected the town alongside a private brigade operated firstly by the Leicestershire Fire Insurance Company, before it was bought by the Sun Fire Insurance Company in 1844.[9]

Leicester Watch Committee first established a fire brigade sub-committee in 1869 to investigate the proposed separation of its police and fire departments. A separate fire brigade was officially instituted three years later as a result of sustained complaints from ratepayers about the lack of organisational co-operation between the 'fire police' and the private brigade at large fires. Establishing a separate fire brigade also involved a merger with the Sun's force, with the new municipal body placed under the supervision of that brigade's superintendent, John Johnson, an experienced local fireman. Johnson reported his firemen's activities to the sub-committee, which comprised a cross-section of the Watch Committee's membership and was a permanent feature of its proceedings from 1872 until the Second World War. As a municipal employee, Johnson was not permitted to attend its monthly meetings, but he would present written reports on the fires in the town, inspections of the hydrants and, when prompted, recommendations on proposed additions to the brigade's equipment or personnel. The sub-committee debated his reports before forwarding any substantive recommendations or amendments to the full committee for its comments and approval. While bureaucratic procedure shielded the full committee's members from the every-day minutiae of policy implementation, cross-membership maintained administrative and financial stability.[10]

Sub-committees were integral components of municipal administration. Those that enjoyed sufficient powers could normally formulate and implement policy, pass resolutions, devise financial estimates, and maintain 'general control' over the activities of departmental staff. Municipal administration undoubtedly became more complex and reliant upon sub-committees for a host of functions from the early 1870s. In 1871, for example, Leicester Town Council devolved authority for administering the lighting department to its Watch Committee, which itself passed departmental responsibility to a permanent sub-committee. By the 1890s, the committee had assumed responsibility for a variety of public protection services, which included enforcing child protection legislation, licensing theatres, regulating hackney carriages and tramway cars, supervising cabmen's shelters, managing the public mortuary, enforcing fire safety regulations, governing the storage of petroleum and explosives, and regulating the use of bicycles.[11]

4.3, 4.4 Industrial fires. Leicester suffered a number of catastrophic fires as in the Imperial Cotton Mills in Lower Brown Street on 5 May 1914 (4.3) and the Great Fire on 5 October 1911 in Queen Street that destroyed the factories of R. Rowley & Co. (4.4) and Spiers.

Source: Record Office for Leicester, Leicestershire and Rutland, DE3736, Box 20, Lower Brown Street.

In Affectionate Remembrance

OF

P.C. Stephens,

Who passed away on April 4th, 1908,

Aged 48 years.

He did 22 years' Service on the Leicester Police Force,
and was acknowledged to be England's Heaviest
Constable, his weight being over 24 stone.
He also served his Country in the Zulu War, 1879.

Poor old Stephens, how we'll miss him
From his customary beat;
Never more his stalwart figure
Or stern, but kindly face we'll greet!

"REQUIESCAT IN PACE."

4.5 England's heaviest constable, PC Stephens. Physical fitness and stature were part of the requirements of policing. PC Stephens was presumably a conspicuous figure.

Source: Leicester City Council.

4.6 Special Constables lined up for wartime duties in the Market Square, 1914.

Source: Record Office for Leicester, Leicestershire and Rutland, DE3736, Box 21, Market Place, Folder 2.

The sub-division of administration saw policies placed under the responsibility of either temporary sub-committees, which sat until a specific issue was resolved, or permanent bodies that enjoyed more formalised powers and administrative longevity. For example, a Promotions Sub-Committee was formed in 1872, which sat on an occasional basis until 1891, following which it was merged with the Police Accounts Sub-Committee (which had itself existed since 1874). A General Purposes Sub-Committee was established in 1897, which was responsible for a range of police functions, including accounts, discipline, promotions and uniforms. It was annually re-appointed until 1919, when it was disbanded following the transfer of certain police regulations to the Home Secretary. Ten permanent sub-committees were constituted between 1900 and 1939 to deal with an increasing workload, ranging from traffic control to cinema inspection and film censorship.[12]

The proliferation of committees and sub-committees, the extension of existing powers into new areas of service provision, and the accelerated growth and expansion of urban areas intensified existing pressures on urban local governments between the 1870s and mid-1930s. Writing during the inter-war years, experts in the emerging discipline of public administration subsequently identified lack of time and specialist knowledge as considerable constraints on the traditional freedoms of town councils:

> A council … may direct policy and decide principles, but is an impossible body to give judgement on the multifarious problems falling to the lot of local government authorities to solve in these days. It has neither the time nor the knowledge.[13]

Leicester was not immune to this burgeoning workload. In 1926 the long-standing Conservative councillor, Walter Lovell, bemoaned the spiralling number of sub-committees of the full council, which had risen by 38% alone between 1922 and 1926.[14] Having joined the Watch Committee and its Fire Brigade Sub-Committee in 1910, three years after his election to the Wycliffe ward, Lovell chaired both consecutively from 1919 to 1934, also serving on the lighting (1914–36), police accounts (1920–36), inspection of public buildings (1913–15), shop acts (1913–15), emergency (1916–34) and traffic (1923–31) sub-committees.

As a whole, the workload of Leicester Watch Committee was divided among 21 sub-committees between 1918 and 1939, with five of them serving permanently throughout.[15] Such a proliferation of

4.7 Walter Lovell (1857–) Wholesale sweet manufacturer; Conservative councillor 1901; Chairman, Watch Committee; Lord Mayor 1918–19. During his first two days in office, the Armistice was declared; in the first five weeks 1,270 deaths occurred from influenza epidemic; and the first election in which women could vote took place. The title of 'city' was also conferred on Leicester during the royal visit of 10 June 1919 during Lovell's period of office.

Source: Leicester City Council.

responsibilities demanded additional administrative time and expertise than individuals like Lovell could guarantee. In its published duties, issued in November 1934, the committee had assumed regulatory and supervisory powers for a growing volume and range of tasks. These included certifying the safe storage of celluloid, inspecting cinema fire safety, licensing Sunday entertainment (including film censorship), and enforcing the factory and workshop legislation (particularly the 1901 Factories Act, which introduced certification of means of escape from factories). It was also responsible for licensing gang masters, pawnbrokers, game dealers, street porters, metal dealers, street collections and public advertisements, as well as supervising the use of steam whistles and trumpets in factories. Existing responsibilities such as the regulation of traffic had escalated with growing levels of road use and successive road traffic legislation. A motor transport and patrol department was formed in 1930, to supervise road traffic in and around the city's congested centre and its arterial roads. A city-wide police box system was adopted in 1931 to improve communication between the police and members of the public, who also used the boxes to report fires. Moreover, the management of both the police force and fire brigade had intensified in response to the rising volume of administrative circulars, policy recommendations and standard operating procedures trafficked between Whitehall, the local authority associations and the various service associations. The Watch Committee was not unique in this fragmentation because the workload of all town council committees was becoming more extensive and cumbersome, involving greater numbers of stakeholders and encompassing a growing variety of fields.[16]

In response to this growing workload, councillors complained of the council's repeated failure to regulate its own affairs by increasing its size and labour force. Since 1871 the Town Council had only increased by nine members and was fixed at sixty-four councillors and aldermen in 1905, while Watch Committee membership was statutorily streamlined from two-thirds of the council's membership in 1871 to one-third under the terms of the 1882 Municipal Corporations Act. Following further reductions, by 1931 the Watch Committee was composed of one-quarter of the town's councillors and aldermen.[17]

This disparity between a growing workload and a streamlined membership inevitably led to more frequent and longer meetings. Various proposals were mooted by senior aldermen to reduce their workloads to manageable proportions. The most publicised came from the city's departing mayor and Labour MP for Leicester East (1922–24), George Banton, who was also the chairman of the local Labour party. Banton suggested transferring additional operational responsibilities to chief officers and junior officials to lessen the burgeoning administrative workload; otherwise, he warned, 'the situation in the municipal sphere is destined to become intolerable' and policy would lack coherence:

The fact has been recognised that the work of the city, owing to its growth and its many activities, is rapidly increasing and the difficulty will have to be faced unless we are prepared to leave more and more of the work in the hands of the permanent officials.[18]

Banton's warning resonated across the English and Welsh county boroughs during the inter-war years. The pressures of an expanding urban and suburban area, coupled with the intensification and diversification of social and economic activities, brought increasingly acute policy demands on Victorian bureaucracies constituted under legislation passed between 1835 and 1888, when the county boroughs were formed under the Local Government Act. Added to that was a shifting policy emphasis towards social welfare during the Edwardian and inter-war years, which demanded additional financial and organisational resources. This was, as identified by J.A. Chandler, the era of 'growth with decline' in local government, but only in terms of the Victorian approach, which had conventionally emphasised the efficient and economical delivery of local services. As Chandler notes, 'The 1930s was not only a decade in which local authorities became institutionalized as more of an agency for undertaking central services but also as bureaucracies that implemented these services in-house through professional officers, who often could determine the direction of an authority more adroitly than its councillors.'[19] Lovell's and Banton's criticisms merely reflected these broader structural changes.

4.8 George Banton (1856–1932) coal merchant; elected councillor for Wyggeston Ward 1896, Mayor (1925), and Labour MP for Leicester East 1922–27.

Source: Leicester City Council.

Notwithstanding the growing burdens of council and committee business, Leicester Watch Committee retained its administrative prestige and status into the inter-war years. Thus, although the frequency of its meetings declined from 1899, it continued to meet, on average, one-and-a-half times every month between 1902 and 1938; local standing orders stipulated that standing committees should meet monthly. Combined with the high frequency of sub-committee meetings, these continued to be the preferred basis for negotiating resources and discussing policy. The complexity of committee business was also reflected in a more than doubling in the length of Watch Committee meetings between 1900 and 1930. Contemporaries defended these broad trends, contending that weekly or fortnightly meetings did not necessarily produce 'better results' than monthly meetings, which were more attractive to 'busy public men' wary of the growing burdens of municipal work on their time.[20]

| Leicester: a modern history

Attendance rates remained stable throughout the period, countering assumptions that early twentieth-century elites did not regard municipal work as highly as their Victorian counterparts. Between 1868 and 1914, the attendance rate at watch committee meetings was 70%, while between 1918 and 1938 it was marginally higher at 71%.[21] Walter Lovell's attendance was more consistent than most, with an attendance rate of 81% from 1917 to 1932. Sub-committee attendance was proportionately lower, but also remained similarly stable across the period. The attendance rate for the Fire Brigade Sub-Committee was 64% between 1893 and 1914 and 62% between 1917 and 1938. For the General Purposes Sub-Committee, the respective rates showed a rise from 56 to 66%.[22] The persistence of high attendance indicates that the members did not class their work as being of diminishing value. Rather, attitudes towards formal organisational networks remained durable well into the inter-war years. If the traditional municipal elites were supposed to be losing power and prestige after 1914, their attitude towards their burgeoning workload did not reflect this.

Consequently, town councillors aspired to Watch Committee membership. In so doing, they were elected through a bi-partisan consensus between the local Conservative, Labour and Liberal parties, which placed patronage on the basis of long and distinguished civic service, rather than party loyalties. The equity of patronage distribution among political parties has been identified as one of the defining characteristics of twentieth-century urban local government, and the representation of political parties on Leicester Watch Committee was roughly proportionate to their strength on the Town Council.[23] It was this sense of fairness that contributed to a longevity of service on the Watch Committee with active members 'who were as much experts in police management and policy as many of the sergeants and above in the force'.[24] Combined with a strong local personality, experience was a considerable tool regularly deployed by Leicester Watch Committee in its negotiations over the allocation and deployment of resources within the full council, with other committees, and with central government departments such as the Home Office. The impact of local personalities on Watch Committee administration was particularly evident when experienced individuals retired from local politics. Between 1888 and 1891, for example, the level of experience on the full committee fell from a peak of 10.8 years to a trough of 2.9 years (4.9). This followed the retirement of Thomas Almond, George Anderson and Samuel Wheeler, all former chairmen, after twenty-five, thirty and thirty-seven years' committee service respectively.[25]

Following this trough, the level of experience rose steadily, peaking at 15.8 years in 1933. Watch Committee membership was increasingly seen in vocational terms, rather than in its traditional sense as a privileged reward for civic duty. Membership demanded the time, energy and knowledge of a committed membership for two decades and longer. In its peak year of 1933, more than half of its members had served for at least ten years; a third of

4.9 Length of service of Leicester Watch Committee members, 1867–1936 (average number of years).

Source: Record Office for Leicester, Leicestershire and Rutland, CM42/10–32, Watch Committee Minutes, 1867–1936.

them for over twenty years, including, among others, Walter Ernest Wilford (since 1915) and Edwin Hincks (since 1901), who were leading figures in the local Labour and Liberal parties respectively, and both having performed senior roles within the committee and its many sub-committees.

This organisational stability reinforced the dominant position of the more experienced committee members over those with a shorter length of service. Those serving for more than ten years used their overwhelming knowledge of procedure to influence policy-making. Experience undermined partisan voting, with experienced members forming close working and personal relationships among themselves. Wilford and Hincks, for example, were bitter enemies during the

4.10 Walter Ernest Wilford (1879–1950) boot and shoe factor and shopowner; elected councillor 1912; Alderman 1928; JP 1932; Lord Mayor 1931, and granted Freedom of the City 1949. Chaired the Health Committee 1921–25; vice-chairman of the Watch Committee from 1928–34, then chairman until 1945. Philanthropic work with Citizens Aid Committee, meals for children during winters, 1904–06, organised 'ye olde Englishe Faire' in 1916 to raise funds for disabled servicemen. *Source*: Leicester City Council.

4.11 William Edwin Hincks OBE (b.1870) Secretary, Leicester Branch of the Amalgamated Society of Engineers (1897); Secretary, Charity Organisation Society from 1903. Councillor 1900; served as Watch Committee vice-chair, 1921–28 and 1934–35, and Lord Mayor in 1929–30.

Source: Leicester City Council.

annual municipal elections, berating each other at the hustings during a fiercely contested campaign in 1911. Hincks, a former trade unionist and member of the Leicester Trades Council, remained a staunch Liberal throughout his career, criticising socialism as an 'intellectual delusion'.[26] Wilford, the chief whip of the Leicester Labour party, criticised Hincks and other leading Liberals for recent rate relief policies.[27] Yet the intrusion of party politics was largely restricted to the annual election periods. There were few chances for partisan voting on the Watch Committee, particularly since party leaders like Hincks and Wilford formed a close working relationship over three decades, which enthused other committee members to overcome factionalism with a commonly shared civic vision of inclusivity and co-ordination.[28]

Experience and seniority could sometimes be an obstacle to new initiatives, but they encouraged innovative ideas through members' individual and collective knowledge of administrative procedures and working relations. Experienced members claimed social and administrative authority in representing the Watch Committee publicly. Edwin Hincks, for example, made references to his knowledge of local fire fighting in a speech to the Institute of Fire Engineers at its annual conference in Leicester's Town Hall in 1930. Through his association with the fire service over the previous quarter of a century, Hincks felt knowledgeable enough to make various suggestions to the delegates concerning community fire prevention and brigade recruitment strategies. His experience and expertise was reinforced by the town's Chief Fire Officer, Henry Neal (1909–38), who publicly proclaimed that, 'I doubt if there is any other municipal legislator who has a deeper insight into, or knows more about, our Service.'[29]

The rise of the chief officer

A growing administrative and operational workload was paralleled by a corresponding rise in the powers and privileges of appointed officials. The chief official was obviously a long-standing feature of urban local government, but the observable shift in his public status from municipal servant to professional officer was discernible around the turn of the twentieth century in the language used to describe his actions and responsibilities in print culture. The establishment of professional associations, with annual meetings held in the larger provincial towns, and the diffusion of best practice through technical periodicals, helped normalise working conditions, while constituting a municipal culture founded upon claims to professional expertise and experience.[30]

Alongside the Town Clerk, the Borough Surveyor and the Medical Officer of Health, the Chief Constable and the Chief Fire Officer emerged as leading progenitors of this professionalising municipal dialogue. Indeed, by the 1900s the Chief Constable was 'one the most powerful chief officers in England and Wales', his professional authority being 'original, not delegated,' and exercised 'at his own discretion by virtue of his office'.[31] This shift was discernible in Leicester where successive chief constables Herbert Allen (1913–28) and Oswald B. Cole (1928–55) acted as authoritarian bulwarks against encroachment by the Watch Committee into operational affairs. When Leicester City Police celebrated its centenary in March 1936, Cole sat at 'the top table' of the civic dinner alongside the Lord Mayor and the Watch Committee chairman, Ernest Wilford. However, although the Chief Constable was increasingly autonomous in the performance of his constitutional police duties, a position that was reinforced after 1918 when a new Police Act invested him with significant controls over police personnel, he still depended upon the Watch Committee's support to maintain the professional legitimacy of his office. An intelligent chief constable thus co-operated with his committee, which sometimes meant acceding to administrative interference, rather than dismissing their views.[32]

The adoption of the standardised title 'Chief Constable' itself signalled a shift in the way in which his administrative and operational authority was reflected in language. Leicester Watch Committee did not formally adopt it until 1914, one year after Herbert Allen had succeeded James Hall-Dalwood (1907–13) as 'Head Constable'.[33] Indeed, Hall-Dalwood, who left Leicester to become 'Chief Constable' in Sheffield, and his predecessors, James Duns (1882–94) and Thomas Lumley (1894–1907), used the title in their internal management of the force from at least 1892.[34] Leicester Watch Committee preferred to use the title of 'Head Constable' in its minute books, which was accompanied by a sense of social and professional inferiority within the committee's formal relations.[35] Chief officials like the Head/Chief Constable thus had to first assert their operational authority before they were in a position to establish administrative parity with their elected committee. This had clear repercussions for the chief's position within municipal government and the embryonic police profession because, as David Wall has shown, county constabularies preferred the standard term 'Chief Constable' which elevated them to a higher professional status than their borough counterparts. Late Victorian and Edwardian professionalism

4.12 Central Police Station, Charles and Northampton Street, built in 1931, and a reflection of the expanding work and influence of the Chief Constable and the role of policing. Architect G. Noel Hill.

Source: Colin Hyde,

was not, therefore, completely immune to traditional ideas of patronage and wealth.[36]

A similar attitude of service traditionally existed towards the head of the fire brigade, who was given the subordinate title of 'Superintendent of the Fire Brigade', rather than the incumbents' preference for the more formal 'Chief Fire Officer'. This placed him on a nominal par with the 'Lighting Superintendent', 'Markets Superintendent' and 'Police Superintendent'. Multiple levels of professional prestige, coupled with the inevitable differences in remuneration and other tangible benefits, reflected ingrained social attitudes towards the degree of skill demanded from specific occupations. The 'Superintendent of the Fire Brigade', for example, performed an important role in leading his firemen during fires, and in maintaining discipline within the fire station through daily drill, but he suffered a lower professional status because fire fighting was generally seen by Victorians as a semi-skilled vocation. Whereas the Head/Chief Constable enjoyed a measure of freedom through the doctrine of constabulary independence, the Fire Brigade's superintendent continued to be seen as a municipal servant, subservient to his employers and the town's ratepayers.

In order to attain profession legitimacy, chief officers first had to cultivate what has been described as 'a core of esoteric knowledge' regulated by professional integrity and strict codes of conduct.[37] Inevitably, status came with experience. This can be seen in the case of William Ely, who was appointed 'Superintendent of the Fire Brigade' in 1889, and retired twenty years later as 'Chief Fire Officer'. The Fire Brigade Sub-Committee formally adopted the new title in 1908, along with the junior titles of 'Second' and 'Third' Officer, as recognition of his brigade's burgeoning professional profile. Ely was credited with improving Leicester's organised fire safety within public and professional circles, having actively stewarded his firemen in their efforts to extinguish fires, according to newspaper reports. For example, in reporting a fire in a china merchant's shop in 1895, the *Leicester Daily Mercury* narrated that 'after more than half-an-hour's hard work, Mr. Ely had succeeded in getting behind the smoke and driving it out sufficiently to allow of an entrance to the cellar to be made'.[38] In a similar manner, the professional journal *Fire & Water*, in an 1893 article reflecting on reforms to Leicester's fire protection following the extension of the town's boundaries two years previously, publicly lauded Ely for having 'done more towards making the Leicester Fire Brigade an efficient organisation than any other person'.[39]

The construction of expert knowledge, combined with the increased responsibilities of urban local government, assisted in the diffusion of this culture of municipal professionalism. Like other municipal services whose delivery was contingent on the generation and accumulation of knowledge, notably public health, the professional knowledge generated by leading firemen like William Ely and his successor, Henry Neal (1909–38), accompanied by the practical deeds of fire fighting, was socially constructed by interested individuals and their representative associations. Both Ely and Neal played formative roles in establishing and expanding the fire service's professional associations, the Association of Professional Fire Brigade Officers (1902) and the Institution of Fire Engineers (1918). The latter was formed during a meeting of senior chief fire officers in Leicester's Central Fire Station who were determined to formalise the technical credentials of professional fire fighting. Neal was elected its founding president.[40]

Chief officers increasingly asserted their claims to being professionals, that is, of being 'laymen to the other professions', in order to strengthen their professional authority, as well as to improve their salary and fringe benefits. They argued that their knowledge was specialised to the extent that it demanded intensive on-the-job training and the cumulative experience of extinguishing fires or maintaining law and order. Expertise was, however, dependent on existing and past administrative relationships between chief officers and elected municipal elites. The rise of 'bureaucratic authority', as well as the intensification of municipal work, between the 1870s and 1930s ultimately contributed to the separation of policy-making and operational administration as chief officers earned their Watch Committee's trust. In return for their professional commitment and political neutrality, they accumulated unprecedented administrative and operational responsibilities.[41]

Reassessing the decline of urban local government

It is commonly assumed that the rise of the chief officer heralded the decline of the traditional checks and balances of urban local government. Inter-war English policing, for example, has been consistently identified as witnessing

4.13–15 The scale and complexity of municipal management.

4.13 (*above*) **and 4.14** (*below*) Fire Brigade
Headquarters, Lancaster Road, 1927, and Fireman's
housing. Architects: A.E and T. Sawday.
Source: Colin Hyde.

4.15 Wyvern. The legendary bird with a
dragon's head is said to breathe fire and have a
venomous bite.
Source: Colin Hyde.

increased centralisation within the operational and administrative decision-
making processes, and an inevitable by-passing of watch committees in
favour of a direct linkage between the Home Office, H.M. Inspectors of
Constabulary and the office of Chief Constable.[42] Studies of fire service
reform, in which minimum standards of service delivery were adopted
under the terms of the 1938 Fire Brigades Act, have similarly taken a
'top-down' approach by focusing overwhelmingly on the role of government
ministers and senior civil servants.[43]

The reality of service administration and regulation was more nuanced. Individual watch committees and their memberships retained considerable prestige and autonomy within the administrative bureaucracy of urban local government, notwithstanding sporadic amendments to their size, membership and powers. In fact, many of the rules and conventions of municipal administration remained strikingly similar between the 1870s and 1930s. The committee structure of municipal government provided the administrative link between the police and fire services, while the proliferation of single-issue sub-committees to deal with the minutiae of administration remained a deliberate response to 'the [increasing] volume and complexity' of work during the inter-war years.[44]

That Leicester Watch Committee assumed additional responsibilities throughout the period, by means of both permissive and prescriptive legislation, as well as local standing orders, reaffirmed its enduring influence on policy-making. Much of its enduring capacity to act and inform was contingent upon the experience and skills of its senior members. The chairman and other experienced members were well-known individuals, regularly attending civic functions, parades and meetings, which was recognised in the chairman's attendance at the annual inspection of the police by the Inspector of Constabulary. Indeed, in 1911 the Home Secretary had deemed it 'in the interests of good administration' for his inspectors to 'confer personally' with the Watch Committee chairman, reinforcing the interdependency between national and local institutions. Similar conventions governed the annual Civic Sunday procession, which involved the City Fire Brigade drilling and marching in public. These cultural rites, which also included the force's participation in civic processions, continued into the 1930s and were capped by the force's centenary celebrations, which were held to public fanfare in 1936.[45]

Leicester Watch Committee continued to perform a managerial role within municipal administration during the inter-wars. Although it had devolved much of the daily operation of its police and fire departments to the chief officers, it retained responsibility for their overall management. Regular committee and sub-committee meetings, at which both the Chief Constable and Chief Fire Officer attended after 1918, provided the formal basis for departmental scrutiny. Although the Watch Committee worked within increasingly fixed regulatory boundaries set by central government and the professions, the role of individual local personalities, the creation of a bi-partisan administrative consensus, the integration of chief officers within local decision-making structures, and the contingency of urban development reinforced its pivotal position within the administration of public protection services.

5

'The Taming of the Soar': Leicester transforms its river environment

About four o'clock on Wednesday morning, a very heavy thunderstorm broke over Leicester and rain descended in torrents for more than an hour. Leicester, as usual, suffered from severe inundations in the lower parts, and, as the morning continued showery, the flood in various districts assumed alarming proportions. Humberstone Road, Belgrave Road, and the adjoining streets were the greatest sufferers. In most of them pedestrian traffic was rendered impossible. Many houses in Martin, Bardolph, Catherine and Dorset Streets were invaded by the water, and the last-named thoroughfare assumed the appearance of a river.[1]

T HE *Leicester Chronicle* opened a four-column report on the 'Great Floods in Leicestershire' with this account in mid-July 1880. The floods resulted in two fatalities in the county, and major damage to property, including the destruction of three railway bridges. The wording 'as usual' indicates that flooding in times of heavy rainfall was not uncommon to Leicester, but the scale of this flood in 1880 surpassed previous ones. The issue of recurrent flooding in the lower parts of the city was arguably the single most important environmental issue in the nineteenth-century history of Leicester.[2] It draws our attention to the river and waterways running through Leicester, particularly the River Soar and the Leicester Navigation which were then incapable of absorbing excessive rainfall when very high volumes of water from upland Leicestershire flowed towards the city, breaching the banks and overflowing into low-lying areas of the city close to the river.

This hazard and the measures undertaken by the Corporation to address the problem by large-scale flood prevention works are the central topic of this chapter. How was the problem perceived? What were the obstacles to be surmounted? Did the measures undertaken contribute to a major physical transformation of Leicester's urban landscape along the river and canal? Can the legacy and lessons of this environmental disaster be identified in the Leicester landscape of today? Although Leicester is obviously an inland town[3] and her river, the Soar, can hardly be termed a major waterway; nevertheless the problems surrounding city–river relations are highly topical. How to regulate and manage rivers in order to prevent costly damage as a result of recurrent floods without losing the economic potential of the river and its city waterfront remains an on-going issue, on the River Soar, as elsewhere.

The setting

The valley of the River Soar in which Leicester is situated dominates the topography of the county. Forming a wide flood-plain over most of its course the river first runs almost in a straight line from south-west to north-east until it passes Leicester and then, behind the confluence of its main tributary, the River Wreake, turns towards the north-west until it joins the Trent south of Nottingham. The river valley provided a transport corridor in Roman times and continued to do so as a natural route for railway lines in the nineteenth century, and for motorways in the twentieth. Leicester, the Roman 'Ratae', was founded where major Roman roads crossed the River Soar. Meadow lands on the flood-plain were fertile and essential for the agricultural economy to provide hay for winter feeding. Settlements, on the other hand, and roads tended to avoid the flood-plain

5.1 Medieval packhorse bridge (Grade II star Listed Building) dates from the fifteenth century and was originally 200 yards long (now about 50 yards) with 11 arches straddling the Soar valley in Aylestone.
Source: Richard Rodger.

and were established on gravel terraces about 19 feet, or 6 metres, above the plain.[4] The Soar has been prone to rapid and serious flooding due to two natural reasons: firstly, the low fall, only 3 feet (1 metre) over a 13 mile (21 km) course; and, secondly as any local farmer, gardener or sports person will confirm, the dominant character of the topsoil in its main catchment area is boulder clay and is almost impervious in heavy rainfall. The result is a very rapid run-off which the gently graded river has frequently been unable to absorb.[5]

The economic significance of the Soar was closely linked to shipping in order to promote regional economic integration. When in 1778 the neighbouring town of Loughborough was linked to the Trent by canal, the breakthrough caused a 'canal mania' in the entire county due to the evident economic success of the Loughborough canal. Eventually, in 1794 the Leicester Navigation between Loughborough and Leicester was opened, and the new canal route led to a dramatic fall in commodity prices in Leicester, especially of coal, and promoted the rapid growth of the city in the late eighteenth and early nineteenth century.[6] With the opening of the Grand Union Canal in 1812, Leicester was linked to the Thames and to London, with its market potential for the already well-established hosiery industry of Leicester.

The economic effects of these canal developments were considerable in the first half of the nineteenth century.[7] For example, in the late 1820s people could travel from Leicester by boat to London, Liverpool, and Nottingham; the journey to London took 60 hours and was certainly more comfortable than on the turnpike road.[8] The Soar and the investment in the

5.2 Limekiln Lock: Leicester Navigation and the canal network.

Source: Dieter Schott.

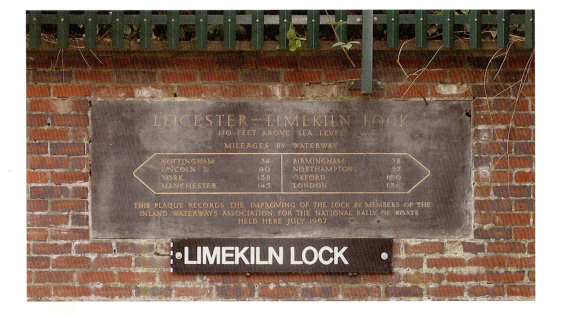

canal system assisted the economic development of Leicester, transforming a disadvantaged inland town some distance from the sea into part of a fully integrated national economy, increasingly dependent on coal as the dominant fuel. Leicester joined a national and global economic system based on markets and the division of labour.

Urban expansion on natural floodplains

How far did the River Soar and the canal affect Leicester's physical development? The Leicester Navigation, as the canal was known, had not created an entirely new channel but rather had developed branches of the river and installed a series of locks so that narrow boats could use them. A rather complicated system of natural stretches of water combined with new stretches of canal constituted the Leicester Navigation, sometimes involving rather tight bends. As the Soar entered Leicester from the south at St Mary's Mills Lock, the river and canal were split only to be re-united below the railway bridge at Bede House Meadow. Near Swan's Mill Lock the system was particularly complicated, and once past West Bridge the river and navigation re-joined until separating again at Hitchcock's Weir, where they flowed on both sides of Frog Island, only to be linked again approximately where today St Margaret's Way is located.

For centuries floods had been a constant threat as well as benefit to these areas around Leicester.[9] Already in 1742 the race course, which had originally been on the Abbey meadows next to the river, had been relocated to higher ground, first to St Mary's Meadow, and again from 1806 to what was to become Victoria Park.[10] Few houses had been erected in flood-prone areas and building development on the western bank of the Soar was very limited until the

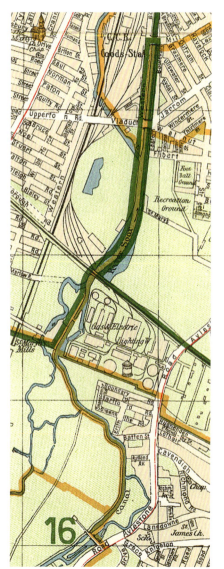

5.3 Southern section of the Leicester Navigation (in brown), 1911, showing its intersections with the meandering River Soar. The green area either side of the river and Navigation illustrate the extent of the flood plain which the formed the basis in the 1980s for the linear path through Aylestone Meadows.

Source: NLS, Thornley's Pharus Map of Leicester, *c*.1911.

1880s so that until the mid–nineteenth century the effects of flooding was largely limited to reducing agricultural yields of adjacent meadows.[11] On the other hand, by the 1860s the perennial problems of the natural drainage of the Soar with its very low fall and impervious clay soils had been aggravated by human intervention. Major problems were caused by the unrestricted and uncoordinated building of mill-dams and weirs, the construction of railway embankments within the flood plain, and the silting up of the river due to increased discharges of industrial waste and household sewage.[12]

When William Cobbett visited Leicester in the 1820s the town of about 30,000 inhabitants was still contained within its medieval area and stood apart from the river: 'Standing on the hill at Knighton, you see the river winding down through a broad bed of most beautiful meadows that man ever set his eyes on.'[13] Between the publication of Cobbett's travel accounts in 1830 and 1860 Leicester's population more than doubled, and the vacant flood-plains were increasingly developed. This land was predominantly used for industrial purposes and working-class housing of a rather poor quality and limited infrastructural facilities such as drains, water supply and

5.4 Flood level marker on the River Soar, 1812.
Source: Colin Hyde.

5.5 View from Knighton Hill, 1846.
Source: Richard Rodger, private copy.

sewerage. Hygienic conditions in these quarters were hostile to human life so that in the 1840s Leicester was one of the unhealthiest places in Britain, with a death rate of 30 per 1,000.[14]

In the 1860s development accelerated with an unprecedented population growth of 40% during the decade – the highest growth rate of larger British cities. This was due to an industrial boom, as the traditional family-based workshops in the hosiery industry increasingly gave way to steam-driven hosiery mills (see chapter 1). In a complementary way, a light engineering industry developed producing machines and tools for hosiery as well as for boot and shoe factories. This contributed to a significant diversification of the town's industrial structure. In the course of this industrialisation, river locations became attractive to these new factories; access to the canal facilitated the transport of coal as the principal energy source for the factories, as well as water use to cool machines and clean products in a variety of industrial processes.[15] Thus the areas close to river and canal, such as Frog Island and the area between Belgrave Road and the canal, increasingly became built up, especially with factories, and also with working-class neighbourhoods. The environmental problems linked with developing potential flood land increased.

In reaction to severe floods in the spring of 1867 the Corporation, after several inconclusive attempts, finally decided to improve the hydrological situation and undertook to get local Acts of Parliament for the improvement and drainage of the Soar passed in 1868, 1874, 1876 and 1881.[16]

The Corporation starts to act

A major problem for action in this area was that the Corporation exercised very little effective control over the river and canal; indeed, it was faced with a bewildering array of owners and user rights along river and canal. Leicester Navigation was owner of the navigation channel, the locks, and loading and unloading facilities on the shore. At several points along the river ancient mills remained and although they were no longer active, the owners still had the right to make use of the water power for their industrial premises and put up weirs for that purpose. At other points owners of plots adjoining the river had the right to extract water for their own purposes, to dispose of their sewage, and to use the river for transport. Thus there were many interests, often contradictory, in relation to the use of the river, as well as a variety of installations that were vulnerable during floods, and some of which contained dangerous and harmful products. Before any physical improvement could be undertaken, ownership and access questions had first to be clarified and could take years if owners decided to drag their feet and aimed for higher compensation.

To pursue their goal of legal clarification the Corporation submitted a series of private acts of parliament from 1868 onwards. The problem with

| Leicester: a modern history

these parliamentary acts was, however, that they had to spell out very clearly which measures were to be taken and which properties were to be purchased in order to execute these improvements. The acts, however, left a rather restricted time window in which to carry out these measures, usually three years for the purchases and seven years for the engineering measures. In 1872 Leicester Corporation managed to purchase both Castle Mill and Belgrave Mill, and their water rights. Belgrave Mill was critical to any flood improvement scheme and so with the purchase completed work started in 1873 near Belgrave locks. In the same year, the Corporation sought an extension of time from parliament in order to carry out the measures approved, and to extend flood control works towards the central and southern section of the river within the town boundaries. Given royal approval in 1874, this act gave the council the required extension and mandate for work on other sections of the river and navigation channel and by December 1874 a contract had been signed for the construction of a flood channel from Whitwick Dock to North Bridge. These works were adversely affected by further floods in 1875 and, on their completion, in 1876

5.6 Abbey Meadows and the River Soar, 1875.

Source: Record Office for Leicester, Leicestershire and Rutland, DE3736, Box 1, Abbey Park Folder 6.

brought a significant relief 'for the western portion of the town in times of heavy rainfall'.[17]

A further act, the Leicester Improvement Act 1876, gave the Corporation additional powers for flood works, and power to purchase the Abbey Meadow and St Margaret's Pastures. Further powers included the widening and deepening of the Soar between the North Bridge and Belgrave Lock, as well as the authority to improve the Willow Brook, a tributary to the Soar that entered the Leicester Navigation near Limekiln Lock. In 1877 measures to widen and deepen the Soar between Braunstone Gate Bridge and Bow Bridge were started for which again property rights from owners keen to extract the maximum compensation had first to be secured. These various river improvements and flood prevention proposals reached such a scale that during the very severe winter of 1878–79, and following interventions by the Charity Organisation Society and discussions with the Mayor, a large number of jobless workers were employed to clear out debris from the channel of Willow Brook. The 1876 Act had also given the Corporation powers to acquire the water rights of North Mill, the owner of which, Mr Hitchcock, received £8,000 as compensation for the adverse impact of the council's improvements on his water rights. Water rights obviously constituted a real asset, assessed as they were at £200 p.a. and capitalised over a period of 25 years to provide Hitchcock with a lump sum of £5,000.

The acquisition of water rights and compensation payments to owners was both complex and financially demanding. Inserted in the Leicester Improvement Act, 1876, were special clauses drafted to protect the mill owners on Frog Island. Given the difficulties, the Corporation had at first decided not to undertake improvement measures for this stretch of the river. However, after negotiations with the mill owners, the Corporation eventually produced an agreement in May 1879 making it possible to include the entire stretch of the river from North Mill to Belgrave in the flood works scheme. In May 1879 work on that larger scheme, estimated at £32,375, was begun. In the same period Swan's Mill and adjacent properties were purchased, including some plots near Belgrave Mill needed for flood works, at the price of £18,000.

In the summer of 1880 a situation arose when the powers granted by the acts of 1874 and 1868, for which a period of seven years had been given, were about to lapse. But the programme approved in these acts had been only partially completed. In addition to the difficulties faced in securing the properties, the Corporation were not particularly energetic in pushing forward with the scheme, which presumably did not have the highest priority for the Council. Then the disastrous floods of July 1880, referred at the start of the chapter, put the issue of flood prevention very high on the municipal agenda. Crisis management galvanised municipal action.

Leicester Council used this emergency for a comprehensive reappraisal

| Leicester: a modern history

and reformulation of the improvement programme. The Corporation engineer for the flood works submitted a plan that would greatly increase the capacity of the river and navigation channel within Leicester and help pass flood waters through the city at a much faster rate without flooding the low-lying ground adjacent to the river.[18] The scheme was positively assessed by experts and approved after thorough discussion in the Council. In a meeting of rate-payers called to discuss whether the cost of parliamentary legislation should be paid out of the borough rates, the Mayor emphasised the health aspects of the programme:

> The floods that had so repeatedly invaded the town had been followed by disease, suffering and death; many homes that would otherwise have been healthy having been attacked by wasting sickness, while the inhabitants generally had been exposed to great inconveniences.[19]

But the scheme would also be a wealth-creation programme. The Mayor expressed his hope 'that sites now almost valueless would be transformed into good building land'. In the same meeting, Alderman Chambers, who had proposed the bill in Town Council, envisaged 'that when the works were completed Leicester would become one of the most prosperous, healthy and beautiful towns in the kingdom." Thus, in an age when beneficial reforms were generally expected to bring long-term dividends, flood protection was promoted as an investment in town development.[20]

Dissenting voices in the meeting drew on what might be called an early version of an ecological argument: the fact that Leicester was not isolated from the world and that by improving and speeding up the flow of water through the city, Leicester would create a more difficult situation for its downstream neighbours. Thus the opponents of the flood prevention scheme proposed to solve the flooding problems by forming organisations based on the basis of watersheds. Enshrined in legislation, these bodies would be responsible for organising flood protection in a coordinated manner. However, the overwhelming majority of the meeting considered their primary duty of care was to Leicester and its inhabitants. The Mayor, in a realistic assessment of the pace of national progress in that matter, said: 'We shall have to wait till next century for it [a national scheme].'[21]

The resulting Leicester Improvement Act, passed by parliament in 1881, gave the Corporation powers to acquire land within three years but, in the light of previous negative experiences, set no time limit for the measures to be carried out. The Corporation was entitled to borrow £85,000 for these works with repayments over 70 years, and this unusually long repayment period clearly shows the exceptional and extraordinary character of these measures. The Act also authorised the use of £15,000 from the property sales fund for the construction of roads and bridges to improve communications between the western districts and the town centre. River improvement, thus, was not only a counter-measure to flooding; it also became part of a general development policy, enhancing new districts of the town.[22]

Flood debates in the county: natural or cultural disaster?

As the dissenting voice in the ratepayers' meeting showed, flooding and flood-defences were not just a problem for the city of Leicester. Representatives of county interests met at about the same time to discuss their flood protection strategy since the flooding had also caused extensive damage to agrarian interests. They sent a deputation to London to urge the government, and particularly the Local Government Board, to support legislation that would enable the county to take flood prevention measures and to pay for these by raising local taxes through the rates.[23] Reports of these meetings show a fairly complex assessment of factors: flooding was not just blamed on freak, excessive rainfall, but also human failures such as badly maintained weirs and dams, installations in disused canals, narrow railway bridges, disused mills and obstructions due to the silting up of rivers. Major responsibility was also attributed to changes in agricultural practices: recently improved drainage of upland fields had led to the much faster run-off of rainwater so that heavy rainfall resulted in much higher water tables. The lack of an overall authority to manage the river as a whole was particularly criticised. It was also revealed that there were intrinsic difficulties in mobilising a flood protection programme for the county as a whole. Landowners on the higher ground refused to accept flood improvement measures as their responsibility and resented paying higher rates for such capital works. Accordingly, landowners from the low-lying areas asked the government to step in and force everybody to share the burden.[24]

But while the county pleaded for government legislation, Leicester got down to work. Leicester Corporation carried out its programme of improving and restructuring the river in the 1880s once fierce resistance from some owners had been overcome. The major change was a completely new course for the navigation channel from Freemen's Lock in the south to the West Bridge. The bed of the channel was deepened and its course was straightened completely, creating a stretch of one mile, locally known as 'Mile Straight', and particularly suited to the activities of a rowing club, long associated with this new stretch of water. The general water management principles were to reduce water levels at flood times, and to enhance the capacity of the system to absorb excess water in times of heavy rainfall. All locks and weirs were arranged to be self-acting in times of flooding to allow excess water to be carried off without the need of human intervention.

The outcome of this programme was a comprehensive re-shaping of the river and canal in the area that bounded central Leicester. This improved the capacity of the waterways, reduced the risk of flooding, and made

5.7 Fishing on the 'Mile Straight' at Upperton Bridge. This was another activity encouraged by improved water quality. The Liberty Building is in the background – see chapter 15.

Source: Record Office for Leicester, Leicestershire and Rutland, DE3736, Box 29, Upperton Road.

the river area usable for leisure, industry and housing. Furthermore, the programme entailed the construction of new bridges and roads across the flood-plain which would allow a much greater volume of water to pass in times of flood. Previously, bridges had acted as severe obstacles where debris had accumulated and water backed up as if blocked by an artificial dam. These new bridges and roads, such as the new West Bridge, opened in 1891, and North Bridge, significantly improved communications between the city centre to the east and new neighbourhoods developing on the west bank. This range of flood improvement and water management measures on the Soar was the largest capital project undertaken by the Corporation during the nineteenth century and cost £300,000, equivalent to £29 million in 2014 prices. It represented 'a monument of the courage and enterprise of the Council of Leicester', and relieved almost 20% of Leicester's inhabitants from the omnipresent fear that their houses would be inundated.[25]

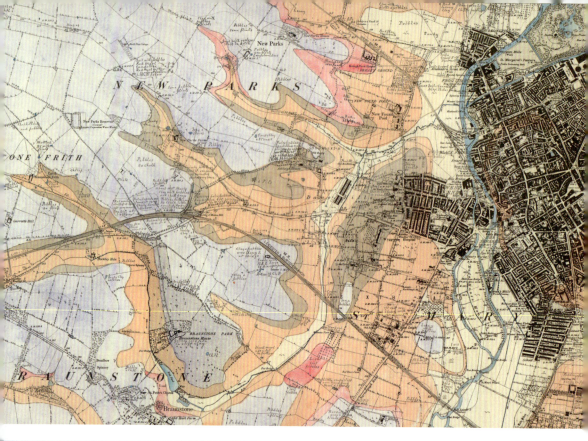

5.8 The course of the River Soar showing the extent of the flood plain and the route of the Leicester Navigation, also known as the Leicester and Northampton Canal and the Grand Union Canal, 1893.

Source: reproduced by permission of the British Geological Survey © NERC.

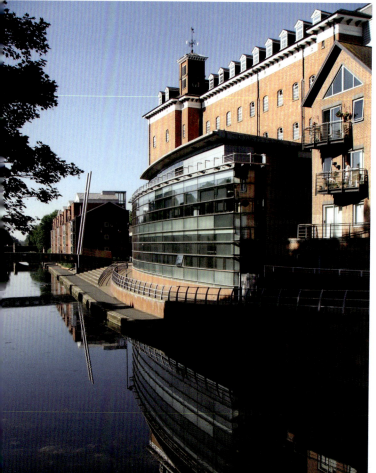

5.9 The 'Mile Straight' from the West Bridge with modern developments undertaken as part of the Bede Island City Challenge improvements on Western Boulevard.

Source Colin Hyde.

5.10 West Bridge during reconstruction, 1880. The gable end of the house on the right reads 'G.A. Fearn Plumber, Glazier, Gas Fitter', whose premises were 8 to 10 Applegate Street.

Source: Record Office for Leicester, Leicestershire and Rutland, DE3736, Box 31, West Bridge Folder 2.

5.11 and 5.12 Completion of the West Bridge memorialised in 1891 (margins). The plaque records the names of Mayor William Kempson (Mayor), Henry Thos. Chambers (Chairman of the Flood Prevention Works Committee), John Underwood (chairman of the Highway and Sewerage Committee), John Storey (Town Clerk), and the firm of S&E Bentley and J. Butler and Co (contractors).

Source: Dieter Schott.

Leicester transforms its river environment |

Turning a swamp into a people's park

A major effect of the flood prevention scheme was to open a large section of the land along river and canal to the Leicester public. In 1878, a local act of parliament authorised the Corporation to spend £25,000 on a new park, called Abbey Park, since the ruins of the former abbey were included within the park. That the flood works had not just been carried out exclusively as an engineering and water management project, but had resulted in this park was also due to the intervention of the former landowner, the Earl of Dysart, who obliged the Corporation under the terms of the 1878 Act to turn the land into a park, despite considerable opposition from the public.[26] The ceremonial opening of the park by the Prince and Princess of Wales on 29 May 1882 was a major public festivity for Leicester, and a relative rare appearance of members of the royal family in the city. (See also chapter 7). The Mayor of Leicester recalled the recent history of the site:

> Only three years ago the ground upon which we stand today was a low swampy meadow, flooded two or three times a year; but by widening and deepening the river-course and raising the whole level of the land, we have now nothing to fear from floods, and only those who knew it formerly can judge what a transformation has taken place. Now we have four miles of delightful walks and drives, a

5.13 Abbey Park Bridge.

Source: Record Office for Leicester, Leicestershire and Rutland, DE3736, Box 1, Abbey Park Folder. Photography by Alfred Newton & Sons, 17 King Street Leicester.

lovely lake of four acres, and archery and croquet grounds with many thousands of trees, shrubs, and flowers in rich variety and beauty … here we trust that many will gain strength and courage to carry on the battle of life, and that purer thoughts and nobler aspirations will be enkindled by the quiet and beautiful scenes which we all may enjoy. We earnestly hope that this Park will afford means for rational recreation and healthy exercise to future generations, and be to them the source of strength and gladness.[27]

In the Mayor's speech the dual functions of the park are clearly identified. Having originated from the flood control project it also became a new public open space, charged with all the educational overtones and moral baggage of Victorian municipal elites. In social terms Abbey Park located in the north served to counter-balance the extensive Victoria Park that had been established 1866 close to the developing middle-class neighbourhoods south of the town, between the end of New Walk and the prestigious suburb Stoneygate. For the thousands of workers living close to mills and factories by the River Soar, Victoria Park was too distant to function as green space suitable for their leisure time. Abbey Park quickly became very popular and hosted major civic events, including the Leicester Pageant in 1932. Furthermore, in times of severe flooding the park area could also serve as a planned overspill area where the damage would remain comparatively low, as opposed to built-up areas.[28]

New horizons: river pollution, the sewerage system and municipal extension

The last phase of the flood works, the construction of new and wider bridges over the Soar and the Navigation, particularly West Bridge and Newarke Bridge, was carried out at the end of the 1880s and early 1890s at a time when the whole posture of municipal activity had acquired a more energetic and interventionist character. The Corporation embarked – after failure in 1885–86 – on a renewed attempt to extend the municipal boundaries and incorporate several villages and small towns, which had grown significantly due to Leicester's economic rise to manufacturing prominence. It had become clear that the infrastructural problems of these small municipalities could not be solved in a satisfactory and efficient manner by the limited means and capacities of their councils and up to 80% of owners in these municipalities declared in favour of incorporation with Leicester.[29] However, any successful absorption of neighbouring communities depended to a considerable degree on an improved environmental performance by Leicester City Council. Whereas the flood risk for the city itself had been greatly reduced by the costly flood works, and the Soar reshaped to reduce the flooding hazard and to create pleasing and leisure-related urban landscapes, such as in Abbey Park or along the Mile Straight, the water quality had not been significantly improved.

In 1884 sustained protests were made by residents downstream of Leicester, and also by the Belgrave Local Board of Health. The Local Government Board, as the national agency responsible for the supervision of councils, sent an inspector to Leicester. On his visit to the Sewage Works and after an inspection of the river above and below Leicester he found, that 'the state of the River at Belgrave and for some miles below was, the representatives of the Corporation could not attempt to deny, most deplorable'.[30] Such a verdict in an account written in 1895 by John Storey, the former town clerk of Leicester and not normally critical of his employers, suggests a catastrophic state of the water quality in the town.[31] As a result of this inspection and the indictment of its water quality that followed, Leicester was under considerable pressure to improve the situation. Although the council pointed out to the Local Government Board that there were also other polluters responsible for the state of the river, it could not dispute its major share of responsibility.

The situation resulted from a long history of neglect and delay. In the 1850s Leicester had, at first as a private venture, installed a sewerage system which aimed at producing manure out of sewage. Much in the line with recycling ideas as proposed by Edwin Chadwick, the sewage was collected at a station near Leicester Abbey where it was treated to extract water, to deodorise the water, and to produce saleable manure while the effluent was supposed to be tolerable for the river into which it was discharged.[32] The scheme, from which the planning engineer had promised profits of £10,000–£20,000 from the sale of the manure, proved to be an utter failure. The Corporation was forced to take over the works and incurred considerable losses because the manure could not be marketed at cost prices. From 1869 there were debates about introducing an irrigation system; reports by experts established the feasibility of such a proposal and in 1873 Leicester held a competition 'for the best scheme for dealing with the sewage and storm waters of the town'.[33] But in 1874 when Leicester, on the basis of the prize-winning scheme, submitted a project to Parliament asking for powers to carry out the project, the Local Government Board strongly criticised it so that the sewage section of the bill was withdrawn and only the flood prevention measures pursued. In response to this rebuff, Leicester asked the eminent sanitary expert Sir Joseph Bazalgette, designer of the London main drainage and sewer system in the 1850s and 1860s, to plan for a Joint Sewerage Scheme together with the neighbouring Sanitary Authorities. But this proposal was quickly abandoned when it became clear that the rural sanitary authorities could not secure sufficient finance. When Bazalgette, obviously used to thinking on a metropolitan scale, came up with an overall scheme costing £300,000, the council refrained from going to Parliament with such an expensive project and preferred to keep the system working by incremental small additions to the existing sewage works. The fact that the Sanitary Authority of Leicester had adopted the pail closet system in 1871 – which collected faeces separately – brought temporary relief since the quantity of sewage did not then increase in line with general population growth. But Storey clearly highlights this as a policy of 'dragging on' without properly solving the questions at hand.[34]

With the full pressure of national government on Leicester Corporation to clean up the river, the Borough Surveyor, Joseph Gordon, who had been in charge of planning most of the flood prevention works since taking office in December 1880, produced a comprehensive report with eight alternative schemes detailing how to prevent the pollution of the Soar. After consultation with the Local Government Board the decision of the council finally fell in favour of an irrigation farm at Beaumont Leys and after the contracts over lease and purchase of the required lands were concluded in 1887, the technical installations were carried out.[35] In 1890 the irrigation farm

5.14 Abbey Pumping Station façade (1891) pumped sewage to the treatment works at Beaumont Leys. Closed in 1964, the Pumping Station opened as the Museum of Science and Technology to display the industrial, technological and scientific heritage of Leicester. Architect: Stockdale Harrison.
Source: Colin Hyde.

5.15 Four beam engines built by Gimson & Co. pumped over 200,000 gallons of sewage per hour to Beaumont Leys treatment works.
Source: Colin Hyde.

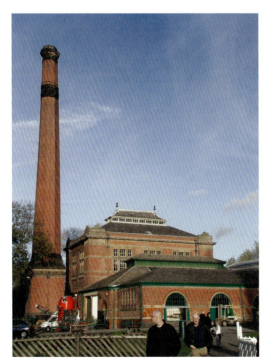

commenced operations and after some initial problems the effluent proved fairly acceptable.[36] From 1887 onwards, the entire sewage system of Leicester experienced an overhaul with new trunk sewers and greater capacity installed in all parts of town. The neighbourhoods previously equipped only with pail closets were now linked to the combined sewerage system.

Progress over the issue of river pollution proved essential, therefore, for the municipal boundary extension that was embarked upon in 1890. In 1886, a select committee of Parliament had rejected a similar bill and in hearings before committee the defective state of the Soar had been a major argument advanced by critics of the bill. In 1890 Leicester fared better; it had secured more allies for its project, and could also point to the fact that the Corporation had invested heavily in the improvement of water quality by setting up Beaumont Leys sewage farm and improving the sewer network. Because the opponents of the bill again criticised the sewage farm and the state of the river, the committee inserted provisions in the bill obliging Leicester to deal efficiently with the sewage 'within six months' and 'that the River Soar throughout the limits of the Borough shall be effectually cleansed by them [Leicester] within twelve months of the passing of the Act'.[37] Eventually, the bill was passed with very few alterations and received royal assent on 3 July 1891. The extension of Leicester's boundaries meant a significant increase in the municipal area which almost tripled from 3,030 acres in the old borough to 8,534 acres. In terms of population the

5.16 Castle Gardens after the drainage scheme 1926. Leicester Castle and St Mary de Castro church in the background.

Source: Record Office for Leicester, Leicestershire and Rutland, DE3736, Box 6, Castle Gardens. Photography by Leicester City Council.

| Leicester: a modern history

5.17 Castle Gardens from the Newarke Bridge prior to the drainage scheme 1926.

Source: Record Office for Leicester, Leicestershire and Rutland, DE.3736, Box 6, Castle Gardens. Photography by Alfred Newton & Sons, 17 King Street Leicester.

leap was not quite so dramatic: it increased by 32,630 (23%) from 142,051 to a total of 174,681 inhabitants, and the rateable value increased by just under 20% to reach £641,269. Leicester now also comprised the parishes of Humberstone, Evington, Knighton, Aylestone, Braunstone, Newfound Pool, Freake's Ground, Leicester Abbey and Belgrave.

In his report to the Parliamentary Committee of the Town Council, the Town Clerk John Storey highlighted that the main aim to have coterminous areas for all parts of municipal activities, except parliamentary representation, had been fully achieved and thus created a clearly improved arena for further municipal work.[38]

One such area for environmental improvement was around the Castle and Newarke Houses which continued to be subjected to flooding into the twentieth century and were the subject of a further drainage scheme in 1926.

Postscript: work never done – the return of flooding

After a prolonged period of relative quiet in terms of flooding, the hazard recurred in the late 1960s, although at different locations within the city. After extensive floods in southern parts of Leicester, which had undergone more extensive development during preceding decades, the Council set up a Special (Flooding) Committee to inquire into the circumstances of the flooding and possible actions to prevent further such disasters. After hearing many experts and witnesses, the committee came to the following conclusion:

> It is axiomatic that rivers and streams will flood. Nevertheless, your committee have had no difficulty in reaching the conclusion that the time has come when the Council must undertake more works to reduce this risk. It is intolerable that people should have to live in this fear. … The expenditure of the sum of £300,000 in the 19th century has served the City well, as has the expenditure on the schemes in more recent times. If any further justification is needed for action other than the harrowing experiences of July and November, 1968, then the relationship between the scale of the present development in the areas of the watersheds and the calculations made in 1910 for the works on the principal streams and culverts is in itself a clear pointer to the course the Council must now take.[39]

Considering that this Special (Flooding) Committee was set up in the late 1960s when the public still retained some belief in the capacity of human society to plan and control nature by technical means, it is remarkable that no engineering measures are foregrounded in its recommendations. Rather, in a relaxed manner the central concept of the committee was 'to help nature do what it normally would', and their remarkable approach towards the threat of flooding was

> to direct the excess water to land where the minimum danger to life and property would occur. Such areas of washlands, in suitable circumstances, can be used as balancing ponds and thus reduce the rate of flow downstream for a period of time. This enables the stream to contain the more intense storms by spreading their effect and thereby reduces the risk of flooding.[40]

Coupled with this approach to slow down run-off by keeping some land free from development, was a suggestion to install gauging stations on the brooks most affected in order to better control water levels and anticipate flooding hazards. Obviously, the council's powers of intervention to check development where it might have hazardous effects on flooding were quite limited. Nevertheless, the Committee commented: 'Your Committee do not consider it sufficient that this important aspect should rest upon the Engineer of the River Authority "keeping an eye on" developments which might have a marked effect on water courses flowing into the City.'[41]

It is not apparent from the records of the Special Committee whether the suggested measures were actually implemented, and recent problems with flooding in many urban areas seem to indicate they were not.

Rediscovering the river and canal: from backyard to prime location

It can be seen from the statements by the mayor and leading experts in the 1880s that the riverside was demonstrably unhealthy. This was entirely consistent with a long tradition in ideas associated with public health thinking that shunned damp and low-lying places as foul-smelling ('miasmatic') and favoured more elevated sites, with their better ventilation and light, as healthy places to live. The extensive flood works, while offering relief in terms of flooding, did not bring about a major change in the public perception of the river area, although with Abbey Park as a local recreation site and the Mile Straight as the locus for a rowing club the merely utilitarian aspect of river front was somewhat modified. But the fact that water quality still remained poor and that river fronts were densely occupied by factories and industrial facilities such as gas works, power stations and rail yards, each frequently burning quantities of coal and emitting gases and noxious fluids into the river, did not enhance the amenities of the area.

By the 1970s, however, we can observe in many British cities first, tentative initiatives to direct the attention of municipal planners to rivers and riversides. This was largely because water transport had declined appreciably due to rail and road transport, and this resulted in a noticeable neglect in the state of maintenance of river banks and related industrial installations. Whereas during the high tide of industrialisation the riverside and canal banks had been bustling, if grim, by the 1970s they increasingly appeared dead and decayed. Since planners realised that these river fronts were, at least in part of their length, often located close to the city centre, and that there was considerable potential for high site rents where former industrial building stock were cleared and the area re-branded with a new image, there was cause to believe that some form of urban regeneration might be feasible. In Leicester this process started in earnest in 1973 when the Planning Commission of the Council approved a 3-year programme of improvements to the River Soar. In 1978 the Planning Department took stock in a publicly distributed brochure designed as a large A2 poster with many pictures and a text, which discussed the general problems and explained potential improvements in an imaginary walk along river and canal. The document stated the dilemma involved in transforming the economic use of an area: 'We are now confronted with the problems of a waterway whose function is in transition, the legacies of its original use both helping and hindering the development of its new recreational function.'[42]

However, developing this function met with problems due to the unattractive state of the river:

> One of the major problems is the dumping of rubbish both into the waterway and along its banks, by adjacent premises and by some

thoughtless members of the public. More than any other action, the Riverside would show improvement with the disappearance of litter and rubbish and volunteers, under the aegis of the Leicester Civic Society, have been cleaning the Canal and its environs, but it is a task that has to be continuously repeated.[43]

Thirty years on, in 2008, the stretches along river and canal present themselves in an entirely different state. Continuous 12-mile walkways have been created on the former tow-paths which allow access almost along the whole length of river and canal, and there is clearly no more pleasant and safer way to traverse Leicester on foot or bike over the entire length from north to south than along river and canal. While there are at some places, particularly to the north of Abbey Park, neglected and decaying industrial sites still, in the section near the city centre re-development has worked wonders. The turn-around in the 'imagineering' of the riverside seems to have been successful. We can observe fashionable new housing, converted industrial buildings with exclusive lofts and studios, student bars and halls of residence, the Space Centre, and glittering office buildings. Leicester City proudly invites residents and tourists to 'Discover Leicester's Riverside Park' in an attractive 3-part brochure covering the different sections from north to south and explaining historical sites and monuments to the visitor.[44] The river and canal, to be sure, are in their physical shape much the same as was produced by the flood works of late nineteenth century, but their aesthetic appearance, the architecture on their banks, and usage patterns have changed dramatically.

5.18 Space Centre.

Source: Colin Hyde.

6

Radical departures? Changing landscapes of death in Leicester

E ACH CEMETERY has a distinctive history. In every community, the decisions made around the need to dispose of the dead constitute an eloquent commentary on that society's emotional, spiritual, political and economic well-being. In Leicester, changes in cemetery provision and the early introduction of cremation aptly reflected a city in which the radical had a dominant voice and found a ready audience. This chapter reflects on three developments: the opening of the Welford Road Cemetery in 1849; the establishment of the Gilroes Crematorium in 1902; and the faltering steps taken towards the laying out of a new lawn cemetery at Saffron Lane in the early 1930s. These sites marked the transition from a centuries-long tradition of reliance on the Church of England for burial space to the emergence of a self-consciously modern landscape of death. In each of these developments, Leicester was among the first cities to adopt new practices which were – on occasion – perhaps too radical for the local population to accept easily.

This chapter draws on a combination of sources including administrative records, the often rich commentary available in Leicester's local newspapers, and industry press including the publications of the institution which represents the interests of cemetery managers. Time has precluded the possibility of exploring changes in Leicester's burial culture using oral histories or other written personal testimony, which would constitute an exciting project. However, it is hoped that this chapter will provide a useful framework for further local research, and contributes by setting the city's experience within the broader national context.

Welford Road Cemetery: a quintessential Victorian cemetery

The study of Victorian burial is often overshadowed by the ring of grand cemeteries which, from the 1830s, began to encircle the capital: All Souls at Kensal Green, West Norwood, Nunhead, Brompton, Abney Park and Highgate. However, if one site could be said to have epitomised the conflicting meanings that could be ascribed to burial space in mid-nineteenth-century Britain, then that would be Leicester's Welford

Road Cemetery. Conceived initially as a joint-stock enterprise that would protect Dissenting interests, the cemetery was finally laid out as a public health measure with due regard to its contribution to the recreational facilities of the city. The site neatly summarises in one example the prevailing themes underlying much of cemetery establishment in the second quarter of the nineteenth century.

Although the Welford Road Cemetery was opened by Leicester Town Council in 1849, the enterprise was originally conceived as a cemetery company. The company prospectus was issued in the *Leicester Chronicle* on 27 September 1845, announcing that the enterprise aimed to raise capital of £6,000 through the sale of £10 shares. The aim was to lay out a new cemetery, a measure deemed 'not only highly desirable, but indispensably necessary'.[1] This development was by no means unusual. Indeed, in the same year, cemetery companies were being floated in Hull, Birmingham, Gainsborough, Canterbury, Norwich, Wakefield and Northampton.[2] The mid-1840s was notable for a degree of mania in financial speculation which was driven in part by the profits that were thought to be made from the expansion of the railway network. A commentator on the mania, looking back from 1855, noted that enthusiasm had been unlimited: 'All the gambling propensities of human nature were constantly solicited into action, and crowds of individuals of very description ... hastened to venture some portion of their property in schemes of which scarcely anything is known except the name.'[3]

The joint-stock cemetery company, which had come into existence in Manchester in 1821, had proved to be a reasonable investment. However, the Liverpool Necropolis, which opened just four years later in 1825, was generally reckoned to be the most successful: interments there had reached over 700 a year within three years of its opening, with annual income exceeding £1,800.[4] By 1840, dividends were reported as being 'not less than 5 per cent, at times reached 20 per cent and averaged at 12 per cent'.[5] It is probable that none of the cities where cemetery companies were floated in the 1840s had profit motivation as their principal concern. The mid-1840s particularly was evidently a propitious time to float any joint-stock endeavour, and for many rapidly growing towns and cities this financial format was the best mechanism for funding essential urban improvements.[6] Indeed, the push for public works was evident through the 1840s in Leicester. In the *Leicester Chronicle* in 1844, editorial comment called for enlarged streets with better drainage and other measures to add to 'public health, comfort and convenience'. Indeed, the city was, shamefully, falling behind Liverpool, Birmingham and even Ashby-de-la-Zouche, which were all 'on the stir, or about to be'. The editor suggested a cemetery for the city, commenting that 'such an undertaking might be made to pay its way, and therefore form no cause of taxation to its inhabitants'.[7] The joint-stock cemetery company was evidently an outcome.

The respectability of Leicester's General Cemetery Company was underlined by the fact that in its prospectus, the provisional committee of over a hundred gentlemen was listed by name. The failure of a prospectus to name directors or committee members was perhaps the most telling indicator that speculation in shares was the principal intention. However, despite this promising beginning, the General Cemetery Company dissolved in acrimony some months later. The explanation lay with the fact that the company was composed principally of Dissenters. Again, this was not an unusual development. The majority of the early cemetery companies had been established by nonconformists. Indeed, the first cemetery company in Manchester had arisen as a consequence of the city's Dissenters, empowered by a successful battle against the compulsory payment of the church rate to the Church of England, reviewing other grievances. The issue of burials was evidently a priority since it encompassed a number of complaints. Having an independent burial ground meant that Dissenters' own ministers could preside at funerals, since such ministers had no right to officiate in churchyards. Burial in an independent cemetery would not be denied to Baptists and Unitarians, who could be excluded from the churchyard by a minister not persuaded that the deceased had been properly baptised; and the land could remain unconsecrated, a ceremony that was deemed by some Dissenters to be unnecessary and even Popish. Perhaps more importantly, independent burial space also reduced clerical incomes from burial fees, which in some areas constituted a substantial sum.

Of all the Dissenter-led cemetery companies, Leicester was probably the most vigorous in its statement of independence from the established church. Other Dissenting cemetery companies, including the General Cemetery Company in Nottingham, had sought to lay out cemeteries that would be open to all denominations and so had arranged part-consecration of its site. In Leicester, this level of compromise was clearly inconceivable. The prospectus of Leicester Cemetery Company included a lengthy address 'to the inhabitants of Leicester'. In the address, the company's committee expressed its views in adamant terms:

> They [i.e. the Company] have been induced, or rather compelled, to adopt this course, in consequence of the apparently great and insuperable difficulties, in the way of reconciling the various and conflicting views of Churchmen and Dissenters. They find it impossible for Dissenters to act in concert with Churchmen in this matter, without making such extensive concessions for the purpose of obtaining their concurrence, as would compromise their own religious feelings of independence. This being the case, the establishment of a Cemetery jointly by Churchmen and Dissenters is not only undesirable, but, to a large majority of Dissenters, would be positively objectionable.[8]

If the cemetery were operated for the benefit of all denominations by the Town Council, then part of the site would have to be consecrated, and, furthermore, the council would itself have to pay the wages of appropriate clergy to attend funerals *and* recompense Church of England clergy in the city who had lost burial fees as a consequence of the cemetery's opening. Clauses to this effect had been inserted in the Acts of Parliament establishing some of the earlier London cemeteries: for example, the West of London and Westminster Cemetery Company was compelled to pay the vicar of any parish within a ten mile radius a sum of 10 shillings for any interment taking place in the cemetery that would otherwise have gone to the local churchyard.[9] Leicester nonconformists, notoriously radical, were unlikely to countenance what would essentially be a public subsidy for the Church of England.

The cemetery plans progressed, and the Leicester Cemetery Company was established in early 1846. In January 1847, the *Leicester Chronicle* reported on the 'Sale of Knighton-hill to Dissenters'. The land was owned by the Town Council, and was to be sold to the company for £365 an acre. The newspaper noted acidly that the land valuers had been company shareholders, and that 'if the land had been sold to an indifferent person it would have made more money'. Furthermore, pressure had been building to effect improvement to the worsening conditions in the city's churchyards, but the Dissenters' cemetery looked set to accommodate no more than a quarter of the city's dead. Moderate Dissenter and ex-mayor Joseph Whetstone commented that 'the dissenters had forgotten what was their duty as public citizens, as members of the Council and had chosen … to form a cemetery for themselves only.'[10]

Religious and political issues attached to the cemetery began to be overtaken by more prosaic concerns. Cemetery establishment in the first half of the nineteenth century was also a public health issue. 'Fever', poorly understood by medical experts in the 1840s, was said to be caused by bad smells that were a consequence of ill-drained and -ventilated overcrowded accommodation for the living and for the dead. The *Leicester Chronicle* noted in February 1847 that, of the nineteen graveyards in Leicester, fourteen were 'quite full'.[11] A more detailed assessment of the situation emerged in the 1851 Board of Health inspection report for the city. The inspector was William Ranger who, with a team of inspectors appointed under the sanitary reformer Edwin Chadwick, had surveyed conditions in over 200 county towns. In Leicester, Ranger took oral evidence on conditions in the churchyards: St Martin's was 'not in the state in which he [the incumbent, Reverend William Vaughn] could wish, nor was its condition such that interments should continue'; and Mr Underwood, living adjacent to St Mary's said that 'he did not think the sexton could dig more than 3 or 4 feet from the surface without meeting with coffins'.[12] Population growth in the city had rendered the city grounds entirely inadequate. In 1801, the city had around 17,000 residents; by 1831, the population had

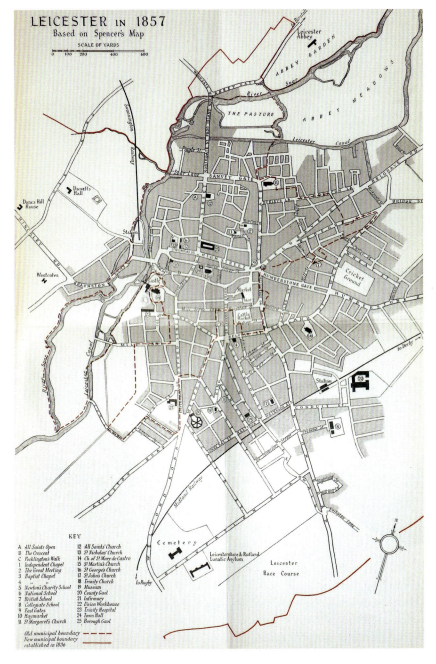

LEICESTER in 1857
Based on Spencer's Map

SCALE OF YARDS
0 100 200   400   600

KEY

A All Saints Open
B The Crescent
C Pocklington's Walk
1 Independent Chapel
2 The Great Meeting
3 Baptist Chapel
4 "   "
5 Newton's Charity School
6 National School
7 British School
8 Collegiate School
9 East Gates
10 Haymarket
11 St Margaret's Church

12 All Saints' Church
13 St Nicholas' Church
14 Ch. of St Mary de Castro
15 St Martin's Church
16 St George's Church
17 St John's Church
18 Trinity Church
19 Museum
20 County Gaol
21 Infirmary
22 Union Workhouse
23 Trinity Hospital
24 Town Hall
25 Borough Gaol

Old municipal boundary ----
New municipal boundary ----
established in 1836

6.1 Leicester in 1857, showing the relationship of the Welford Road Cemetery site to the town centre.

Source: reproduced from A.T. Patterson *Radical Leicester* (Leicester, 1954).

reached 41,000. Burial provision had hardly changed. Mr Macaulay stated to William Ranger that even if there could be no agreement that churchyard 'miasmas' caused disease, it could not be that 'the morals of the people would be better served by increasing the accommodation for burials and doing away with the necessity of too frequently disturbing the ground'.[13]

6.2 Welford Road Cemetery site, showing the Leicestershire and Rutland Lunatic Asylum (now the University of Leicester's Fielding Johnson Building, 1837) in the distance.
Source: not known.

6.3 William Biggs (1804–81), hosier in John Biggs and Sons firm; adopted new elastic web technology in 1840; elected radical councillor to reformed Corporation in 1836; MP for Newport Isle of Wight (1852–57); Mayor 1848, 1859.
Source: Leicester Arts and Museums Service.

Accusations of scandal, concern about the city's churchyards, and increasingly impassioned calls for an end to 'sectarian hostility' brought about the end of Leicester Cemetery Company. In debate on the issue, again reported in the *Leicester Chronicle*, William Biggs deployed the liberality of Nottingham's Dissenters against the Leicester Cemetery Company directors who were urged to create a cemetery 'on catholic, liberal principles'. The example of Coventry was also brought forward, where the Town Council was one of the first to establish a cemetery. The cost was wholly met by the ratepayers and, most importantly, no fees were paid to the clergy to compensate for lost burial income.[14] The Leicester Cemetery Company dissolved, and responsibility for a new cemetery was left to Leicester Corporation. New arrangements for the cemetery did indeed follow a

6.4 Welford Road Cemetery, Chapels, Cloisters and Terrace (chapels demolished *c*.1958).
Source: privately owned.

6.5 Elaborate tombstones: Welford Cemetery in winter looking towards Southfields.
Source: Colin Hyde.

principle of absolute equality: the site was half consecrated, and separate Dissenting and Anglican committees were set up to administer the two portions.

However, controversy attached to the cemetery did not end with this decision. The Welford Road Cemetery was remarkably opulent. A competition to design the cemetery was won by architect J.R. Hamilton of Hamilton and Medland, the firm which had designed the Warstone Lane Cemetery in Birmingham. In Leicester, expenditure on its architecture and infrastructure was cause for comment. In 1851, William Ranger was told

6.6 Angel, Welford Cemetery.
Source: Colin Hyde.

that the chapels alone had cost £8,396, when original estimates for that work had been around £2,700; planting and preparing the ground could have been undertaken for £600, but £1,518 had been spent. A basic estimate for the entire works had totalled £6,700, but the final bill was £12,411. Ranger could only conclude that if the council had received proper advice, it would 'never [have] embarked the large sum which has been expended'.[15]

This high level of expenditure reflected the desire, promoted strongly by William Biggs who was Mayor of Leicester at the opening of the cemetery, to undertake public works that would add to the amenity and status of the city. The layout included a double chapel – one for Anglicans, one for nonconformists – sited at top of the hill, and dominating the landscape. The cemetery was deemed to be an essential addition to the Victorian urban landscape, in demonstrating both scientific understanding and moral sensitivity. A cemetery demonstrated that a town had rejected the gruesome brutality of inner-city burial, and understood the moral value of an environment in which grief could be expressed by the graveside, consoled by the beauty of an artfully designed landscape. Furthermore, the cemetery could constitute a healthful promenade. This feature had obviously told with William Biggs who, at the cemetery's opening ceremony, announced his hope that the site would become 'one of pleasurable resort and quiet enjoyment for the living'.[16]

The establishment of Welford Road Cemetery contains within its narrative all the elements essential to an understanding of the significance of the nineteenth-century cemetery: the sometimes uneasy compromises that were made between the Church of England and nonconformists; the urgency created by rapidly worsening urban churchyards; and a self-conscious desire to adorn the city with amenities that reflected civic value and the wealth accumulated by industrial expansion.

Gilroes Crematorium

There is little doubt that the strength of radicalism in Leicester was an essential context for the town's early conversion to the cause of cremation. Gilroes Crematorium was opened by Leicester Corporation in 1902, and at the time constituted a risky endeavour in financial terms. National histories of cremation have only recently been written.[17] Substantial gaps remain in tracing the local history of this fundamental new development, but – as Leicester demonstrates – this history is well worth pursuing.

In the nineteenth century, cremation was considered, simultaneously, an ancient and a very modern mode of disposal. The Cremation Society of England was established in 1874 by Sir Henry Thompson, surgeon to Queen Victoria, who had been impressed by cremation equipment he had seen in a Viennese exhibition. The complex legal framework governing what was permissible in cemeteries and churchyards did not encompass this mode of disposal, and the cremation movement benefited from an early test case.

The cremation of the body of a child by Welsh eccentric William Price resulted in charges brought against Price, with the case being decided by Sir James Fitzjames Stevens at the Cardiff Assizes in 1884. Stevens concluded that cremation was not illegal providing it caused no nuisance to the public. The Woking Crematorium, which had already been built by the Cremation Society, was opened to the public in the same year and in 1902 national legislation set in place the regulatory framework.

Gilroes Crematorium was opened in August 1902. Leicester Corporation was only the second municipality in the country to open a crematorium, and Gilroes was the seventh, after Woking (1884), Manchester (1892), Glasgow (1895), Liverpool (1896), Hull (1901) and Darlington (1901).[18] Aside from Hull and Leicester, other crematoria had been opened by local cremation societies, who had themselves raised capital for the venture. Members of the Cremation Society paid a fee which included 'cremation at death'. The arguments in favour of cremation have shifted over time, and so tend to be wide-ranging. Thompson himself viewed the decomposition of the body after death as repellent, and contrasted the 'tranquil sleep of Death' with the 'forces innumerable' that attack the body at death, acting with the 'rapidity of a vulture'.[19] This style of rhetoric appears to have set the tone for the often emotive and sometimes scientifically dubious propaganda used by the Cremation Society for much of the following half-century.

Cremation was not necessarily favoured at first in Leicester. The *Leicester Daily Post* was unconvinced in 1885: 'Cremation may or may not be the popular system of the more distant future, but it will most assuredly continue to be intensely repugnant to the national sentiment to the close of the present century.'[20] The newspaper was not accurate in its forecast. By the following April, a branch of the Cremation Society had opened at Leicester, with a Dr Blunt as president.[21] During the course of the next few years the society decided that it should raise funds to build a crematorium for the city. It would be very interesting to know more about Leicester's early cremationists, but information is scant. William Samson was the secretary of the Leicester Cremation Society, and later went on to become a president of the Leicester Literary and Philosophical Society. Another early advocate of cremation in the town was John Page Hopps, Minister of the Unitarian Great Meeting. Hopps was notable for his radicalism and his interest in spiritualism. Although he moved to London in 1892, it is possible that he acted as a vociferous and influential advocate of cremation in Leicester in the early years of the Leicester Cremation Society.[22] Indeed, this development reflected the strategy of the Cremation Society generally. Much of its influence came through the involvement of prominent cultural figures, such as John Everett Millais and Anthony Trollope, who gave the movement credibility and even cachet.

An opportunity for the Leicester Cremation Society arose within months of its resolution to build a crematorium in the city. It was clear that, despite additions to city's burial provision at Belgrave, more space was needed and the council settled on the purchase of the Gilroes estate. The Leicester Cremation Society considered that, in seeking powers to provide a cemetery, the Corporation should also seek powers to provide 'an alternative Crematory'.[23] Cremation was, for local authorities, a remarkably risky venture. With the exception of Woking, the six earlier crematoria had not proved to be in any regard successful. Nevertheless, the Corporation secured local powers for the opening of a crematorium, under the Leicester Corporation Act of 1897.

6.7 John Page Hopps (1834–1911) educated at the Baptist College, Leicester; Unitarian minister in Leicestershire, north of England, and then in Glasgow, where he was a member of the Glasgow School Board and advocate of secular state education; returned to Leicester (1876–92). Edited the monthly *Truthseeker* (1863–87), and compiled hymns.
Source: Dr Williams Library.

6.8 Gilroes cemetery and crematorium, opened 1902. Designed by Goddard and Sons, 1898.
Source: privately owned, and reproduced with the permission of Goddard Manton Architects.

The crematorium at Hull had been designed by the borough engineer. Typically, Leicester Corporation felt it could do much better. In September 1899, Goddard & Co., distinguished local architects, were engaged to lay out a new cemetery at Gilroes. Almost immediately, the architects were asked to consider a scheme that would facilitate the addition of a crematorium on the site. Goddard & Co. estimated that the cost of attaching a crematorium to the chapel buildings would be around £3,700, and were advised to go ahead in such a manner 'for the attachment of a crematorium to be carried out whenever the council decide to provide such a building'.[24] By December they had produced an estimate of £7,000 for new crematorium if separate and £3,000 if attached to the cemetery chapel. It is uncertain what prompted the Corporation to take the step of commissioning a crematorium, but by the turn of the century the new building was underway. Recorded in the Corporation minutes in 1901 is a note that the architects were sending along – for inspection – the cremated remains of a sheep, and that letters were sent to the crematoria at Hull and Manchester to ascertain what regulations had already been put in place.[25]

Gilroes Cemetery and Crematorium was opened in August 1902, and the newspaper reporting was not wholly enthusiastic. There was care to announce the cost of the venture: 'The mere fact that the amount already expended …has reached nearly £27,000 speaks to the artistic taste and judicious liberality adopted.' Considerable detail was also afforded to explaining the cremation process:

> The coffin will pass through a small ante-chamber, and, still propelled by the same machinery, will enter the actual cremation chamber, previously raised to great heat by a powerful furnace in a basement directly underneath. The time necessary for the cremation of a body is expected to be an hour and a half, or less. When the process is complete, the ashes will be handed over to the representatives of the deceased persons.

Although the crematorium had already been used prior to the official opening, it was concluded that 'a considerable time must pass before the more scientific method of disposing of the remains of the departed dead can become really popular'. The writer thought that cost remained the principal issue: cremation was more than three times the cost of interment, and 'is proportionately prohibitive to all but the wealthy and well-to-do'.[26]

The newspaper predictions were certainly correct in foreseeing the uncertain popularity of cremation in the city. In the first ten years of opening, the Crematorium completed just 113 cremations, and within twenty years the site was still only dealing with two or three cremations a month. The thirteen crematoria that opened by 1914 had between them dealt with over 13,588 cremations by the start of the First World War; Leicester's share of that total was 149.[27] It is possible that the Corporation had begun to regret its decision. Correspondence to Leicester is missing at the Cremation Society archive in Durham, but council minutes record some of the exchanges. In April 1923, the Corporation accepted the Cremation Society's offer to print 1,000 leaflets to advertise the crematorium, but declined the request to join the proposed Federation of Cremation Authorities. This decision was later reversed after membership charges were placed on a sliding tariff according to the number of cremations completed.[28] In the following year, the Corporation edged towards a more dynamic approach. A letter was received from George Noble, secretary to the Cremation Society, commenting that newspaper advertisements alone were not likely to persuade numbers of people to change their minds. He suggested a more direct approach, and requested 'a marked Directory of the residents in the City of Leicester and vicinity who would [be] most likely to adopt Cremation, also, a list of the prominent people who have been cremated at the Leicester Crematorium.' This measure again reflected the greater strategy of Cremation Society activity, in seeking to influence the 'opinion makers', and draw the middling classes into aspirational emulation. It is not recorded whether the list was sent, but in the following month the Corporation abolished the charge of 3d. to inspect the crematorium, and Mr Addison was thanked for by the society for his assistance with a 'cremation' stand at the Leicester Home Life exhibition.[29]

Cremations at the Gilroes Crematorium were limited in number until 1938, but this was fairly typical among provincial crematoria. Nationally, cremations did not exceed burials annually until 1964. The reasons why Leicester Corporation became such an early convert to cremation are as yet uncertain. Further research is required, but it is certain that a propitious context was provided by the strength of radicalism in the town in the second

6.9 Chart of Cremations.

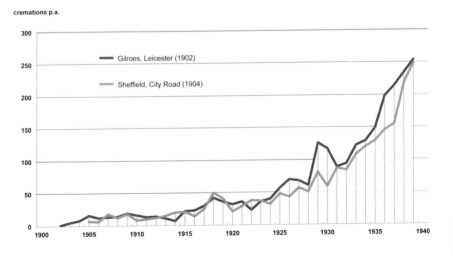

cremations p.a.

Gilroes, Leicester (1902)

Sheffield, City Road (1904)

| Leicester: a modern history

6.10 Gilroes Cemetery, 1988 showing the extent of the burial ground and its associated crematorium. Glenfrith Way is on the left of the picture with Severn Trent's Leicester Water Centre in the top left.
Source: Leicester City Council.

half of the nineteenth century. The Town Council's commitment to the development was without doubt substantial in terms of finance, although it may be the case that the decision was regretted. This pattern was to be repeated again with Saffron Hill Cemetery.

Saffron Hill Cemetery

Limited progress has been made in researching the history of cemeteries in the twentieth century.[30] Modern times demanded a modern aesthetic for cemeteries, very different to the muddle presented by the Victorian burial landscape. By the 1920s, Leicester Corporation was in further need of new burial space to serve the Aylestone ward. In common with cities all over the UK, the sprawl of urban development had absorbed outlying settlements; the extended suburbs needed their own facilities. At the opening of the site on 21 October 1931, the mayor accepted the key to the cemetery from its architect Edward Prentice Mawson and declared that Saffron Hill, a new type of lawn cemetery, was 'one of the first of its kind on the country'.[31] Again, Leicester had been radical in its approach to disposing of the dead

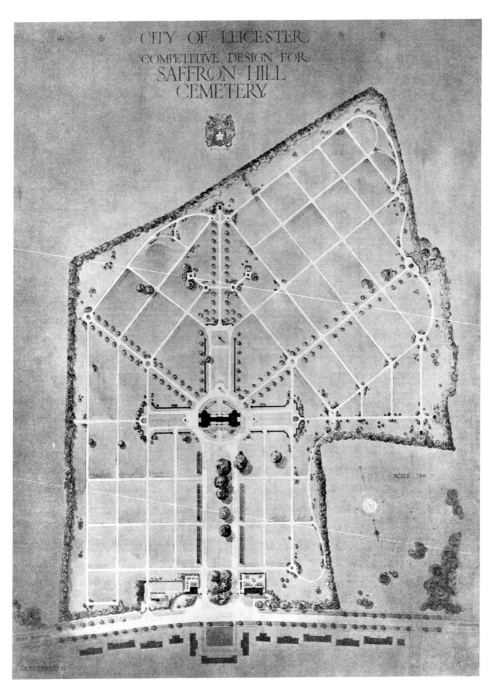

6.11 Saffron Hill Cemetery plan by E. Prentice Mawson (1885–1954), founder member of the Institute of Landscape Architects, and awarded Royal Institute of British Architects (RIBA) Soane medallion in 1908. Grade II listed park and garden of historic interest.

Source: Reproduced from *Landscape and Garden: A Quarterly Journal Devoted to Garden Design and Landscape Architecture*, 2 (1935), and reproduced by permission of the Landscape Institute.

and again, as will be seen, the boldness of this radical first step was followed by a series of faltering stumbles.

Cemetery development in the inter-war period was marked by a number of new trends. Notably, 'cemetery managers' had emerged within local government as distinctive officers whose skills involved mastery of what was remarkably arcane burial and cremation legislation; horticulture; considerable administrative skill, given the tight regulation around burial and cremation regulation; and the softer 'personal' skills appropriate to someone who frequently has dealings with bereaved families. Indeed, many cemetery managers were also nonconformist lay ministers.[32] In 1913, the National Association of Cemetery Superintendents had become established to further and protect the interests of cemetery managers. When Mr A.C. Addison accepted the post of Superintendent and Registrar of Burial Grounds in Leicester in 1923, he was the first generation of Leicester managers to have a strong connection with what is now the Institute of Cemetery and Crematorium Managers.

Cemetery managers during the inter-war period set about expressing their authority by taking control of the cemetery landscape. The history of the earliest cemeteries in the nineteenth century has tended to overshadow later cemetery developments, as new sites were created and extensions added to existing cemeteries. The scale of the maintenance task was formidable, made much more onerous by the complexity of the landscape in question. Grass cutting was the main difficulty, and cutting by scythe was the only feasible option. Graves were cluttered, and each could include the monument itself, a kerbset 'boundary', railings on top of the kerbset, planting or glass chippings inside the kerbset, and a glass immortelle. Where families or friends could not meet this level of expense, it was typical for the grave to be mounded with a permanent earth platform to indicate that burial had taken place. The entire landscape became dilapidated over time: marble monuments fared ill in the British climate; ironwork rusted; broken glass, pottery and floral tributes – displaced from the grave by the weather – became litter. By the inter-war period, it was felt by many that the Victorian cemetery landscape was neither dignified nor decent. Cemetery managers were inspired by a new aesthetic: the Imperial War Graves Commission cemeteries in Europe. J.D. Robertson – speaking to the National Association of Cemetery Superintendents in July 1920 – looked towards 'grounds laid out on park-like lines', 'with beautiful stretches of well-kept lawns', while 'certain portions should be devoted to graves on which no memorial would be erected'. He concluded: 'I am sure that no Superintendent with advanced ideas would for one moment say that he is satisfied with conditions that present a cemetery with its entrance all that could be desired, and with the remainder a wilderness.'[33]

When a new cemetery was proposed for Leicester in the 1920s, it was likely that the modern aesthetic would be a consideration. The architect who won the competition was Edward Prentice Mawson, who had a very strong view of how the cemetery should appear. His proposed plan was reproduced in *Landscape and Garden* in 1935, where he also discussed the principles underpinning the new design:

> To almost everyone of refinement and artistic perception the very word 'cemetery' brings to mind all that is ugly and monstrous. Otherwise they would never permit the appalling monstrosities in stones of varying hues and sizes in the closest proximity and without the slightest idea of orderly arrangement, which mitigates against economy of upkeep and all the other points which should be so carefully considered in the creation of a restful, artistically satisfying composition.[34]

There were a number of elements in Prentice Mawson's approach to cemetery landscape: efficiency in land use, where open lawn could be created as soon as possible after interment; standard monumentation with regimented headstones erected without accompanying kerbsets; and restrictions in families' ability to plant in or otherwise embellish the grave.

What Prentice Mawson had not appreciated was both the tenuous hold of the poor on any level of visibility in the cemetery landscape, and the tremendous importance that was attached to the grave. Nineteenth-century cemeteries are remarkable for their vistas and promenades of fine monuments. Prime locations on corners and rotundas were secured by families willing to pay the additional cost, and pauper burials were relegated to the periphery, in boggy ground beyond where the mass graves were left, quite deliberately, unmarked. In some instances, evident in Sheffield's Burngreave Cemetery for example, the main roadway of the cemetery was fringed with unmarked graves, giving the eye the impression of opulent spaciousness, and heightening the importance of the monuments on the visible 'front row'.[35]

Studies produced in the 1980s discussed the foundation of new cemeteries in terms of class, and concluded that cemeteries were little more than a bourgeois invention to display middle-class sensitivies, with ponderous monumentation to demonstrate social status.[36] What these studies tended to overlook was that the dead of the poor were the mainstay 'bread and butter' business of every nineteenth-century cemetery.[37] Arrangements with the local workhouse provided a steady supply of interments for the common graves: these were the graves which were dug deep enough to accommodate anything up to twenty coffins, each coffin succeeding the next, and the whole finally backfilled and turfed with no memorial. The dignity of this arrangement was called into question in an editorial comment in the *Leicester Mercury* in 1889:

> We do not say that persons who bury their dead in ordinary graves can expect the same privileges as those who purchase freeholds, but

this plan of indiscriminate burial is not what we desire. It matters not who introduced it, or what is done in other towns. In Leicester we can afford to have the burial of the dead conducted a little more in conformity with order and decency, and to say the methods saves a hundred pounds a year simply makes the thing more offensive still.[38]

Many cemeteries offered a complex range of burial options. The more expensive options served to underline the delicate gradations of status of the families involved, but the lower levels enabled the working classes to find themselves a level of interment that could take them one or two stages away from the indignity of an unmarked common grave. For example, recent research on death among the working classes showed that where a family had been able to purchase a burial right, the right became a kind of currency that could be sold or even loaned to another family who had been unable to purchase a burial right themselves; and when families were able to afford to do so, they would disinter relatives from common graves and rebury them in purchased graves.[39] Levels of monumentation were similarly graded: again at Burngreave in Sheffield, small and relatively inexpensive footstones were allowable as a replacement for more costly headstones; and Leeds Beckett Street had 'guinea graves'. These were common graves surmounted by a headstone where the bereaved were allowed a single line on which the name of their loved one could be carved, with a dozen or more names on each stone.[40]

Prentice Mawson had expected to be able to impose his plan for a simplified 'lawnscape' on what was remarkably complex and emotional territory. It is evident from the Corporation's burial committee minutes that the plan almost immediately floundered. In Leicester by the 1920s the Corporation had developed a compromise system for poorer families who were unable immediately to purchase a burial right.[41] Essentially, the Corporation interred in a grave and charged the standard 'unpurchased' interment fee. However, the family was given a promise that the grave would be 'reserved' for that family for a period of time. If further family members died then they could be interred in the same grave, which became in essence a 'family grave'. In 1927, the Corporation reviewed its options: a 'fill up' system of continuing the use of common graves with perhaps four or five unrelated bodies in a grave; or a 'period' system which allowed families fourteen years' grace to inter family members before the unpurchased grave was used for other interments. This latter system meant that the cemetery had to be bigger, since half-filled 'period' graves were perforce used more slowly. Indeed, Prentice Mawson estimated that the scheme would require 27 acres rather than 17, as per his original estimate.[42] Nevertheless, there was substantial opposition to the plan.

There was similar difficulty with Prentice Mawson's plan for Saffron Hill to be a 'lawn cemetery'. By 1927, he had persuaded the burial committee that 'the Cemetery be laid out upon the "Lawn" principle as this system is the modern one, and contributes largely to the appearance and beauty of the cemetery'.[43] In May, 1930, when the scheme was close to completion, Prentice Mawson expressed the wish for the cemetery to be 'the best of its kind in the country, which it certainly promises to be'.[44] However, by June 1931, these plans had been overturned. The committee had concluded:

> Careful consideration has been given to the method to be adopted in order that the Cemetery may be worked upon the lawn principle, and it is found upon investigation that the suggestions contained in the report of Mr Mawson, although desirable in many respects, presented difficulties and restrictions to which it was felt that the citizens would raise considerable objections.[45]

The committee resolved that kerbsets would be permitted, but that headstones were not to exceed six feet. Other restrictions were put in place, including a prohibition on iron railings, immortelles, and other 'unsightly receptacles'. Families were also not allowed to plant trees or shrubs on graves, although small, hardy flowering plants were allowed. No raised mounds would be permitted. However, Prentice Mawson's principles had been entirely undermined. He complained years later in *Landscape and Garden* that monumental masons, who had looked set to lose out substantially on restrictions in monumentation, had contrived their way on to the cemetery committee in November 1927 and overturned the earlier, more radical, resolve:

6.12 Gilroes Cemetery: postcard of landscape with body mounds and immortelles.

Source: postcard, Friends of Welford Road Cemetery.

| Leicester: a modern history

What might have been an outstanding example of a modern cemetery in a beautifully naturally timbered area has gone by the board and white Italian marble crosses, columns, Angels, ivy and doves are now vying with polished red granite in infinite variety, complete with kerbs, case iron railings and spiked chains. Within a few years it will be simply another collection of toppling headstones and leaning monuments, sunken graves, weeds and grass in luxurience.[46]

However, the lawn principle did finally prevail. In 1948, Leicester Corporation decided that all new cemetery sections in the city would be laid out on the lawn principle, and in this instance any local objections were over-ruled.[47] Saffron Hill was one of the earliest examples of a local authority that sought to lay out a new cemetery entirely on the modern 'lawn' principle. In other authorities, the movement towards lawnscaping had been more piecemeal: a prohibition against immortelles had perhaps been followed by a flattening of body mounds, and then successive restrictions on kerbsets and the size of headstones.[48] Existing landscapes were generally altered in order to prepare cemetery visitors for the introduction of a wholly lawnscaped cemetery section. By the 1960s, lawnscaping was beginning to make even more dramatic inroads, as local authorities sought to remove in their entirety monuments that were deemed to be abandoned or neglected.

Conclusion

Leicester has been and continues to be exceptional in its willingness to experiment with 'radical departures'. Indeed, it could be argued that the establishment of the Muslim Burial Council of Leicestershire in 1994 echoes the nineteenth-century concern that the city's burial landscapes adequately serve the needs of a religiously diverse population.[49]

Again and again, Leicester Corporation has been persuaded to aim for the very best and most impressive landscape of death. It is uncertain why the Corporation was minded to be so radical in the matter; further and more detailed research is required. Interest in family history has forged new links between the cemetery and the city, as families seek meaningful connections with their ancestors. This chapter highlights the virtue of the study of cemeteries in themselves: they give evidence of the ways in which communities negotiate tricky pathways between competing religious orthodoxies and between the traditional and the modern. However, it is perhaps the over-riding attraction of what is familiar and consoling that remains the quieter but more eloquent theme in Leicester's cemetery history.

7

Representing the city: the opening of Abbey Park (1882) and the Leicester Pageant (1932)

I N June 1932 the Leicester civic authorities in partnership with the county and with the help of local voluntary associations staged the Leicester Pageant, a 10-day spectacle of historical enactments and public ceremony. Over 4,000 local people participated actively in the Pageant, while many more took part in related events. A purpose-built amphitheatre was filled to capacity every night and crowds of both locals and visitors thronged to watch the civic and industrial processions. The occasion represented Leicester both to its own residents and outsiders as a prosperous and confident city; a place which had a working relationship with its hinterland and where the different groups that comprised the city population were united under a shared civic identity.

7.2 Speeches at the Opening of Abbey Park.

Source: W. Kelly, *Royal Progresses and Visits to Leicester* (Leicester, 1884).

Some commentators have associated the popularity of civic ceremony in provincial towns more particularly with the Victorian and Edwardian period.[1] However, the Leicester Pageant of 1932 was significantly more ambitious than previous civic events held in the city. An earlier and spectacular civic occasion in Leicester, the opening of Abbey Park in 1882, had been celebrated with a royal visit by Albert Edward Prince of Wales and Princess Alexandra. Local residents had demonstrated their support for this event by turning out in their thousands to welcome the royal visitors. The success of the Leicester Pageant in 1932 showed that fifty years later the enthusiasm in Leicester for civic ceremony still remained and although the support for the 1882 event had been substantial, the level of participation by Leicester townspeople in the Pageant celebrations of 1932 was far greater both in numbers and depth of involvement.

This chapter explores and compares the form, organisation and symbolism of these two civic events: the opening of Abbey Park in 1882 and the Leicester Pageant of 1932. The similarities and differences between the two occasions are highlighted, as is the way in which civic ceremony was adapted by 1932 to reflect the changing social environment.[2] The years between 1882 and 1932 had seen the progression to universal franchise and the widespread acceptance of the democratic ideal. This ideal of a more socially inclusive society was reflected in the high level of participation by Leicester residents in the Pageant.

The opening of Abbey Park, 1882

The backdrop to the opening of Abbey Park in 1882 was the growth of Leicester as an industrial centre.[3] During the 1860s and 1870s the civic authorities had undertaken a variety of schemes to improve the town including the construction of Granby Street, new municipal buildings,

Representing the city |

bridge building and flood prevention measures.[4] (See chapters 1 and 5.) The development of Abbey Park for the enjoyment of town residents was part of this series of improvements and the royal visit provided an opportunity for the Town Council to showcase recent achievements and to represent Leicester as a successful modern town.

The decision to mark the opening of Abbey Park with a royal visit was made in January 1882 and agreed with Buckingham Palace in a matter of days. The prince stopped at Leicester a week later on his way to stay with the Earl of Stamford and was presented at the station with an address of loyalty and a formal invitation to open the park on 29 May, the Whitsun holiday.[5]

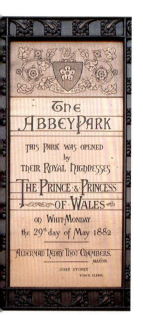

THE
ABBEY PARK

THIS PARK WAS OPENED
by
THEIR ROYAL HIGHNESSES
THE PRINCE & PRINCESS
OF WALES
on WHIT-MONDAY
the 29th day of May 1882

ALDERMAN HENRY THOS CHAMBERS.
MAYOR.

JOHN STOREY
TOWN CLERK.

7.3 Abbey Park memorial plaque, 29 May 1882.
Source: Colin Hyde.

7.4 Aerial view of Abbey Park, no date. The 57 acre park was acquired from the Earl of Dysart as part of the flood prevention works in 1876 (and a further 35 acres in 1925) and laid out by the renowned landscape designer William Barron. The outline of the medieval Augustinian abbey can be seen at the bottom left corner; the straight line of Belgrave and Melton Roads bisects the photograph with Rushey Fields recreation ground and the Great Northern Railway station (Tilton and Leicester Branch) beyond.
Source: Record Office for Leicester, Leicestershire and Rutland, DE3837, Box 1, Abbey Park, Folder 3. See also Aerofilms, RCAHMS.

A formula for royal visits had already been developed in other industrial towns and much of this was copied in Leicester.[6] The royal couple were received formally at the station by the Mayor, Mayoress, members of the Corporation, and the Leicestershire Regiment. They then processed with the civic authorities, representatives of various Leicester friendly societies and the Lord Lieutenant of Leicestershire, the Duke of Rutland, through the newly constructed town centre. Subscriptions of over £3,000 had been raised to pay for the public decorations[7] and triumphal arches had been specially erected for the royal visitors to pass through while shops and other buildings were elaborately decorated. An extended stop was made in the market place for a ceremony led by local freemasons, and over 6,000 schoolchildren from voluntary and board schools accompanied this ceremony with patriotic songs. The climax of the day was an opening ceremony in Abbey Park itself. The mayor presented a golden key to the Prince of Wales, who then declared the park open. Princess Alexandra was then invited to plant a tree and was presented with a silver spade by the Mayoress on behalf of the 'ladies of Leicester'. This ceremony was followed by a civic luncheon for selected guests, the programme of which included a mayoral speech and a schedule of toasts proposed by the Prince of Wales and various aldermen, local justices of the peace, military representatives and county dignitaries. The royal couple

7.5 The Prince of Wales in Masonic regalia.

Source: F.S. Herne (ed.), *The Historical Pageant of Leicestershire: Official Souvenir* (Leicester, 1932).

7.6 The procession entering Leicester Market Place, 1882.

Source: W. Kelly, *Royal Progresses and Visits to Leicester* (Leicester, 1884).

7.7 Evening
crowds at the
Clock Tower for
the Prince of
Wales' previous
visit to Leicester,
January 1882.

Source: Courtesy
of University of
Leicester, Special
Collections, www.
myleicestershire.
org.uk

then took a formal departure from the station and the evening was given over
to the enjoyment of spectacular fireworks and illuminations.

The Leicester Pageant, 1932

The Leicester Pageant and related civic activities of 1932 were, in comparison,
a much longer and more complex affair. Ten days of public events and
Pageant performances were originally planned and then, when consistently
large crowds attended, an extension of three days was announced.[8] There
was a series of themed days during the fortnight: Civic Day, Day of
Industry, County Day, Day of the British Empire, Pageant Sunday, Shops
Display Day and Children's Day. The civic authorities, as in 1882, used
the occasion to showcase their recent achievements and arranged for the
opening of Charles Street, a major new Leicester thoroughfare, to take
place on Civic Day. Other outstanding events during the fortnight were
an industrial exhibition, the trades' procession and the civic procession.
The Pageant itself, with its thousands of performers, was directed by a
professional Pageant master, Frank Lascelles,[9] and the narrative traced a
history of Leicester through seven episodes starting with the arrival of the
Romans and concluding with the 1882 opening of Abbey Park by the Prince
and Princess of Wales. Performances were staged every evening and on a
number of afternoons in the specially built amphitheatre in Abbey Park.[10]

7.8 Pageant
performers in
Tudor costume.

Source: Record
Office for Leicester,
Leicestershire and
Rutland, DE8438/3.

7.9 Pageant
performers in
seventeenth-
century costume.

Source: Record
Office for Leicester,
Leicestershire and
Rutland, DE3736,
Events 252/4.

The industrial exhibition was held in the municipal concert hall, the De Montfort Hall, opened by Viscountess Snowdon[11] and remained open throughout the Pageant period. Fifty city and county firms representing the hosiery, boot, engineering and a range of other industries took stands, and the trades' procession, which took place the next day, was still more comprehensive, including tableaux from ninety Leicester and Leicestershire industries and firms.[12] The procession, which drew very large crowds of spectators, was nearly two miles long and included marching groups of trade associations and trade unions. With the encouragement of the Lord Mayor of Leicester, workers' organisations had invited national trade union leaders and representatives of the TUC to the event. These were invited by the mayor to a civic lunch at the municipal art gallery along with representatives of the Industrial Relations Department, the Ministry of Labour and the Leicester and Leicestershire Chamber of Commerce.[13]

For the procession on Civic Day a half-day's public holiday was declared.[14] The Lord Mayor of London and the mayors of thirteen other provincial towns accepted an invitation to the event. After a civic lunch, again at the municipal art gallery, they processed, with the Leicester civic authorities, through the town, past streets lined with spectators to Abbey Park. Full ceremonial dress was worn and the 400-year-old Leicester city mace was carried. The Lord Mayor of London brought up the rear in his ceremonial coach, while the procession was led by the 4,000 Pageant performers, in full costume and forming a column a quarter of a mile long. At a ceremony in the centre of the city, the Lord Mayor of Leicester invited the Lord Mayor of London to open the recently constructed Charles Street. The Lord Mayor of London did this, cutting a silken cord with silver scissors, close by an archway formed by the fire escapes of the local fire brigade. The ceremony completed, the procession continued on its way to Abbey Park. Here, the Lord Mayor of London drove around the Pageant arena to the tumultuous applause of those in the amphitheatre before all settled to watch a performance of the Pageant.

Pageant fortnight included a wide variety of other events, such as a carnival, variety performances, Scout displays, and the transformation of Leicester market into an Elizabethan market with stall-holders in full Elizabethan costume.[15] In the last days of the fortnight, a large number of children's street parties were also held in the rundown Wharf Street area of the city.[16] When Pageant fortnight closed it was amid reports of financial success and hailed as a demonstration of the public spiritedness and civic awareness of those who had taken part.[17]

7.10 Pageant poster.
Source: F.S Herne (ed.), *The Historical Pageant.*

7.11 Horse drawn carriages on Charles Street, Civic Day, Leicester Pageant, 1932,
Source: Record Office for Leicester, Leicestershire and Rutland, DE3736, Events 276.

7.12 Fireman's Arch, Leicester Pageant.

Source: Record Office for Leicester, Leicestershire and Rutland, DE3736, Events 272.

7.13 The Civic Day procession passing along Charles Street during the Leicester Pageant, 1932.

Source: Record Office for Leicester, Leicestershire and Rutland, DE3736, Events 295.

7.14 The Lord Mayor of London and Lord Mayor of Leicester, Arthur Hawkes (1871–1946), prepare to make a presentation at the Leicester Pageant 1932. The Town Mace is in the background. Arthur Hawkes was educated at Wyggeston School, founded a firm of shop-fitters, and was the managing director of a boot company. Elected as a Liberal for the Westcotes ward in 1912, and served on the Watch, Water, Highways committees, and supported the improvements to Charles Street.

Source: Record Office for Leicester, Leicestershire and Rutland, DE3736, Events 293.

The events of 1882 and 1932 compared

The choice of honoured guests at both the 1882 and 1932 events was a matter of symbolic significance. The royal visit of 1882 was one of a series of visits by royalty to industrial towns in the mid- to late nineteenth century and was in step with contemporary support by both private and public institutions for promoting a sense of tradition, even when that tradition had to be invented.[18] A sense of tradition provided a counterbalance in a time of rapid social change.[19] The rise of a more organised working class was perceived to be a growing cause of class division and the expansion of the franchise had brought with it the emergence of mass political parties. These developments were significant at both national and local level with national and civic identity providing an alternative to both class and partisan loyalty. Moreover, as wealth and status were progressively more centred on the capital, local identity was increasingly envisaged within a national framework.[20] With the monarchy now removed from any real political power, it was no threat to the national state to present the royal family in splendour and by means of public spectacle to emphasise tradition.[21] Likewise, from a local point of view, loyalty to the monarchy provided a relatively neutral way of representing a local community within a wider national one. The seeming ease and speed with which the royal visit to Leicester was arranged suggests that there was now a general consensus both at national and local level, as well as with the royal family themselves, that this type of spectacle was a desirable way to promote local and national allegiances.

National and local identity were celebrated and represented as being in partnership rather than polarised, suggesting that diversity within unity was the ideal. This aligning of the two identities, separate but united, was made evident in many ways. Prior to the royal visit, a local newspaper report emphasised the valuable unifying role that the Prince of Wales was able to play, remarking that he had proved himself to be non-partisan and 'a representative of the country at large'.[22] Unity was physically demonstrated in the procession that linked the Prince of Wales, the Leicester civic authorities and also the chief symbol of the county, the Duke of Rutland. The image of national and local in partnership was also expressed in the toasts offered at the luncheon in Abbey Park. First, loyal toasts were made to the royal family and then to the Mayor and Corporation and the prosperity of the town of Leicester. Later toasts included 'the House of Lords and Commons' but also 'our municipal institutions'.

The decorations that bedecked the town also proclaimed national and local partnership. Buildings and triumphal arches bore symbols of the Borough of Leicester, the Borough Arms and the Wyvern, but were also emblazoned with heraldic symbols representing the Prince of Wales. On one arch the unity of nation, counties and towns was depicted by the allegorical figures, Britannia, Commerce and Agriculture. The keynote of the partnership portrayed was loyalty combined with civic pride. Loyalty was represented by the first arch through which the Prince of Wales passed, an arch composed of the evergreens of fir and yew, and it was echoed by the many mottos of welcome displayed on shops and buildings, at the same time the parade through the civic centre to the park demonstrated pride in the achievements of the local state.

The use of heraldic symbols was also one of a variety of ways in which a sense of historical and traditional reference was created. The day chosen for the event was itself symbolic, as 29 May was Oak-Apple Day, the traditional anniversary of the Restoration, and whether this was fortuitous or not, it was commented on by the press. In addition, the Princess of Wales planted an oak as part of the opening ceremony, a possible further reference to the day as well as a reminder of a traditional national symbol. Historical symbolism also served to highlight Leicester's heritage as well as that of the monarchy. While the procession through the new centre of town was seemingly a celebration of progress, the new park, named after Leicester's medieval abbey, the place of Cardinal Wolsey's death, was a clear reminder of the town's historical past. This was underlined again by the memento given to the Prince of Wales of the opening ceremony, a gold key 'massive in character and designed in the Gothic style' as being suitable to the ancient abbey.[23] Historical reference was an inspiration for the design of a number of the triumphal arches in the town. These included a Renaissance arch suggesting the rebirth of Leicester as a modern industrial town, while an old English arch celebrated deep historical roots and enduring tradition.

Fifty years later at the celebrations of 1932 the same ideal of national and local partnership was projected but this time the representation of civic identity was even more upbeat and less deferential.[24] The Pageant had two main guests, the Lord Mayor of London who attended the Civic Day and was accompanied by the mayors of a number of other provincial cities, and Viscountess Snowdon, who opened the Industrial Exhibition. At a time when national government increasingly dictated social policy while burdening local authorities with the responsibility of implementation, it is not perhaps surprising that a representative of civic government was invited as an honoured guest.[25] The choice of the Lord Mayor of London gave the occasion a national dimension but the value of localism was continually emphasised. Welcoming the Lord Mayor of London, the Lord Mayor of Leicester exalted local government proclaiming: 'Your presence is a … symbol of the value of civic life and local government which means more to the homes and lives of our people than anything.'[26]

Next, promoting an invented tradition by referring to the local connection with Simon de Montfort, he represented Leicester itself as the model for government, referring to the city as 'the birthplace of freedom and civic government'.[27] Viscountess Snowdon was not the first choice to open the Industrial Exhibition. The organisers, with their characteristic confidence, had hoped for the higher profile Lloyd George.[28] However, as wife of the ex-Labour Chancellor Philip Snowdon, it was likely thought that she had a relevance to industry while symbolising an approach to labour organisations that highlighted partnership rather than class conflict. Again, at the opening of the exhibition, the Lord Mayor of Leicester represented the city as a model for the nation, emphasising its relatively easy progress though the depression and hailing its success as a manufacturing centre as the most fortunate in the country and probably, for a town of its size, the most fortunate in the world. This success he attributed to the excellent choices made by their forefathers.[29] The hyperbole, seems to have been a little too much for Viscountess Snowdon who, while she congratulated Leicester on its achievements, chose to reinforce a more national sense of identity asking the audience to remember that citizens of Leicester 'were also Britons and citizens of the world'.[30]

Leicester's international connections were also emphasised by the organisers. The celebrations included an Empire Day at which trade representatives from the Dominions were present. Moreover, letters of congratulation from the prime ministers of South Africa, Australia, Southern Rhodesia and New Zealand were read out at the end of the civic procession on 21 June. This showcase of international contacts implied that Leicester could in fact hold its own as a trading centre within the Empire and that in the partnership of local and national the junior status of Leicester as a provincial city should not be over emphasised.[31]

7.15 De Montfort Hall laid out for the Leicester Pageant Display of Industries, opened by Viscountess Snowdon, 16 June 1932.

Source: Record Office for Leicester, Leicestershire and Rutland, DE3736, Events 269.

| Leicester: a modern history

The Mayor of Leicester, councillors, aldermen and borough officials were of course at the heart of the celebrations both in 1882 and 1932. However, in 1882 there was no exaggerated show of ceremonial dress on the part of the Lord Mayor. While the civic authorities may have wished to assert their authority on this occasion it was not done visually with a display of official robes. A line drawing of the opening ceremony shows the Lord Mayor simply wearing his chain of office.[32] The break between the old and reformed administration in 1836 had been so bitter that all the civic paraphernalia was considered symbolic of corruption and was disposed of previously.[33] A compromise was reached in 1867 with the acquisition of a new mayoral chain; however, it is clear that in 1882, the traditions associated with mayoral costume were still not ones with which the civic authorities wished to be associated.[34] In contrast, in 1932, the Lord Mayor of Leicester and the visiting mayors dressed in full ceremonial costume and the town mace was displayed. Possibly, this was a renewed assertion of authority or possibly, with the electoral principle now firmly established, it was now acceptable to use costume as just another theatrical contribution to the invention of tradition.

As already observed, the major contrast between the 1882 and 1932 celebrations was the increased level of participation by Leicester residents. The numbers involved were one aspect of this. The extension of the celebrations over a far greater length of time gave greater scope to the organisers, as did the elaborate range of events organised from the Pageant with its 4,000 performers to the Civic Day and trades' processions to the displays from schools and youth associations. However, what was also notable, was the depth of involvement by those who took part and was particularly evident in the production of the Pageant itself which was facilitated by the mechanism of the city's associational network.

Voluntary associations in Leicester played a prominent role in mobilising local residents to take part in the Pageant. In the decades between the opening of Abbey Park and the Pageant the number of associations in the town including philanthropic, commercial, religious, educational and

7.16 Ethel Annakin (1881–1951), Viscountess Snowdon: suffragist, Christian socialist, and Independent Labour Party member; teacher training at Edge Hill College, Liverpool; freelance lecturer; a BBC governor, and wife of the Labour Chancellor of the Exchequer, Philip Snowden.

Source: F.S. Herne (ed.), *The Historical Pageant.*

Representing the city | 167

recreational groups increased and this growth continued into the inter-war years. In the mid- to late nineteenth century the Leicester local press dedicated extensive column space to reporting the calendar of small, regular civic and associational events that helped shape the urban year. By 1932, at the time of the Pageant, this was still the case and, moreover, this calendar of events had become denser, reflecting an associational life that had become more inclusive of the different sub groups that comprised the local population. It was this regular associational life that underpinned the success of the Pageant providing a vehicle by which local residents could be recruited and organised.

At the heart of associational life was a meeting culture – the formation of committees, reports, debate and decision-making through voting. At one level these procedures were a pragmatic way of doing business but at another they symbolised the ideal of wide participation and social inclusiveness and could be characterised as the rituals of democracy. With the implementation of the universal franchise in the inter-war years, these ideals were further institutionalised. The forms of meeting culture were demonstrated in 1932, in the display of democratic practice and coordination in the lead-up to the Pageant. This was so intensively covered by the local newspapers that the process could be justifiably considered as part of the spectacle itself. Public meetings were a hallmark of this process. The initial public meeting was described by the *Leicester Evening Mail* as 'a meeting of the citizens of Leicester attended by representatives of almost every social, industrial and religious movement in the city and county'.[35] Other meetings followed to appoint a pageant master and delegate work to committees and to embark on the task of compiling a full list of local societies and associations from which performers could be drawn.[36] Then there were further meetings to ensure that county cooperation could be relied on in this city-led project[37] and also to report on work in progress.[38]

The choice of leading Pageant committee members shows that preferred qualifications for the job were involvement in Leicester associational life and influence in the county as well as practical, commercial or artistic skills. Members of leading associations such as the Rotary Club, the Leicester Drama Society, the Leicester Orchestral Union, the Women's Conservative Association, the Leicester Society of Artists and the Chamber of Commerce were all appointed.[39] Reports show how the committees organised small communities at 'grassroots' level to prepare for the Pageant, sometimes placing very diverse groups together. For example, in April 1932, it was reported that plans for episode one of the Pageant had been implemented.[40] The organisations involved were: the Catholic parishes of Leicester, the British United (Shoe Company) Drama League, the Glen Parva Army Barracks, and the Leicester Women's Athletic Club. A further committee was established, including representatives from each of these organisations, with the headmistress of Sacred Heart Catholic School as the committee secretary. This committee was to work with a stage manager and two assistants, cooperating with the Pageant Master to produce the episode. Self-reliance and economy were to be practised, with each player responsible for buying his or her costume from a range of approved costumes, chosen by an expert with a view to historical accuracy, and obtainable at a modest expense. Thus, unlike the Abbey Park event in 1882, the Pageant of 1932 involved sustained hard work over months and expense for large numbers of people. This was not just a matter of transposing associations like the Freemasons, various friendly societies and the Rifle Volunteers, who already had ceremonial props, such as banners and insignia or uniforms, into a procession. Producing the Pageant required preparation and cross communication between separate associational communities. The successful staging of the Pageant, by these means, showed that the meetings were not empty symbols of participation and demonstrated how democratic practices could facilitate social cohesion and produce a convincing display of civic community.

It is, of course, impossible to say why so many people were willing to commit themselves to this depth of involvement over a sustained period of time. The city authorities of course, from the outset, promoted the official reasons of public spiritedness, civic awareness and the advertising of Leicester both nationally and internationally throughout the Empire.[41] On the other hand, the chance to socialise was as likely a reason for taking part as any, especially as amateur dramatics were a popular pastime in the inter-war period.[42] The very nature of pageantry, however, enabled maximum scope for inventing tradition and it may well be that alongside the more prosaic reasons for participation the performers were inspired by the narrative of Leicester history presented by the Pageant. The connection of Simon de Montfort with the city, in particular, permitted a notion of Leicester as 'the birthplace of civic freedom and local government' to take hold.[43] As well as being a means by which Leicester could be marketed as a leader and a model within the nation, it may also have promoted the desired feelings of local pride and loyalty. Moreover, the city had managed to obtain the services of Frank Lascelles, a 'top' professional Pageant Master, to produce the event and so it is very likely that his expertise had a motivating effect. A fashion for civic pageants had been established since the turn of the century and Lascelles had already produced a great many.[44] These had included a very ambitious and successful Pageant of London with 15,000 performers, as well as huge extravaganzas in South Africa and India.[45] The excitement of taking part in a professionally produced event, coupled with Lascelles' ability to keep momentum going probably produced both enthusiasm and feelings of social solidarity among the cast which may have in turn manifest itself as a communal sense of civic identity.

Besides the Pageant, the older form of civic ceremony, the civic procession used to effect in 1882, was adapted for use in 1932. A characteristic of

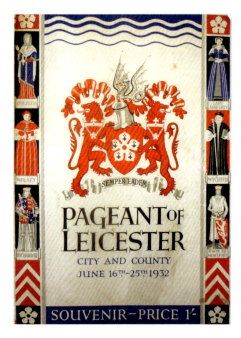

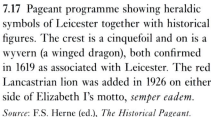

7.17 Pageant programme showing heraldic symbols of Leicester together with historical figures. The crest is a cinquefoil and on is a wyvern (a winged dragon), both confirmed in 1619 as associated with Leicester. The red Lancastrian lion was added in 1926 on either side of Elizabeth I's motto, *semper eadem*.

Source: F.S. Herne (ed.), *The Historical Pageant*.

7.18 Simon de Montfort (1208–65) 5th Earl of Leicester, as represented on the Clock Tower, 1868, to commemorate Simon de Montfort, credited with forming the first Parliament; William Wyggeston, wool merchant; Sir Thomas White (benefactor); and Alderman Gabriel Newton, wool-comber and mayor in 1732. Designed by Joseph Goddard, sculptor Samuel Barfield. Other Leicester contemporary references to de Montfort include the De Montfort civic hall, and De Montfort University, previously Leicester Polytechnic.

Source: Colin Hyde.

invented tradition has been the use of old models for new purposes.[46] The 1882 civic procession, with its combination of royalty, civic authorities and friendly society members, seemed to represent a society with class divisions since the order of the procession, with the friendly societies placed in the least prestigious position at the front, stressed a definite class hierarchy. In 1932, a different effect, more suitable to the growing sense of egalitarianism in society, was achieved by substituting the overtly working-class element at the front of the procession, with the Pageant performers in full costume. A group in theatrical costume could be seen as a classless representation of the people and a symbol of civic unity representing an undivided civic identity with roots in the past and continuing into the present. This was, moreover, a way of incorporating into the event representatives of voluntary societies that had rituals in the form of meeting procedures but which lacked a ceremonial style that could enhance the spectacle of a procession.

The increased mobilisation of voluntary associations for the 1932 celebrations also incorporated substantial numbers of women into the events. The Victorian style of civic celebration has been characterised as entirely male dominated.[47] This was true of the civic celebrations for the opening of Abbey Park in 1882, although it should not be overstated. Women were represented in small numbers both at the opening ceremony and at the celebratory luncheon, and both the mayoress and the Princess of Wales played leading roles. In addition, women as well as men played an important role as spectators. However, the 1882 civic procession was almost exclusively male and the more active aspects of the day were male dominated. In the 1932 event this imbalance was altered as women were extensively involved in both the preparation of and performance in the Pageant. Moreover, while the councillors and aldermen who participated in the civic procession in 1932 were almost exclusively male, the inclusion in the parade of the Pageant performers and the mayoresses of visiting towns, as well as the Mayoress of Leicester, ensured a more balanced representation.

The trades' procession, like the Civic Day procession, used symbolism to model beliefs and values. As the *Leicester Evening Mail* reported, the display 'drove home, as the written word could not', the success and further potential of Leicester's industry.[48] Marketing Leicester as a commercial success had been a major argument for staging civic celebrations in 1932 and the trades' procession as well as the Industrial Exhibition was part of the process of 'talking up' the city as a business leader nationally, within the Empire and beyond. While the broad-based nature of Leicester's economy had no doubt given it an easier ride through the depression than many other cities there had also been room for anxiety. In January 1932 an editorial in the *Leicester Evening Mail* had stated that 'Leicester's industrialists are showing their courage. Things seem better all round this year but conditions of trade are generally far from ideal.'[49] A belief that civic ceremony could create a positive profile of the city that would attract business was a driving force behind the event. At the initial meeting called to discuss the proposed celebrations, the mayor and other supporters of the cause had pointed to neighbouring Northampton. It was said that Northampton's pageant had made it 'the hub of the commercial universe for a week' despite the industrial depression.[50] Likewise, a pageant staged in Bradford had received extensive international advertising as flyers were left 'in every British consulate and travel office and in leading hotels, steamships and railway offices all over the world'.[51] All this, it was said, was possible for Leicester and it was the diversity of its trades that was to be the main selling point. The trades' procession, with its tableaux of ninety Leicester and county industries, was one way in which the point was made. Arguably, the audience for this display was mainly the local community itself who formed the great mass of spectators on the actual day. However, this dovetailed with a second driving belief behind the celebrations, that the self-belief embodied in a strong sense of civic spirit could help bring the city prosperity. The trades' procession also satisfied the need to represent the separate identity of 'labour' and its contribution to the city. The civic procession avoided representing distinctions of class in hierarchical form, and the trades' procession emphasised the products of 'labour', representing both industrial and agricultural workers as integral partners in the production of wealth rather than emphasising opposing interests or an inferior class identity. The incorporation of trade unions into this parade further played down any suggestion of class conflict and militancy. Moreover, the attendance of trade union leaders at a civic luncheon alongside members of the local Chamber of Commerce and representatives of the Ministry of Labour completed the image of partnership between employer and employee.

The inclusive style of the 1932 events was also evident in the approach to those who did not play a leading part in the proceedings. In the 1882 celebrations for the opening of Abbey Park, there was little formal means of participation for spectators beyond cheering and waving and making decorations. However, in 1932, efforts were made to involve spectators to a greater degree. This was partly done by advance preparation. For example, in the six months prior to the events, a series of lectures was organised in relation to the Pageant.[52] A Leicester resident, Laurie Pears, remembered that there was a sense of great anticipation and excitement fostered in schools long before the Pageant fortnight. The Pageant song, which also showcased Leicester's history, was taught to schoolchildren in advance and special Pageant badges were distributed.[53] Moreover, the historical scenes to be portrayed were extensively described and explained by a very supportive local press ensuring that many who attended the performances arrived with minds that were already involved and receptive to the narrative that was to be related.

The use of photography in reporting the 1932 celebrations was also a means by which a deeper level of involvement on the part of spectators was suggested. The 1882 newspaper reports, working only with words, largely conveyed the crowds as a homogeneous mass. However, in June 1932, the *Leicester Evening Mail* reports focused extensively on photographing the audience as well as the performers.[54] The faces of those seated in the amphitheatre are easily picked out in newspaper photographs. No doubt this was a good way of selling papers, tempting Leicester's residents to try and 'spot' themselves as well as friends and neighbours. However, it also had the effect of suggesting that those attending were not an anonymous mass but a group of individuals who were willing to support the way the city was being marketed.

An increased level of spectator interaction was also introduced by some of the supporting events arranged during the Pageant period. There were, for example, several occasions of massed singing by schoolchildren in the Pageant amphitheatre.[55] School choirs had also been featured in 1882 but in 1932 their participation was extended and while in 1882 the singing had been used as an accompaniment to the Freemasons' ceremony, in 1932 it was an event in itself. There was also a massed inter-denominational religious service in the amphitheatre on Pageant Sunday creating the impression of a united religious community in Leicester.[56] A further important interactive event was the transformation of Leicester market into an Elizabethan market where people could shop and chat to costumed characters apparently from Leicester's past.[57] This project again showcased the city's long history while offering an opportunity to participate to yet more people.

The Pageant was successful in that events were staged without major problems, prestigious visitors were welcomed to the city, and the occasion mustered enough local support to attract large audiences and cover itself financially. The celebrations were reported in *The Times* with a favourable review stating that 'The Pageant is worthy of the communal exhilaration it has produced'.[58] The projected image of the city as a united and prosperous community that deserved to be recognised as a substantial player within the nation and the Empire went largely unchallenged. Moreover, the strength of the local economy, of which so much was made during the Pageant period, was to a great extent confirmed by the League of Nations statistics of 1936 that rated Leicester as the second most prosperous city in Europe.[59]

However, the ambitious and sustained nature of the project meant that inevitably obstacles arose which, although dealt with, indicated some underlying weaknesses in the façade. For example, the organisers' attempts to have Lloyd George open the Pageant failed.[60] The opening day had been grandly named Statesman's Day and although Viscountess Snowdon was a national figure, her presence perhaps did not bestow the recognition that the organisers were seeking to convey. Other obstacles that arose included squabbles about the level of recognition given to the county,[61] and an argument with Catholic Church leaders about an offending verse in the Pageant song, which almost resulted in Catholic performers being forbidden to participate.[62] There were also a significant number of businessmen who objected to the three-day extension of the Pageant, claiming that the events were drawing their customers away.[63] However, despite this disruption, these problems were resolved through negotiation suggesting that there was strong drive among the parties involved to present a united local front.

Two incidents, however, showed disaffection among sub-sections of the population. First, on the Saturday night of the first Pageant week, youths fought with police at the Leicester Clock Tower in the city centre. It was reported that 'these were the types who habitually hung around the town jeering at Pageant performers returning from their rehearsals'.[64] Second, a plan to disrupt the Civic Day procession was discovered and stopped. A sign saying 'Welcome to the Slums' put up in a poor area of town was removed.[65] In both these cases police action was taken. It is difficult to assess fully the significance of these disruptions, but it is clear that some voices more critical of the Pageant were not being heard. The numbers of people involved, however, seem minor in comparison to the 4,000 people who took part in the Pageant, the show of organised labour at the trades' procession, and the 100,000 people who bought Pageant tickets.[66] Generally, it seems the civic project was a success and was welcomed by the majority of local residents.

This chapter has compared two major civic celebrations in Leicester, one in 1882 and one in 1932, and has explored how the symbolism of these two events served to define a strong sense of local identity as well as a harmonious relationship between local and national. There were similarities between the form of the two occasions, notably the presence of guests from London, the staging of a civic procession and opening ceremony, and the emphasis on creating a sense of tradition. However, as well as similarities there were also major contrasts, most strikingly the outstanding level of participation by Leicester residents in the Pageant of 1932 as well as the inclusion of a wider cross-section of the local population both in the production and in the events organised during Pageant fortnight. The role of voluntary associations in mobilising local people to participate has been emphasised as well as the demonstration of meeting culture that was at the heart of the organising process. Britain had moved to a more democratic polity in the years between 1882 and 1932. The taste for civic ceremony remained but it had adapted to fit the changed social context.

PART II

Reinventing Leicester

Freemans, Hardy Willis 1940 —   Kenneth Holmes

8

Reinventing the city after 1945

ON 30 April 1946 King George VI and Queen Elizabeth visited Leicester. Around the Clock Tower the streets were packed to welcome the royals, and at Spinney Hills Park more than 6,000 children greeted them before the royal party made a series of visits to Leicester factories.[1] At De Montfort Hall, the king's speech acknowledged the contribution of Leicester citizens to the war effort:

> Leicester may well be proud of the contributions of her citizens to the final victory. Your men and women served in all arms of the fighting services, in the many sided activities of Civil Defence, and in many branches of industry. I thank them all for they did and I would like to express my sincere appreciation to the householders of Leicester who welcomed in their midst, refugees and evacuees from areas which were subject to heavy bombing attacks. This was a work of practical sympathy which was particularly close to the heart of the Queen.

The king's speech was a direct reference to the 30,000 people, including 10,000 unaccompanied children, evacuated to Leicester in the early weeks of the war. For the most part the assumption that German bombers would not pay much heed to Leicester since it was not a major producer of armaments was correct, although the worst air raid on 19 November 1942 resulted in 11 factories destroyed and 72 damaged; 550 houses destroyed, and 4,200 damaged; and there were 102 fatalities with 203 further injuries.[2] Though guns, ships and tanks were not produced in Leicester, the Corah factory converted its engineering workshops so as to manufacture 80,000 gun parts and 30,000 components for tank landing craft, and the Leicester textile industry made very significant contributions by producing uniforms and clothing for the armed forces – the Corah factory alone manufactured 17 million pairs of socks and 0.5 million ant-flash helmets for the troops.[3]

In one sense, post-war adjustment for Leicester was straightforward. There were relatively few bombed sites; the physical scars of war were less visible than in nearby Coventry and other British cities. Yet industrial plant and buildings were exhausted, depreciated, and in need of maintenance and re-investment for peacetime production. The government understandably identified higher priorities in the war-torn cities of the West Midlands,

8.1
(*opposite*)
The Freeman, Hardy and Willis factory on Rutland Street and Humberstone Gate was destroyed in 19 November 1940.

Source: reproduced by permission of the Imperial War Museum.

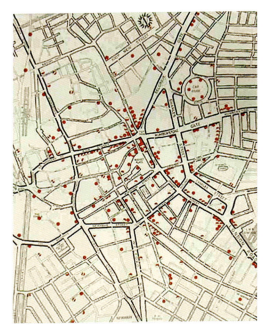

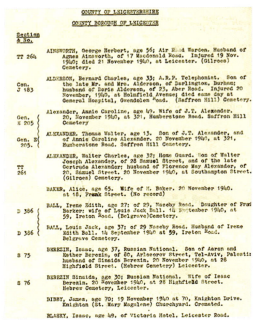

COUNTY OF LEICESTERSHIRE

COUNTY BOROUGH OF LEICESTER

Section & No.	
TT 264	AINSWORTH, George Herbert, age 56; Air Raid Warden. Husband of Agnes Ainsworth, of 17 Macdonald Road. Injured 19 Nov. 1940; died 21 November 1940, at Leicester. (Gilroes) Cemetery.
Con. J 183	ALDERSON, Bernard Charles, age 33; A.R.P. Telephonist. Son of the late Mr. and Mrs. Alderson, of Darlington, Durham; husband of Doris Alderson, of 23, Aber Road. Injured 20 November, 1940, at Holmfield Avenue; died same day at General Hospital, Gwendolen Road. (Saffron Hill) Cemetery.
Gen. K 205	Alexander, Annie Caroline, age 49. Wife of J.T. Alexander. 20, November 1940, at 321, Humberstone Road. Saffron Hill Cemetery
Gen. E 205.	ALEXANDER, Thomas Walter, age 13. Son of J.T. Alexander, and of Annie Caroline Alexander. 20 November 1940, at 321, Humberstone Road. Saffron Hill Cemetery.
TT 261	ALEXANDER, Walter Charles, age 32; Home Guard. Son of Walter Joseph Alexander, of 28 Samuel Street, and of the late Gertrude Alexander; husband of Florence May Alexander, of 28, Samuel Street. 20 November 1940, at Southampton Street. (Gilroes) Cemetery.
	BAKER, Alice, age 65. Wife of M. Baker. 20 November 1940. at 18, Frank Street. (No record)
D 386	BALL, Irene Edith, age 27; of 29, Naseby Road. Daughter of Fred Barker; wife of Louis Jack Ball. 14 September 1940, at 59, Ireton Road. (Belgrave)Cemetery.
D 386	BALL, Louis Jack, age 37; of 29 Naseby Road. Husband of Irene Edith Ball. 14 September 1940 at 59, Ireton Road. Belgrave Cemetery.
B 75	BEREZIN, Isaac, age 37, Russian National. Son of Aaron and Esther Berezin, of 80, Arlosorov Street, Tel-Aviv, Palestine; husband of Sinaida Berezin. 20 November 1940, at 28 Highfield Street. (Hebrew Cemetery) Leicester.
B 76	BEREZIN Sinaida, age 30; Russian National. Wife of Isaac Berezin. 20 November 1940, at 28 Highfield Street. Hebrew Cemetery, Leicester.
	BIBBY, James, age 70; 19 November 1940 at 70, Knighton Drive. Knighton (St. Mary Magdalene) Churchyard. Cremated.
	BLASKY, Isaac, age 49, of Victoria Hotel. Leicester Road.

8.2 Air raid shelters.

Source: Record Office for Leicester, Leicestershire and Rutland.

8.3 Wartime civilian casualties in Leicester. At least 120 people were killed and 300 injured in the air raids.

Source: Leicester City Council.

Clydeside, and in the London boroughs. In that sense Leicester was forced to be self-reliant and the independent spirit that had been a feature in its early development surfaced again.

In 1944, even before the peace was won, the city was quick to address housing needs unencumbered, as in other British cities, by the elaborate and ambitious reports of internationally renowned town planning experts.[4] The Leicester Reconstruction Committee was set up under Councillor Charles Keene in 1944 with the brief to develop a post-war planning strategy. By identifying the accommodation shortage and focusing on short-term goals, council housing projects at New Parks, Scraptoft Valley and Thurnby Lodge were developed, as well as a quick fix – 800 bought-in chalet-style 'pre-fabs' with a ten-year life expectancy for several locations owned by the city (8.5; 8.6).[5] This responsiveness was also evident in the adoption of

8.4 Sir Charles Keene (1891–1977) managing director; JP, knighted 1969; local methodist preacher from 1910; elected Labour councillor (1926), alderman (1945), mayor (1953); wartime responsibilities for the city's air raid precautions, and regional fire service; chair of Planning Committee, and of Education Committee; Art and Technology College; Gateway School.

Source: Leicester City Council.

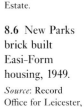

8.5 New Parks housing built by the British Iron and Steel Federation. Further steel-framed housing was erected at Eyres Monsell at a cost of about £1,350 each.

Source: Record Office for Leicester, Leicestershire and Rutland, DE3736, Box 25, New Parks Estate.

8.6 New Parks brick built Easi-Form housing, 1949.

Source: Record Office for Leicester, Leicestershire and Rutland, DE3736, Box 25, New Parks Estate.

new 'Easi-Form' all-steel housing designs by the Iron and Steel Foundation which were approved by the City Architect, J.S. Fyfe and the City Engineer and Surveyor, John Beckett, to overcome post-war materials shortages. Each day, four of these aluminium-framed houses could be built, financed by Treasury subsidies for 75% of the costs, spread over 60 years. By Christmas 1948, 58% of the planned 2,450 houses on the council's flagship estate, New

Parks, had been built. Council house building was also treated flexibly by
sub-contracting work to small builders, as at Thurnby Lodge. Elsewhere,
the officially commissioned master plans for a number of British cities had
only just been, or were still to be, published in 1948. The City Council
then approved further new council building, first of all at Stocking Farm
in 1950, and then from 1952 at the extensive Eyres Monsell estate. Between
the end of the war and Christmas 1952 the City Council had built 5,155
houses. Initially the post-war priority in the reinvention of Leicester relied
on volume building, that is, on increasing the number of housing units as
quickly as possible; then a more long-term structured approach emerged
through a programme of planned demolition and replacement.

The reinvention of Leicester entered a new post-war phase from 1949.
By then slum clearance plans were in preparation. Again Leicester was
ahead of the Ministry of Housing and Local Government announcement by
preparing to demolish almost 20,000 houses and a number of factories. The
implications were, first, that an extension to the city area was essential given
the scale of the demolition and re-housing; and, second, that in keeping
with an emerging vision of the zoned modern city, industries would also be
relocated at the edge of the city so that fewer families lived in the polluted

8.8 Warrington Street, 1958, demolition of 4-room terraced homes for factories between Northgate and the canal.

Source: Leicester City Council.

shadows of a factory. Both approaches required delicate negotiations with the County Council over Leicester's overspill – decanting the city's rising population beyond the city boundaries disrupted revenues and demand for amenities. The need to move population around the country to meet changing labour force requirements was a central principle of the Barlow Report (1940) and indeed there was a high degree of wartime compliance with public interventions in daily routines as a result of planning and rationing. Post-war reconstruction and the more overt social welfare, nationalisation and economic management plans of the Labour government after 1945 built on such interventions in private lives, and on earlier slum clearances in the 1930s, and so the Leicester plans for relocating residents were not as controversial as might have been expected, though very disruptive locally.

Over the next twenty years, from 1954 to 1975, the City Council demolished an average of 550 houses each year (8.9). The results of slum clearances on such a scale were the many vacant sites – scars on the physical and psychological landscapes – that contributed to the sense of loss and displacement for those families ejected from their homes for what seemed like little or no progress. However modern the council accommodation to which they were assigned, the destruction of their area, family folklore and

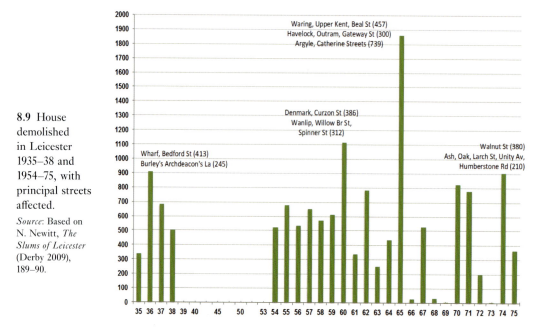

8.9 House demolished in Leicester 1935–38 and 1954–75, with principal streets affected.

Source: Based on N. Newitt, *The Slums of Leicester* (Derby 2009), 189–90.

Chart labels:
- Waring, Upper Kent, Beal St (457)
- Havelock, Outram, Gateway St (300)
- Argyle, Catherine Streets (739)
- Denmark, Curzon St (386)
- Wanlip, Willow Br St, Spinner St (312)
- Wharf, Bedford St (413)
- Burley's Archdeacon's La (245)
- Walnut St (380)
- Ash, Oak, Larch St, Unity Av, Humberstone Rd (210)

X-axis: 35 36 37 38 39 40 45 50 53 54 55 56 57 58 59 60 61 62 63 64 65 66 67 68 69 70 71 72 73 74 75

8.10 Highfields redevelopment. Planned demolition and redevelopment of the St Peter's Housing Estate Project, begun 1964. The multi-storey tower blocks were given the names of the former streets in the area. According to the City Architect 'The Rank Hobson factory (est. 1886) is to stay … because it is a highly skilled workforce'. It produced precision lenses and precision measuring equipment.

Source: Leicester City Council.

cross-generational talking points, reference markers and navigational aids was equivalent to a bereavement for those displaced. The collective memory was devalued. The old medieval town of Leicester with its chimney stacks, familiar street patterns, human building scale and the jitties that gave a porous character to the town was lost, as were quaint street names – Blue Boar Lane and Red Cross Street – and neighbourhoods. Visitors thought the vacant sites within a few hundred yards of the Clock Tower were the result of wartime bombing so extensive that it took a many years to repair the damage.

The reinvention of Leicester in the 1950s and 1960s received another stimulus from traffic plans and the transformation of the town centre associated with them. Peripheral council estates, middle-class suburbanisation, vacant downtown sites, displaced factories, Treasury subsidies for improved road layouts, rising car ownership, an infant motorway system on the Leicester boundary and a new planning paradigm inspired by 'Modern Movement' architecture guaranteed that from the 1950s Leicester town centre would never be again the same (8.11; 8.15). In the 1930s a new thoroughfare, Charles Street, had been constructed to ease traffic congestion so Leicester residents were not entirely unfamiliar with the concept of revised traffic flows, and in 1955 Newarke Street was reconstructed to ease the traffic circulation (8.12). However, from the late 1950s, the scale of intervention

8.11 Abbey Street Car Park. The building was typical of Modern Movement designs with its horizontal lines, and represented the power of the motor car to influence the character of the city centre.

Source: Colin Hyde.

Source: Leicester
City Council.

was entirely different. Cleared sites around Burley's Lane in 1957 and Great
Central Street created the beginnings of an inner ring road, to be followed
soon after by the demolition associated with the city's historic areas around
St Nicholas Street and Southgates to form another part of the inner ring –
Vaughan Way. In 1960 the City Engineer's transport master plan proposed
further central and outer ring roads mindful of the construction work
already underway on an 11-mile stretch of the M1 motorway immediately
to the west of the Leicester city boundary. By the 1960s it was evident that,
despite the cleared and increasingly vacant industrial sites, the city centre
still retained its retail and commercial primacy. The streets converging on
the Clock Tower and the Market continued to attract shoppers, cinema-
goers, a thriving theatre audience, and a pub, club and social life, as well
as football and rugby fans. Public transport was inadequate, and rising car
ownership simply produced more congestion. Clearly early Park n' Ride and
public transport provisions were inadequate.

The city was reinventing itself in terms of housing and the use of space,
but it was not until Konrad Smigielski replaced John Beckett in 1964 as the
City Planning Officer and recognised the traffic paralysis he had inherited
that this reinvention took on a more striking form (see also chapter 11).
Smigielski's uncompromising views on traffic were public knowledge long
before his Leicester appointment, as he explained at a press conference
after winning £1,000 as second prize in the Roads Campaign Council's
'New Ways for London' competition in 1958.[6] He claimed that the highly

esteemed Professor Patrick Abercombie's 1944 London Plan for a ring road would actually increase city-centre congestion, was a 'mere palliative', and already obsolete. In 1960, in a glimpse of Leicester's future, Smigielski claimed that a more scientific and long-term approach to traffic was essential for large cities, with 'forceful government intervention' and interdisciplinary research teams involving town planners, architects, landscape artists, traffic engineers, sociologists and economists' engaged at a regional level. More specifically Smigielski explained: 'the plan for elevated motorways ... would solve the problem of traffic congestion and parking [by the provision of multi-storey garages] for the next 30 years.'[7] At a meeting of the Town and Country Planning Association in 1966 the Minister of Transport, Barbara Castle, appealed to local authorities 'to use guts and intelligence' to address urban traffic problems yet described 'Mr Smigielski's passionate attack on the motor car [as] unpopular with anybody who ever rode in, drove or owned one', and that the 'surrender of cars in cities was politically impossible and socially undesirable'.[8] Smigielski then entered the contentious national political arena, stating that if improved public transport was part of the traffic solution 'the economics of urban transport' required urgent investigation.[9] These were highly charged comments in the mid-1960s when the 'Beeching Axe' aimed to cut the rail network mileage overall by 55% and 30% of stations.[10] Only four stations remained in Leicestershire; city and regional policy were in direct opposition.

The transport situation was summarised in the Leicester Traffic Plan. Smigielski's explained: 'This is the dilemma: the city centre or the motor-car.'[11] His solution: an 'Integrated Transport System'. This demoted the primacy of the car by elevating – literally – the road traffic on a 5-mile inner city motorway to replace three ring roads. In his own display of 'guts and intelligence' Smigielski proposed interchange car parks; electric 'rickshaw taxis; short 'crush buses' for the city centre with standing only; 'bus-trains' – an early form of 'bendy bus'; a moving 'pedestrian pavement' or beltway; improved road networking, and significant upgrading of public transport including a elevated monorail system. One-way systems were proposed as part of the traffic management plan, and underpasses, flyovers and designated feeder roads were further elements designed to improve traffic flow and handle increased volumes (8.13). Leicester's bold transport planning assumed centre stage as the first local perspective in a national debate associated with the Buchanan Report, *Traffic in Towns* (1963) that juxtaposed 'complete motorization and limited entry to central areas'.[12] The overall costs for Leicester were estimated at £135 million over a 30-year period. One element of the local proposals, approved by the City Council in 1967, was an extensive scheme to address the traffic bottleneck at the West Bridge and this was scheduled to take 20 years and cost £30 million. Further traffic schemes faltered, or at least were incomplete; some, such as the Eastern Ring Road Project, were abandoned, in 1974. The 'Park 'n

8.13 Burley's flyover, 1976.

Source: Colin Hyde.

Ride' slogan for local motorists was taken a step further at a regional level, however, with stress placed on Leicester's future economic health linked to a role as a midland transport hub with radiating roads, good M1 access, two regional airports, four seaports within a 100 miles, frequent rail transport to London, and efficient rail freight handling potential.[13]

How did the experience of such transport planning proposals affect the shopper? A visitor to Leicester in 1969, Carol Wright, provided a snapshot of the city. The centre was described as 'straggly, drab and non-definitive' and the shopping centre around the Clock Tower was 'a snarl of one-way streets'.[14] Positive impressions, however, prevailed. There was a tight cluster of 'good department stores and chains', access by car had been 'programmed' by the council with 'inexpensive' multi-storey car parks, while the 2*d.* bus fares, among the cheapest in Britain, 'encourages the use of public transport and the bus company makes a profit'. In 1969 the 200 Leicester buses carried 72.5 million passengers. The Co-op introduced 'self-service shopping' in 1942 and was singled out for its 200 parking spaces in the High Street, with charges refundable on purchases. The challenge of out-of-town shopping was also noted when the new Woolco store at Oadby opened four miles away in 1967 with 90,000 square feet of floor space and free parking for 750 cars. Town centre shopkeepers contributed to their own problems with confusion over half-day closing – some chose the traditional Thursday and others Mondays – and another complication for retailers was the availability of clothes direct from factories at well below shop prices. The Holiday Inn, under construction in 1969, was intended to attract businessmen and overseas visitors, and city-centre attractions were to be improved with completion of the Rank Ballroom in the Haymarket Centre. Carol Wright concluded that Leicester had 'a live centre' which would only be improved with the proposed walkways between the station and main shopping thoroughfares.

In a striking headline – '"Smigielskiville" halts the process of decline' – *The Times* extolled the Leicester Chief Town Planner's tactics to shock the local population into action by drawing attention to the 'clutter, litter and vandalism' he observed on his arrival in the city, especially in the Georgian pedestrian promenade of New Walk.[15] 'It was a degraded environment. When I first came to see it I was really depressed,' Smigielski recalled. A decade later his environmental clean-up was shortlisted for *The Times* Royal Institution of Chartered Surveyors Award Scheme. The Chief Planner's ability to curb the encroachment of cars – the Transport Minister described Leicester as 'Smigielskiville' – was the prelude to the improvement of New Walk and the surrounding central area. Smigielski adopted shock tactics. He made what he described as 'a very rude speech' in 1967 about prosperous Leicester's lack of concern about its 'dilapidated, shabby, dirty, chaotic' environment. He observed the chicken wire around De Montfort Square and commented that 'town planning cannot be done by one man, but by a conscious and cooperative effort of the whole society'.[16] The modest expenditure of £25,000 by the city resulted in replacement lamps, seats, railings, paving, and by lifting the road blight property owners responded by repairing and repainting in approved colours so that the process of decline was reversed. New Walk, so nearly a defeat for conservation, was an object lesson in success. Most importantly, this success paved the way for Leicester's embrace of environmental issues, the greening of the city, the development of a 12-mile linear park along the valley of the River Soar begun in 1974, in Smigielski's last year. In addition to local legacies, Leicester also became Britain's delegate to the Rio summit on the environment in 1992.[17] However, though New Walk was a success it was short-lived and Smigielski's tempestuous personal relations with council officials, specifically over his efforts to preserve the Victorian Sun Alliance building in Town Hall Square, resulted in the resignation of Leicester's 'radical planning officer'. Never noted for being mealy-mouthed, Smigielski announced 'Leicester as Clochemerle' – an analogy with a small French town's stumbling bureaucratic attempt to build a public urinal.[18]

In some respects, Smigielski was fortunate. He inherited a programme of unprecedented housing clearances and new estate building, and a crisis in local industry in Leicester (see below). It was an environment, and a mood, that demanded change in the 1960s. However radical Leicester had been in social and intellectual terms in the nineteenth century it reinvented itself physically and culturally in the second half of the twentieth century. New Modern Movement buildings with their strong geometric shapes appeared during Smigielski's period in his newly created post as Chief Town Planning Officer (1962–74). The Modernist buildings included the City Council offices at New Walk (1971–75) – revised by Smigielski and described by Pevsner as 'a disappointing group of speculatively-built offices'[19] – the 'unexceptional' Haymarket Centre (1971–73); Lee Circle multi-storey car park (1960s); and

8.14 Lee Circle in the 1950s. The cleared area previously occupied by Lee, Alfred and neighbouring streets is visible in this aerial photograph from 1955 and which subsequently formed the site for the largest Tesco and the largest multi-storey car park in the UK.

Source: Leicester City Council.

8.15 New Walk Centre, Leicester City Council offices, 1971–75. Built speculatively as office blocks, 'there is nothing to distinguish these two 14-storey grey concrete blocks' (Pevsner), and demolished 22 February 2015.
Source: Leicester City Council.

8.16 Cornmarket and Market Place canopy, 1966–70.
Source: Record Office for Leicester, Leicestershire and Rutland, DE3736, Box 25, New Parks Estate.

8.17a Rowlatt's Hill flats and the surrounding low-level housing. Demolished 17 July 2013.
Source: Leicester City Council.

8.17b Victorian terraces of Highfields and low-rise inter-war housing and industrial building of North Evington compared with Rowlatt's Hill flats in the distance.
Source: Leicester City Council.

the Market Place canopy (1966–70).[20] Rising to 180 feet, the two council office blocks at Welford Place were accompanied by skyscrapers elsewhere in the city and redefined the otherwise low level townscape of Leicester – Telephone Exchange 275 feet; St George's Tower 269 feet; and the tower blocks of Merton, Oriel, Marston, Goodwin and Goscote Houses each of 21 to 24 storeys and between 220 and 230 feet. Elizabeth House with 60 flats, 151 feet seems almost modest by comparison. Unlike the clustered La Défense in Paris, or the Chicago Loop, or the City of London, Leicester skyscrapers were scattered and introduced an almost random and unplanned appearance for the city. The tower blocks of the St Matthew's, St Peter's Highfields and Rowlatt's Hill dwarfed their surrounding estates and, against the background of four deaths in a London skyscraper at Ronan Point, a backlash against tower block dwelling resulted.

The local economy

Paradoxically, one of the key strengths of Leicester's economic success, and unusual in British industrial history, was the persistence into the twentieth century of small-scale family owned businesses. This characteristic became its weakness during and after the Second World War. There were two reasons for this: conscription had denuded small firms of key workers; and the Concentration of Industry Scheme required a minimum level of production to qualify for government contracts. The diversity of Leicester – 'the city of a thousand trades'[21] – that had been an insurance against peaks and troughs in earlier times exposed it and its manufacturers to absorption into larger units of production after 1945. For a wartime emergency the arrangement functioned efficiently; in peacetime, when decommissioning industrial concentration took place, it was disastrous. This was because, firstly, many small firms simply did not restart due to the absence or age of family personnel and insufficient capital to invest in new plant; and, secondly, because new start-up firms were restricted by the Board of Trade in an effort to protect older businesses from competition. The effects of wartime and post-war policies were evident: in the hosiery industry in 1938, over 130,000 people were employed and by 1946 there were just 68,000.

Partly as a result of the decommissioning process and partly because Leicester knitwear and footwear firms lost contracts to foreign competition short-time working was introduced by well-established firms like Wolsey and Tomkins in the early 1950s. Sound business sense suggested mergers as a solution: by combining order books and re-tooling plant future profit-ability and employment prospects might be secured. This also presented opportunities for aggressive corporate take-overs, as in the case of Bentley Engineering. The sting in the tail, though, was that the Bentley family lost overall control when almost a quarter of its shares were stealthily acquired by another interest, Prince's Investments, a holding company that had

8.18 Bentley Engineering, Braunstone Gate, and at Parker Drive. This was one of more than 50 engineering firms in 1940 that built and supplied hosiery and footwear machines. In the 1960s Bentleys supplied an estimated 90% of British requirements for knitting machines. The firm eventually accumulated debts of £7 million and went into receivership in 1988.

Source: Colin Hyde.

8.19 Freeman, Hardy & Willis advertisement.

Source: Manufacturing Pasts, University of Leicester.

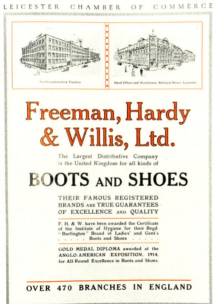

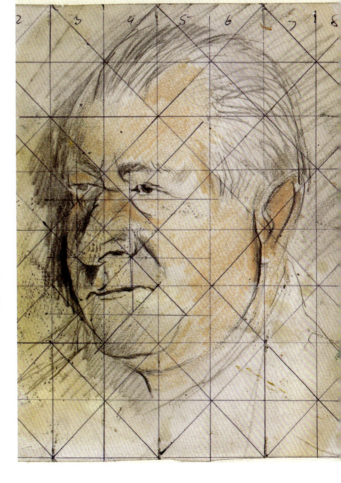

8.20 Sir Charles Clore (1907–79) owned British Shoe Corporation, Lewis' department stores, and Selfridges through his company, Sears Holdings. His trust, the Clore Foundation, is a major arts donor and supporter of Jewish community projects.

Artist: Graham Vivian Sutherland, pencil, crayon and biro, 1967. *Source*: © National Portrait Gallery, London.

also obtained control of J. Sears' (Tru-form Boot Co.) several factories and 900 retail outlets, and which owned 99% of Leicester's largest shoe manufacturer, Freeman, Hardy & Willis with its chain of 500 shops. By 1958, and after another spate of acquisitions, Sears Holdings owned the household names of Tru-form, Dolcis, Manfield's, Freeman, Hardy & Willis, Curtess, Character and Phillips Bros, and so controlled six manufacturing plants and 1,500 shops. Trading profits tripled to £3 million between 1954 and 1958 and a £30 million bid in 1962 brought Saxone and the Lilley & Skinner Group into the Sears' fold, together with two more Leicester factories. This, then, was the provenance of the restructured British Shoe Corporation with its 2,000 shops and warehousing at Braunstone. It provided the owner, Charles Clore, control over the previously independent British shoe industry in the space of fifteen years. Not content with this, Clore then used his financial power to buy the knitting machine-making firm of Mellor Bromley and so removed a major competitor to his original acquisition, the Bentley engineering interests. In this sense Clore's financial restructuring consolidated interests in footwear, hosiery and engineering and introduced an alarming shift in the industrial structure and pattern of retailing in Leicester by the 1960s.

By the mid-1960s Leicester industry seemed to be in free-fall. Just as the wartime Concentration of Industry Scheme did small industrialists no favours, so in 1960 the Board of Trade introduced a requirement that an Industrial Development Certificate was a pre-requisite for factory rebuilding. The high profile test case involved Fox's Glacier Mints and their wish to relocate as a result of a compulsory order to purchase their property. Their case was rejected despite the willingness of the City Council to agree to relocation. A Birmingham-based Board of Trade bureaucrat was immoveable. Government agencies, not local government, influenced many small and medium-sized firms – there were 272 firms considering relocation within the city in 1960. Fox's moved out; Whitbread's brewery just moved away – to Loughborough. By 1965 the Leicester Footwear Manufacturers' Association and the National Hosiery Manufacturers' Federation issued pessimistic statements about the future of their industries, and the columns of the *Leicester Mercury* carried stories of foreign competition, falling production and factory closures. New workflows were explored, including re-tooling to reduce labour costs by simplifying the number of stages in production; different materials were introduced, such as PVC for shoe uppers and linings, as well as better adhesives and stitching. Polyester fibres increasingly invaded the clothing industry and this required new investment and capital restructuring for many firms and by 1975, within not much

8.21 Fox's Glacier mints, advert 1954, insert to margin.
Source: private copy.

THE FINEST PEPPERMINT IN THE WORLD

FOX'S
Glacier
MINTS

| Leicester: a modern history

more than a decade, the fashion fad for circular spun polyesters was already in retreat. Increasingly, too, the advance of the multiples meant firms like Debenhams and Marks & Spencers were able through their purchasing power to cut manufacturers' margins. Altogether the complementary nature of industrial production that had insulated the Leicester economy was in double jeopardy.

Two serious and direct consequences of the restructuring of Leicester businesses from the 1970s were the rapid decline of the works social, sporting and cultural activities; and, the retreat of a manufacturing class and the self-employed from the public sphere. Business pressures and changing family structures adversely affected their ability to make contributions to elected council and voluntary arenas. Constrained by personal and employment conditions, the customary independent and radical voices of Leicester were also crowded out by the reform of local government in 1974 when a culture of thickening regulation was accompanied by a class of career administrators with ample professional qualifications but limited historical grasp of local circumstances. Trust between bureaucrats and the public was ruptured. Indeed, the term 'planner' was increasingly derided as wasteful and locally ill-informed. Nationally, the introduction of rate-capping (1985) and the poll tax (1989) employed the language of localism but yielded little of the necessary authority and financial independence to encourage urban regeneration. The 'block grant' algorithm used by Whitehall to assign central taxation to local councils was in reality a blocking grant in the 1980s that constrained the scope for independent action and in so doing handed the initiative for city-centre change to the private sector, rendering one High Street much like any other in the country. The personality of place was homogenised in the process, and Leicester suffered – like most cities.

Business amalgamations and town planning initiatives altered the complexion of Leicester. The partnership between public and private interests, between corporate and council, and the balance between voluntary and compulsory

8.22 Rate-capping demonstration, Town Hall Square 1985.

Source: Leicester City Council.

changed. As a result, Leicester was reinvented but with its independence and radicalism diminished though not extinguished. Beginning in the 1950s, new housing estates, cleared central sites, modernist architecture, a high-rise skyline, redesigned roads, and a shift in the local economy moved Leicester decisively away for from its century-long dependence on the knitwear and footwear formula.

Migration and the reinvention of Leicester

For some, familiar patterns of authority – at home and work, in schools and churches – were weakened as the 'swinging sixties' brought them face to face with modernity and new forms of popular culture and behaviour. For others, it was given a further fundamental, even uncomfortable, shock as substantial numbers of South Asian immigrants grafted their skills and capital on to the prevailing, if ailing, local economy. The availability of cheap properties with multi-occupancy potential was a further Leicester lure, particularly as these had been regarded in earlier decades as among the best-quality terraced homes in England. They were scheduled for demolition not because they had deteriorated in quality or had reached the end of their lifespan, but because they impeded the onward progress of the motor car. In Highfields and Belgrave terraced houses sold at less than £1,000 in the 1950s, blighted by the threatened intrusion of an inner-city ring road. The migrant's choice of Leicester was not one of chance, therefore, and its central position offered convenient and cheap travel to meet family members and village friends and relatives in other midland and northern towns.

The census term 'foreign born' might mischievously have been considered by Leicester folk to refer to nineteenth-century incomers from Northamptonshire or Warwickshire since residents originating from outside the British Isles were few in number. In 1881, the non-British born accounted for less than 1% of the Leicester population; of those 1% a third originated from North America, a fifth from India, and a tenth from each of France, Germany, Southern Europe and Australasia.[22] Few migrants from northern Europe, the West Indies or South America found their way to Leicester, and the influx of Irish had never been as numerous as in many towns and cities in Victorian Britain. Between the wars, little changed and even after 1945 it was more a matter of a different European composition. The European Voluntary Workers and Displaced Persons programmes brought Serbs, Ukrainians and Latvians to Leicester and locally their churches provided a community and cultural identity within the city, as did the Polish migrants at St Paul's Catholic church on the corner of Dale and Melbourne streets.[23] Poles came to Leicester in large numbers and accounted for one-seventh of the foreign born population in 1951 and 1961, before plummeting as Caribbean, then Asian and finally East African Asian migrants arrived in the city (Table 8.1) in very large numbers.

The 'Windrush' ship that docked in Tilbury in 1948 brought the first of many Afro-Caribbeans seeking work in Britain in the 1950s. A mostly Christian influx, they obtained manual jobs in transport, catering, and cleaning services and relatively few came to Leicester compared to the West Midlands and London. However, the Commonwealth and Immigration Act, 1962, sought to limit entry only to those whose passports had been issued in Britain; for others an additional voucher was required. Subsequent

Table 8.1   European and New Commonwealth
born populations in Leicester, 1951–1991

	European foreign born		New Commonwealth born	
	Total	%	Total	%
1951	3,705		1,178	
1961	3,920		2,815	
1971	4,275	1.5	23,280	8.2
1981	3,582	1.3	42,459	15.0
1991	3,005	1.1	43,348	16.3

Source: K. Burrell, *Moving Lives: Narratives of Nation and Migration among Europeans in Post-War Britain* (Aldershot 2006), 12.

Commonwealth Immigration legislation in 1968 and 1971 introduced further controls designed to limit numbers – those whose parents and grand-parents were born outside Britain were denied, and virginity tests were introduced for prospective brides. These were responses to a surge of immigration in the 1960s and reduced immigration to a trickle with the important exception of refugees from East Africa where Africanisation programmes, most notably in Idi Amin's Uganda in 1972, and also in Kenya, Tanzania and Malawi, sought to reduce the economic dominance that South Asians had acquired under British rule and expelled or pressurised them to leave.

One consequence of the South and East Asian immigration was a period of intense racial tension in Leicester – a 'whites' only policy in pubs; Ku Klux Klan inspired activities in Highfields; a 'no lettings' policy from landlords towards black and coloured students; and street demonstrations in the 1970s. The situation was not helped by Enoch Powell's inflammatory remarks, known subsequently as the 'Rivers of Blood' speech to the West Midlands Area Conservative group on 20 April 1968, which vehemently criticised Commonwealth immigration and anti-discrimination legislation. In Leicester tensions ran high. The city became a focus for confrontations between National Front, black and South Asian communities in the 1970s, and there were riots in Highfields in 1981, though this had as much to do with social injustice, deprivation and mistrust of the police.[24]

Seared in local memory is the strike in 1974 at Imperial Typewriters, the world-renowned factory with a typewriter brand name founded in Leicester originally in 1902 by Hidalgo Moya in partnership with the Leicester business dynasties of Chattaway and, later, in association with

Imperial Typewriter Co. Ltd.
Head Office and Works: LEICESTER, ENGLAND
Telephone: 27801 (5 lines)   Telegrams: "Typewriter, Leicester"

8.23 Imperial Typewriters, Leicester.
Source: Manufacturing Pasts, University of Leicester Special Collections.

Goddard and Evans. In 1974 discrimination by Imperial Typewriters against Afro-Caribbean and Asian employees, specifically over equal opportunities and pay, was complicated by the persistent refusal of the Transport and General Workers Union to allow the election of shop stewards. It was a copycat complaint of the dispute in Loughborough involving Mansfield Hosiery two years earlier and in Leicester it resulted in a 12-week strike of 370 of Imperial's 1,650 workers, 1,100 of whom were Asian.[25] Frustration led to 'ugly scenes' at Imperial's East Park Road factory when 150 sacked pickets confronted police; six Asians were subsequently found guilty of assault.[26] As G.S. Sanghera, the national secretary of the Indian Workers' Association, noted, 'Discrimination against coloured people is becoming institutionalised and there are no positive steps being made to remove discrimination.'[27] Eventually the Race Relations Board was involved, though not before another group of Leicester women at Kenilworth Components plastics factory successfully complained about their pay in what was a landmark achievement for Asian women. These were Leicestershire predecessors of the Grunwick dispute in Willesden, London, where in 1977 the predominantly Asian workforce in a film-processing firm were again victims of lower pay rates.

8.24 Leicester Strikers demonstration.

Source: Leicester Mercury, 13 May 1974.

The *Leicester Mercury* consistently focused on incidents related to racial conflict, and surveys in 1975 and 1978 among the white Leicester population concluded that there existed negative attitudes and a high degree of intolerance toward the Asian populations. To an extent this was understandable: some employment opportunities were taken by Caribbean and Asian immigrants, and as the Leicester Health Committee identified, with an immigrant population numbering between 14,000 and 16,000 in 1968, considerable strain was placed on its resources. Similarly, the Education Committee reported that, due to immigration, up to 80 new school places were required every month. Their American-style solution was to bus pupils to schools at Thurnby and Beaumont Leys, though the Education Minister, Ted Short, promptly prohibited this.[28]

South Asian settlement in the 1960s and 1970s was initially in the eastern inner-city area of Highfields previously colonised by European migrants and before that by fragments of the Leicester middle class. Large Victorian terraced houses already in need of repair and often sub-divided provided affordable accommodation within walking distance of the hosiery mills and new factories. To the north, the Belgrave area, already blighted by a proposed ring road and demolition planned for over 1,000 properties, provided large family accommodation for Sikh and Hindu families in the 1960s. By contrast, less numerous Pakistanis and the more recent Bangladeshi immigrants who were scattered across several city wards in the 1970s tended to converge during the 1980s on the central areas. By 1991 a quarter of Leicester wards had a white minority, most conspicuously in Spinney Hills ward where just 17.5% were from a white background.

Conversely, the Eyres Monsell and Braunstone council estates had only 1.9% and 2.8% respectively of their populations from Black minority ethnic groups. The spatial polarisation of 'us' and 'them' was captured in the term 'white highlands' – a specific reference to the dominance of whites in the outer council estates.

What was just as significant was the emergence of a spatial segregation defined by religion. The largest non-Christian religious group in 1983 were Hindus (62%), mostly concentrated in north Leicester; Muslims (18%) in the east central areas of Highfields increased by 220% between 1983 and 2001 in Spinney Hills and this vector became a largely self-contained and autonomous area dominated by Muslims. Sikhs constituted 17% of the religious affiliation of South Asian immigrants in 1983. It was not just the institutional structures of mosques and Muslim academies, temples and gurdwaras that defined an area. It was also the commercial structures associated with faith since Muslim families relied on Muslim lawyers, accountants and financial agents, and were the customers of Muslim builders, heating engineers, driving schools, banks and credit agencies. Estate agents sold principally to their sub-group, excluding others, and so reinforced the religious homogeneity and identity of the area. The process was replicated among Hindus and to a lesser extent among Sikhs. As the cultural and religious networks gained density and complexity so the areas became even more strongly associated with a spatial segregation. Where

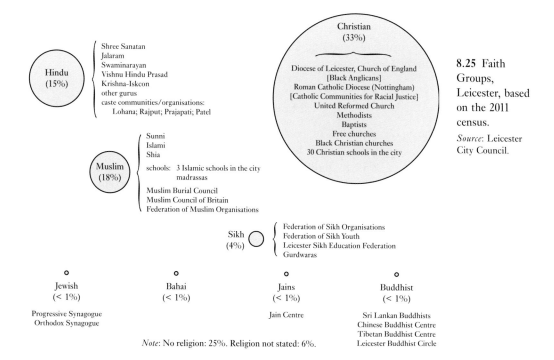

8.25 Faith Groups, Leicester, based on the 2011 census.

Source: Leicester City Council.

the English Catholic population of Leicester had once worshipped at St Paul's on Dale Street, boosted by a large post-1945 Polish congregation, the decline in worshippers by 2000 resulted in the church being deconsecrated and becoming a mosque.

The phases of immigration were highly concentrated. The main influx from India (138,000) and Pakistan (68,000) was between 1965 and 1974, although there were some arrivals post-partition in the 1950s; East African Asian immigration (25,000) between 1965 and 1967 was followed by another pulse (27,000) between 1967 and 1974; Bangladeshis (23,000) arrived between 1980 and 1984. Since the 1990s recent migrations in smaller numbers have included refugees from Bosnia, Iraq, Iran, Afghanistan, Turkey, Kurdistan, Somalia, Eritrea, Tamil-speaking Muslims from Sri Lanka, and Africans from Nigeria and Zimbabwe. Some 6,000–8,000 from the new European Union states arrived between 2004 and 2011. Immigrants from South Asia came to Britain from very specific places – Punjabi Sikhs from Jullunder Doab; Muslim Punjabis from Mirpir, Jhelum, Rawalpindi and Gujurat; Bangladeshis mainly from Sylhet.[29] In short, immigrants were connected more with districts, cultures, kin and commercial networks rather than with the nation state and that in part explains the clustering on arrival in British cities, Leicester included. In that sense the pattern was not very different to earlier migrations of Irish and Jews with their receiving networks, cultural and religious practices. Their orbit of social interaction functioned principally around the workplace and place of worship, but as employment became more fragmented and casualised the decline of the workplace as basis for sociability has resulted in greater emphasis on the 240 faith groups in the city, of which there were 36 Muslim mosques, 22 Hindu temples, 7 Sikh gurdwaras and one Jain temple. These and some of the 121 Christian churches have been the real magnets for Leicester migrants.[30]

The quality of Leicester

The main emphasis of post-war urban policy, nationally and locally, was unashamedly on volume housebuilding – Harold Macmillan's Conservative pledge in 1951 to build 300,000 new houses annually was trumped by Harold Wilson's and Richard Crossman's Labour Party commitment in 1965 to a yearly figure of 400,000. Treasury financial incentives encouraged the construction of multi-storey tower blocks in the 1950s and 1960s and Leicester acquired a modest number of these to adorn its skyline. However, a gas explosion in 1968 at Ronan Point in east London shook more than the tower block – faith in multi-storey housing was undermined.[31] This coincided with Crossman's concerns for the nature of development in historic towns and he commissioned a report which led within months to the Civic Amenities Act, 1967.[32] That Act enabled consideration to be given to groups of historic buildings – not just to a single structure – and placed a responsibility on Leicester City Council, as others, to review such buildings in their area:

> Every local planning authority shall from time to time determine which parts of their area … are areas of special architectural or history interest the character or appearance of which it is desirable to preserve or enhance, and shall designate such areas (hereafter referred to as 'Conservation Areas') for the purpose of this section.[33]

The result was that government provided modest grants to councils for townscape and conservation projects in the 1970s and 1980s, and encouraged property owners to repair their historic buildings.[34] It was indicative of a more flexible approach to the urban environment.

A greater awareness of historic buildings signposted an emerging policy theme: the quality of the urban environment. In some respects, Leicester was alert to this shift of emphasis under the Civic Amenities Act, 1967, through Smigielski's plans for New Walk, the cathedral/Guildhall area, and Castle each designated in 1969 as Conservation Areas, and the Victorian suburb of Clarendon Park assigned Housing Action Area status. Significantly, post-war planning, which operated initially at a city-wide level with Konrad Smigielski as its Leicester missionary, mutated to stress a different local or neighbourhood scale designed either to relieve or revive smaller areas such as Beaumont Leys Master Plan (1967) and Beaumanor Comprehensive Development Area (1971). Following Smigielski's resignation, John Dean as chief planning officer continued within a general planning framework under the Town and Country Planning Act, 1968, which increasingly recognised that local area improvement schemes provided a more nuanced scale of development.[35] This resulted in a rash of such local plans, including Vann

8.26 Local area improvement was increasingly recognised in plans of the 1970s and 1980s.

Source: private copies.

8.27 Walkers Crisps. The snack food company was founded in Leicester in 1948 and accounts for 58% of the crisp market (2014). The plant produces 11 million bags of crisps daily and uses about 800 tons of potatoes to do so.

Source: Leicester City Council.

Street Redevelopment Area (1974), Albion Hill-Belvoir Street Planning Policy (1976); Ross Walk (Belgrave) Improvement Zone (1984); Three Gates (Belgrave, Church, and Humberstone) Commercial Improvement Plan (1985); St George's Industrial Improvement Areas (1987); and East Hamilton Planning Brief (1987).

Though not planned as a local housing strategy the Conservatives' 'right to buy' legislation encouraged a privatised or 'stakeholder' mentality after 1980 as tenants were able to purchase their rented council homes on the basis of a generous discount amounting to 33–50% of the value of the house, capped at £25,000 discount.[36] Predictably there were council estates that proved more attractive – Eyres Monsell has the highest proportion of purchases of former council houses – and 'right to buy' proved divisive within individual estates as front doors, colour schemes, garages and window designs were introduced by the new private owners as marks of distinction. In the 1980s sales under the right to buy legislation averaged 750 yearly; in the 1990s the figure had fallen to an annual average of 350, and in 2011–12 sales were just below 100 with serious consequences for the City Council's Housing Department and its ability to find accommodation for those on benefits.[37] In a statement blind to both the origins of council housing (1919) and William Beveridge's welfare state proposals (1942) to counteract the five giants of poverty, Michael Heseltine, Secretary of State for the Environment, immodestly claimed that the 'right to buy' Act laid 'the foundations for one of the most important social revolutions of this century'.[38] The appeal – or bribe? – of a cash discount channelled to the Treasury rather than Leicester City Council was obvious. The decline of social housing in the city commenced; the policy limited the council's flexibility since tenant turnover was reduced, necessitating a return to new council house building in recent years.

Because of the local emphasis, Conservative regeneration schemes in the 1980s constituted a £4 billion patchwork of initiatives that included Enterprise Zones, Urban Development Corporations, Simplified Planning Zones, and City Grant. Where there were coordinating schemes, such as City Action Teams and Task Forces, these concentrated on a 'bricks and mortar approach'. It was an approach that drew withering condemnation from the Public Accounts Committee, forcing the Department of the Environment to commission a report in which the authors concluded that 'resources were channelled to areas with commercial potential' and that the poor 'largely stood by – very occasionally rebelling', subjected as they were to 'increasing unemployment, greater polarisation, and apparent intractability of problems in the worst areas'.[39] Nowhere was this more apparent than in the Urban Development Corporations where capital investment was directed towards regenerating buildings, an initiative that resulted in 'islands of renewal in seas of decay'.[40] The City Challenge programme (1991) and Single Regeneration Budget (1994) that emerged were precisely designed to provide a more coordinated and less wasteful response, and to reinstate local government involvement that had been largely by-passed by central government. In the event, City Action Teams and Task Forces gave central government even more control of local projects, and between 1990 and 1995 the overall level of urban funding was cut by 40% according to the Association of Metropolitan Authorities with the City Challenge programme in retreat from 1994.[41]

Inner-city riots around the country in 1981, and in Leicester, made it plain that merely replacing buildings was no guarantee of vibrant communities. The Conservative emphasis on urban regeneration and its focus on the built environment receded and by 1990 the policy priorities had switched to improvements in the social, cultural and environmental fabric of an area. In Leicester this took three forms: firstly, housing policies showed greater awareness of life-cycles, families, pensioner, disability and special needs; secondly, an environmental policy gave prominence to green issues, notably the linear Riverside and Watermead parks; and, thirdly, under the leadership of Peter Soulsby, Leicester with the 12th worst deprivation index of 55 urban districts successfully competed for City Challenge funding in 1992. Over £400 million was eventually secured for a strategic approach to revitalise defined areas based on partnerships with the private sector, the Health Authority, and the universities, and Leicester City Challenge Ltd was formed in 1993 to deliver the challenge of economic, social and cultural regeneration over a five-year period.[42]

The West End, Bede Island, and Raw Dykes Road areas of south-west inner Leicester contained 25% of the derelict land in the city; 15% of residents were unemployed and more than 50% of the households were in receipt of benefits; 66% of the households were not car owners in 1990. With excess through traffic, lack of open space, and a high proportion of private rentals the area was in urgent need of improvements to the quality of life. Creating new homes and jobs, increasing open and green space and access to training, and improving community facilities were the criteria for City Challenge cash. The area also included historic buildings, such as the iconic Pex and Liberty buildings, a waterfront, and aspirations within the city to build racial harmony, build on its reputation as Environment City, and to promote Leicester as a city of European significance. No longer were 'islands of renewal in seas of decay' acceptable. There were, of course, substantial phases of new construction, but a central element in the regeneration of the area was the involvement of local residents in the Bede Island Community Association (BICA), an umbrella organisation serving over 60 different local organisations and groups engaged in the regeneration process and updated through their newsletter, *The Challenger*. The integrated nature of planning in the area was on a scale never previously attempted in Leicester, and rarely elsewhere. Bede Park (0.77 hectares) opened in 1999 and was a pivotal development (8.28). It featured a plaza with seating around a central performance space, dog-free toddler and junior play areas, and one of the largest slides of its kind in Britain. Bede Park was developed close to extensive new and existing housing, with footpath and cycle ways linking it through the Great Central Way and Riverside corridors to the city centre. The park and its maintenance package with the Council's Environmental Services meshed with numerous council priorities framed by a Community Plan, a Local Cultural Strategy, and Landscape and Countryside plans. In 2002 Bede Park received a 68% approval rating in a neighbourhood survey.[43]

Bede Park, sandwiched between the River Soar and Grand Union Canal, was one of the most recent in a sequence of green spaces developed by the city that began in the 1880s when Abbey, Victoria and Spinney Hill parks provided over 80 acres of public parks on the fringe of the built-up area at that time.[44] Other major parks were added – notably Western (1899), Humberstone (1925), Braunstone (early 1930s) and Knighton (1953) and a spate of small park developments and play areas then infiltrated the densely packed streets to provide recreational space. The hierarchy of parks and gardens in 2013 includes one city park, two country parks, eight district parks, and 39 local parks and gardens within the city boundaries. From 1974 a 12-mile Riverside linear park of almost 1,000 hectares was developed from Bluebank Lock on the Grand Union Canal to Watermead Country Park in an innovative combination of ecological, historical and recreational interests. The north–south axis of the park provided a realistic alternative to a central park for Leicester. Simultaneously it provided a wealth of industrial heritage – coal wharves, gasworks, a pumping station, Stephenson's railway line to Swannington, mills and warehouses, as well as weirs, a medieval packhorse bridge, Victorian mileposts and parish boundary markers – and recreational

8.28 Bede Park.

Source: Leicester City Council, Parks and Recreation.

activities for rowers and runners, cyclists, dog-walkers, orienteering, and narrow boat enthusiasts. Leicester's Riverside Festival is centred on Bede Park with its arts and craft stalls, live music, food stations from around the world, and activities for all ages. As an experiment in social reconstruction Leicester's City Challenge project pointed a way forward, though whether it leveraged an economic regeneration remains doubtful.[45]

The 'quality of Leicester' was not confined to images of Leicester; there was substance, too.[46] Nowhere was this more evident than in the environmental dimension. The City Wildlife Group made a comprehensive study of habitats between 1983 and 1987, and with further advice from the Ecology Advisory Group, an empirical basis for environmental policies

8.29 HRH
Prince Charles'
statement, 1991.

Source: Leicester
City Council
development plan.

> **"I** *have been particularly interested and pleased to see the splendid progress being made here in Leicester under the flag of Environment City. I am impressed by all the people who have got together in such an energetic fashion to make it happen.* **"**
>
> ## H.R.H. Prince Charles
> ## November 1991

developed. These studies provided details of the land in Leicester, 35% of which was undeveloped in the 1980s, and the 189 miles of canals, rivers, streams, railway verges and hedges that were part of the city. What was more convincing was the detail: Welford cemetery supported 25 types of lichens on the gravestones, and 130 species of wildflowers – about the same number as disused allotments at Blackmore Drive, Braunstone. The ecological survey in the 1980s recorded that almost one-fifth of birds on the official British list were seen in land-locked Leicester; there were over 500 wild plant species, 27 species of mammals, and 23 butterflies in the city. To raise awareness of this rich biodiversity within Leicester the Watermead Bioblitz event (2010) was sponsored by seven different agencies, including BBC TV, and involved 1,600 members of the public recording the flora and fauna of Watermead over a 24-hour Bank Holiday Monday. The total of 653 species included 200 flowering plants, 85 species of moth, 149 invertebrates, 77 species of birds, and 44 lichens.[47]

Perhaps this was unsurprising since in 1990 Leicester was designated 'Environment City' by the Royal Society for Nature Conservation as a result of initiatives that included Riverside Park (1974), an Ecology Strategy (1986) and Eco-House show homes (1989). Two years later the city received an invitation to discuss local communities' contributions towards environmental sustainability, organised by the United Nations Conference on Environment and Development (UNCED) at the 'Earth Summit' in Rio de Janeiro.[48] Further local sustainability initiatives followed – kerbside recycling (1997); an audit scheme for environmental management (1999); 'Beacon status' (2001) for 'maintaining a quality environment' and for 'sustainable energy (2005); and 'Fairtrade City' status (2002). Progress on these and a raft of related sustainability initiatives resulted in Leicester advancing from 14th in 2007 to 2nd in 2010 in a sustainability league table comparing the twenty largest British cities. Driven largely by environmental factors, the economic and educational prospects reflect a much bleaker outlook for Leicester.

Table 8.2   Sustainable British Cities 2010: Leicester rankings (in brackets) compared to the 20 largest British cities*

Environmental performance indicators	Quality of life indicators	Future-proofing indicators
Air quality (18)	Employment (16)	Climate change (9)
Biodiversity (1)	Transport (3)	Local food (2)
Household waste (1)	Education (20)	Economy (5)
Ecological footprint (1)	Health (15)	Recycling (6)
	Green space (8)	

Note: ranking: 1 is high; 20 is low.

* Top ten overall rankings in 2010 were Newcastle (1); Leicester (2); Brighton (3); Bristol (4); London (5); Leeds (6); Coventry (7); Plymouth (8); Edinburgh (9); Sheffield (10).

Source: details of how the sustainability indicators were calculated can be found at http://www.forumforthefuture.org/project/sustainable-cities-index/overview

The comparative survey of sustainability concluded:

Leicester, in 14th place four years ago [2007], is second [in 2010] and leads on environmental performance. It has the lowest ecological footprint, produces the least household waste and is best at managing its biodiversity. It has a strong climate change plan, a high recycling rate and an emerging new business sector pursuing opportunities in sustainability and environmental management.[49]

The quality of Leicester, therefore, depended in no small measure on the environmental or Green Space Strategy that incorporates 1,250 hectares or one-sixth of the entire administrative area of the city. Of these green space areas, parks and gardens account for 31%; natural areas 24%; cemeteries, 'green corridor', and other uses 17%; informal open space 12%; outdoor sports 8%; allotments 7%; and children's play and young persons' areas 1%. Overall, the city has a generous 20% surplus of green space using the prevailing assumptions about needs, though this is a little misleading since ward boundaries and green space access bear little relation to one another and considerable inequalities exist between wards (8.30). For example, seven wards have no allotments; six have no parks and gardens; and Stoneygate, with the greatest deficiency of green space, enjoys the most generous of private gardens and, within a few hundred yards, access on three sides to Knighton and Victoria parks, and the Arboretum at Shady Lane. Some wards are in a state of equilibrium with the overall supply of green space roughly in keeping with population levels – as in the Freemen, Humberstone and Hamilton, Knighton, and Eyres Monsell wards – but

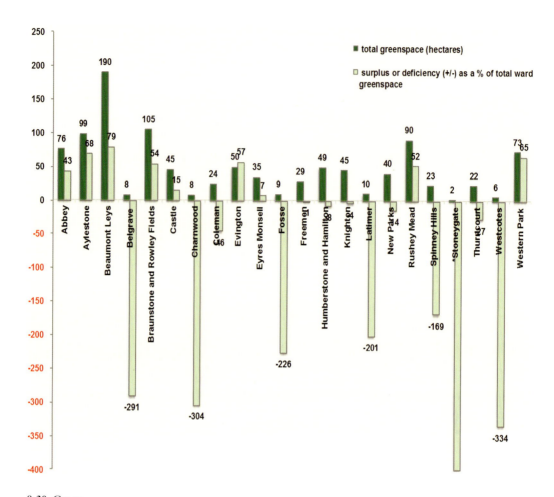

Legend:
- total greenspace (hectares)
- surplus or deficiency (+/-) as a % of total ward greenspace

8.30 Green Space by Ward, 2009. Note: Stoneygate ward: the deficiency relative to total existing green space is 3470%.

Source: Leicester City Council, Green Space Strategy (2009–2015), Appendix 1.

others have a deficiency of provision across all categories, as in Latimer, Westcotes, and Stoneygate. Generally, though it is Westcotes, Charnwood, Belgrave, Fosse, Latimer and Spinney Hills wards, in that order, that have disproportionately the greatest shortfall of green space, understandably because of their inner area location, dense population, and limited scope to create new parks.

The qualitative assessment of Leicester as a place to live is also directly associated with the built environment. Where particular historical or architectural interest exists then Conservation Area status is designated so strict limitations apply to proposed alterations or developments. Conservation Areas represent an investment in 'cultural capital' – desirable features that enhance the character of a neighbourhood and therefore cannot be reproduced – and may include some of the 350 buildings in Leicester listed by English Heritage as Grade II, that is, of national importance or of special interest. These areas (8.31) were first recognised in 1969 during Smigielski's period of office as City Planning Officer and then, in a flurry activity, over

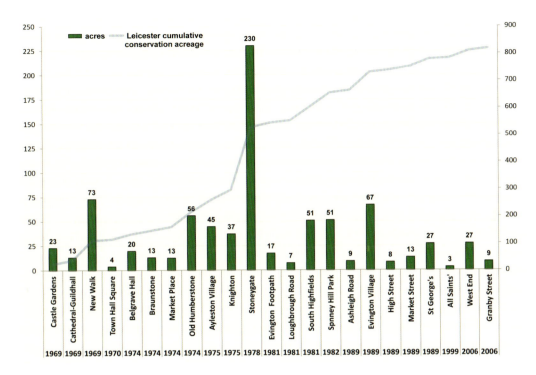

8.31 Conservation Area Status, 1969–2006 (acres). Note: Dates indicate when conservation status was approved, and numbers are the acreage of each area, rounded. Both vertical axes are in acres.

Source: http://www.leicester.gov.uk/your-council-services/ep/planning/conservation/conservationareas/
conservationareasleicester/

95% of Conservation Areas were designated between 1969 and 1989, and all together account for just over 11% of the Leicester area.[50] When the major district parks are included, accounting themselves for 9%, then over 20% of the Leicester administrative area is protected in ways that developers and planners alike must take into account.

The inequality of Leicester

In 1936 a League of Nations study observed that Leicester was the 'second most prosperous city in Europe'. By 2011, according to Office for National Statistics, Leicester was ranked the 12th most deprived unitary authority out of 348 in England. Tower Hamlets (13) and Wolverhampton (11) were Leicester's nearest statistical neighbours based on four major indicators. Put differently, in only 3% of major English administrative areas was deprivation worse than in Leicester. More specifically, in 2011 only one-third of Leicester households were not subject to some form of deprivation in one of the four dimensions: (i) unemployment; (ii) educational attainment (lack of 5 Grade GCSEs at C pass (8.32)); (iii) 'bad health' or a long-term health condition;

(iv) overcrowded or amenity-deficient housing. The consequence of this social deprivation meant that for Leicester men, though the probability of reaching the age of 75 improved from 45% to 60% between 1983 and 2007, compared to England overall the gap widened since the chances in the rest of the country of reaching 75 rose from 47% to 67% over the same period.[51]

The obvious conclusion is that the city lost ground nationally and internationally in terms of mortality and morbidity. Of course, the data for 1936 and 2011 are not directly comparable; the city can be both prosperous and have starkly different levels of wealth and poverty as seen in the incidence of deprivation between different wards and sub-districts. New Parks, Braunstone, Beaumont Leys, Spinney Hills, St Matthews and Saffron Lane estates were all in the 5% of most deprived areas in England; Stoneygate was in the top 3% of most affluent. So in 2011 although four out of five people in Latimer had some form of deprivation, in Knighton only one person in two did, and to a lesser degree (Table 8.3). Although the situation improved across Leicester wards between 2001 and 2011, other East Midlands towns made better progress in this respect. Perhaps of greatest concern is that three out of every five Leicester households is amongst the 30% most deprived in England – and three out of every four in the 40% most deprived.[52]

The pattern of deprivation in Leicester was not, as some might assume, simply associated with ethnicity; concentrations of poverty at the ward level do not correspond with patterns of ethnicity. In Leicester the proportion of Asians in the most deprived areas is not very different to the proportion elsewhere in the city, and is in stark contrast to Derby, Bradford and Preston, for example, where Asian deprivation in 2005 was almost seven

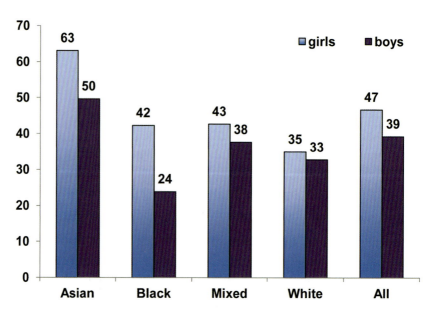

8.32 Leicester GCSE results: 5 or more A*–C passes, 2005

Source: Department for Education and Skills, http://www.dfes.gov.uk/rsgateway

Leicester: a modern history

Table 8.3   Deprivation* in selected Leicester wards, 2011 (%)

Areas	Not deprived in any dimension %	Household deprivation in			
		1 dimension %	2 dimensions %	3 dimensions %	4 dimensions %
Leicester	33	34	24	8	1
East Midlands §	43	32	20	5	0
Selected wards					
Spinney Hills	18	33	33	14	2
Latimer	20	33	33	12	1
Belgrave	23	33	31	11	2
Eyres Monsell	26	34	29	10	1
New Parks	26	35	28	10	1
Stoneygate	32	35	24	8	1
Evington	36	36	23	5	0
Aylestone	41	34	20	5	0
Knighton	53	31	13	3	0

* Dimensions of deprivation are indicators based on the four selected household characteristics: Employment (if any member of a household not a full-time student is either unemployed or long-term sick); Education (no person in the household has at least level 2 education, and no person aged 16–18 is a full-time student); Health and Disability (any person in the household has general health 'bad or very bad' or has a long term health problem); and Housing (the household's accommodation is either overcrowded, with an occupancy rating – 1 or less, or is in a shared dwelling, or has no central heating).

§ The figures for England and East Midlands are identical.

Source: ONS, Households by Deprivation Dimensions, 2011 (QS119EW)

times higher than in Leicester, and more concentrated geographically. Given that 34% of the Leicester population was born outside the UK, and 50% of the population and 57% of pupils in the Leicester school system are non-White in 2011 – a level three times greater than in Nottingham and Derby – there is no simple social deprivation correlation with ethnicity in Leicester. Indeed, the performance at Key Stage 2 and in GCSE exams by Asian and mixed race candidates was significantly better than that of White boys and girls.[53] As indicated by overall literacy rates (68%) and educational attainment levels (KS2 and GCSE) for Leicester, multiple deprivation is not exclusively associated with ethnicity.

Until they were incorporated into a composite benefit in 2013, Leicester claimants for Job Seekers, Lone Parent, Incapacity and Housing Benefit were all significantly above the national and regional averages, often by a third.[54] Two very sensitive measures of poverty – free school meals and infant mortality – showed one Leicester child in five provided with a free school meal and infant mortality 50% higher than the English average.[55] The net effect of these and other measures of poverty indicate that the gap in life expectancy between people living in Leicester and those in the rest of England has doubled in the last ten years and that there has been very little improvement for the most deprived segment of Leicester society since 2001.

Just as there is a hierarchy of educational attainment so there is with unemployment. In 2006 Leicester's white population had the lowest rate (2.3% unemployed); Asian, Asian British and Mixed Race were next (2.9%); non-White unemployed (3.4%); Black and Black British (6.3%); and other ethnic groups were most likely to be unemployed (8.0%). Where an ethnic element does exist in relation to deprivation it is within the Asian grouping since Pakistanis and Bangladeshis have higher unemployment rates and lower participation rates in the work force, and are more likely to be concentrated in the wards with greatest deprivation.[56]

Manufacturing matters

Fundamental to inequalities in Leicester was the nature of industrial performance. Employment in textiles as a percentage of the total manufacturing sector continued to decline from 38% to 29% and leather and footwear from 17% to 13% between 1950 and 1964. The industrial malaise was arrested to some extent by growth in the engineering trades from 32% to 40%, and unemployment was cushioned by an increase in office-based work where the levels of Leicester rents and taxes in the 1970s and into the 1980s were well below those of most major cities.[57] However, Leicester was not exempt from the downward spiral of manufacturing which nationally

> ... fell back by 17% in the 1970s, as manufacturing employment in Britain as a whole fell by a quarter (1.9 million jobs altogether). Much of this was concentrated in the period 1979–81 (when 1.2 million jobs were lost) and linked to the stringent policies of the government towards exchange rates and interest rates which made it very difficult for manufacturers to compete abroad and induced a deep recession across the country.[58]

In Leicester, the tell-tale sign of industrial depression was that vacant industrial floor space increased to about 1.75 million square feet in the mid-1980s.[59]

Nationally, the manufacturing sector fell from 30% of all employment in 1981 to 21% in 1991, and to 18% in 1996; in crude numbers, it had fallen from 6 million to 4 million between 1981 and 1996. The rate of decline was greatest in the conurbations – Liverpool, Sheffield, Glasgow and Manchester, suffering most, in that order.[60] However, Leicester, among the provincial

210 | Leicester: a modern history

cities, between 1981 and 1996 experienced a 35% decline in manufacturing employment in contrast to a decline of just 4% in total employment (figure 8.7). Nearby, Nottingham, with a similar production structure, shrank by much the same in its manufacturing sector but expanded its overall employment by 12% in the same period; Coventry suffered a contraction of over half its manufacturing employment in the fifteen–year period, and an shrinkage of 10% in total employment. In short, a third of manufacturing workers in Leicester were laid off in a fifteen–year period, 1981–96, and a further third laid off in the thirteen years, 1995–2008.[61] The towns and cities of the North were not the only ones enduring steep industrial decline.

The phenomenon of inequality and the multiple deprivation on which it was founded had more to do with the nature of the labour market and the decline of industry than with ethnicity or any other single factor. In Leicester the decline in manufacturing took place at precisely that moment in time when immigration was at its greatest; it was the least propitious time to be a new entrant to the labour market, whether black, Asian or white. It is easy, therefore, to understand why kinship networks maximised cultural

8.33 British United Shoe Machinery Company's 25-year service certificate to E.R. Johnson, August 1963. This type of recognition soon became a thing of the past.
Source: British United History Group.

8.34 Apprenticeships at BU and other Leicester companies were in decline from the 1960s.
Source: British United History Group.

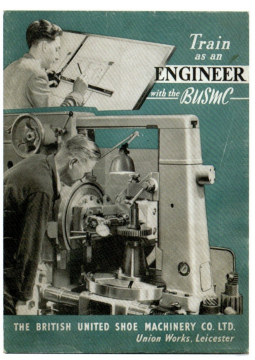

capital to improve work opportunities irrespective of whether the jobseekers were immigrants, refugees, white lads with low educational attainments, or students who had completed a degree and returned to the family home and the bank of mum and dad. The matrix of work and poverty, wealth and health, were defining factors in terms of multiple deprivation.

The implosion of manufacturing in the last three decades has been particularly serious because of three related characteristics. Firstly, manufacturing provides indirect contributions to other parts of the economy through its extensive linkages and spillovers; secondly, it is a sector that has relatively high employee incomes; and thirdly, disproportionate export earnings from manufacturing add greatly to the significance of the sector.[62] Indeed, manufacturing has indirect effects at the urban and regional scales beyond the immediate and direct contributions to the economy because 'the more advanced or modern the production process, the longer and more complicated the chains of linkages'.[63] There is, then, a qualitative and a quantitative dimension to manufacturing that is not matched in terms of multipliers by service and commercial activities. Leicester's engineering sector emerged from the demand for tool-making and machine building to enhance the productivity and profitability of the hosiery and footwear interests. This emphasis on engineering skills and knowledge-rich local economies was a crucial element in the ability of many British towns and cities to diversify production, limit risk, and move seamlessly into related areas of production

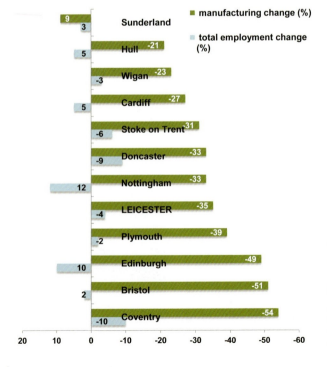

8.35 Changes in Manufacturing and Total Employment, 1981–96 (%).

Source: Adapted from I. Turok and N. Edge, *The Jobs Gap in British Cities* (Bristol, 1999).

in the twentieth century.[64] In short, manufacturing added long-term value in wages, human interactions in the workplace, and developmental potential through linkages with cognate areas of production and service. In addition, it has been argued that manufacturing historically provided the main source of manual jobs in the city, and that this enabled those individuals to make an important contribution to the local economy. The inability of Leicester, like most British cities, to find suitable manual employment for a workforce, and particularly a male workforce, who previously would have been employed in manufacturing remains an on-going source of inequality and social deprivation.[65] For all these reasons, the notion that an advanced economy can abandon manufacturing as a primitive form of wealth creation is a myth, and misleading.

8.36 Interdependencies: industry was embedded in the housing estates around Blackbird Road and Parker Drive, with racing and betting associated with a greyhound track (opened 1923), and a motorcycle dirt-track constructed within it (1928). The Stadium also hosted side car and stock car racing.
Source: Leicester City Council.

The future of the past –
conservation and the twenty-first-century city

Leicester citizens elected Sir Peter Soulsby to a four-year term in the mayoral election of 2011. In a pledge reminiscent of an earlier Labour election theme of 'joined up government', Soulsby's platform firmly embraces the theme of 'Connecting Leicester'. In his own words, 'some developments in the city, such as the ring road, have created barriers that make it difficult for people to move from one area to another and enjoy all the exciting things Leicester city centre has to offer'.[66] The legacy of the omnipotent car has cast a long shadow over Leicester's central districts. So 'Connecting Leicester' seeks 'to greatly improve connections between key places within and next to the city centre'. That vision relies on interconnections between shopping, leisure, heritage, transport and housing linked by means of pedestrian routes through the city. Where central city sites were either pockmarked in the 1960s and 1970s by planned demolition programmes or lined by ghostly warehouses and factories vacated by defunct firms now the vision is to retain, renew and reconnect Leicester folk with their past. This vision has a drive and a direction and replaces a previous elusive logo – 'One Leicester'.

What is Leicester like? How do people describe it? Some think it has an image problem, in the sense that there is not one. Is the recent discovery of King Richard III really sufficient and desirable to identify Leicester, and is it wise to link the destiny of a city to some partially understood persona; Simon de Montfort was hardly the best ambassador; 'Robin Hood Country' has not been an unambiguous success for Nottingham; and Warwickshire's 'Shakespeare's Country' is problematical too. When asked 'Where are you from?' does anyone proudly reply: 'I'm from Robin Hood Country.'

So in this second part of *Leicester: A Modern History* the authors explore different aspects of Leicester as a means to understand its qualities and characteristics. Ritual and ceremony, clubs and societies, home life, the battle over an iconic statue, imaginative planning ideas, Asian communities, popular music, and healthcare provision all figure as a means of understanding the personality of Leicester – individual, civic, and associational.

Jack Simmons, historian and an 'incomer', described Leicester as 'unromantic' with 'nothing that catches your eye' and 'the most midland of all Midland towns'. Konrad Smigielski characterised Leicester as a typical provincial English city, architecturally not very interesting 'but behind the unimpressive façades Leicester is not a Florence but there is a willingness to accept new ideas, with religious, political and racial tolerance'. How apt. Leicester: radical, independent, tolerant – that is what characterised Leicester residents in the nineteenth century. These were the qualities Mayor Edward Wood identified in presenting Leicester's case for city status to Queen Victoria in 1889 and, as the centenary of Leicester's city status approaches, it is important to remember how confident, though not complacent, Mayor Wood was about Leicester's achievements over the preceding generation. Queen Elizabeth II's choice in 2012 to begin her Diamond Jubilee visits in Leicester could not conceivably have been accidental; it denoted a distinctiveness about the city, and that place-making is about values and ideals not buildings alone.

So though Leicester's motto, 'Semper eadem' ('always the same') seems most inappropriate when the focus is directed towards the ever-changing built environment, it could not be more appropriate when the focus is on the values and ideals – the moral environment – exhibited by Leicester folk since 1800. Radical, independent, and tolerant are the qualities of Leicester that in the twenty-first century will assist the city towards a high quality of everyday life for every citizen.

9

The transformation of home?

Hₒₘₑ has an essential role in people's lives and a person's experiences of home affects other areas of their life. It is also important in the life of the city because housing 'accounts for more than half of the total land use.'[1] Over the centuries what 'home' meant and how its inhabitants experienced it have changed constantly, but many aspects of home life we now take for granted emerged during the period 1880–1970. This chapter therefore has two main aims. The first is to examine the experience of home for Leicester people between the 1880s and the 1960s and to assess how these experiences were influenced by the material and spatial attributes of the home (size, layout, amenities and location), and by the social and economic profile of the inhabitants. The second aim is to address the issue of the transformation of homes, drawing out both the changes and continuities in domestic life during the period.

This chapter focuses on the following attributes of home: house size and the way in which people used domestic space; amenities and utilities and the impact that their absence or presence had on domestic experiences and routines; the contribution which various members of the family made to household chores; and different forms of domestic entertainment. There are many aspects of home life which this chapter does not cover. For example, family relationships are not considered; nor are domestic activities which occurred around the home, such as gardening, playing on the streets, or shopping.

The main sources for the chapter are autobiographical and oral reminiscences of some thirty Leicester people which provide revealing insights into the viewpoint of the home-dweller. Reminiscences allow us to understand in more nuanced ways how people from different periods and different backgrounds behaved while they were 'at home'. When using memoirs of home life it is important to bear in mind the impact of age on experiences of home. People are frequently more positive about their childhood home than their adult home, and this is partly because children do not notice their material environment as much as adults and are less likely to be critical about home. However, there were adults happy with their domestic circumstances just as some individuals had unhappy childhood memories.

The chapter begins by providing details of types of dwelling which were popular in Leicester and how house form and housing standards were

9.1 *(opposite)* Highcross Street, mid-Victorian back courts.

Source: Record Office for Leicester, Leicestershire and Rutland.

217

affected by the location of a dwelling within the city. House form, in terms of its size and layout, was an important factor in the experience of home as well as in its transformation during the twentieth century. The chapter then goes on to consider amenities the dwelling had to offer and the utilities that were available at different times during the period. Finally it finishes with an examination of time spent in the home both in terms of housework and domestic leisure.

9.2 Plan of two houses for Mr J. Stevens, Walnut Street, 1873.

Source: Record Office for Leicester, Leicestershire and Rutland, 4091, 1873.

9.3 Plan of two houses on Welland Street/ St Peter's Road, 1880.

Source: Record Office for Leicester, Leicestershire and Rutland, 13865, 1880.

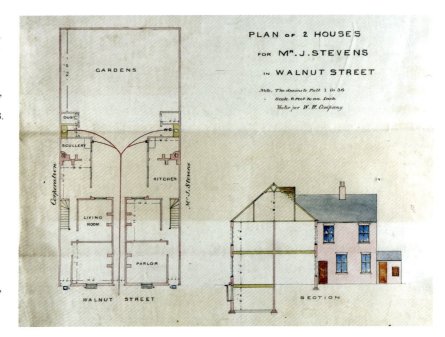

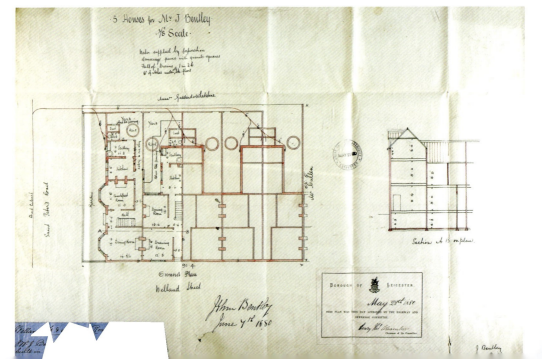

9.4 Plan of semi-detached dwellings on Baden Road: (*below*) front elevation; (*right*) ground floor.

Source: Record Office for Leicester, Leicestershire and Rutland, 19698, 1915.

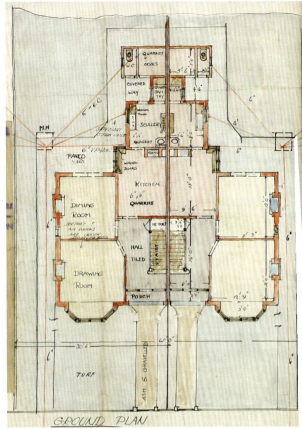

9.5 Plan of 20 proposed semi-detached dwellings on Stanley Road, 1934.

Source: Record Office for Leicester, Leicestershire and Rutland, 46059, 1934.

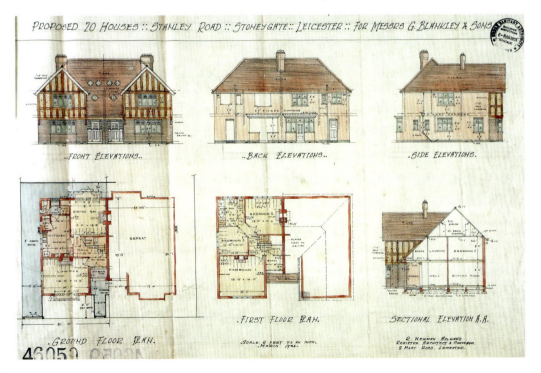

The transformation of home? | 219

House types and plans in Leicester

The dwelling types available to Leicester people between 1880 and 1970 had a substantial impact on living conditions. Little house building took place during the two world wars so the main phases of house building in the period covered here were between 1880 and 1914, 1919–1939 and 1945–1970.

In the 1860s, Leicester's rapid population increase resulted in the construction of around 35,000 houses between 1871 and 1911. This relatively late expansion of the town meant that its homes were of a better quality than those in towns which had industrialised earlier, such as Birmingham, Nottingham and the northern textile towns. Leicester's terraced houses were largely 'through' type, having a front and back entrance (that is not back-to-back) and with generally at least four or five rooms and often more, as in figure 9.2.[2] This had an impact on living conditions because there was more space and better ventilation than in earlier nineteenth-century workmen's homes.[3] The kitchen or scullery was nearly always located at the back of the house or was the furthest room from the front door in houses sited on street corners (9.3). The largest and most ornate room was closest to the front door and faced the street. These houses formed new 'suburbs' on the edge of the town such as in Highfields, the West End, Belgrave Road area and Clarendon Park.

These nineteenth-century dwellings continued to dominate the Leicester landscape well into the twentieth century and remained the main form of housing until 1945. However, building did take place in the inter-war period, and these homes differed from their nineteenth-century counterparts. An important change was the introduction of state-funded housing as a result of the Addison Housing Act of 1919 and most council houses (as opposed to flats) were built with three bedrooms, a bath of some kind, and a garden.[4] Leicester Corporation built 9,000 council homes during the inter-war period and aided the construction of 3,000 more. However, this was a far smaller number than neighbouring Nottingham which built almost 17,500 council homes in the same period and thus Leicester depended more on privately constructed homes. Private housing frequently took the form of suburban 'semis' of the kind featured in figures 9.4 and 9.5. In these, the kitchen continued to be located at the back of the house but was often a smaller 'working' kitchen. The drawing room or 'lounge' was either at the back or front of the house and there was generally a small third bedroom over the hall. The earlier floor plan from 1915 is a hybrid between the inter-war and nineteenth-century floor plans.

The next main phase of building occurred in the 1950s and 1960s. Throughout Britain during the 1940s, there was a desperate need for housing. Although Leicester had lost hardly any homes to bomb damage, little building had taken place during the war while the population had continued to increase. In 1946, it was estimated by Leicester's Housing

Department that 10,000 homes were needed immediately and 56,000 in the longer term.[5] While some post-war estates were located on the edge of town as had been the practice in the 1920s and 1930s, such as New Parks (1940s and 1950s), Stocking Farm (1950s) and Beaumont Leys (1970s), others were now constructed closer to the centre in 'slum' clearance areas. St Matthew's estate, for example, was built during the late 1950s on a cleared area to the north-east of the city centre. This estate consisted mainly of maisonettes and flats which diverged further from nineteenth-century floor plans as illustrated (9.6). The kitchens might be either at the front or back of the dwelling and the 'front room' and dining room were replaced with a 'living room'. Later in the 1960s two tower blocks were added to the estate, as was the case with other estates but, compared with towns such as Birmingham, Leicester's council homes were in the main low rise.

However, it was not just the period when the house was built which had a substantial impact on the layout and size of the home, but also in what part of town, and even on what kind of street within a district, it was located. This was especially the case for nineteenth-century housing. In St Margaret's, constructed between the 1830s and 1860s, houses on the main streets were more substantial than those on side streets which in turn were larger than the courtyard housing. Dwellings on the main streets had higher status because of their size and location. The plans for two houses on the corner of Welland Street and St Peter's Road, Highfields (9.3), illustrate this point well; the rooms in the house which fronted on to Welland Street, the

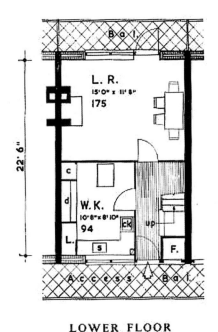

LOWER FLOOR   **UPPER FLOOR**

9.6
St Matthew's maisonette floor plan. These 4-person, 2-bedroom flats had a floor area of 675 square feet (approx. 80 square metres). Upper flats were accessed from a common staircase and a projecting balcony; lower flats were accessed through a small private garden.

Source: Ministry of Housing and Local Government, *Flats and Houses* (1958), 108, figure 97.

The transformation of home? | 221

side street, are smaller. In Highfields there were many substantial villas for better-off families as well as smaller houses on the side streets. After 1945 the larger houses were increasingly turned into lodgings and bedsits and rented by Polish immigrants.[6] In the 1950s they became inhabited by Pakistani and Indian migrants who, once they had been joined by their families, moved to terraced housing vacated by established Leicester residents. The latter took up the opportunity to move to new council estates, a move for which many migrants did not qualify under Corporation rules.

Space and room usage

9.7 Evington Hall interior: (a) sitting room and (b) billiard room. In upper-middle-class homes, such as that of an elastic web manufacturer John Faire in Evington, house size allowed for even greater room specialisation.

Source: private copy, Richard Faire.

House plans are useful in providing an idea of the layout of the house and space available, but they tell us little about how people actually used the rooms, the names they gave to them, and what they felt about their domestic space. As would be expected, class and income were important in determining the level of space in the home and the way it was used. In working-class homes, the kitchen or living room was the central living space and consequently used intensively. George Smith, born in 1919 on Chestnut Street, explained, 'The living room was just that – a living room – where all activities took place.'[7] These activities often included cooking, but washing-up was generally done in a 'back kitchen' or 'scullery', especially in pre-1914 housing. Positive feelings about the kitchen or living room usually reflected positive feelings about family life. Room usage was more specialised in middle-class homes, at least until the 1950s, as Kenneth Ellis observed about his home on New Walk in the 1890s. The kitchen was for the maids and had a separate entrance, while the family had the choice of three sitting rooms, a dining room, a drawing room, and a breakfast room.[8]

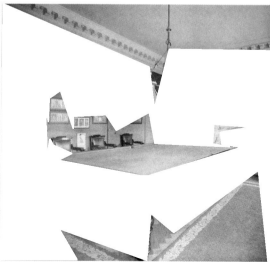

9.8 Loughborough Road house. Servants were summoned by interior bells, which also reflect greater room specialisation, in middle-class homes.

Source: Colin Hyde.

9.9 Stoneygate Court, interior, London Road. Built in the 1930s these substantial flats housed the middle classes and were affordable due to low mortgage interest rates and steady jobs during the Depression.

Source: Record Office for Leicester, Leicestershire and Rutland.

Parlours, or front rooms, were found in lower-middle-class and working-class homes and had a different function from middle-class sitting rooms, at least until the 1940s. For example, they were often only used on special occasions. Roy Battsion lived in inter-war North Evington, and remembered that the fire was only lit on Christmas Day and Boxing Day: 'It was always kept as a special room.'[9] Front rooms were 'special', largely for adults who wanted a place of retreat or a best room for invited (and especially) uninvited

The transformation of home? | 223

guests.[10] They acted as a barrier between the family's living space and the outside world. A resident of the Walnut Street area provided a description of their 'front room'. It had 'a sofa, two easy chairs, we had a side-board in there and an aspidistra ... the biggest aspidistra in the world. They [the aspidistra] used to be ever so popular, I mean, nearly every house had one.'[11] Not all families had a parlour. Those living in smaller nineteenth-century housing with one or two rooms downstairs generally had to do without and some inter-war council houses also had none. After the Second World War, not only were council homes increasingly built without front rooms, but improved heating, rising incomes, and the arrival of television in the home all increased front room usage and turned it from a best room into one that was used every day.[12]

In Leicester, bigger houses and lower family size meant that overcrowding became less of a problem in the last decades of the nineteenth century. However, for large families among the lower middle and working classes, sleeping arrangements were often cramped. Several siblings, as in Roy Battison's inter-war North Evington home, shared bedrooms. Roy was one of ten and two of his brothers shared one big bed in the back room and there was a double and two single beds in the middle room: 'it was a matter of top and tail in the beds,' but '[w]e managed it anyway.' His parents had the front bedroom to themselves but other parents were less fortunate.[13] This contrasted with Kenneth Ellis' 1880s home where there were 'adequate bedrooms' on the first and second floor and an upstairs sitting room just for his two brothers. Although some council homes were built with four bedrooms, pressure on bedroom space was eased more by falling household size throughout the twentieth century: in 1911 the average *family* size in Leicester was 4.1 persons compared with an average *household* size of 3.1 in 1951 and 2.9 in 1971.[14]

Amenities

The age of the home determined to an extent the amenities present in it and absence of certain facilities generated particular routines and experiences within the home. The introduction of piped water into the majority of homes was the greatest improvement in housing during this period and it allowed for a number of other important transformations – hot taps, baths and the flushing toilet.

Leicester's water supply only really became sufficient for its population in 1911. In the 1880s, many people shared taps and even in 1951 around 15% of Leicester households shared a water supply and nearly 3% had none. Shared taps were generally found in courtyards where they were shared between the homes facing on to the yard. This situation was transformed in the 1950s so that by 1961 only 2% of households were sharing, which was almost identical to the national average at this time. Access to a hot water tap was recorded by the census only from 1961, denoting its low priority before then. At this point nearly 30% of Leicester homes lacked a hot water tap – nearly 8% higher than the national average – but by 1971 this figure had fallen to 10.5%.[15] From 1951, the census also recorded the number of homes with a fixed bath: 53% of Leicester households had sole use of a bath. This figure included baths located in rooms other than bathrooms and it included baths without taps. By 1971 84% had baths or showers, all of which had their own water supply. The 1960s was thus a decade of substantial change for bathing experiences, too. These figures underline that for a certain section of the population the transformation of home was a long process which stretched well into the second half of the twentieth century.

Table 9.1   Households entirely without or
sharing a facility in 1951 (%)[16]

	Piped water[a]	Cooking stove[b]	Kitchen sink[c]	Water closet[d]	Fixed bath[e]
Leicester	18	9	12	18	47
Nottingham	13	8	9	11	50
Birmingham	17	11	12	22	46
Sheffield	10	7	6	12	49
Manchester	13	8	8	10	41
Leeds	10	6	4	32	33
London	31	8	16	35	62

[a] Inside tap either from tank or mains.

[b] Any type of cooking stove, range or fixed grate using gas, electricity or other kind of fuel provided it had an oven.

[c] Inside the house with a drain to the outside. It did not need to be in the kitchen nor have piped water. Basins 'for personal use' were excluded.

[d] It had to flush by water into a sewer or cesspit using a cistern or by hand.

[e] A permanent fixture anywhere in the home with a waste pipe to the outside. It was still counted even if the bath lacked any piped water.

Leicester Corporation terminated its night cart collection in 1895, and the shift from earth to water closets was completed around the same time that Nottingham Corporation passed a law instructing all new dwellings to have flushing toilets. In the 1880s for the overwhelming majority of Leicester residents the WC was located outside and often shared. Early council housing continued the practice of the external WC and in the Coleman Road estate houses built in 1919, the WC was accessed through an external lobby. New middle-class homes built at the same time had external WCs often supplemented with an upstairs WC (see figure 9.4b and c). The different location of the WC in middle-class and working-class houses reflects the assumptions of architects and local authorities about working-class standards of hygiene: external WCs had more ventilation. However, plans for parlour-type council housing produced by the Ministry of Health in 1918 and intended for better-off working-class families, did include an upstairs WC. The 1951 census found that 17% of households in the city shared WCs but this had fallen to around 6% in 1971. The concern shifted therefore to households lacking an internal WC and the 1971 census recorded that over a quarter of households had access only to an external WC.

Although these figures give us an idea of the access to amenities, or lack of them, over the period, they tell us little about how this affected the experience of home, nor how people used the facilities once they acquired them. An external tap in a yard caused many problems for its users. Water had to be carried into the house when needed and was often stored in a bucket under the 'sink'. In winter, braving the elements was another drawback and the pipe easily got frozen. William Abbot explained how he would defrost the water pipe in the morning before filling the kettle. One way round this problem, he noted, was to fill the kettle the night before, something that, as a boy, he generally forgot to do. William's home did possess a sink in the 'kitchen' but it lacked taps.[17] The majority of homes in Leicester did have their own tap which was located in the scullery or kitchen (the names given to the rooms varied much more widely before the 1960s).[18] Gerald Morris' home in the 1910s had two different sources of piped water: the ordinary piped water and a pipe connected to a rain-water tank on the coal place roof which was used when washing clothes.[19] Rainwater was also collected in pits or 'wells' in Clarendon Park gardens.

While the outside WC was considered more hygienic by architects of council homes, memories of external toilets suggested there was little to recommend them. In winter they were cold, dark and draughty because of the 'good' ventilation and absence of lighting. Mrs Allen remembered her North Braunstone WC freezing in winter.[20] Children often found the trip to the WC at night terrifying especially if it was some way from the house. Distance generated other problems: 'imagine how quick we had to run if we had tummy trouble!'[21] Thus in homes with outside lavatories, it was standard practice to use a chamber pot at night. Perhaps one of the few benefits of the external WC was that it provided a place for peace and quiet in homes that were often overcrowded. Children would choose the WC as a place to read books while fathers often read the newspaper there on Sunday.

Sharing a WC had its own particular experiences. The houses most likely to have shared toilets were situated in courtyards in pre-1870s areas such as St Margaret's and Wharf Street. This meant walking across the shared yard and it could involve quite a trek: 'You had to go down this yard, right down that yard, round again and round into the toilet. There would be many a night I took a candle holding my hand round it, stop it going out 'cos it were so dark …'[22] Sharing the WC caused a great deal of embarrassment: people disliked the fact that others in the yard could see that they were going to the toilet, and there would often be someone waiting outside. Albert Hall (born 1907), who lived in Fleet Street Terrace where there were two toilets between eight houses, recalled 'there was always conflict about the state in which they were left' and this led to another problematic feature of deciding whose turn it was to clean it: 'The two neighbours were supposed to take it in turns but my mother used to do it most of the time. She used to scrub that seat. It were one of them wooden seats, you know.'[23]

It is easy to assume that once people acquired indoor WCs they immediately started to use them in the same way we do today. This was not the always the case. In Phyllis Orange's home on Southgates the outside WC 'wasn't used as such'.[24] In a detailed description of the rooms in her home, she does not mention another WC. Later in the 1920s, Michael Green's parents continued to use chamber pots at night even though they had an upstairs WC: 'They were distressed that my brother and I scorned chamber–pots and insisted on going to the bathroom.'[25] His parents claimed that practice was 'hygienic', but Michael considered their behaviour as 'old-fashioned even by standards of the time'. It was by no means 'old-fashioned' in the many homes that still lacked an indoor lavatory at this time. Furthermore, although the claims to hygiene sound thin, it was not impractical: at a time when few houses had central heating, using a chamber pot could be far more pleasant than a chilly walk to the WC.

Water was mainly heated on the stove, fire or range. The range, introduced by the late nineteenth century into the majority of homes, transformed cooking and heating of water since it had an integral boiler and an oven. The acquisition of hot water was a significant change in people's lives, especially when attached to a bath. The first fixed baths in Britain appeared in wealthy homes from the 1840s but were not found in most homes until the 1880s or later. These bathrooms often had no hot water supply.[26] Certainly in Leicester the middle classes were acquiring bathrooms in the 1880s: plans for an extension to a house on New Walk from 1880 consisted of a bathroom with WC plus a separate WC on the first floor.[27] Less wealthy middle-class families living in older parts of town were still without bathrooms at the turn of the century. None of the ten rooms in Phyllis Orange's home was a bathroom, and they bathed once a week in a tin bath in front of the kitchen fire. The residences erected in the last two decades of the nineteenth century in areas such as Clarendon Park and Highfields were more likely to have a fixed bath in a bathroom than houses built before the 1880s, but there were still many without one. Eric Tolton, who lived in Highfields in the 1930s, explained that having a bathroom was 'quite unusual for those days really'.[28]

It was during the inter-war years that homes with fixed baths became available for working-class families in large numbers. The Tudor Walters

Report (1918) set the standards for early local authority housing and it recommended three house plans: one with an upstairs bathroom; one with a downstairs one; and one with a bath in the scullery.[29] The 1923 Housing Act made baths a requirement and by 1924 these had to be located in a bathroom.[30] The Act was aimed at private building but houses for the lower middle classes were already being built with bathrooms at this time. This is illustrated by the 1915 plans for infill houses on Baden Road seen in figure 9.4c.

The acquisition of a bath or bathroom was greeted enthusiastically. Elsie Sutton appreciated the bathroom in their Saffron Lane council house. The bath did not have taps but was filled by water heated by a copper, located under the kitchen draining board, which then had to be pumped into the bath. This arrangement lasted for years and Elsie praised the fact the pump never broke.[31] This system seems to have been common for inter-war council housing and was used on the Braunstone Estate, too. The system was not popular with all tenants: the water would take around half an hour to heat up and the pump required some elbow grease and would often break. Braunstone's Tenants' Association came across many cases of residents having to fill the bath by bucket.[32] Norman Pilgrim commented that '[i]t was quite a messy and long protracted business. It probably accounted for the fact we didn't have all that many baths.'[33] The complexities of filling the bath, the expense involved, and the adherence to the weekly bath among those working-class families still without bathrooms, ensured that council tenants between the wars stuck to the traditional weekly bath.

Council tenants were at least generally able to let the water out through the plug hole. In privately rented inter-war housing inhabited by working-class families, bathing still took place in a tin bath or in 'slipper baths' at the public bathhouse.[34] The latter consisted of individual baths, so-called because they were shaped like a slipper and were partially covered to ensure the modesty of the bather in front of the bath attendant. Using the municipal 'slipper' baths was really only a practical option if you lived close by. Frank Brooks, born in 1929, used the slipper baths in Vestry Street and claimed it was quicker than bathing at home.[35] Sandy Coleman hated

BATHROOM EQUIPMENT

| Baths and Lavatory Basins, W.C. Suites in White or Colour | Kitchen Sinks in Stoneware, Stainless Steel and Enamel |

BATHROOM FURNITURE AND FITTINGS

FIREPLACES AND COOKERS

| The most varied Stock in the Midlands | Aga, Raeburn and all modern Cooking and Heating Stoves |

We invite you to visit our Showrooms.

R. POCHIN & SON LTD.

GRANBY STREET, LEICESTER

'Phone 21263.

9.10 Pochin's advert for Bathroom.

Source: Leicester of the Future (1947).

bathing in the Vestry Street baths because the water was too hot and only the attendants were allowed to work the taps.[36] Washing in the kitchen had the advantage of being warm but the steam made the kitchen walls damp, and the bath was difficult to empty. Moreover, the last person to get in got tepid, dirty water. One resident of the Walnut Street area had the task of clearing the mess up: 'I were the last one so I had all the cleaning up to do. By that time I were that sweaty I wanted another bath.'[37] Privacy was also a problem, especially for teenagers who could not wait until everyone else had gone to bed as their parents might choose to do.

After the Second World and into the 1960s many families continued to live without a fixed bath. Brett Pruce, born in 1955, lived in a house without a bathroom for the first 13 years of his life. The landlord converted the fourth bedroom to a bathroom in 1968. Brett did not appear to see this as a reflection of poverty but commented that 'when you're thirteen and sitting in a tin bath in front of an open fire it's a bit embarrassing'.[38] Likewise an inhabitant of the Walnut Street area of Leicester had their bathroom extension built around 1962 'maybe as late as that. So I suppose we were poor but frankly we never noticed it.'[39] The continued use of tin baths into the 1960s indicates that there was a continuity of domestic experience that stretched across the entire period from the 1880s until the 1960s, though by the 1960s bathing in a tub was no longer a cross-class experience and was confined to working-class families.

Although many homes lacked basic amenities, people in Leicester still felt 'at home' in them. One inhabitant of the Walnut Street area lived in a two-up, two-down house on a communal yard with shared toilets, tap and washhouse: 'It was a horrible place! But it was home, we didn't know any different.' Likewise, Elise Sutton who lived in St Margaret's in the 1920s, felt quite positive about the house, which was large for the area: '[t]o me and to lots of people who lived there we never thought of them as slums because we'd never known any other house ...' However, in both of these cases, the families became aware of the deficiencies of their homes once they moved out. For Elsie, whose family was offered a council house on Coleman Road they 'couldn't get away quick enough. ... When we saw the house, well to me it was like living in a palace, because it had got electric light and a bathroom.'[40] The other family moved into a three-bedroom house, close to their existing house: 'Well, we were living in luxury then, weren't we? Still never had an indoor bathroom nor hot water.'[41]

Many of the amenities we now take for granted took a long time to spread through the population. While upper-middle-class homes were acquiring bathrooms and upstairs WCs in the 1880s, working-class families living in older areas of Leicester often had to wait until the 1960s and even 1970s before they had these amenities. So although the acquisition of these totally transformed experiences of home life, the transformation was protracted.

Utilities

While the spread of water-related amenities took a long time, gas and electricity were introduced into the home more quickly. However, once acquired, gas and electricity did not necessarily generate an instant transformation and for practical and financial reasons old practices coexisted with the new.

Leicester Corporation had acquired its gas works in 1878 and at this point was supplying around 19,000 consumers. By 1904 this figure had increased to 52,802. Many of these customers were industrial as well as domestic users. Leicester Corporation also provided electricity but in 1904 it only had 2,357 consumers, indicating that electricity had yet to supersede gas as the main form of lighting in the urban home.[42] Only in the inter-war period was this change in emphasis of energy source achieved, in Leicester and around Britain. A Leicester guide from 1937 recorded that around 58,000 houses, or three-quarters of dwellings, had electricity. This still left one-quarter of the homes unconnected. The guide also boasted that '[s]everal innovations have been introduced by the department, including a system of payment by slot meter for purchasing house wiring, which has been copied all over the country'. Such a system would have appealed to poorer families and landlords alike. The Gas Department had also designed its own cooker and supplied 'gas fires, wash boilers, geysers, multi-point water heaters, and gas-heated circulators, for fitting to existing hot water systems.'[43]

9.11 Wright's New Century Eureka Cooker c.1910.

Source: National Gas Museum, Leicester.

9.12 Advert for 'Regulo' 1923. Issued with accompanying song 'Trust the Regulo': Text – it will make your wife and daughters happy.

Source: National Gas Museum, Leicester.

Different points of view...
same choice...
RENOWN Six

★ High-level grill with big plate-rack.

★ Four self-lighting boiling burners.

★ Easy-clean design throughout.

★ Extra-large, drop-door oven.

★ Chromium plated safety shelves which will not tip.

★ Ajusto has low setting for slow cooking and warming.

★ Flush taps — choice of five colours.

See the **RENOWN Six** at your Gas Showroom
CASH PRICE £47.19.6 (fixing extra)
Finished in white or cream. *Available on Hire Purchase*

Trade-in your old Gas Cooker!
SPECIAL OFFER: £2 will be allowed for your old cooker when placing an order for a new model. Full details from all Showrooms of the EAST MIDLANDS GAS BOARD.

MATURE experience and youthful enthusiasm agree that the Parkinson Cowan Renown Six is just the partner they want. It's practical because of the easy-to-cook layout and easy-to-clean finish. It's the last word in design —just what a modern kitchen needs.

PARKINSON COWAN

Best of the Gas Cookers

PARKINSON COWAN APPLIANCES LIMITED (GAS DIVISION) STECHFORD BIRMINGHAM **33**

9.13 Advert for Parkinson Cowan cooker.
Source: Leicester Mercury, 11 September 1958, 18.

The Corporation claimed to have installed 41,664 gas cookers by 1904, which left around 5,000 households without one.[44] Having a gas stove did not mean that it was actually used as Bel Weldon (born 1923) recalled of her grandmother: 'She did have a gas stove, but seemed to prefer the open fire.'[45] In other households the stove was used alongside the fire or only in the summer months. This was mainly the case in working-class homes where families could only afford to heat one room: the kitchen range acted as source of heat as well. In middle-class homes heating the kitchen was

9.14
a) Gas mantle
and light;
(b) Gas mantle
and clothing
dangerously
close;
(c) gas mantle
gauze, lit by
match.

Source: National
Gas Museum,
Leicester.

less important because before the 1950s it was used only rarely as a living room. Indeed, the 'living kitchen' is one example of middle-class adoption of working-class room usage. Coal fires remained the main source of heating; maisonettes in St Matthews were built with fireplaces in the 1950s (9.6). Gordon Baker recalled that his parents installed a gas fire in the front room in about 1927 which he thought was 'ahead of its time'.[46] However, the fire was only used twice a year. It was not until the Parker Morris report *Homes for Today and Tomorrow* (1961) that central heating began to be viewed as particularly important, and the report stressed that there should be heating in all rooms so that they could be used during the winter.[47] The introduction of central heating was an important factor in the transformation of room usage in the working-class home after the 1960s, although financial constraints often meant older patterns persisted.

Gas lights, like gas stoves, were also combined with traditional forms of lighting. Gas was often only piped to certain rooms; an inhabitant of the Walnut Street area explained that there was a gas mantle in the front bedroom but the stairs were unlit.[48] This meant that candles and lanterns had to be used in the rest of the house. Elsie Sutton, living on Sandacre Street during the 1920s, remembered using paraffin lamps with their gas mantles until the house was wired. This was a common pattern around Britain. However, families also used candles and lanterns to save money and to avoid having to replace the gas mantles which, William Abbott recalled, broke nearly every week. The use of mixed lighting continued in poorer households even after they had got electricity.

Electricity, and to a lesser extent gas, enabled 'time-saving' technology, first in the form of lighting and later as electric appliances, to enter the home. This was to have an important impact on housework and domestic leisure, though not necessarily always for the better.

Household chores and domestic routines

Although the majority of time-saving electrical appliances were available by 1900, their assimilation into the home took much longer, and for much of the period domestic appliances in the home were limited. This applied to middle- and working-classes families alike, though for different reasons. While working-class families could not afford to buy appliances, for upper-middle-class families until 1939, it was still cheaper to pay someone else to do time-consuming tasks.

A prime example of this was the washing machine, which was only widely adopted by the 1960s. 'Washing-machines' of some kind were on the market before 1880. Ada Jackson described the arrival of their 'washing machine' in her diary of 1883. Ada did not explain how it worked but she noted: 'Mother has tested the washing machine today, I am sure she has got her washing done quicker.'[49] The 'washing machine' was probably quite basic because even the 'Housewives' Darling' (9.15), produced somewhat later in the 1920s, was still a far cry from the 'twin tub' popular in the 1950s and 1960s and required the user to act as the motor. Washing machines powered by electricity were rarely found in homes until the 1950s and even then they were often only semi-automatic. In 1956 nearly 20% of households had some kind of electrical washing machine but they were mainly found in middle-class homes.[50]

9.15
Housewives'
Darling washing
machine.
Source: author's
copy.

Consequently for much of the twentieth century washing was done in a copper and it was the most time consuming of household chores. The copper consisted of a metal bowl bricked into a corner under which a fire would be lit. It had no drainage so the water was bailed out once washing had finished. Coppers continued to be built into both privately owned and council-rented homes in 1920s, although gas coppers were also available at this time (9.16). It was usually located in the kitchen, scullery or back room but in some homes could be found in a communal washhouse or cellar.[51]

9.16 Dean Gas Copper, typical enamel boiler with gas ring below water. The other utensils are a puncher, dolly (left), and iron.
Source: National Gas Museum, Leicester.

9.17 Washing lines in the back court.
Source: Colin Hyde.

Norman Pilgrim, who lived on the Brauntsone estate, remembered washing being 'a very steamy business' with doors and windows flung open whatever the weather. His mother used a mangle for wringing the water out of the clothes, a dolly tub and sometimes a 'puncher'. The washing would take most of the day. Blanche Harrison remembered that 'on that day we always had cold meat if there was any left, and mashed potatoes, or something makeshift in other words, for dinner because Mum was so busy.'[52]

The absence of appliances and certain amenities partly explained the distinctive housework routines practised during the period.[53] In Leicester, washday was usually Monday, at least by the inter-war period. Until 1939 this was the case around the country and among all classes, though of course wealthier people, including some better-off working-class families, were able to pay someone else to do it. In Ada Jackson's late Victorian home, washing seemed to take place more randomly, often on Wednesdays but sometimes on a Monday. However, their day for cleaning the house was consistently Friday and this was a popular day for cleaning among the working class in inter-war Britain, too.[54] Another working-class routine at this time that had a national pattern was bath night (as opposed to the middle-class bath time) which generally fell on Friday or Saturday and continued into the 1950s even for families with bathrooms. Exceptions to this general rule were miners, who would bathe daily.[55] D. Connolly who worked at Desford colliery in the 1940s described how he and his father took turns using the tin bath after they returned home from their shift.[56]

Families also followed daily routines that were in part the consequence of the kinds of dwellings in which they lived. Such routines would entail collecting water from communal taps, emptying out night-time chamber pots or cleaning the wicks of paraffin lamps. Other routines were more the result of environmental conditions and ideas of respectability. One Leicester resident commented: 'Nobody left their front unclean. It was considered your obligation ...'[57] Elsie Sutton remembered people scrubbing the step once a week, and this would suggest that as a routine it was less dominant in Leicester compared with northern industrial towns where it often happened on a daily basis at least among the older generation.[58] This was probably because Leicester's industries generated less pollution and soot and this would have reduced the frequency of other cleaning tasks also.

9.18 Victorian flat iron, A heated triangular piece of iron (margin).

Source: National Gas Museum, Leicester.

Another daily routine was the provision of a hot meal in the middle of the working day. This applied to all classes but the timing of the factory operative's 'dinner hour' was 12 noon to 1 p.m., while for office workers and grammar school pupils 'lunch' was generally between 1 and 2 p.m. Mary Essinger, who worked in an underwear factory in the early 1950s, went home at 12 each day for 'dinner' which 'was a cooked meal, with my three brothers and Mum and Dad'.[59] Thus, the family came together in the middle of the day as well as for the evening meal. Although this routine continued into the 1950s and 1960s for all classes, it became harder to maintain once more people moved to new estates outside the city and were no longer close to their workplace, especially for those who did not or could not drive to work. Other factors contributed to the decline of hot midday meal: with more women going out to work there was no one at home to get the meal ready and rising incomes made eating out more feasible.

Annual routines feature less in reminiscences, but spring cleaning was hard to forget. It involved cleaning the entire house and meant a lot of upheaval as Ada Jackson noted on 12 June 1883: 'We are in a mess this week, we are having the house cleaned so we are topsy-turvy. ... I managed to stay at work all day, at night I was cleaning some of the furniture ...' Mona Lewis described it as one to two weeks of 'sheer hell'.[60] Spring cleaning could entail repainting certain rooms because of flaking paint, an annual task rendered less necessary by the introduction of emulsion paint. Before this, walls were lime-washed using

9.18 Gas heated iron.

Source: National Gas Museum, Leicester.

a mixture of slaked lime and water, or 'white-washed' which was lime-wash with size added to give longer life. The reduction of domestic smoke omissions with the Clean Air Act of 1956 combined with the increasing affordability of vacuum cleaners, contributed to the eventual demise of this annual event.

While much of the household management in working-class homes fell upon mothers and wives, the lack of time-saving appliances and domestic servants meant that the rest of family had to help out. As was usually the case around Britain, fathers were expected to light the copper fire. It was an important task because '[s]ometimes it was a job to get the fire going'.[61] George Miles, who lived in the Newfoundpool area of Leicester, recalls his father waking up in a panic because he had overslept and had not lit it.[62] Fathers also mended shoes, cut children's hair, fetched in the coal or wood, and did various DIY tasks. Boys were not exempt, either: William Abbot scrubbed the bedroom floors with carbolic, filled the kettle up from the outside tap first thing to make his parents tea, got rid of the bed bugs with paraffin, and claims he generally had to do 'everything'. Roy Battison, son of a North Evington butcher, remembers turning the mangle while his father fed in the clothes. Predictably, girls helped out too. Ada Jackson wrote on 19 January 1883: 'I must do more cleaning at home because Mother has so much to do. I tell her I'll have the parlour to clean all to myself, she says that will just suit her.' She sewed shirts for her father and also took turns with her mother to stay at home on Sunday to get the dinner. However, on Bank Holiday her father got up early to get her breakfast: 'He is good when I am going out.'[63] One of the negative consequences of the acquisition of domestic appliances in working-class homes was that family members felt less obliged to help mothers out.[64]

In upper-middle-class homes, housework, cooking and some of the childcare could be left in the hands of servants. This was the case for less wealthy families such as Phyllis Orange's who could still afford a nurse 'to help' when Phyllis's mother had her fourth child in 1886: 'she was with us for thirteen years, she made life a lot easier for my mother.' However, although the family had servants, the Orange girls were still expected to help; one had to close the shutters at dusk while Denzil 'was so helpful to Mama, and was so good keeping we two youngest amused'.[65] By the 1930s, lower-middle-class families were able to afford electric appliances, such as vacuum cleaners and irons, and this was particularly the case in places such as Leicester where 'new industries' kept unemployment lower and rates of pay higher than in the parts of the country where 'old industries' prevailed.[66] By the 1950s the upper middle class was making do with just a 'daily' and thus were forced to take advantage of other more expensive 'time-saving' appliances on offer. Any time saved by these appliances, however, was offset by higher expectations of parenting: mothers of all classes were expected to spend more time with their children.

While the 1950s is considered a time when women's paid employment in Britain increased rapidly, many married working-class women in Leicester had long been accustomed to do paid work. Margaret Skinner in *Married Women's Work* (1915) recorded that in 1901 a quarter of all married women in the town 'were engaged in occupations' and that in two 'typical' working-class wards nearly half the married women were earning. At this time, and afterwards, working women were seen by middle-class observers to have a detrimental effect on family life. For example, the Medical Report of Leicester in 1908 blamed the high infancy death rates on working women. Skinner pointed out that in fact the reverse was often the case: 'In point of fact we find, as we have said, that the intelligent woman capable of earning a good wage usually manages her home well – she sets out to earn money that she may manage it better.'[67] Throughout the period, and for the same reason, married women worked at home doing out-work for the shoe and hosiery trades. One mother living in the Walnut Street area in the 1950s 'used to sit up all hours of the night working on shoes and that, you know, and sewing buttons on and all that sort of thing just for some money ... to keep the house going and my father was at work.'[68] Sandy Coleman recalled her mother, who was a sample machinist, doing her work at home while she was young. Other married women took in washing or did part-time cleaning jobs and these were also popular ways to supplement family income in other parts of the country. Working at home, however, helped to maintain the illusion that women 'didn't work'. Gerald Morris born in the 1900s, for example, explained that his mother 'didn't go out to work of course' but admitted that she did take in washing.[69] Given the hard labour involved in washing, and the time it took, it was a substantial undertaking, but it was unlikely that this kind of work was officially recorded in the census.[70]

Home entertainment

Access to leisure was clearly affected by class and gender, with working-class housewives having the least clearly defined 'leisure time'. While evenings, Saturday afternoons and Sundays were considered leisure time for working men, women spent them on domestic tasks necessary for everyday life. For many working-class wives 'leisure', if they used this term, often meant doing slightly less arduous domestic tasks, such as sewing and mending. Clare Langhamer has argued that in order to find a wider range of 'leisure' experiences of women when at home, different terms are needed, including those such as 'spare time', 'pleasure' and 'enjoyment'.[71]

In theory working-class men had more clearly defined leisure time, and many of them did spend this time doing recognisable leisure activities such as going to the pub or watching a match. However, as well as the domestic tasks mentioned in the previous section, many men were involved in other family-related activities such as DIY, entertaining children, or working on the allotment, and these tasks were performed during their 'leisure' time. It depended on the point of view of the individual concerned whether these activities were viewed as work and/or leisure. Such activities were less likely to be carried out by better-off, middle-class men, especially in the earlier part of the period.

For children of all classes it was easier to find time for leisure, but there were still class differences. As the previous section explained, the absence of time-saving appliances among the working classes meant that working-class children were expected to help out more than their middle-class counterparts whose parents could afford hired help. Working-class boys were also more often likely to do paid work before and after school hours. However, once these boys left school, their leisure time expanded and they had the added advantage of having more disposable income. This contrasted with those who stayed on at grammar school after they were 14 (15 after the 'Butler' Education Act, 1944). Not only were these boys expected to do homework in the evening but also they lacked the purchasing power of their contemporaries in full-time employment.[72] This was the case to a lesser extent for girls for whom parents often placed greater restrictions on their non-domestic leisure activities and for whom wages were lower.

However, many forms of domestic leisure were experienced across all classes and all ages. One form of leisure that featured prominently in the autobiographical data was the production and consumption of music. As George Miles recalling his 1930s childhood commented, '[p]robably the most popular hobby of all, involved music in its many forms, either playing an instrument, or listening to primitive 78 rpm scratchy records. Even the tiniest child could turn the handle on a wind-up gramophone.'[73] This central role of music in domestic life stretched from 1880s to the 1960s. Ada Jackson recalled in the 1880s singing songs in the evening and playing the piano,[74] while Phyllis Orange, remembering the following decade, described her own and her four sisters' 'thirst for classical music'. Her sister Dorothy was given a real violin in her Christmas stocking.[75] Music was important in Valerie Tedder's late forties home near St Saviour's Road. They had a second-hand piano which 'had seen better days' and was played by her father. Although it had many 'scars from years of misuse' Valerie explained that 'it was our pride and joy and after a good clean and polish by Dad, it gave us many years of pleasure'.[76] The production of live music in the home continued until the end of the period, but it was increasingly supplemented with a mixture of pre-recorded and transmitted music.

Singing with family and friends was an especially popular Leicester activity for Sunday evenings and this was the case in many areas of the country. One of the reasons for its popularity was that in nonconformist households Sunday activities were strictly regulated: 'In my younger days, say up to the time I was fifteen. [sic] Sunday observance was very strict. Children had special toys, special books and one did not play cards, sew or work in the garden. In fact, nearly all activities were bound up with religious service in some way.' Kenneth Ellis was writing about the last decade of the nineteenth century and he saw the regulations easing around 1900.[77] However, Sunday observance continued to be important in the twentieth century. Cecil Bell, remembering a nonconformist childhood from around 1915 to the 1920s explained how he was not allowed to play 'common songs' on a Sunday evening and had to stick to religious songs and ballads. Cecil saw the 1920s and 1930s as a time when people began to lose their faith and Sunday observance went into decline.[78] Nonconformist Sunday observance cut across classes because while Kenneth and Cecil came from different backgrounds, both families viewed Sunday in the same light.

9.19 'Know your Bible' game. The price is still attached.
Source: author's copy.

Radio not only brought music into the home but it offered other forms of entertainment as well. 'The wireless' was introduced to the domestic environment in 1922 but during the early years listening was a solitary activity because early radios or crystal sets required headphones. This was remedied with the introduction of valve wirelesses with speakers ensuring that family arguments now centred on what programme to listen to, rather than who got the headphones. However, it could be a communal activity with the family sitting around the wireless on a Sunday night, as one resident of the Walnut Street area remembered.[79] Radio ownership developed rapidly in the 1930s and according to the 1937 *Official Guide*, there were 73,047 wireless licences issued to Leicester residents and businesses.[80] Central government considered radio as vital to the war effort and it did play an important role in people's lives during the 1940s and early 1950s. Valerie Tedder, living in wartime Wigston, described it as 'our greatest company and amusement', while in the 1950s Mary Essinger's family listened to *Worker's Playtime* during the weekday midday meal.[81] A spin-off entertainment was making your own crystal set. According to George Miles this was a popular hobby because it was cheap and very satisfying when it worked.

Radio generated an important transformation in people's home entertainment and it served to bring the family together as well as being a source of tension. This was also the case for television, which was to produce an even greater change in domestic leisure. TV came to Leicester in 1949 and for many people their first experience of it was watching through a shop window. Norman Pilgrim, who worked for Goodman's on Leicester High

Street, explained: 'we put a consol receiver in the arcade of the shop so that people walking by on the pavement could see the picture. And it was such a draw. People had never seen a television picture in their lives.' Coronation Day 1953 was the first time that many people watched television actually in the domestic environment. Mary Essinger's family was able to rent one for the event, but Valerie's family did not rent a set until around 1957. Her family watched the coronation on her aunt's set and she remembers being 'absolutely enthralled with the occasion'. 'It had made us long to possess a television set as soon as possible, but finances were such that we were not able to purchase one.'[82] Valerie's experiences reflected the national patterns of TV ownership during this decade. In 1952 TV ownership in the UK was highest among the upper class and upper middle classes, of whom 27.2% owned a set, indicating that TV at this point had yet to become a classless experience. However, with the reduction in TV prices and the spread of Independent TV coverage across the UK, by 1958 ownership had become equally distributed among the three classes.[83]

From the early years of TV there were concerns about the impact it had on family life. One fear was that it would limit family interaction. Advocates of television argued that it in fact fostered family relationships by providing common talking points and encouraging husbands to remain at home rather than spending time and money in the pub.[84] Another fear was that television was a time-waster, but mothers were quick to point out how much more housework they could achieve while their children were occupied with the TV.[85] This was one of the reasons why televisions were acquired for the home before 'time-saving' appliances such as washing machines.[86]

Two forms of family entertainment that television was thought to threaten

9.20 Advert by Wathes for 'The Sensational Decca' TV.

Source: Leicester Mercury, 11 September 1958, 18.

9.21 Wathes High Street Showroom: 50 years in operation selling electrical appliances.

Source Colin Hyde.

was the playing of games and reading. Board games and cards certainly appear to have been a family activity as George Miles recalled: 'parents initiated their children into the wonders of card games such as Pontoon, Brag, or Solo Whist … in pre-T.V. [*sic*] instant entertainment days.' He also remembered his father making a game of skittles in the 1930s which gave 'many hours of fun and games, for both young and old'.[87] George's memories reflect his working-class background in which the playing of games often involved fathers more than mothers who were too busy with domestic chores to join in.[88] Furthermore, it reflected the lower incomes of working-class families who relied on home-made games more than wealthier middle-class families.

Like playing games and music, reading was a popular form of domestic leisure across the period. In her diary for 1883 Ada Jackson mentioned how much she enjoyed reading *Pomeroy Abbey*, while Phyllis' Orange's mother read Shakespeare and the classics as a young wife in the same period.[89] Despite TV's arrival, reading (or at least an interest in books) increased during the post-war period and this was reflected by a rapid rise in library loans and book sales. Between 1939 and 1962 the number of books issued by libraries increased by 86.2% while the sale of books rose by over 900%.[90] Certain kinds of literature were more favoured than others, with magazines and newspapers being most commonly read. Even among teenagers reading newspapers was considered a common activity in the 1960s.[91] Comics, such as *The Magnet* and *The Gem*, were popular with children, and national newspapers had sections for children, with Rupert Bear featuring in *The Express* and Pip, Squeak and Wilfred in *The Mirror. The Mirror* even had a dolls house built for its three imaginary characters and published a book about the making of the house.[92] Locally in the 1930s, a section of the *Leicester Evening Mail* was dedicated to the 'Tom Thumb Club'.

However, unlike playing games and music, reading was a form of domestic leisure that was largely individual, though family members did read to each other. The increasing popularity of reading as the twentieth century progressed was in part to do with the changes in domestic circumstances described in this chapter. Improvements in heating and lighting, for example, meant that people could find space in the home to do individual activities whatever the season away from the noise and activity of the main living room. This change accompanied an increase in personal domestic space which was largely the consequence of a fall in household size among the working class: in 1951 there was an average of 0.7 persons per room in Leicester; by 1971 this figure had fallen to 0.6. These changes enabled activities which had been traditionally more communal, such as making and listening to music, to become more individualised too. Thus while Ada Jackson and her friends sang together in the parlour, her 1960s counterparts were able to disappear into their own rooms, which they increasingly had to themselves, to play the guitar or listen to records. This expansion of personal space in the domestic environment brought working-class domestic leisure more in line with that of the middle class who had had access to individual space at the start of the period.

However, there were changes in domestic leisure that were not related to material conditions at home but importantly to the time available for leisure. One important factor which resulted in greater similarities in leisure between the middle and working classes was the convergence in leisure hours which started to take place after 1950. Thus, the reduction in hired help meant that middle-class women in particular had far less leisure time in the 1950s than in the 1880s while, conversely, leisure time for much of the working class increased as the official working day was reduced.

Experiences of home are influenced by a number of factors. Some of these are material, such as the condition and form of the home. The size and layout of the house had an impact on the way that people used rooms

9.22 Shop bought games: botanist (1900s), wooden construction game (1890s), and 'Hopla', indoor crocquet set (1890s?).
Source: author's copy.

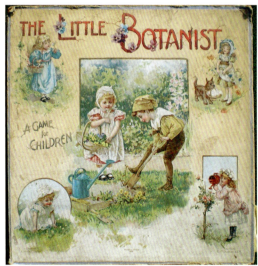

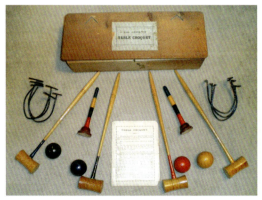

Leicester: a modern history

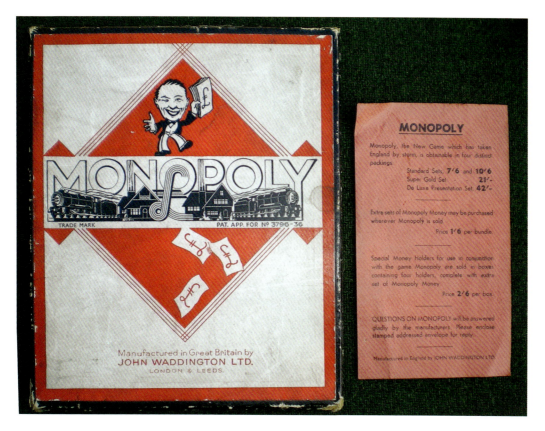

while amenities and utilities influenced domestic routines. Other factors were the social and demographic characteristics of the dwellers, such as their income and class, and the historical period. Thus as we would expect, wealthier families were able to afford more space and more amenities and this was more the case at the start of the period covered here than at the end. During the period working-class families acquired more space, mainly due to a reduction in family size, while upper-middle-class families were forced to scale down.

This chapter has also shown the ways in which domestic life transformed during this time, and this occurred at all levels, from the physical condition of the home to domestic labour and home entertainment. However, while the changes were substantial, the rate of change was erratic and even in the 1960s there were families who had domestic experiences similar to their nineteenth-century counterparts. Such experiences were partly to do with class but also to do with the age of the home. Thus those working-class families residing in nineteenth-century homes were far more likely to lack 'mod-cons' than working-class families in post-1918 council and private housing.

9.23 Monopoly, 1930s version with price list. *Source*: author's copy.

10

Wealthy city, healthy people?

T HIS CHAPTER provides a broad and accessible overview exploring
the health of the people of Leicester through the twentieth century.
It focuses on public health policy and practice, and is organised in four
sections: 'Social investigation and social reform, 1900–18' traces the
development of public health services in the early 1900s as an important
area of local authority activity; 'The high point of municipal medicine,
1918–48' concentrates on the zenith of municipal medicine in Leicester,
as elsewhere in England and Wales; 'A National Health Service, 1948–74'
explores how in the post-war period, Leicester came under the aegis of the
Sheffield Regional Hospital Board (RHB); and the final section, 'The new
public health', traces the revival of public health as a medical specialism
from the late 1980s, including the move from health authorities to primary
care trusts, and the establishment of the post of Director of Public Health
(DPH). The overall argument is that Leicester was, for most of the
twentieth century, a comparatively wealthy city, and its experience is an
important corrective to studies that have focused on local authorities in
economically disadvantaged regions.[1] Nevertheless even in Leicester, differentials in income were reflected in trends in health status.

Social investigation and social reform, 1900–18

The development of public health services in Leicester took place within the
context of wider medical provision. From the early part of the nineteenth
century, for example, the sick poor in the community had received out-relief
from the parish medical officer as administered by the Relieving Officers,
and many sick clubs and friendly societies gave access to a doctor as part
of their benefits. The Dispensary that was opened in 1830 as a charity,
and became a Provident Society in 1867, also provided health care through
its main site in Bond Street and the branches scattered throughout the
city. Although the National Insurance Act of 1911 disrupted the work of
these organisations, the Dispensary regrouped as the Leicester Public
Medical Service and continued to work from the same premises. Medical
treatment was also provided by the District Nursing Service, midwives,
and pharmacists, and by alternative practitioners such as herbalists and
homeopaths who charged relatively low fees.

New institutions for the insane had been established in the late eighteenth and early nineteenth centuries, including the Leicester Infirmary Asylum (1794) and the Union Workhouse (1839). But by far the most important of these was the Leicestershire and Rutland Lunatic Asylum (1837), later replaced by a new mental hospital at Narborough (1907). Like many provincial urban centres, Leicester had a voluntary hospital, founded in 1771, which gradually grew in size and was rebuilt several times. The hospital as a whole had only 200 beds for a population of 211,581 in 1901, but even so, the expansion of the Royal Infirmary helped to foster the growth of a medical elite (10.1). Funds and money-raising were continual preoccupations for many of the voluntary hospitals, but in Leicester the Saturday Hospital Fund was a successful source of income with regular payments by local workers.[2]

Local authority public health provision was thus only one strand within the wider provision of medical services. Indeed it may have partly been as a reaction to the inadequacies of hospital services, and to compensate for the shortage of general practitioners, that the local authority developed extensive public health services. Environmental health had been a major preoccupation of sanitary reformers in nineteenth-century Leicester, and developments after 1900 were built on these foundations. There were continuities of personnel and in priorities, and the traditions established at that time, notably the emphasis upon dissent in the field of health, illustrated by the campaign against vaccination, were still very influential.

The character and outlook of the Medical Officers of Health (MOsH) undoubtedly mattered, and Leicester had three in the period 1901–74 who influenced and reflected the trends of their respective periods of office. Their involvement in the East Midlands branch of the Society of MOsH gave some indication of how Leicester compared to other urban centres in terms of health services. In addition, their membership of the Leicester Medical Society revealed the changing status of the MOH within the city's medical elite. In 1901, the Sanitary Committee appointed a new MOH, Dr Charles Killick Millard, public health doctor for Burton-on-Trent, whose earlier work at the Birmingham Fever Hospital indicated that he was opposed to compulsory vaccination (10.2; 10.3).[3] While the twentieth century also witnessed the growth of new personal health services, environmental regulation and the battle against infectious disease remained important aspects of the work of the Sanitary Committee. Millard's first annual report as MOH reflected the impact of the investigations of Rowntree and Booth (10.5).[4] He subsequently noted the striking differentials in birth and death rates between the affluent and more deprived wards; the latter included Newton and Wyggeston.[5] In the late nineteenth century, sanitary inspection had begun to include both lodging houses and working-class housing in general. The MOsH had become increasingly concerned about domestic sanitation and with private houses, although overall it was thought that Leicester's housing was relatively good, with few houses being classed as unfit for habitation. It was perhaps

10.1 Leicester Royal Infirmary, founded 1771 by the Rev. William Watts. Many of the modern buildings are named after royal residences: Windsor, Balmoral, Osborne, and Sandringham.

Source: Colin Hyde.

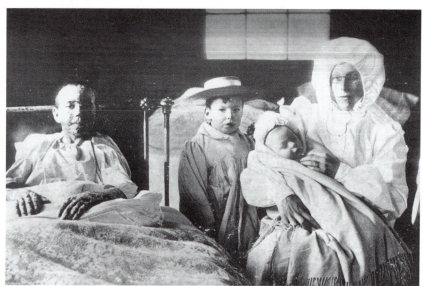

10.2 Dr Charles Killick Millard (1870–1952), Leicester's MOH (1901–35) previously held posts in Birmingham and Burton. He was a powerful advocate for the Voluntary Euthanasia Legalization Society founded in 1935 (now Dignity in Dying).

Source: private copy.

10.3 A pock-marked, vaccinated smallpox patient visited by Dr Milllard's wife and family. Previously vehemently opposed to compulsory vaccination Millard later showed his confidence in it through this photograph.

Source: C.K. Millard, *The Vaccination Question in the Light of Modern Experience* (1914), plate 1.

for this reason that Millard was ambivalent about the Housing and Town Planning Act of 1909, which instituted a system of closing and demolition orders, and made Sanitary Committees responsible for listing houses 'unfit for human habitation'.

Occupational health was another issue at this time. There had been outbreaks of anthrax, for instance, among the city's furriers, tanners, and upholstery workers, and especially in the wool trade, in 1880 and in 1886–87. Moreover it was well known that workers in the city's boot and shoe industry had a high incidence of illness and death from pulmonary tuberculosis. Indeed, although manufacturers emphasised the healthy nature of their premises, the incidence of tuberculosis rose rather than fell with the replacement of the smaller workshops by factories in the 1890s. Interest in occupational health faded as the MOH became preoccupied with other issues, and it only re-emerged in 1915 because the first report of the new Medical Research Committee focused on tuberculosis in the boot and shoe industry.[6] But the local branch of the National Union of Boot and Shoe Operatives, concerned about the impact of a high sickness rate and mounting losses on the union's sick and funeral fund, also campaigned on this issue.

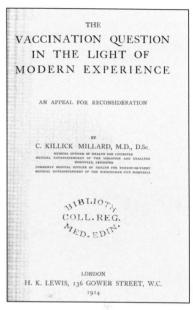

THE

VACCINATION QUESTION
IN THE LIGHT OF
MODERN EXPERIENCE

AN APPEAL FOR RECONSIDERATION

BY

C. KILLICK MILLARD, M.D., D.Sc.

MEDICAL OFFICER OF HEALTH FOR LEICESTER
MEDICAL SUPERINTENDENT OF THE ISOLATION AND SMALLPOX
HOSPITALS, LEICESTER
FORMERLY MEDICAL OFFICER OF HEALTH FOR BURTON-ON-TRENT
MEDICAL SUPERINTENDENT OF THE BIRMINGHAM CITY HOSPITALS

BIBLIOTH
COLL. REG.
MED. EDIN.

LONDON
H. K. LEWIS, 136 GOWER STREET, W.C.
1914

10.4 Title page of C.K. Millard's *The Vaccination Question in the Light of Modern Experience* (London, 1914).

Apart from occupational health, tuberculosis was a key infectious disease, and the centrepiece of the efforts to tackle it was the tuberculosis sanatorium. The Isolation Hospital at Groby Road began to admit tuberculosis patients in September 1903, but it did not match the stereotype of these institutions. Neither located on a mountain top nor surrounded by pine forests, it was situated on a slight hill on one of the major roads leading out of the city. Yet some features of its regime do fit with what is known about other institutions of this kind. The routine of the institution was based on a process by which patients graduated to progressively more demanding types of work. Moreover, although the sanatorium consumed much of the resources devoted to the treatment of tuberculosis, its effectiveness was questionable. In comparison, prevention, notification, and after-care were all allocated a more minor role. By the 1890s, the MOsH had begun to take action on prevention – signs prohibiting spitting were put up in trams, workshops, and other public places – but the Sanitary Committee also delegated much of the responsibility to the local branch of the National Association for the Prevention of Tuberculosis (NAPT). It was NAPT that organised and paid for health education, and tried to keep in touch with patients after they had left the sanatorium.[7]

As with other infectious diseases, both prevention and treatment depended on the existence of an efficient system of notification. Pulmonary tuberculosis

10.5 Municipal Wards, Leicester, 1906.

Source: Record Office for Leicester, Leicestershire and Rutland, L A12 938.

had been voluntarily notifiable since October 1902. Compulsory notification was extended to patients in hospital from May 1911. Subsequently the Local Government Board stated that pulmonary tuberculosis was compulsorily notifiable, from January 1912, and this was extended to all forms of the disease in February 1913.[8] In this period, the main innovation in the diagnosis and treatment of tuberculosis was the dispensary opened in 1911.

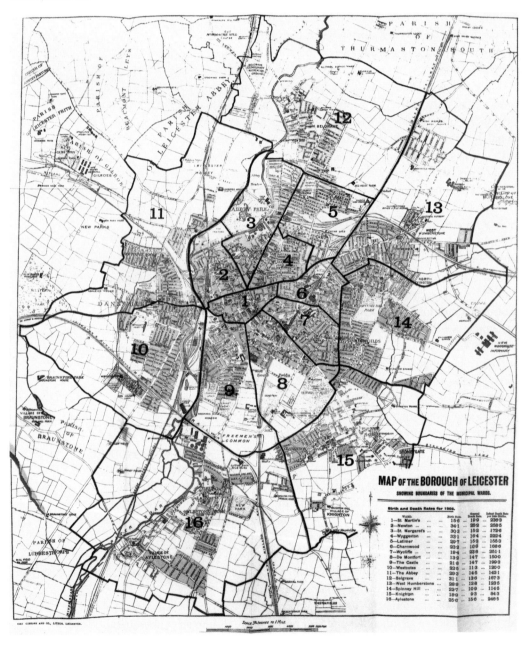

| Leicester: a modern history

Based in three rooms in a former shop, its staff distributed tuberculin, advised patients, and examined cases for admission to the sanatorium. It was claimed that the dispensary acted as a 'clearing house' in the campaign against tuberculosis. With the introduction of compulsory notification, all cases were registered and card-indexed, and were visited by nurses or health visitors. They made enquiries, inspected houses, gave advice, supplied pocket spittoons or spitting cups, and advised patients to apply to the dispensary.[9]

It was a system of policing that placed a heavy emphasis on education, and tended to ignore wider economic and structural factors. The fear of infection meant that individual liberties were often overridden in the interests of preventive medicine. Public health doctors regretted that there were not enough beds to enable advanced cases to be isolated permanently. But the greatest fear was of the patient who remained undetected, and who moved around the city infecting others. Although all tuberculosis patients suffered from this sense of stigma, it was at the sanatorium that their humiliation was most complete. The purpose of the sanatorium was education rather than cure, and responsibility for the disease was successfully transferred to the patients themselves.

In the late nineteenth century, Leicester had been second only to Preston in the urban league table in terms of infant mortality, with a mean figure of 208 deaths per 1,000 live births (see 1.29). By 1910, this was more in line with trends for England and Wales, at 126.4 deaths per 1,000 live births.[10] Nationally at this time, there was a greater focus on the health of children, and as in other local authorities the development of health services for mothers and infants, and for schoolchildren, were important milestones in the move from environmental health to the new personal health services (10.7). The new committee set up after the 1902 Education Act moved quickly on the issue of child health, and in 1905 appointed Dr Allan Warner as the city's first School Medical Officer (SMO). His initial duties included responsibility for the sanitation, heating, and lighting of schools, but it was medical inspection that remained the mainstay of the School Medical Service throughout this period. Medical inspections revealed that many children had head lice and skin diseases such as ringworm, but it was not until January 1912 that the Education Committee considered funding treatment. The local authority remained cautious about encroaching on the territory of general practitioners, and the provision of free treatment was closely controlled by means-testing. In 1919, for example, charges for operations ranged from 1s. to 10s., for dental treatment from nil to 1s., and for spectacles from nil to 2s.[11] Earlier activity in the field of sanitary reform meant that the city already had several public baths. The provision of swimming lessons for schoolchildren was followed by the formation of voluntary leagues – a Leicester Schools Swimming Association had been set up by 1909 – and by the provision of cricket pitches and tennis courts.

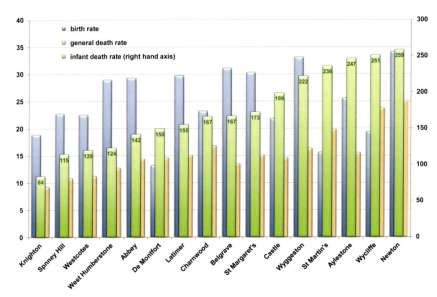

10.6 Birth, Death and Infant Mortality Rates per 1,000 population, Leicester 1906.

Source: Record Office for Leicester, Leicestershire and Rutland, L A12 938.

10.7 The Milk Depot at 217 Belgrave Gate was opened in July 1906.

Source: Record Office for Leicester, Leicestershire and Rutland, A12 937.

The high point of municipal medicine, 1918–48

As elsewhere, the period 1918–48 in many ways represented the high point of municipal activity in the field of public health. Under the 1929 Local Government Act, the Health Committee appropriated the North Evington Poor Law Infirmary and renamed it the City General Hospital (10.8). Although a Poor Law infirmary, this had been one of the most modern

10.8 The City General Hospital (*c*.1930) shortly after it had been transferred from the Poor Law authorities.

Source: Record Office for Leicester, Leicestershire and Rutland, A13 183.

hospitals of its kind when opened in 1905, with 538 beds in 16 large wards. From 1930, the City General dealt with more patients, and it also bridged the gap between the local authority and the voluntary hospital. One of the most pressing needs was to improve the quality of medical care. The local authority remedied this by making a number of part-time appointments from among the Royal Infirmary's consultants and specialists.[12]

In the inter-war period, the development of some aspects of public health was influenced by ideology, and by the new science of eugenics, with its emphasis on good breeding and the need to stop the 'unfit' from reproducing. In the field of mental health, for example, an After-Care sub-committee supported legislation embodying the principle of segregation; the concept of the 'social problem group' was influential in local medical circles, and the Eugenics Society sponsored the work of some local figures. Birth control was more a religious and moral issue than one that divided local councillors on party political lines, but Millard was influenced by the local surgeon and eugenicist C.J. Bond, and was in contact with national figures such as Marie Stopes. The issue of housing and slum clearance is surprisingly revealing of the ideological debates that underlay the development of public health policy at the local level. Millard had distinctive ideas on the question of overcrowding, but he was forced to concede defeat on his proposals for improvement areas when he encountered opposition within the Health Committee. The slum clearance episode, and in particular a meeting in November 1933 when Millard threatened to resign, indicated the limits to the authority of the MOH.[13]

With regard to the School Medical Service, the scale of medical inspection expanded during the inter-war period, from 4,114 routine inspections in 1918, to 14,248 in 1938.[14] Services were affected by financial retrenchment in the 1920s, but advances in research and medical technology ensured that individual aspects of treatment, such as orthopaedics, developed quickly (10.9). Children regarded as anaemic or malnourished received 'artificial sunlight' therapy, while gas was used for tonsil and adenoid operations, and X-ray treatment for children with ringworm. In the late 1930s, there was more discussion about the failures of services such as dentistry, and wide-ranging debates about how school clinics might be run in future. Deaths of children during operations remained alarmingly common, suggesting that facilities at the smaller clinics continued to be primitive. Moreover, the extension of the city boundary in 1935 forced a reappraisal. Many people were no longer living near the city centre but in the new suburban housing estates. From 1938 it was suggested that treatment could be provided at a central health centre, and by nurses working in decentralised school clinics, such as on the Braunstone and New Parks estates. The SMO drew up a five-year plan which included nine clinics, and a prominent local architect was appointed to design an elaborate and expensive health centre.[15]

10.9 The School Medical Service tested hearing with a gramophone audiometer from 1936.

Source: Record Office for Leicester, Leicestershire and Rutland, A13 102.

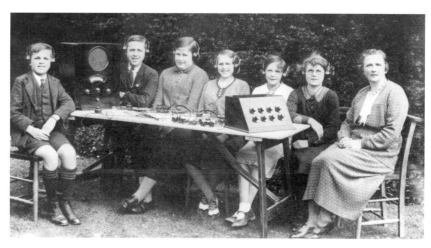

10.10 The open-air school was opened in Western Park in November 1930.

Source: Record Office for Leicester, Leicestershire and Rutland, A13 099.

Although, in the end, the health centre was not built, advances in nutritional science percolated down to the local level and generated concern about the effectiveness of medical inspections in detecting malnutrition. This marked a turning point after which the Education Committee set up a central kitchen, drew up new menus, and expanded the provision of school milk, from 112 'meals' in 1912, to 19,576 in 1938.[16] As elsewhere, physical education gradually became a minor but important aspect of the School Medical Service. The physical education organisers set up short courses for teachers, and there were some signs that, by the late 1920s, physical education had become more liberal. The School Board had provided special classes for 'defective' children from the 1890s, and the local authority slowly established schools for deaf, blind, 'feeble-minded', and 'backward' children at St Mary's Fields, Haddenham Road, and Duxbury Road. The 'open-air' movement was first apparent in the treatment of children with tuberculosis of the bones and joints, and in November 1930 an open-air school finally opened in Western Park (10.10).

Since Leicester had a reputation as a forward-thinking local authority, there was fierce competition for the post of MOH when Millard retired in 1935. The Health Committee subsequently appointed Dr Kenneth Macdonald, previously MOH for Keighley, Barnsley, and Stockport, to the combined post of MOH and SMO (10.11). Macdonald was a more liberal figure than Millard, more committed to the expansion of health services, and in touch with national developments in rapidly changing fields such as nutrition. He played an important leadership role nationally, in 1946, in

10.11 Dr Kenneth Macdonald (second right) seen here with wartime ambulance crews was Leicester MOH from 1935 to 1960.

Source: Record Office for Leicester, Leicestershire and Rutland.

trying to rally MOsH who were pessimistic about the prospects of public health under the early National Health Service.[17]

Even when the influence of the local boot and shoe industry is taken into account, mortality from pulmonary tuberculosis declined, to 70 deaths per 100,000 population by 1939.[18] There were some minor changes to both prevention and after-care. Under the 1921 Public Health (Tuberculosis) Act, the prevention and treatment of tuberculosis was consolidated and rationalised. The dispensary moved to larger premises on Regent Road in 1929, and a new After-Care Committee used nurses to follow up notified cases, while in the same year a seaside convalescent home finally opened at Holt in Norfolk. In the early 1930s there was a belated recognition of the links between pulmonary tuberculosis and poor housing conditions. In 1929, for example, when the mortality rate for pulmonary tuberculosis for Leicester as a whole was 108 deaths per 100,000 population, the rate in the different wards varied from 208 in Wyggeston, to 90 in West Humberstone.[19] It had long been realised that the mortality statistics fitted a pattern in which the 16 wards formed 5 concentric rings, ranging from the deprived inner-city wards to the suburban middle-class residential areas. In 1936, when the mortality rate for pulmonary tuberculosis for Leicester as a whole was 127 deaths per 100,000 population, the average for seven new housing estates was 78.[20]

10.12 Record form for the physical condition of new patients at the sanatorium, 1943.

Source: author's copy.

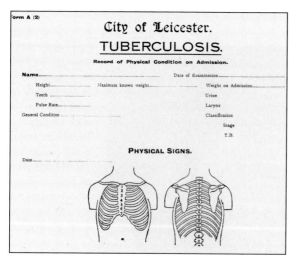

The 1920s were marked by an increasing emphasis on work therapy in the treatment regime at the sanatorium. Patients were increasingly involved in poultry farming, bee-keeping, gardening, and handicrafts, and a special fund was set up to organise expenditure and income from the sale of handicrafts. Despite these efforts, however, the light, outdoor jobs thought ideal for these patients were difficult to obtain and poorly paid, and former patients faced problems in obtaining suitable employment throughout the inter-war period. Perhaps related to this, in the late 1930s, there was greater emphasis on the development of more sophisticated forms of treatment. The MOH reports heralded the alleged value of artificial pneumothorax, in which air was deliberately injected into the pleural cavity to collapse the lung and allow the tuberculous areas to heal (10.12).[21] However, the focus on modern treatment methods could not disguise the fact that for many a diagnosis of tuberculosis remained a death sentence.

| Leicester: a modern history

Health education had been a function of the local Sanitary Committee since the 1880s, and was an important aspect of maternity and child welfare activities, both voluntary and statutory, including health visiting, the milk depot, and clinics for mothers and infants. Health education was also regarded as of great potential significance in the battle against individual diseases, notably pulmonary tuberculosis and venereal disease. The Health Committee began in the 1920s to hold annual health weeks and engage in other educational activities. It distributed handbooks, put up posters, screened films, got doctors and nurses to give health talks, and arranged exhibitions and tea parties for mothers and infants. In addition, from the early 1930s, the Health Committee began to use materials produced by the Health and Cleanliness Council, and from 1933, the poster sites of the defunct Empire Marketing Board. These efforts culminated in the 1937 national health campaign, when it publicised local health services, arranged talks, and published newspaper articles.[22]

A National Health Service, 1948–74

In the post-war period, there were fundamental changes in the medical, policy, and administrative context in which public health services operated. First, the period saw dramatic changes in medicine, with new vaccines and antibiotics for infectious diseases such as pulmonary tuberculosis and poliomyelitis, and breakthroughs in epidemiology which included the discovery of the connection between lung cancer and smoking. Second, new policies emerged for older people, children and adults with learning disabilities, and the mentally ill, including an emphasis on care in the community, and these again raised questions about geographical variations in the extent of services (10.14). Third, the fact that local authorities had lost control of most of their clinics and hospitals to the National Health Service meant that in this period MOsH had to come to terms with changes in their responsibilities.[23]

From 5 July 1948 Leicester was subsumed in the Sheffield Regional Hospital Board (RHB). Its principal hospitals were divided between four Hospital Management Committees, and the local authority lost control of those hospitals and clinics that it had previously run (10.13). Relations between the city's Health Committee, local Hospital Management Committees, and the RHB remained poor in the post-war years. The RHB showed little interest in such issues as health education, mental health, old age, or in planning for the challenges posed by ethnicity and health, and the local MOsH were kept at arm's length at regional level. Sheffield possessed the only teaching hospital and tended to dominate the region, and Leicester, isolated at its southern end, was very much on the periphery of hospital medicine. It was only with the creation of new medical schools in the 1960s and 1970s that the balance of power in the region shifted more towards Nottingham and Leicester.[24]

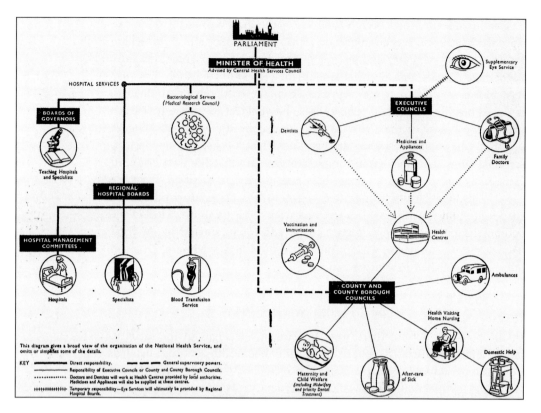

10.13 Diagram explaining the structure of the National Health Service to the general public.

Source: author's copy.

10.14 The Health Committee coordinated the MOH's work in public health.

Source: MOH Report for 1952.

As public health declined in importance, general practice gradually revived. Macdonald had considered health centres in the late 1930s, and during the war had included 15 district centres in his plans for reconstruction. His colleagues also seemed enthusiastic. However, in the 1950s, instead of health centres, general practitioners set up group practices. Encouraged

by their experience in group practices, family doctors were much more interested in health centres by the 1960s, and the restrictions on capital expenditure that had hampered building in the 1950s had gradually been relaxed. By April 1974, five health centres had been opened in Leicester – St Peter's, the first and most expensive; Westcotes; Pasley Road on the Eyres Monsell housing estate; Rushey Mead; and Charnwood Street.[25] The local authority could now close the clinics previously held in church halls. However, in other respects the health centres merely provided further evidence of the revival of general practice, and the relative decline of public health as a local authority responsibility.

While mortality from pulmonary tuberculosis declined in Leicester in the post-war period, from 60 deaths per 100,000 population in 1945, to only 2 by 1970, notifications of new cases increased immediately after the Second World War, from 355 cases in 1945, to 555 in 1950, suggesting that further progress would depend on continued improvements in nutrition and living standards.[26] The slum clearance schemes and construction of new council estates that had been such a feature of inter-war Leicester had come to an abrupt halt in September 1939 (10.15). In the post-war period, the local authority's preventive measures included the dispensary and mass radiography. The dispensary staff recorded new cases and deaths, examined and referred patients for treatment, while health visitors visited patients at home and linked the dispensary with the chest clinic. The mass radiography unit surveyed specific groups like schoolchildren, cases referred by doctors, and particular geographical areas including the new housing estates (10.16). While the dispensary and mass radiography remained important, from 1953 the main weapon in the prevention of tuberculosis was BCG vaccination. In the inter-war period, preventive measures had been limited to fresh air

10.15 Slum clearance was postponed by the Second World War and was slow to resume in the 1950s.

Source: Record Office for Leicester, Leicestershire and Rutland, A12 123.

10.16 Mass miniature radiography began in September 1946 and improved tuberculosis diagnosis.

Source: Record Office for Leicester, Leicestershire and Rutland, A12 116.

10.17 Sanitary inspectors monitored the state of the city's housing.

Source: Record Office for Leicester, Leicestershire and Rutland, A12 125.

and checks on the milk supply, and BCG therefore marked an important step forward.

One of the most striking demographic features of Leicester after the Second World War was its growing ethnic minority community (see Chapter 14). Migrants tended to settle initially in cheap lodging houses in the Highfields area, then later in adjacent owner-occupied areas. The local public health department tackled the perceived high incidence of tuberculosis among migrants in a number of ways. Mass radiography units were set up in Highfields and in Belgrave Gate, the areas where migrants had settled, and were publicised by leaflets delivered to local houses. From 1965, migrant children were offered tuberculin skin tests – subsequently all newly arrived migrant children were given these tests, with BCG vaccinations for those where the test proved negative.[27] What was common to these tactics was that they focused on surveillance and biomedical intervention. Moreover, even this limited response was to a degree undermined by the naiveté (and explicit racism) of staff in the local public health department. There was little contact between staff who were monitoring notification rates and those who were more concerned with housing conditions and overcrowding. When tuberculosis was looked at within the wider context, it was from the perspective of sanitary inspectors concerned about the 'multi-occupation' of lodging houses (10.17).

In the post-war period, health services for the city's schoolchildren were affected by the 1944 Education Act and the establishment of the National Health Service. Wider social and economic changes that included rising living standards and improved nutrition led to an improvement in child health. This served to revive the long-running arguments about the usefulness of routine medical inspections. The local authority treated fewer schoolchildren than previously, and some diseases, including rheumatic fever, were no longer seen by school doctors. More children were treated through general practitioners and hospitals, and the School Health Service increasingly targeted its resources at areas of deprivation. Even so, clinics still treated substantial numbers of children and were often overcrowded, indicating that they remained popular with some mothers. In 1953, for example, 23.2% of the children having routine medical inspections, and 5.6% of all the children inspected, were thought to require treatment.[28] Other consequences of improved living standards, such as cigarette smoking, drugs, and wider car ownership created new threats to child health, and demonstrated that a School Health Service was still necessary. The emergence of a large ethnic population presented the School Health Service with new challenges. By 31 December 1971, for instance, 14.2% of the school population was of 'ethnic origin'.[29]

Rising living standards led to a reduction in the number of undernourished children, and the Second World War had seen the creation of a consensus on school meals that survived until the early 1970s. The problem became one of obesity rather than under-nourishment, and a new clinic provided children from the lower-income groups with a controlled diet and exercise. For schoolchildren in general, physical education, games, and swimming lessons had become an integral part of the primary and secondary curriculum. As the local School Health Service spent less time on routine medical inspection and treatment (special inspections declined from 43,951 in 1950, to 20,492 in 1970, while routine inspections remained stable in the same period), it was able to concentrate more on psychological and psychiatric

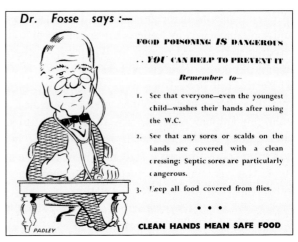

10.18 The general public were sceptical about the School Psychological Service (cartoon that appeared in the *Leicester Mercury*).

Source: Record Office for Leicester, Leicestershire and Rutland, A12 962/1.

10.19 The cartoon figure of 'Dr Fosse' was the winning entry in a local competition.

Source: Record Office for Leicester, Leicestershire and Rutland, A13 184.

services, and on special schools.[30] Overall Leicester can be seen to have retained its position in the forefront of the provision of 'special education' through the post-war period (10.18).

Dr Macdonald retired in 1960 and was succeeded by his deputy, Dr John Moss. Moss had ambitious plans for public health, notably in the emerging field of care in the community, and he supervised important management reforms for nurses and other groups of health professionals. On the other hand, his period of office coincided with an era of crisis and change for public health. Moss was not as active as his predecessors in the East Midlands branch of the Society of MOsH, nor in the Leicester Medical Society, illustrating that the post of MOH was no longer as prestigious as it had once been.

With regard to health education, the Health Committee had set up a specialist department, appointed a Health Education Officer, and created the character of 'Dr Fosse', a cartoon that was the winning entry in a local competition (10.19). Through the 1950s, the Health Education Officer promoted exhibitions, films, window displays, courses, lectures, leaflets, posters, cards, and lantern slides in local cinemas. The Health Committee organised health exhibitions on food hygiene and diphtheria immunisation, and local shoe manufacturers paid for small exhibitions during the 'national foot weeks'. The annual Leicester Show included health exhibitions, a film was made of the city's health services, and in the late 1950s there were important campaigns on clean air and polio vaccination (10.20). From the

10.20 City centre air quality in the 1950s was similar to the previous century. The Clean Air Act (1956), the decline of coal for domestic heating, and the reduced manufacturing scale contributed to the improvement in air quality.

Source: Leicester City Council.

1960s, Moss argued that health education should be directed towards lung cancer, tooth decay, and mental health, and the wider issue of lifestyles. In some respects, this reflected his confidence that the traditional enemies of public health had been contained.[31] Nevertheless on the specific issues of water fluoridation, family planning, and cigarette smoking, progress was less impressive. In general the local authority simply reacted to circulars and statements emanating from central government, and on these issues it showed little zest for policy-making independent from Whitehall.

The emergence of care in the community in Leicester in the 1950s was only the latest stage in the longer-term history of provision for those with mental health needs and learning disabilities. One of the main achievements was that the Occupation Centre for children was replaced by a specially designed school, the Emily Fortey School, in Western Park. In the early 1960s, the MOH argued that the 1959 Mental Health Act would lead to an expansion of Junior and Adult Training Centres, residential accommodation, day centres, social clubs, and domiciliary care.[32] The local authority went some way towards achieving these aims. It began a mental health social club, and in 1965 opened Runcorn House, a short-stay hostel for adults, and the Fosse Industrial Unit, an Adult Training Centre. Further institutions were opened in the late 1960s and early 1970s, including Langley House, a

10.21 District nurses visiting older people in their own homes, 1940s.

Source: Leicester City Council.

hostel for adults with learning difficulties, and a new Junior Training Centre at Netherhall Road. Following legislation in the early 1970s, the Junior Training Centres, schools, and special care unit were transferred to the Local Education Authority (LEA), while the social work and community care elements of the mental health service were absorbed by the new Social Services Department from April 1971.

On the ground, the local authority slowly began to provide services for the city's older people. Dr Joan Walker, a physician based at the Royal Infirmary, had begun a clinic for diabetics in 1945, and she deployed health visitors to teach diabetics in their own homes. She subsequently went on to conduct important research on the incidence of diabetes (10.21).[33] Many local women had always worked in the local hosiery industry, and after 1945 the Health Committee recruited large numbers of part-time home helps. Voluntary organisations also had an increasingly important involvement with older people and the chronic sick. The Marie Curie Memorial Foundation, for instance, was involved in the care of cancer patients, the local branches of the Old People's Welfare Association and Women's Royal Voluntary Service (WRVS) organised a laundry service, while the Red Cross operated a medical equipment loan scheme and provided some chiropody treatment (10.22). The meals-on-wheels service was administered by the WRVS from the 1950s. Overall, voluntary organisations were often more imaginative than the Health Committee in initiating new services.

Leicester: a modern history

10.22 Local branches of the Old People's Welfare Association and the Women's Royal Voluntary Service organised a laundry service for the city's older people.
Source: Leicester City Council.

The new public health

At the time of health service reorganisation in 1974, Dr Alan Buchan, the MOH for Leicestershire, was appointed to the post of Area MOH. As Area MOH, Buchan was more concerned with administrative issues that ensued from health service reorganisation, with 'community medicine', and with the opening of the Medical School.[34] After 1974, the series of annual MOH reports stretching back to the 1880s came to an abrupt end. It was only in the late 1980s that they reappeared following the Acheson Report of 1986, and the appointment of a Director of Public Health (DPH) by the Leicestershire Health Authority.

In Britain it was only from the late 1980s that public health returned to the political agenda, following a period of relative decline. By the mid-1970s, concern about the rising costs of hospital treatment, awareness of demographic changes, and critiques of medicine by feminists and others created conditions in which the role of preventive medicine began to be reassessed. The World Health Organisation played an important part in this process, as did individual governments. In Canada, for instance, the Lalonde document, *A New Perspective on the Health of Canadians* (1974), ushered in a new emphasis on individual lifestyle and health education. Similarly in Britain, prevention came to have a more prominent place in policy documents.[35] It was a theme that was picked up by reports which increasingly tried to establish priorities for future health provision in the light of a decline in the rate of growth of health spending. This trend was accelerated during the 1980s by pressure from different ends of the political spectrum. On the one hand, local authorities benefited from the argument put forward in the Black Report on inequalities in health

(1980), that resources for public health should be shifted towards care in the community.[36] At the same time, successive Conservative governments sought to re-fashion the philosophy and patterns of provision in public services such as health, and aimed to roll back the frontiers of the state.

Nonetheless concern over AIDS, salmonella poisoning, and outbreaks of Legionnaires Disease served to direct attention to public health, and culminated in the decision to set up a committee to consider the future of public health, including the control of communicable diseases and the specialty of community medicine. Its recommendations included the appointment of regional DsPH, the revival of the annual MOH reports discontinued in 1974, and greater co-operation.[37] The new specialism of public health medicine was, as its name suggested, very medical in its orientation. Nevertheless, the publication of the Acheson report coincided with activity at the grassroots level, since a number of local health authorities appointed DsPH in the late 1980s. In Liverpool, a city in the forefront of this movement, academics sought to re-examine the history of the philosophy of public health, arguing in support of a 'new public health'.[38]

By the 1990s, policy documents such as the *Health of the Nation* indicated that prevention had become an increasing priority, even for a Conservative government. Outbreaks of infectious disease exposed how the watchdog role exercised by earlier public health doctors had been seriously weakened. The outbreak of *Escherichia coli* food poisoning in Scotland in 1997, for example, was followed by calls for the restoration of MOsH who had the skills and authority to take action in a public health emergency. Moreover, plans to modernise local government tentatively acknowledged the responsibility for health that it had lost in the 1974 health service reorganisation. The White Paper on public health, *Saving Lives: Our Healthier Nation* (1999) outlined a range of priority areas comprising cancer, coronary heart disease and stroke, accidents, and mental health, and stressed the importance of partnerships between people, communities, and government. Apart from Health Improvement Programmes, Health Action Zones, and Healthy Living Centres, a new Health Development Agency, a Public Health Development Fund, and a network of Public Health Observatories were all established.[39]

At the local level, Alan Buchan had become the first DPH and District Medical Officer for the Leicestershire Health Authority. His first annual report was published in 1988. Dr Gillian Morgan was appointed DPH in 1991, to be succeeded by Dr Bernard Crump in 1995. Their annual reports were more thematic than previously – in 1990 the report focused on children; in 1991 on older people; in 1992 on lifestyle, disease, and health; in 1993 on deprivation, disability, and mental health; in 1994 on environmental factors; and in 1995 on the impact of cancer.[40] Ten years later, the focus had moved to health inequalities. The annual report of the Director of Public Health and Health Improvement for 2007 noted that the key health challenge for the city was reducing health inequalities. There were gaps in life expectancy between Leicester and England, and variations in life expectancy within Leicester. The key factor in this inequalities gap was perceived to be deprivation, and between 2004 and 2007 Leicester's position had worsened from the 34th most deprived local authority in England to the 20th most deprived. This underscored the importance of continuing to improve the wider determinants of health, such as education, unemployment, housing, and environmental health. The key areas of activity under the *Choosing Health* White Paper (2004) were smoking, obesity, mental health, alcohol, and health inequalities.[41]

Conclusion

Such indices as infant mortality, and the heights and weights of school-children, indicate that the health of certain groups in the city was improving over the period covered in this chapter. Mortality from infectious diseases such as pulmonary tuberculosis also declined rapidly, particularly after the Second World War. In some cases, the timing of these changes in mortality can be related quite closely to the introduction of specific therapies, as in the case of tuberculosis and streptomycin. But in many cases, mortality rates were already in decline as a consequence of improving living standards and nutrition. Changing systems of disease categorisation create problems when attempting to chart patterns of disease over a long time period, and the issue of natural modifications in disease virulence is similarly complex. Overall it remains extremely difficult to decide to what extent improvements in the health of specific age and gender groups can be attributed to public health policies, and to separate them from the wider context of advances in nutrition and living standards.

The city's standing compared to other urban areas of similar size, and its visibility at the national level, underwent dramatic change during our period. By the end of the nineteenth century, the city had gained some notoriety on account of its high infant mortality, and following its prominent role in the anti-vaccination campaign. To some extent, it retained this reputation in the early decades of the twentieth century. Local figures were active in London-based organisations such as the Eugenics Society, and also attracted attention through their publications. But in many ways the distinctive character of the city evaporated in the course of the twentieth century. While its population continued to be compara-tively large, social surveys showed that across a range of indices the city's performance was average compared to other county boroughs. Although infant mortality remained slightly high compared to the national average, it declined dramatically after 1900, and little seemed to survive of the proud nineteenth-century radical tradition. By the mid-twentieth century, the city had become comparatively anonymous in health terms – a change that, if anything, was exacerbated by the economic decline that set in from the early 1970s.

It is less evident to what extent public health services have been able to mediate health inequalities between the different wards within the city. As we have seen, there were movements of population following the building of large housing estates from the 1920s, slum clearance in the city centre, and also changes in ward boundaries. Areas such as Highfields that had been popular in the nineteenth century had become less desirable by the 1950s, so much so that it was there that migrants first settled, in large Victorian houses that had become lodging houses. But on the other hand, there is evidence of important continuities in the health experiences and expectations of successive generations of people living in the different wards. The annual DPH reports, for example, have indicated that it is the wards with large housing estates – North Braunstone, Eyres Monsell, and Mowmacre – that remain the most deprived. Despite a century of municipal activity in the field of public health, the wards with the highest mortality in 2007 were the same as in 1907.[42]

| Leicester: a modern history

11

Between modernism and conservation: Konrad Smigielski and the planning of post-war Leicester

MID-TWENTIETH-CENTURY LEICESTER was not considered an attractive place by visitors, who depicted it as plain, humdrum, workmanlike. According to the writer, J.B. Priestley, in *English Journey* (1934), it lacked a distinct character; Leicester, he wrote, 'seems to have no atmosphere of its own'. Priestley's opinion was echoed in the early 1960s by the architectural critic Ian Nairn who was commissioned by the City Council to undertake an architectural analysis of the city. 'There are no high spots, no dramatic sites and gestures and no obviously endearing local traits,' he remarked, before listing the many unsuspected qualities of the townscape.[1] By the mid-1960s, however, this self-effacing image was altering under the impact of urban planning. A new city had begun to be envisaged and at least partly created. In this respect Leicester paralleled other British cities where the decades after the Second World War saw a major attempt to plan the urban environment and to bring into being a brave new world, free from the nineteenth-century legacy of squalid housing, grimy streets and urban sprawl. Even so, Leicester's planning experiment was exceptional for the period. In the 1950s and more especially the 1960s the city emerged as a pioneer of new traffic solutions and approaches to the preservation of the historic environment, an original mix of modernist planning and conservationism.

One man above all was associated with Leicester's changing reputation, Konrad Smigielski, head of the City's Planning Department between 1962 and 1972. Smigielski was a controversial figure, within Leicester and outside. He was notorious for making highly coloured statements; soon after arriving in 1962, he shocked respectable opinion by declaring at a public meeting that 'a little bit of vice would make Leicester a truer city'. On retiring in 1972 he reflected, tongue-in-cheek, on his time in office: 'I would really have liked it to be a little duller. I have enjoyed it too much; it has been too exciting.'[2] In Leicester Smigielski has often been identified with the worst

11.1 The planner as publicist: *Leicester Mercury*, 1963.

LEICESTER · CARDINAL · T.E.

11.2 Leicester modern: the Telephone Exchange, Humberstone Road, 1967.

excesses of 1960s modernism, from high-rise blocks to concrete car parks. But his contribution to the cityscape of Leicester was more complex than this simple condemnation suggests. He accurately diagnosed many of the problems which have continued to bedevil town planning since the 1960s while pointing towards at least some solutions. Moreover, the manifold failings of the period were as much a product of political and financial problems as personal hubris. The figure of Konrad Smigielski has to stand at the centre of any account of the postwar planning of Leicester. To evaluate his contribution properly, however, he must be placed in relation to the planning situation he inherited and the larger social and political conditions of the time.

Early plans

Although the planning of Britain's cities is normally understood as a product of reconstruction following the Second World War, its roots lay earlier. It was part of a generalised reaction immediately before and after the First World War against the chaotic, laisser-faire urban development which had the attended rapid industrial and population growth of the nineteenth century. In the 1920s and 1930s the vogue for planning reflected

Leicester: a modern history

11.3–11.7 This selection of photographs shows a variety of street improvements undertaken before the Smigielski era.

11.3 Last building standing: Rodwell's shop, 84 High Street, 1889. The widening of the High Street required demolition on a grand scale. Rodwell's was last to be reduced to rubble.

Source: Record Office for Leicester, Leicestershire and Rutland, DE3736, Box 16, Folder 10.

11.4 Laying tram tracks in London Road.

Source: Record Office for Leicester, Leicestershire and Rutland, DE3736 Box 20, Folder 1.

11.5 Laying tram tracks in Melton Road.

Source: Record Office for Leicester, Leicestershire and Rutland, DE3736 Box 20, Easygates Folder 1.

11.6 Road improvements near Welford Road Prison, 1926.

Source: Record Office for Leicester, Leicestershire and Rutland, DE3736, Box 30.

11.7 Charles
Street pre-1920s
improvements.
Source: Record
Office for Leicester,
Leicestershire and
Rutland, DE3736,
Box 7, pre-1932,
Folder 1.

an increased concern with urban sprawl, which seemed to be engulfing the
countryside, as well as with the effects of traffic on towns.[3] In Leicester the
first plan for a ring road around the city was mooted in 1922 and two years
later a fifty-year Reconstruction Plan was put to a town meeting, which
rejected it on grounds of cost. However, a regional plan involving all the
local authorities covered by Leicestershire County Council was published
in 1932. Its proposals announced many of the themes of the post-1945 era:
zoning of urban functions (industry, residence, shopping and so on); slum
clearance and the provision of public or 'council' housing for workers; ring
roads around built-up areas; and the containment of the city through the
provision of a 'green belt'.[4] A number of proposals from the interwar plans
were implemented. In Leicester, for instance, a major new through-road,
Charles Street, was constructed between Belgrave and London Road at
a cost of £1 million, opened in 1931; and new council estates were built
at Braunstone and Saffron Lane, the peak in terms of new council-house
building being achieved in 1925–26.[5] But on the whole, inter-war initiatives
were piecemeal and little was achieved by way of systematic planning of the
city as a whole.

It was not until the Second World War that a coordinated plan for
Leicester was successfully put forward, largely the work of the City Engineer
and Surveyor, John Beckett. Reflecting over twenty years' experience in
municipal works, Beckett's 1944 plan was solid rather than inspirational and
included the creation of further council housing estates and modernisation

11.8 Leicester Development Plan 1952. This continued to influence the renewal of Leicester until the late 1960s.

Source: author's copy.

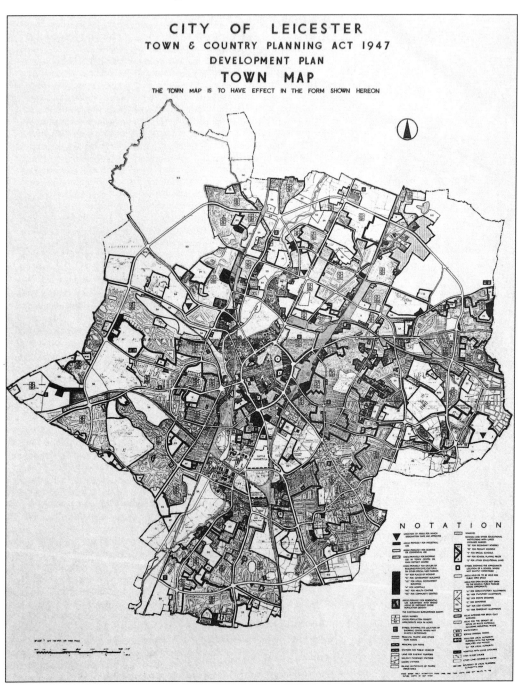

Leicester: a modern history

of the city's markets. It was quickly overtaken, however, by the Labour government's stipulation under the 1947 Town and Country Planning Act that all local authorities should produce a twenty-year Development Plan, based on a detailed survey of land use in their urban area.[6] Before it could be implemented, the Development Plan had to be approved by the Minister of Housing and Local Government, approval being granted in Leicester's case in 1952.

The result was a document extending to almost two hundred pages, based on detailed projections for factors such as population growth, industrial development and employment up to 1971. The Development Plan contained a large number of proposals affecting the city's future physical size and population distribution. Land use was to be rigorously zoned by removing industry from the city centre and residential areas. Housing was seen as the top priority, with 40,000 new homes planned over the twenty-year period and 126,500 people to be re-housed. Of these, over half would represent 'population overspill', 'working-class' households who would be 'decanted' (such were the terms used) to new purpose-built estates on the urban fringe, like Beaumont Leys – a sewage farm in 1952, but already being eyed as a potential site for a new suburban community. Industry, the plan's second priority, was to be dispersed to new industrial estates while additional land was to be made available to meet the needs of the city's major employers in hosiery, footwear and engineering. The urban conglomeration as a whole was to be connected by three ring roads, outer, inner and central, which would speed traffic between different zones while relieving congestion in the city centre. Beckett's vision for Leicester reflected Labour's post-war ideal of modern, rational efficiency. Indeed, such was the plan's presumed efficacy, that its 'ring and radial' system of traffic management became known in the Ministry of Transport as the 'Leicester solution', an early index of the city's reputation as a model of progressive practice.[7]

What was achieved from the Beckett plan of the 1950s? The programme of slum clearance begun between the wars continued, accelerating from the later 1950s: 3,250 houses were cleared in the 1920s and 1930s, a further 9,250 in the years between 1952 and 1968.[8] Demolition concentrated in particular on old working-class districts around Wharf Street and Highfields. In their place new council estates were developed, some on the urban fringe, such as Eyres Monsell, others close to the city centre, as in the case of the St Matthew's estate on the old Wharf Street site. The principle of zoning functions was also instituted, assisted by the 1947 Town and Country Planning Act which enabled the City Council to regulate all new building development. This meant that industrial uses – mid-twentieth-century Leicester had substantial numbers of small factories and workshops – would gradually be removed from residential areas and the city centre.

Road construction was slower, work on the ring roads not beginning until 1960. Construction started on a section of the inner ring to the west of the city centre between the Cathedral, Vaughan College and Castle Gardens. Here in Leicester's Old Town, where the ruins of the Roman forum still remained, the new highway resulted in the destruction of a whole series of historic streets and buildings, including medieval inns and Victorian mills. The 1952 Development Plan conceded that a number of listed buildings would be affected but blithely argued that 'none are of sufficient interest to justify retention'.[9] Writing in 1974, the Leicester historian Jack Simmons was damning in his view of the destruction wrought by Beckett's road-building:

11.9 Central Leicester in 1962.

Source: Leicester Traffic Plan.

> The Old Town in its former state was grimy, and in many respects an inefficient anachronism. Nevertheless, it was full of interest, of oddity; it was lovable and contained surprises. Not one of those

11.10 Belgrave
Road
improvements in
the 1960s.
Source: Leicester
City Council.

things is true of its successor. It has become a passage-way, a mere hyphen between larger units. Can anyone feel the smallest interest in such a place?[10]

Nevertheless, if a blueprint was in place, only limited progress towards urban transformation had been made by 1960. Leicester remained a workaday industrial city, in which the legacy of the nineteenth century, in the form of factories and terraced streets, overlay and obscured the city's longer and more varied history.

Konrad Smigielski and the Leicester Traffic Plan

This was the backdrop to the major phase of Leicester's post-war redevelopment, which occurred broadly in the years between 1962 and 1973. The new phase was associated with the arrival of Konrad Smigielski as Chief Planning Officer. Smigielski was born in Poland, trained in architecture and became Senior Planning Officer in the historic city of Kraków before the Second World War. During the war he served in the Polish army under British command and subsequently took a series of academic posts in architecture and town planning, notably at Leeds University between 1952 and 1962. In 1959 he attracted wider attention among urban planners

11.11 The urban designer: Smigielski and the model of Market Square.

Source: Leicester City Council.

with his proposal for London's road system. On this basis he applied for the post of deputy to the Chief Planner of the London County Council, but was later informed that the appointment board had been put off by his 'outrageous, arrogant manner'.[11] Leicester's decision in November 1961 to establish a Planning Department under a Chief Planning Officer was itself a daring one. It broke with the tendency in post-war cities to leave planning in the hands of a City Engineer (John Beckett's title) or, more rarely, a City Architect. As Kenneth Bowder, chair of the Town Planning Committee, explained in his report to the City Council, 'the Committee do not accept the view that planning is subordinate and subsidiary to engineering. ... It is a specialised profession and a positive science which can shape the social as well as the architectural pattern of a city's life and it will grow in importance as and when the full implications of this are realised.'[12] Leicester was second only to Newcastle-upon-Tyne in establishing a City Planning Department: by 1964 it had a total of 49 staff divided between five separate sections, such as Design and Re-Development. Smigielski's appointment in 1962 from a list of 33 applicants was likewise a bold stroke, masterminded by Bowder with whom he was to have a difficult yet crucial professional relationship over the next decade.[13]

11.12 Major traffic proposals, 1966.

Source: Leicester Illustrated Chronicle, 3 August 1966.

11.13 *Traffic in Towns* cover.

Source: author's copy.

11.14 *Leicester Traffic Plan* cover.

Source: author's copy

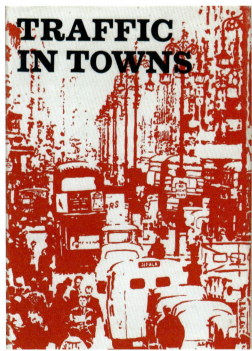

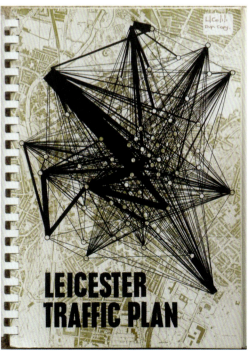

Smigielski's first move in office was to put on hold a number of the projects initiated under Beckett, while his new Planning Department undertook a review of the 1952 Development Plan. Traffic control quickly emerged as the most pressing issue, reflecting Smigielski's interests from his London roads proposal. The 1952 Development Plan had been based on a projected doubling of traffic volume in Leicester by 1971. By the early 1960s this appeared a serious underestimate; Smigielski's team showed that car ownership alone was more than doubling in each decade. Concern with what Smigielski called the 'motor revolution' was increasing at the period. In 1963 a major government report, *Traffic in Towns*, was published by Colin Buchanan, a planner employed by the Ministry of Transport. Buchanan's report was a milestone, signalling the emergence of 'traffic' as a dominant issue for British urban planners and defining a crucial conundrum of modern urban governance – how to reconcile the benefits of expanding car ownership with quality of life in towns. In Buchanan's view this could only be done by a trade-off between changes to the urban infrastructure, notably the construction of new road systems, and restrictions on traffic in certain areas such as congested city centres.[14] Smigielski's earliest report for Leicester, the *Leicester Traffic Plan* (1964) was regarded as the first city transport plan in Britain to operationalise Buchanan's principles of traffic management.

Smigielski's plan was pioneering in several ways. Unlike the previous Development Plans it took account of Leicester's history and its architectural heritage as well as the city's existing economic and social priorities. It was written in a jaunty style and illustrated with a variety of images including cartoons and colour drawings. At the same time the Traffic Plan was methodologically innovative, informed by an awareness of international trends in car ownership and urban transport policy. It followed North American examples by basing analysis not simply on a survey of traffic volume but on qualitative home interviews aimed at revealing people's complex patterns of transport use. The scientific status of the study was bolstered by the application of computer analysis, carried out at the Birmingham Data Centre of IBM.[15] In substance the document contained what for the time were radical solutions to the problems of traffic pollution and congestion. 'It was the first city plan,' Smigielski proudly asserted, 'to say NO to the motor car scientifically.'[16] As such, the Leicester study prefigured the environmental and conservation-conscious urban transport policies of the late twentieth century. All in all it was a formidable technical and creative achievement, which as Smigielski later admitted 'nearly kill[ed] the department and my wife in the process'.[17]

The *Leicester Traffic Plan* took at its starting point the 'motor revolution', the rapid and seemingly irreversible spread of motorised vehicles, especially the private car, as the predominant form of transport in and between cities. As well as a status symbol, according to Smigielski, the car had become the equivalent of a pet in the suburban home. 'In Leicester, as in

11.15 Press coverage of the Leicester Traffic Survey:

Source: Leicester Traffic Plan, 28.

any other city, the car is considered a sort of "domestic animal" and every weekend the ritual of washing the car, in which the whole family frequently participates, takes place in every third household.'[18] Awareness of the rising expectations of car owners, however, required to be balanced by recognition of the impact of increasing traffic on the urban environment. Hence the essential principle announced at the beginning of the Leicester study: 'in the hierarchy of the urban planning problems, *Environment* comes first and *Traffic* afterwards.' A second priority stemming from this principle was the protection and conservation of 'Inner Leicester', an area defined more broadly than the central area of Beckett, including New Walk and Victoria Park to the south and part of the river Soar to the east. Along the newly defined boundaries would run the Inner Motorway, a 4–6 lane freeway, carrying traffic around the city centre and which was presumed to obviate the need for any other ring roads. For those wishing to access Inner Leicester private transport would be restricted. Instead, Interchanges would be provided on the Inner Motorway, comprising multi-storey car parks and, in some cases, entertainment facilities such as bowling alleys and sports centres. Within Inner Leicester transport would be provided by various means, old and new, including buses, electric 'rickshaw-style' taxis and pedestrian conveyor belts. Most controversially, the city would install an overhead monorail, operating on a north–south route between Beaumont Leys and Wigston with the Clock Tower as the centre-point. This transport

11.16 Scale model of the Inner Ring Road.
Source: Leicester Traffic Plan, 75.

11.17 The ill-fated monorail (Kenneth Browne sketch).
Source: Leicester Traffic Plan, X.

11.18 The walking city: Gallowtree Gate imagined.

Source: Leicester Traffic Plan, 60.

network was referred to as the Integrated Transport System – a means, in other words, of envisioning urban movement as an interacting whole rather than as a series of unconnected parts.

Following its publication in 1964 the *Leicester Traffic Plan* attracted national attention, including praise from members of Buchanan's team and papers such as the *Observer* and the *Economist*.[19] But the estimated cost of implementation of £135 million ruled it out; the 'stop-go' policies of the Wilson Labour government before 1967 and the continuing constraints on public expenditure limited the confidence of city councils in embarking on major urban projects. As in other cities, progress on urban motorway construction was intermittent and sometimes fragmentary, with flyovers left hanging and slip roads going nowhere.[20] Parts of the Inner Motorway were built, though not without mounting protest at the damage to neighbourhoods in its path, despite Smigielski's efforts to protect the environs of inner Leicester. The plans for public transport also remained largely unfulfilled. Though supportive at the time, the Chair of the Town Planning Committee Kenneth Bowder was later to describe aspects of the Leicester Traffic Plan as 'abhorrent', singling out the monorail in particular as a 'laughline'.[21]

Our current realisation of the relationship between cars, pollution and climate change, however, should warn against easy dismissal of the Traffic Plan as a costly fantasy. In retrospect it conceded too much to the motorist rather than too little; its proposals for pedestrianisation have largely come about in the city centre, going well beyond Smigielski's modest first steps; and in seeking to preserve and enhance the central area of the city, the Plan not only mitigated many of the destructive effects of the Beckett proposals for road construction but laid the groundwork for more environmentally friendly transport policies in the future. Indeed, had the City Council (supported by central government) implemented the Leicester Traffic Plan, not only would it have been value for money in the longer term, it would also have placed Leicester in the vanguard of the new environmental urbanism. After all, integrated transport systems that include the metro, trams, bicycle and skateboard lanes have become standard features of many cities across the world.

Modernism and Conservation

The Leicester Traffic Plan sought to achieve a balance between the impulse to modernisation in motorway construction and the protection and enhancement of the urban environment. A similar balancing act between modernism and conservation was apparent in other aspects of the work of the City Planning Department during the Smigielski years.

As in roads policy, Smigielski inherited several major housing projects from the Beckett era. His department made a substantial contribution

11.19 Sketch of St Matthew's (Kenneth Browne).

11.20 Model for Market Square.

Source: Leicester Traffic Plan, 163.

to two of these, the council housing estates of Rowlatt's Hill and St Matthew's. Both estates combined modernist tower blocks – it was boasted that Rowlatt's Hill had the highest prefabricated towers in Europe when they were opened in 1967 – with socially and environmentally sensitive low-rise housing, together with a shopping centre and other amenities. The housing itself was designed by the City Architect, Stephen George, but the estates were nevertheless produced by the Planning Department and bore Smigielski's imprint.[22] Within twenty years they were beginning to suffer the problems of a deteriorating fabric, poverty and neglect, but in this they differed little from other high-rise council estates nationwide.[23] Smigielski himself remained distanced from the major housing disaster of the period, St Peters, where the high-rise blocks were beset by financial and structural difficulties, resulting in the dismissal of the City Architect, Stephen George, in 1970.[24] He contributed to the planning of Beaumont Leys, Leicester's own 'new town' on the north-eastern fringe of the city, notably the of the Radburn layout, with strict separation of cars and people. But the building of the new town only began in 1972 at the point of Smigielski's departure as City Planning Officer, and the proposed monorail linking Beaumont Leys to the city was never constructed.[25]

In reality Smigielski's priorities lay elsewhere, in the transformation of Leicester's city centre. Here a number of his interests converged, notably a continental European sensibility to the central area as the historic heart of the city and a site for sociability, pleasure and consumption. 'The inhabitants of Continental cities,' he wrote in 1968, 'live and work in cities and spend their leisure in city centres, puffing politics, gossip and garlic at each other in cafés, wine cellars, at fountains or just sitting anywhere on the piazzas and indulging in *dolce far niente*, an important function.'[26] It was characteristic that Smigielski's first proposal in April 1963, on behalf of the newly established City Planning Department, was for the redevelopment of the markets area. The market square, he argued, was 'in the historic past, the main square of Leicester ..., a civic space for the enjoyment of the people'. Here Smigielski echoed the 1932 Regional Plan which depicted Leicester as a 'great mart', whose 'Retail Markets draw thousands of people'.[27] Smigielski's proposal envisaged creating a new piazza in front of the refurbished Corn Exchange while the corrugated-iron roof over the market stalls, considered to make the square resemble a railway station, was to be replaced by a modern egg-box style canopy. The proposal immediately met with trenchant opposition from stallholders in the form of the Leicester Market Traders' Association who pointed out that while rents would rise the amount of space allocated to the market under the plan would shrink. Taking the aesthetic high-ground, Smigielski loftily dismissed the Association as 'barbarians', though he was forced to reduce the size of the piazza to accommodate some of the objections.[28] Nevertheless, the overall result was that the market square was preserved and at least partly enhanced at the heart of the city at a time when retail markets in many other British towns had come to be regarded as a nuisance and moved to premises indoors or outside the central area altogether.

A similar mix of tradition and modernism, albeit in different proportions, was envisaged in the Clock Tower and Haymarket area of the city centre. Smigielski's plan included a further piazza (now termed less contentiously a 'pedestrian square') around the Clock Tower, which was preserved 'for the continuity of tradition rather than its artistic merit' as the symbolic centre of Leicester. The proposed pedestrianisation of this area was bold since throughout the 1960s the Clock Tower remained the most congested traffic intersection in the city, despite repeated efforts to curb the problem. Pedestrianisation of Gallowtree Gate was partly achieved in 1971 – buses still ran down it – but the plan for the Clock Tower was combined with the construction of a 'major shopping and entertainment centre which could be described as Leicester's Piccadilly Circus'.[29] This was the Haymarket Centre, including a night club, ice rink and theatre, which was intended to open up the city at night by bringing people back in to the central area – a modest prototype of the idea of the culture-led '24-hour city' which city councils in Manchester and Leeds were to promote some twenty years later.[30] Again, however, Smigielski's grander vision for the Centre and the area was only partly realised. In 1966 the contract to build the Haymarket Centre was awarded to the private developers Taylor Woodrow, who thereafter took effective control of the project. Although the Haymarket Theatre was built at the City Council's own expense, the more ambitious proposals aimed at revitalising the city at night were watered down or abandoned. When the Haymarket Centre was officially opened by the mayor, Arnold Wakefield, in June 1973, it was presented exclusively as large-scale shopping mall, 'one of the most successful provincial shopping centres in the whole of the country' as Wakefield boasted.[31]

Smigielski's modernism was eclectic and playful, incorporating not only car parks and shopping malls but also pop art. Yet it co-existed with a still deeper appreciation of the historic environment: 'A city without old buildings,' he was fond of saying, 'is like a man without a memory.'[32] Conservation was thus an increasingly important component of Smigielski's planning vision, embodied most triumphantly in the rehabilitation of New Walk. Conservationism was not a new invention of the 1960s. Nationally, a

11.21 Continental-style: the Clock Tower imagined as Circus.

system of 'listing' buildings and monuments of architectural and historic interest had been introduced in 1948. What was new was the designation of 'Conservation Areas' under the Civic Amenities Act of 1967 which Smigielski and the City Council initially applied to New Walk, Castle Gardens, and the Cathedral and Guildhall precinct.[33] Of these the most extensive was New Walk, a late Georgian promenade, three-quarters of a mile in length, stretching from Victoria Park to the city centre. Smigielski was scathing of the 'dilapidation and neglect' into which New Walk had fallen by the later 1960s, noting that it had been 'for several years a source of embarrassment to the City Council and a favourite subject of criticism in the local press'.[34] His proposals were simple but highly effective, including additional tree planting, replacement of concrete street lamps by Victorian lamps, landscaping in De Montfort and Museum Squares, and coordination of colour schemes on housing elevations.[35] The improvements to New Walk, initiated from 1967, were eloquent testimony to Smigielski's imaginative commitment to conservation. It was to New Walk that he would always return on his daily perambulation from the Planning Department, often selecting someone from the office to look with him at Leicester's townscape.[36]

When asked later what he considered to have been his major achievements in his time as Chief Planning Officer, Smigielski nominated the projects involving the Market Place, the Haymarket Centre and New Walk. We might consider the last to have been his most enduring and least ambivalent legacy. While the Haymarket has given way to the Shires shopping centre and a new cultural complex, opened in 2008, and the Market Place canopy was replaced in 1990, Smigielski's renovations to New Walk remain largely intact today. Each of these projects, however, was concerned with the balance between modernism and conservation, categories that were understood to be not separate but indivisible. Thus Smigielski saw the construction of the Inner Motorway as the condition of the preservation of historic Leicester. The bold, even utopian elements in all this are evident in the plans

11.22 Poster advertising Smigielski's lecture on New Walk, 1967.

City of Leicester
The Chairman, Ald. Kenneth Bowder, and Members of the Town Planning Committee invite you to attend

A PUBLIC LECTURE

"Rehabilitation of New Walk"
(illustrated with colour slides and followed by a discussion)

by **W. Konrad Smigielski**
the City Planning Officer
in the Museum and Art Gallery
on Tuesday, 24th October 1967
at 7.30 p.m.

The Exhibition
"Rehabilitation of New Walk"
will be open in the Museum and Art Gallery from 20th October to 12th November 1967

| Leicester: a modern history

Inside the sketch (handwritten notes):

Note doorway (see 8)

7 close up

the intimacy of this path emphasized by the casual way in which the cathedral buttress edges in.

11.23 Kenneth Browne, sketch of St Martin's East.

themselves, displayed in the coloured diagrams of the *Traffic Plan* which echoed the Concept Art of the period, in the scale-models of the city of the future, exhibited to the public and photographed in Council publications, and in Kenneth Browne's wash drawings of sites such as Gallowtree Gate and St. Martin's East. In practice, as I have argued, such visions were very often stymied by public opposition, financial cost and everyday politics; some projects were significantly qualified through the planning process, others never got off the ground. But the Inner Motorway no less than the renovation of New Walk stand as a striking reminder of the ambition of urban planning in Leicester during the 1960s.

The end of the Smigielski era

By the early 1970s, however, problems were mounting on several fronts for Smigielski and the City Planning Department. There was growing public opposition to urban motorways and 'planning blight', symbolised by the numbers of empty office blocks. More serious still, the end of the long postwar boom spelled difficulties for Leicester shops, the prosperity of which was fundamental to Smigielski's plans for a modern, consumer-oriented city centre. In August 1970 the *Leicester Mercury*, ran a two-page special under the banner headline, 'It's time to stop the rot in the High Street'.[37] Echoing the complaints of retailers, it drew attention to the empty shops and bankrupt businesses which were blamed on planning measures, notably the application of over-zealous parking restrictions in the central streets. Matters were exacerbated by the Chief Planning Officer's dismissive response, printed in full in the *Mercury* the following week. According to Smigielski, the problems of city-centre retailers had nothing to do with the planners, 'a vague term of abuse embracing some mysterious and sinister persons to whom unlimited dictatorial powers over all human beings are attributed'. Instead, the blame for the economic predicament lay with shopkeepers' own slowness in adapting to changes in market demand as well as the vagaries of the capitalist trade cycle: 'commercial trends are not controlled by planning but by the laws of supply and demand'.[38] Unsurprisingly, retailers met this retort with charges of high-handedness and failed to be mollified by Smigielski's assurances that the situation would soon be eased by new car parks.

By this period Smigielski was also confronting increased opposition within the City Council itself, sections of which had become disenchanted with what they saw as maverick policies and a confrontational style of public relations. Proposals to build two new high rise office blocks in Belgrave and on London Road were received negatively, despite Smigielski's assertion that encouraging more office workers to the city would help resuscitate the ailing central shopping area. Ominously for the Chief Planning Officer, members of the Council and even the Town Planning Committee were quoted in the local press expressing sympathy with protestors against office block development.

Ultimately, though, Smigielski's dramatic fall from grace was the product of a more bizarre – and in certain respects, more telling – set of circumstances. Part of the city's long-term development plan was to have the Wholesale Fruit and Vegetable Market (separate from the Retail Market in Market Square) relocated. In March 1972 an unidentified party, possibly within the Council, made a successful bid to the Department of the Environment to have the Wholesale Market building listed, scuppering the Planning Department's proposals in the short-term at least and calling into question the Chief Planning Officer's credibility.[39] The following month the long-running saga over the future of the Sun Alliance building came to an unexpected head. In conjunction with the Sun Alliance company themselves, the City Council had agreed to the demolition of the Victorian building in Horsefair Street and its replacement by a modern block. The affair had roused a powerful preservationist lobby, including local history societies and Victorianists from the University of Leicester who described the plan as 'monstrous'.[40] On 6 April 1972, however, the *Leicester Mercury* announced that, as in the case of the Wholesale Market, an unknown individual or group had successfully applied to the Department of the Environment to have the Sun Alliance building listed as of special architectural interest, thus halting demolition. The City Council immediately responded by indicating that the Sun Alliance company could apply to them for 'special listing consent', which, if granted, would overturn the Department of the Environment's decision. The following day, 7 April, however, the *Mercury* dropped a new bombshell through the person of Smigielski who calmly announced that it was the Corporation itself which on his recommendation had applied to the Department to have the building listed a year previously. The Council, however, professed no such knowledge. The chair of the Town Planning Committee, Kenneth Bowder, blamed a 'well-organised, well-informed group of string-pulling conservationists' for this apparent act of treachery, while his deputy, Arnold Wakefield, was anxious to find out 'who has pulled the strings and brought this matter to a head'.[41]

Whoever was to blame, the finger pointed inevitably to Smigielski as the mole within. While the City Council held back from naming him directly, the *Mercury* was less circumspect, identifying him as the 'paid planner-in-chief and committed conservationist' and pointedly noting his absence at the meeting of the Town Planning Committee to discuss the Sun Alliance affair.[42] Smigielski never openly admitted responsibility but as well as revenge for previous slights his actions were undoubtedly fuelled

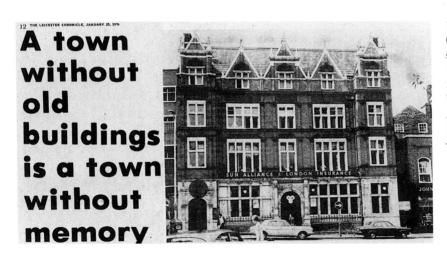

11.24
Conservation struggles in 1976 - the Sun Alliance building.
Source: Leicester Chronicle, 25 January 1970.

by principle: his sustained opposition to the demolition of the Sun Alliance building was well known and fitted with his longer-term commitment to the cause of urban conservation. From the vantage point of the City Council, however, such behaviour on the part of a senior official represented an unacceptable breach of trust. Following a reportedly blazing row with Bowder and Wakefield, Smigieslki was granted 'leave of absence' some eleven months in advance of his formal retirement from office in March 1973. Although his premature departure was the subject of a leader in the *Mercury*, which paid generous tribute to his achievements, his passing does not seem to have been mourned in Leicester; the letters page of the local press remained almost wholly silent on the matter of his dismissal.[43] Not so Smigielski himself, his passing-shot being to label Leicester 'Clochemerle', a popular television series based on a fictional French town noted for its parochial conservatism.[44]

Conclusions

How then should we evaluate the achievements or otherwise of the Smigielski era? An assessment is complicated by the rising tide of opposition to 'planning' from the later 1960s and the subsequent tendency to tar all town planning of the period with the same brush, as leading to sterile, soulless urban environments. Protest against tower blocks, urban motorways and architectural 'vandalism' on the part of planners, became widespread in Britain from the late 1960s, orchestrated through a series of highly-staged campaigns.[45] A similar tide of opinion was apparent in Leicester with hope in what might be created gradually giving way to concern about what was being destroyed. Historians have begun to highlight the significance of conservation in postwar urban planning, even in a place like Newcastle upon Tyne, where T. Dan Smith and his chief planner Wilf Smith were busy trying to recreate the city as the 'Brasilia of the North' in the 1960s.[46] Yet in Leicester especially, planning under Smigielski came to be as much – if not more – about conservation as the modernism with which he is conventionally associated. As Peter Mandler has recently argued, most of the more obvious examples of brutalist city centre development in postwar Britain were carried out by private developers rather than by the planning profession.[47] And it was significant that Smigielski's resignation was prompted by a dispute over conservation in which he was strongly identified with the pro-conservation lobby, not with the modernists.

I have argued in this chapter that the reputation of Konrad Smigielski is in need of restitution. So often held responsible for the worst excesses of 1960s brutalism, a closer inspection of his career and of the record of the City Planning Department under him suggests a more positive assessment. Many of the most obvious eyesores, such as the gyratory road development at St. Nicholas Circle, were a legacy of his predecessor, John

Beckett, and an earlier phase of planning. Equally, he had little to do with the long-running debacle over the siting of the new Civic Centre, whose design was contracted out to a London consultancy while its premises in New Walk did not open until 1976. In other respects, such as the Leicester Traffic Plan, Smigielski's ideas were genuinely pioneering and for a brief time placed Leicester in the vanguard of national urban planning. As his colleague in the Planning Department, Henry Blachnicki, put it, 'Smigielski discovered Leicester for the people of Leicester – [he] transformed it from a market town into a city'. Even those with whom he was frequently in conflict acknowledged his galvanising effect. In the words of Kenneth Bowder, chair of the Town Planning Committee, who was instrumental in both recruiting and dismissing him, 'Smigielski's appointment was good for Leicester. There are other people who should take their share of credit for what has been achieved – councillors and other officers – but I don't think so much would have been achieved had he not been here to provoke it.'[48]

Ultimately, however, Smigielski's most lasting achievements may have been those which were the least determinedly modernist and for which he has attracted least attention. They include the renovation of the historic environments of New Walk and Town Hall Square. Just over a year before his departure Smigielski added his stamp to a further area of the city, a compact neighbourhood of Victorian terraces known as Clarendon Park. Under the Housing Act of 1969 the Council offered grants for home improvements in this area of workers' housing, including the provision of hot water, bathrooms and inside lavatories. Smigielski's skills were employed to design a scheme for environmental improvement, which he undertook with great sensitivity. An extensive process of public consultation was set up, involving innovative use of focus groups (called 'street groups') drawn from local residents to feed back views of the plan. Roads were closed to through traffic, prioritising pedestrian use; new open spaces and play areas were created for children; trees were planted to soften the appearance of the area; mixed use, including shops, small factories and workshops, was encouraged.[49] The result was a design that reversed earlier planning priorities and anticipated many of the ideas later to become associated with the 'new urbanism', encouraging social interaction, visual variety and a sense of the unexpected.[50] Smigielski himself was characteristically ebullient about the Clarendon Park project, asserting that 'historians will judge it a great period in town planning'.[51] Yet it represented, essentially, a modest urbanism that started from the existing historically-formed environment rather than one that sought to impose its own abstract design upon it. In the final analysis this modest urbanism was a more significant part of Konrad Smigielski's legacy to Leicester than the road systems and office blocks for which he is more commonly remembered.

11.25 A modest urbanism: Clarendon Park, 1971.

12

Gonna Rock Around the Clock (Tower) Tonight: Leicester and the coming of 'the Sixties'

Why I decided to pretend I was American, I will never know! I'd never been across the pond and knew nothing of the great Wild West apart from what I had seen on the big screen. All I knew was that I felt an urgent need to put on airs and graces, and pretend to be somebody – anybody – other than who I was.

> Local singer Gerry Dorsey, on meeting his future wife at the Palais de Danse, Leicester in 1956.[1]

THIS CHAPTER is about Leicester and 'the 1960s' and it is written with a number of important assumptions. First, 'the Sixties' is taken here to mean an idea, with a variety of connotations, rather than, literally, as a decade. As Arthur Marwick remarks in his book *The Sixties*, 'we readily think in decades'; he then embarks on a discussion of 'the Sixties' which dates them from 1958 to 1974.[2] Similarly, Julie Stephens has suggested that 'the Sixties' has come to be used 'like a shorthand … variously to denote acts of protest or rebellion, a distinctive cultural mood, a special style or atmosphere'.[3] This chapter uses the term, generally speaking, to refer to a changing 'cultural mood' in Leicester and charts its emergence in the life of the city after the Second World War, chiefly in relation to music and night and/or young life. In this context, it argues that a lot of what came to constitute 'the Sixties' began in the 1950s. Second, historians for some considerable time now have acknowledged that history should not only be about the recorded activities of public figures, institutions and the holders of office; it should be about the lives of 'ordinary citizens, as well as ministers and mandarins', as David Kynaston wrote recently.[4] This, of course, should include patterns of popular leisure activity.

The third assumption is that in the main there is no reason to suppose that Leicester had any special relationship to, say, skiffle music, the contraceptive pill, the Beatles or any other of the core cultural themes of 'the

Sixties'; on the contrary, what is described here is invariably, in effect, a local edition of a sequence of social changes that occurred throughout Britain and beyond. Indeed, it is part of the paradox of the cultural politics of 'the Sixties' that, while a greater validation seemed to be bestowed upon working-class and/or provincial cultures – northern accents, for example, were heard in millions of British living rooms via television's *Coronation Street* (1960–), *Z Cars* (initially 1962–65) or the proliferating number of 'beat groups' interviewed by Brian Matthew on BBC Light Programme's *Saturday Club* (1958–67) – the discourse that was 'the Sixties' usually centred on the doings of a London-based elite. This elite consisted largely, in the words of Dominic Sandbrook, the most painstaking chronicler of British life in 'the Sixties', of 'a relatively small, well-educated minority, usually people who were in their teens or twenties at the time and went on to become well-paid writers, journalists, publishers and so on'.[5] So it was probably a reflex, rather than a recollection of personal experience, that led John Lahr in his biography of Joe Orton (a playwright and recruit to this metropolitan elite from the city's working class) to refer so airily to Orton's need to escape 'the banality of Leicester life'.[6] How, he may have assumed, could it have been otherwise. Indeed, such summary judgements on a town like Leicester might cause inhabitants of such places to be reflexively self-apologetic. The film-maker and social commentator Ray Gosling, born in Northampton, began a documentary about Leicester and Nottingham made for the BBC in 1963:

> I'm a Midlander and that is, I do believe, the most uninspiring, uninteresting, unexciting English tribe to belong to. If your home is Liverpool, then you have something. People, they call you a Whack, a Scouse. … But me, I'm a nobody. No tradition, no proper accent and I'm even worse, I'm not even a Brummie. Home is the other side. The East Midlands is my country.[7]

This account of Leicester and 'the Sixties', then, is drawn from local histories, contemporary coverage in the city's press culled from county archives, documentary footage, and the memories of people who were around at the time.[8]

Before 'the Sixties': family and kinship in central Leicester

Virtually any student who has sought to know something of the social history of Britain after 1945 has encountered the 'working-class community'. This was captured in a number of studies, most notably the celebrated Penguin books *Family and Kinship in East London*, a portrait of the East End district of Bethnal Green by Peter Willmott and Michael Young, and *Poverty: The Forgotten Englishmen*, Ken Coates' and Richard Silburn's exploration of the St Ann's area of inner-city Nottingham.[9] These books, and others like them, told of tightly knit communities based upon local industry, stable family networks, and strong traditions of mutual assistance. Leicester had communities very like these, as recent histories attest. The Wharf Street area, running east from the city centre along the Leicester Navigation Canal was a good example. Many of the terraced streets of this district came down in the 1930s and demolition was recommenced in the 1950s. Houses made way for the new Leicester Telephone Exchange. Residents were dispersed to new estates such as Stocking Farm (begun in 1952), Mowmacre Hill (where 'production line' houses started to go up in 1954),[10] New Parks, Thurnby Lodge and Eyres Monsell, but those who survived forty years later remembered a strong community with little crime, partly, as one reflected, because 'we had nothing much worth stealing'.[11] The Walnut Street area, a little to the south of the city centre, is another example. Colin Hyde uses oral testimony to paint a vivid picture of life in a 'largely self-contained working-class community [where] many factories and places of work as well as scores of small shops [allied to the] closeness of small terraced houses gave people a feeling of security'.[12]

Bentley's Engineering was here, along with Liberty Shoes, Armstrong Siddeley, Morley's hosiery and sundry other factories and dye works – all later superseded by the expanding Royal Infirmary, which bought up many houses in the area, and Leicester Polytechnic, established in 1969. In the 1950s, many of the families who moved out to the new estates left behind, according to one, a 'community in which you lived, you worked and you played, and you shopped, it was all there, that's really what it was all about'.[13]

Forms of play in these substantially closed social worlds varied according to age – street football, summer-time swimming in the canal, and roller-skating for the children; the pub, the cinema or, perhaps, the theatre for

12.1, 12.2 The former Regal Cinema on Havelock Street before and after demolition.

Source: Colin Hyde.

12.3 The
Palace Theatre,
Belgrave Gate.
Originally an
opera house
(1891), it became
a venue for
variety in 1901,
and closed in
1959.
Source: Record
Office for Leicester,
Leicestershire and
Rutland, DE3736,
Box 3.

12.4 Adverts for
Palace theatre,
Oxford Street
and Newarke
Street, seen from
the *Magazine*,
January 1909.
Source: Record
Office for Leicester,
Leicestershire and
Rutland, DE3736,
Box 25, Oxford
Street.

the adults. At one time there were 24 pubs in the Walnut Street area and a popular cinema on Havelock Street called the Regal, built in 1937 to seat over a thousand. 'We went pictures, we were always at pictures,' recalled one resident; 'We never went into the town,' said another – 'We always waited for the film to come from town to the Regal'.[14] Leicester, incidentally, had 36 cinemas in the 1950s.[15]

Of course, the people of these now mythic districts did not play as they pleased. Youngsters would often congregate at youth clubs, for example. Given the policing of the young within families, however, this would not necessarily be constricting. 'It won't sound exciting to you,' said one interviewee reflecting on the PT, woodwork and modelling with clay on offer at St Andrew's church youth club, 'but to them in those days it was terribly exciting to be out of sight of their mums and dads and, you know, they could do what they wanted and it didn't matter'.[16] Out in Belgrave Gate, the main thoroughfare on the city's east side, running through another warren of terraced streets, was the Palace Theatre opened by the famous Stoll Group in 1901. Sir Oswald Stoll had conceived such theatres as a proper riposte to the vulgarity of the music hall, and in the Palace's auditorium was a huge notice which read: 'No whistling or catcalls allowed. Applaud by hand only'.[17] The Palace closed in 1959, having faced increasingly heavy competition from the local Working Men's Club, at which, it is rumoured, the emotionally much less restrained American crooner Johnny Ray had once recently appeared.

Then, of course, there was dancing, an activity about which the common people of Leicester seemed to enthuse and one which usually took them out of their immediate neighbourhood. In the late 1940s and early 1950s couples thronged to dances at De Montfort Hall where there was room for 500 couples, and the local press boasted that the Palais de Danse, on Humberstone Gate in the city centre, was 'one of the biggest and best ballrooms in the Midlands [and] accommodates several hundred couples for six nights of the week throughout the year'. The manager told a reporter in 1953: 'Leicester is a woman's town. Factory and office girls are the smartest dressed in the country. They come to the Palais to enjoy themselves and it gives them a chance to parade their clothes.'[18] This hints at what has been widely acknowledged: that Leicester was a prosperous town in the 1950s and 1960s, with high wages and full employment. Hyde explained, 'it was accepted that there were plenty of jobs available, and if you didn't like one you could easily find another.' ''Cos, you know,' as one of his respondents recalled, 'jobs in those days were so easy to get, they were ten a penny, jobs, they really were, you never had to worry about a job, and when you were in a job, you felt secure.'[19] Many of these jobs, in a town based on light industry, were held, as the manager of the Palais knew well, by young women. These women, though, would not necessarily go dancing simply to show off their new clothes. They were there to meet young men. In the Palais, popular culture was likely to be policed by families with far more strictness than Sir Oswald Stoll could muster. Valerie Tedder, daughter of the boiler man at Wilson's dye works on Nottingham Road, began work at Martha Hills garment factory in 1949. She was a keen dancer and became a regular at ballrooms around the city. One night in the early 1950s she went to De Montfort Hall with a workmate and ended up dancing with a young man she had taken a shine to, called Brian. She agreed to let him walk her home:

> When we reached my gateway we stood outside for a few minutes fixing up another date. Brian then took me in his arms and kissed me. Suddenly the wicket gate opened and my mother was standing there. She stepped through the gate pointing her finger at Brian and told him to get off home. What time did he call this? She smacked my face and ordered me into the house.[20]

It is doubtful that this incident was untypical of its time or place. It was full of sociological implication: the disciplining of young bodies; the zealous protection of the virginity of daughters; the denial of social space in which any independent youth culture might flourish. As David Bell noted, the teenager was still in the process of being invented; meanwhile, young people, in Leicester as elsewhere, were expected to pass from childhood into junior versions of their parents, with nothing in between.[21]

12.5–12.7
Transformations to the site of the Palais de Dance between 1926 and 1960. From Batten and Son (Corn Merchants) to the Palais de Danse, to Mecca.

Source: Record Office for Leicester, Leicestershire and Rutland, Box 19, Humberstone Gate, Folder 2.

'It took over your soul, that music did':
Leicester, the 1950s and the dawn of 'the Sixties'

These restrictions notwithstanding, the material basis for 'the Sixties' – with their connotation of musical exploration and greater personal freedom – was enshrined in the ample wage packets being taken home across the city, which left healthy disposable income for young workers after bed-and-board money had been paid to parents, and the end of rationing in 1954. Increasingly in the 1950s, with the incipient break-up of inner-city working-class culture and many of these young workers living increasingly on new outlying estates, with money in their pockets and purses, entertainment was a bus or motor cycle ride away in the town centre. Much of this new entertainment related to music and, more specifically, in Leicester and across the UK, a relationship developed between young people and the sounds and rhythms of working-class America. Steadily, during the 1950s, popular music and emergent youth culture became awash with what the Chambers has called 'Americanicity' – the desire to imitate or otherwise engage with American-ness.[22]

The popularity of American music in Britain was, of course, not new: American dance bands had had a big UK following before the Second

12.8 The Astoria – a popular social venue in the 1950s. Note the varied nature of the streetscape in 1952 which includes the Antelope Hotel, Astoria, Beehive, Opera House, various shops, and St Martin's.

Source: Record Office for Leicester, Leicestershire and Rutland, Box 28, Silver Street, Royal Opera House, Folder 2.

12.9 The Coliseum (now the Leicester Colosseum) on Melton Road.

Source: Richard Rodger.

World War, along with their resident singers – men such as Bing Crosby and Frank Sinatra, who had gone on to become, in effect, the first pop stars. But this was essentially hip urban middle-class music from the north-east coast of the United States. Sinatra, incidentally, performed at De Montfort Hall in 1953;[23] he was voted Second Best Male Pop Singer in a Leicester poll of 1999.[24] By contrast, the music beckoning British youth was associated principally with the disenfranchised blacks and 'white trash' of the rural South.

On the face of it, in Leicester, as in other British cities, 1956 seems to have been a watershed year in this regard. In 1954 the American country singer Bill Haley, by then twenty-nine, had, with his band the Comets, recorded 'Rock Around the Clock' a record, like a number at the time, blending country music with African American rhythm and blues. It was a Billboard hit in the States in 1955 and was added to the soundtrack of a film of that year called *Blackboard Jungle*, a story of high school delinquency. The song's rapid success, through this film, had led in 1956 to a second film, called simply *Rock Around the Clock* – a flimsy vehicle for Haley and his suddenly popular music. In *Talk of the Town*, a video documentary about Leicester in the 1950s and 1960s, a local man recalled: 'I can remember reading in the *Leicester Mercury* that *Rock Around the Clock* had been shown, I think at the ABC cinema and there'd been Teddy Boys rocking in the aisles and that certainly impressed me.' Another man added: 'One Sunday night at the Colosseum [cinema on Melton Road] I just got out of my seat and danced in the aisles … nobody cared … it was as though it took your soul, that music did.'[25]

The editor of the *Illustrated Leicester Chronicle*, sister publication to the *Leicester Mercury*, was swift to denounce such enthusiasm. In September 1956, beneath the headline 'What We Think of … ROCK 'N' ROLL' he asked, 'What is it that has caused youthful audiences at a Leicester cinema to break out into rowdyism, to dance in the aisles and to worry the police?' 'Rock 'n' roll,' he continued, 'has an insistent, pile-driver rhythm. It is crudely sexy. The band featured in the film … makes noises like a boiler factory. A singing Rock 'n' roll quintet also in the film, is led by a negro who sounds, at times, as if he is about to vomit, or is having hiccups.' The city of Leicester should stand up to the American commercial interests now threatening to exploit its teenagers, and, according to the *Leicester Chronicle's* editor:

We should retaliate! Let us 'send' Rock 'n' roll – back to where it came from! … This is one American import we can well do without. Stem the Rock 'n' rolling tide – and parents, police, cinema and dance managers and most popular singers and musician will all echo: 'GOOD RIDDANCE!'[26]

Although the extravagant use of exclamation marks suggests this article might have been written tongue-in-cheek, it probably met with numerous murmurs of approval in suburban Leicester, especially since, perhaps as a further invitation to outrage, the article carried a still from the film, with a caption pointing out that a female dancer is being 'thrown over her partner's shoulder and through his legs'. Moreover, the dyspeptic reference to the 'negro' with hiccups (apparently, Tony Williams, lead vocalist of The Platters) was suggestive of the tacit racism that often characterised establishment disapproval of this emergent music. Sociologists recognise moments like this one as indicative of a moral panic – a point in the history of a society when an activity and its perpetrators are singled out for condemnation by media and public spokespeople. The activity itself need not be dangerous or noticeably new, but the strong implication is that right-thinking people should be disgusted by it. Rock 'n' roll in 1956 was one of the first in a long line of moral panics about youth in post-war Britain.[27]

However, the phenomenon denounced in the *Chronicle* was not wholly new to Leicester. Although Haley's music, in essence the country-based rockabilly style, was novel for the time, some approximation to Rock 'n' Roll was already established in the town.[28] Beryl Simpson's memories bear this out in her typically Leicester working-class biography: born in 1938 in the Gypsy Lane area of east Leicester, her father was a news vendor in the city centre, her mother worked in a hosiery factory; she began courting at sixteen and was herself employed for forty years in the boot and shoe trade. Beryl remembers the ages of 12 and 13 (1950–51) as her 'rock 'n' roll years':

> I used to go to Cossington Street swimming baths in Leicester. Tuesday under 13. Wednesday over 13. I was quizzed about my age but I managed to bluff my way in. … The band was called the Blue Stars and there was ten or twelve of them. … We also used to go to the De Montfort Hall where there were placards all round the dance floor saying 'NO JIVING ALLOWED'. But before long one couple started jiving and that was it – every one on the dance floor would be jiving like crazy.

This, she confirms, would often entail the now-dreaded over-the-shoulder/between-the-legs manoeuvre: 'We were only thirteen, fourteen. You didn't think it was sexy. You thought it was energetic.'[29] This defiant jiving and jitterbugging among Leicester's young had its origins in the presence of American troops in Leicester in 1944 and from the music played on the American Forces Network.[30] In some sense, perhaps, for Leicester 'the Sixties' began then.

A closer look at the Leicester music scene in the 1950s, as charted in the local press, reveals a complex picture. Like many English towns of the time Leicester people were variously negotiating their relationship to the imagined culture of America's southern states. This had implications for gender relations (while women might remain marginal as performers they would become more prominent, and expressive, as audiences), for 'race' (much of the music had originated among, and/or was played by, Afro-Americans), and for public order ('skiffle' music was generally regarded as permissible while 'rock 'n' roll', for many guardians of civic morality, was not).

In the early 1950s, Leicester newspapers told, principally, two stories about the city's popular musical life. One was the story of show-business – a staple of local journalism, as it remains. Here the local (Leicester) was juxtaposed with the global (the big time – the United States). There was news, for example, that in 1954 Clive Allen, 'employed in a clerical role at a Leicester boot factory' and resident pianist in a local working men's club, had had one of his songs recommended to the famous Beverley Sisters;[31] that Maurice Coleman, son of the licensees of The Coventry Arms on Halford Street, was the same year given a contract to write songs for the American singer Frankie Laine;[32] and that Larry Gretton, formerly a worker at I.L. Berridge's hosiery factory on Sanvey Gate had got a job as a vocalist with the well-known Joe Loss Orchestra.[33] In the later 1950s there was also a steady stream of reports of the 'Leicester singer to appear on TV' variety – often on the talent discovery programme of Carroll Levis.

The second story was about jazz, originally an Afro-American musical form of course, but in the 1950s mostly dispensed in the UK by white, usually male, enthusiasts. The *Leicester Evening Mail* in the mid-1950s ran a column called 'John Cawood's RHYTHM CORNER' – 'Pardon me for a moment while I rave over the jazz scene in Leicester,' he purred in 1954.[34] Here, too, the local met the global. For example, saxophonist Betty Smith, whose parents kept the White Swan Inn in the Leicestershire village of Sileby, became a minor local celebrity, partly because she was a female in a largely male world, and partly because she played in the London-based Freddie Randall jazz band: it was announced that she would be touring the United States with them in the summer of 1956.[35] Similarly, the following year, Sonny Monk and his brother Owen, who came from the Leicester suburb of Wigston Fields and had a Dixieland jazz band, announced that they were going to settle and play in the United States.[36] Peter Bailey, a grammar school boy in neighbouring Coventry in the 1950s, has written evocatively of the local jazz scene. It was fun, he recalls, occupying a 'slender zone between repression and excess'; there was dancing and drinking, along with a quiet envy of the 'social and sexual utopia' apparently inhabited by the working-class kids at the secondary modern schools; and there was an elitism, widespread among jazz people, which saw outsiders as 'peasants', incapable of distinguishing a b Flat from a bull's foot. Jazz, he says, subsided with the arrival of Haley and Elvis Presley in 1956.[37]

Jazz, or jazz-derived dance music, certainly continued to have a place in Leicester's musical calendar. The American jazz performers Sarah Vaughan

(February 1953), Nat King Cole (March 1954), Lionel Hampton (November 1956) and Eddie Condon (1957) all played the De Montfort Hall in the 1950s, and Britain's leading exponent of jazz, Chris Barber, brought his band to the 'De Mont' no fewer than nine times between March 1957 and April 1963. Here they took their place in a crowded schedule that embraced classical concerts by the Hallé Orchestra, local (Jerry Cope, Johnny Lester) and visiting dance bands (Joe Loss, Ted Heath), American pop singers (Guy Mitchell: August 1953, May 1954; Johnny Ray: October 1955, November 1956, March 1959; Connie Francis: March 1959), smiling pub pianists (Winifred Atwell: April 1956; Russ Conway: November 1959, November 1961), crooners (Denis Lotis: October 1955; David Whitfield: October 1957, April 1959; Dickie Valentine: October 1957; Frankie Vaughan: November 1958) and the soothing strings of (Annunzio) Mantovani and his orchestra (February 1957: February 1959, April 1960, February 1961).

If the outrage of the *Leicester Chronicle* was belated and alarmist, something did seem to change around 1956, as Peter Bailey intimated. For one thing, the greased-back, 'DA' haircut, most closely associated with Elvis Presley, began to appear on the heads of young local men photographed for the evening papers – an early example belonged to 17-year-old Alan Sturgess of Hinckley, a singer with local dance bands who had an invitation to appear on the Carroll Levis TV show. Alan was training to be an accountant but the DA soon came to characterise dissident working-class lads – Teddy Boys, or as an Austrian artist living in London described them: 'thin, undernourished creatures … ragged and unambitious, quaff crowned [wearing] spivvish attire with mischief glittering in their eyes.'[38]

These young men may have scared the editor of the *Chronicle* and his readers, but hope was at hand. In December 1956 the *Leicester Evening Mail* discovered skiffle. In its 'Junior Evening Mail' section it announced: 'We were invited to hear a newly formed skiffle group at the Evington Valley Youth Club. "Oh, it takes a worried man to sing a worried song," crooned eight young voices which belonged to eight young syncopating bodies. They had rhythm and enthusiasm – important ingredients for a first-class skiffle group.' The band assured the reporter that they played 'only American folk songs'. 'Rock 'n' roll?' asked the reporter. 'No,' replied lead singer Brian Park, reassuringly.[39]

Skiffle was indeed rooted in the folk songs of the rural American south – 'Worried Man Blues', sung in Leicester youth clubs in the 1950s, had originated as an Afro-American convict song in the early 1900s and had been collected by country musician, A.P. Carter, whose band, The Carter Family, had had a hit with it in 1930. Skiffle was pioneered in Britain by jazzmen, chiefly cornetist Ken Colyer and guitarist Lonnie Donegan.[40] Donegan, who had changed his name from Anthony to Lonnie in a tribute to the black American bluesman Lonnie Johnson, had become the standard bearer for this new wave of 'Americanicity' on the British music scene. His recording of 'Rock Island Line', written by the Afro-American bluesman Huddie Ledbetter (known as 'Lead Belly'), was no. 1 in 1956. 'When it was a hit in the States, we laughed for a week,' said Donegan later.[41]

Skiffle, as historians have noted, was a democratic music; it was cheap to play and drew in young people from different backgrounds.[42] A number of skiffle bands emerged in Leicester, sometimes, such was the domestication of this musical form, under the auspices of the church. In June 1957 a group called The Black Cats won the Leicester Diocesan Youth Fellowship skiffle competition and this qualified them for a heat of the National Skiffle Contest, to be shown on BBC television's *Six Five Special* the following April.[43] In between times they had an audition with Carroll Levis but were reluctant to turn professional because, as Black Cat Roddie Fraser explained, 'if some of the lads give up their present jobs they are liable for their two years in the forces'.[44] Around the same time a three-hour skiffle concert was organised at De Montfort Hall by the National Jazz Federation and Bob Cort, whose band took part and who was the county's leading exponent of skiffle. He was called upon to explain the poor turnout: 'I don't really blame people for not coming to a show of this nature,' he said, 'a quarter of an hour of skiffle during an assorted programme is great fun, but to ask anyone to sit through three hours of it is another matter.'[45]

Skiffle was not rated by the city's young jivers; nor, in all probability, did bleak songs about chain gangs and hopping freight trains appeal to many of the young women of Leicester who, like young women in other towns, were experiencing some kind of emotional and sensual awakening. Karin Patrick (b.1940) remembers going to see Johnny Ray at De Montfort Hall when she was sixteen:

> I had seen articles in the national press about Johnny and all the excited girls screeching and shouting at his concerts and I was looking forward to seeing what all the excitement was about. We had seats on the stage and when this tall brown haired handsome man appeared and started to sing I shouted and screeched with the rest of the audience. Johnny was very emotional and cried during his renditions and all the women were on a high with excitement. ... The only other time I have seen such excitement and emotion was when the film 'Rock around the Clock' ... was shown in The Ritz cinema in Market Harborough and we all rocked in the aisles, much to the disgust of our parents. We had our own version of Bill Haley in Market Harborough, called Norman Carter, who appeared on the Carroll Levis Show and performed on numerous occasions in local venues.[46]

Norman Carter was a local example of a national trend, as impresarios sought British equivalents of the Americans who could trigger this lucrative emotional reaction. One early example was Tommy Steele. As Dominic Sandbrook has observed, Donegan's fans listened in silence, but Tommy Steele's fans drowned him out.[47] Tommy came to De Montfort Hall in February 1957 and there was no sign of the moral outrage that had attended Haley's film the previous year. On the contrary, the *Chronicle* now spoke like a mouthpiece for the local chamber of commerce, announcing that, 'ROCK 'N' ROLL has invaded the hosiery industry in the shape of a special sweater made in Leicester. The sweater, officially called a "Rhythm Pullover", was worn by singer Tommy Steele on Midlands ITV last Sunday.'[48] The local press returned to this theme ten months later, disclosing that the manufacturers, Montford (Knitting Mills) Ltd, had received orders from Scandinavia, where Tommy had been appearing. 'It all means more work for the teenagers who piece the garments together,' added the paper. 'Most of them are young girls, employed as makers up.'[49]

The kids are alright: Leicester embraces 'youth'

'Inside this white body is a black person, trying to get out.' – Dusty Springfield[50]

Tommy Steele was made ostensibly of the same stuff that had caused such moral perturbation at the *Illustrated Chronicle*. While Tommy's musical hero was the American country icon Hank Williams and he had begun as a skiffle player, he is accepted to have been Britain's first indigenous rock 'n' roll star and 'teen idol'.[51] Like the British Elvis, Cliff Richard, who appeared seven times at De Montfort Hall between 1960 and 1965, Tommy Steele soon became an unthreatening family entertainer, though his concerts were still often riotous, so much so that in 1958 hysterical fans stormed the stage at Dundee's Caird Hall and knocked him unconscious. The days when rock 'n' roll and its mythic greasy-haired adherents were seen officially as a menace were now past. The Palais de Danse began running rock 'n' roll sessions on a Friday afternoon. Most apprentices in the hosiery and engineering industries finished work at midday; others had a long lunch break. Roland Stokes remembers:

When I was 17 in 1961 I went into the shoe trade working in the Stead and Simpson factory which was in Belgrave Gate. We used to work 7.30 a.m. until 5.30 p.m. on Monday to Friday, then Saturday 7.30 until 12.30 p.m. These were long hours but you had a long 2-hour lunch break. There was lots of girls working there and we all used to join up on Friday lunchtime and go to the Palais for a Rock and Roll session. This used to cost an old sixpence.[52]

'Go man, Go!' trumpeted an excruciating article in the *Leicester Mercury* in 1957, 'Come on you cats! Is rockin' 'n' rollin' on the way out? The five members of the Craig Rock 'n' Roll Group, the only out-and-out group in Leicester, so it is claimed, laughed at the very idea. Says leader Raymond Craig, 'It's come to stay. It's the beat and the melody that get folk. It should last five years.'[53] In February of 1959 the *Illustrated Chronicle*, by then apparently converted to boiler factory music, ran a special train to London for 'Leicester lovers of "beat" music' so that they could be in the audience for ABC television's rock show *Oh Boy!* On the bill were a five-man harmony group from inner-city Leicester who, in a notable gesture of 'Americanicity', had changed their name from the unpromising 'Dellac Brothers' to The Dallas Boys.[54] By 1960 the *Mercury* had a 'TEENAGE PAGE' on which, one day in March 1960, Roger Kenyon wrote:

> All thoughts of the examinations were soon forgotten and homework took a back seat when 'The Rebels' struck the beat at an after-school rock 'n' roll session. I arrived at Stonehill Secondary School, Birstall just as the G.C.E. trial examinations were finishing last Thursday. Jiving may not be on the school timetable but the lads and lasses were soon to show that they were anxious to tap their toes. Instead of the pale-faced schoolgirls in white blouses and blue skirts I had expected, I saw pretty young ladies in gay cotton dresses and bouffant skirts. The boys had shed their black regulation blazers in favour of Italian suits and narrow-bottomed trousers. ... Said head girl Joyce Henson, 'All the young people are enthusiastic and it reflects unfavourably on those people who have nothing good to say about teenagers.'[55]

Rock 'n' roll had transmuted swiftly from a threat to public order and decency, discouraged in ballrooms across the city, to a legitimate after-school activity in a middle-class suburb. In 1962 in a profile of local band Tony Bart and the Strangers, the *Leicester Evening Mail* exclaimed: 'IN LIVERPOOL THERE ARE 380 ROCK GROUPS; IN LEICESTER A MERE 50 TO 60 – BUT MOST ARE TRYING MAKE THE "BIG TIME" ... A TV APPEARANCE, A RECORD IN THE CHARTS.'[56] By the early 1960s stories about these rock groups were quite frequent, and their teenage admirers a considered section of the readership of the local press. 'Beat is booming,' exclaimed the *Chronicle* in 1964, 'there are about 70 groups, some full time professionals. ... Who goes to the top only the teenagers will decide. At the moment the Leicester Sound is too much of a whisper to oust the Mersey Sound, but you never know!'[57]

Through the 1960s, one by one, clubs began to open in the city which soon acquired specific clienteles within the emergent youth market. The *El Casa* on Castle Street, for example, catered for bikers upstairs and a 'more beatnik crowd downstairs' and it stayed open after the pubs had shut.[58] There was the Il Rondo, a pioneering rock venue on Silver Street; The Pit, a coffee bar on New Bond Street which opened in 1964 and was styled in the local press as 'Leicester's answer to Liverpool's Cavern';[59] and The Burlesque on Humberstone Road which opened two years later. The Palais de Danse now became more of a female space – a place for single girl friends to meet and dance and display the latest fashions. Christine and Phyl were both 16-year-old secretaries in Leicester in 1965. On around £7 a week, they still had £2 spending money after their living expenses had been met. 'We smoked and we drank – not binge drinking, but we were merry at the end of the evening.' For them, Saturday nights at the Palais were 'wonderful':

> Christine: 'You'd spend hours on your hair, your Dusty Springfield eyes. … It was meeting, dancing. It was the girls all dancing in the middle with their handbags. The boys didn't ask you to dance 'til 10 o' clock'.

> Phyl: 'So they didn't have to buy you a drink.'[60]

There was also the Penny Farthing, a night club of the early 1960s on Abbey Street. Sue Chambers (b.1945), a regular, recalls 'They had a DJ. They played Tamla Motown, that sort of thing.' According to Sue, 'the girls from Lewis's make-up department' were often the star attraction, a kind of glamorous aristocracy of female labour.[61] 'They were the bees' knees. They thought they were everything and we thought they were everything.'[62] Shirley Kendall of South Wigston was another keen dancer. She turned 15 in 1961 and found work as an office junior in Leicester. On Friday evenings she caught the bus home to 'get glamorised' and then went back into the city to dance with girlfriends at the Regent Ballroom on Belgrave Gate: 'on Thursday evenings my mum always washed and set my hair (using Amami setting lotion) so that it looked good on Fridays.'[63] Socially and sensually, these young women seem to have had considerably more control over their leisure lives than Valerie Tedder's generation of fifteen years earlier.

There was a substantial Afro-Caribbean migration to Leicester, and the city had, for the time, a reputation for welcoming black workers. 'It was said,' recalled a Caribbean male voice in *Talk of the Town*, 'that if you couldn't find a job in Leicester, you couldn't find one anywhere else.'[64] Yet comparatively little was heard of local 'black' music. However, as in so many British towns, black music was present both as subtext and in white tribute. As to subtext, many conservative commentators of the 1950s denounced black American music because of its sexual and emotional expressiveness. British teenagers and young music makers liked it, for the same reason. As Ian Macdonald wrote of The Beatles: 'The influence on them of black singers, instrumentalists, songwriters and producers was, as they never failed to admit in their interviews, fundamental to their early career.'[65] So it was with Leicester musicians. Brian Rushin, for instance, a drummer with the Leicestershire band Warlock, found himself 'almost trembling with excitement' on meeting the legendary black singer Little Richard at the St Georges Ballroom in nearby Hinckley in May 1964. 'He was a perfect gentleman and chatted to us as if we had been together forever. But when Richard came on stage it was just as if someone had switched him on. His performance was electric.'[66] Fear of sex, it might be thought, had lurked at the heart of the *Chronicle*'s disgust at the 'negro' quintet (The Platters played De Montfort Hall in 1960) and the 'hiccups' of their lead vocalist whose 'hiccupping' style of broken phrasing was seen by some as orgasmic. Just as young women, inspired by Johnny Ray and Bill Haley, had demanded the right to scream, young white artists sought, in a sense, to be black. In March 1963 Douglas John Harris, who drove a lorry for Leicester Corporation Water Department and fronted the band Johnny Angel and the Mystics, told the *Leicester Mercury*:

> I move around a lot when I'm singing. Leap up in the air and come down on my knees ... lie flat on the stage. ... I still keep singing. It's the sort of thing they want nowadays and anyway I like it. But it's very hard on the body and on clothes. I guarantee I rip up two pairs of trousers in an evening.[67]

In the early 1960s local bands enthusiastically pursued black music and, in the America of their musical imaginations, they trawled the rural south and the urban north. Glyn Essex, born in 1944, had another typical post-war Leicester upbringing. Transplanted from the city's West End where most of his extended family had lived in the same neighbourhood, he moved with his parents to a council estate in Evington village around 1950 and was a sixth former at the prestigious Wyggeston Boys Grammar School in the early 1960s. Like many of his generation he embraced Dixieland jazz and skiffle and then got into rhythm and blues. He remembers the Casino Club on London Road and the popular local band The Farinas.[68] A lot of British bands, including The Farinas, strove to play black American music that they could regard as 'authentic'. For many, rhythm and blues – essentially black American dance music dominated by the electric guitar and which came out of northern American cities after the Second World War – was authentic. The most noted exponent of this music was the Missouri guitarist and songwriter Chuck Berry and its leading British interpreters were the south London band, The Rolling Stones. Berry, as the Rolling Stones' biographer observes, 'was the first intimation that Rhythm and Blues might be an expression of youth'.[69] Members of The Farinas and other local bluesmen went to see the Stones at the Il Rondo in August 1963 and realised that their cherished music (R & B and the same rural blues that had inspired Lonnie Donegan) could be a ticket to the (very) big time. When a record company came to Leicester looking for new bands, The Farinas auditioned (playing the music of another R & B giant, Bo Diddley) and so did The Beatniks whose drummer, Rob Townsend, recalled: 'We wanted to wear black leather waistcoats like the Stones, but we couldn't afford them. So we turned up in black trousers and herringbone waistcoats that we'd bought on Leicester market.'[70]

Blue men sing the whites:
Leicester, 'the Sixties' and globalisation

'You call yourself what you want to call yourself,' – Bob Dylan[71]

Much of what defines 'the Sixties' purports to present an egalitarian element, evoking a notion of the young somehow subordinating their differences and communing in some global rock concert that embraced the growing global importance of the visual media, of the image and the sign. Here we see some genuine, if overly visible and ultimately modest social mobility as a few working-class young people made money through music, fashion, or photography. We also see a much more fluid relationship between the local and the global.

In Leicester in some ways the local resisted the global. There is, for example, the charming story of Arthur Kimbrell, a promoter who brought a succession of popular musicians to the De Montfort Hall between the early 1940s and his retirement in 1983. These included Frank Sinatra, Judy Garland, The Beatles, and The Rolling Stones. During this time, far from opening offices in London or Las Vegas, Kimbrell never moved from his modest premises in the west Leicestershire town of Hinckley.[72] Leicester also had a thriving folk club that met in the Red Cow pub on Belgrave Gate. A report in the *Chronicle* in March 1961 suggests that, while performers cast their net far and wide for material, they acknowledged the cultural provenance of these songs based as they were on 'unexpurgated Liverpool sea shanties … an atom bomb ballad from Japan', and so on.[73] Indeed, the guest act that week had been the Ian Campbell Folk Four, and four years later Campbell described the Rolling Stones as 'phoney Americans'.[74]

Part of what defined 'the Sixties', therefore, was the blurring of the relationship between music and place. In the southern states of the USA white and black musicians 'had been stealing and trading ideas and techniques across racial lines for centuries without ever seriously challenging the racial order of their region'.[75] Now this music began to travel across social class and national boundaries. As one writer observed, 'the Rolling Stones passionately embraced roots they, as Britons, never possessed'.[76] Irrespective of their private devotions and acknowledgements, The Beatles and the Rolling Stones, the two principal bands of the time, did not play music that was 'from' anywhere in particular;[77] nor did they play it as an explicit homage to, say, black American artists. They were celebrities, famous through the rapidly globalising media for being themselves; their music was part of a broader appeal or 'image', and hence the concern with waistcoats at the Leicester audition which just might be part of the magical formula with which to unlock the 'youth market'. 'Americanicity' became lost in this process; indeed 'the Sixties' were seen as a British bestowal. Alan Forrest was living in America at the time: 'It was a wonderful time to be a young man in California. All you had to say was "Oh, yes, I'm British. From Liverpool, actually," and the girls would squeal and crowd around, hoping for a date.'[78]

When The Beatles played De Montfort Hall in December 1963 there was screaming throughout the concert. Fifteen-year-old Barbara Corduroy, of Leicester Forest East, told the local paper: 'I didn't hear anything. ... I didn't see anything. But it was fab.'[79] Johnny Angel of the Water Department knew what he was talking about: this was what people wanted nowadays. The girls who shrieked and jostled with police were doing essentially what was now expected of them. The *Leicester Mercury* remained cautious: the day after the Beatles' concert its lead story was of a strike in Hinckley hosiery factories and, with regard to The Beatles, the primary editorial concern was still with public order. 'Squealing Fans in Fight With Police,' grumbled the headline at the foot of page one.

The growing globalisation of previously ghettoised American musical forms enabled some young Leicester men to participate, like their counterparts in dozens of other British towns, in the crossing of class and cultural fault lines. Two contrasting biographies illustrate this.

The short life of Ric Grech was itself an essay in globalisation. Born in France of Ukrainian parents in the mid-1940s, Grech grew up in Leicester and played the violin in the City Schools Orchestra. He also played with the Farinas (later Family) and was recruited, this time as a bassist, to the first 'supergroup', Blind Faith, in 1969. Made rich through his music, he bought an estate in Surrey and spent time in the USA with Gram Parsons, the son of a wealthy Southern family, making country music, previously much despised outside its 'redneck' constituency of farm workers and truck drivers.[80] In July 1969, Ric's father Mykola, a joiner, spoke poignantly to *The Leicester Chronicle* about his son's disappearance into the long-haired middle class:

There's no doubt Ric deserves all his success. But I would still prefer if he went back to something – like the printing trade, for instance. This pop music is such a hard life. Not enough food or sleep. Always on the move ... His world goes up and down but mine is nice and steady. I am a tradesman myself. I can go anywhere and get a job, but not my son. He has no security ...[81]

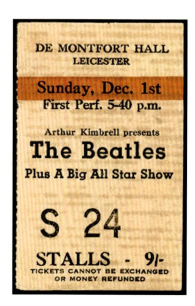

12.12 Original Beatles ticket from their concert at De Montfort Hall.

Source: http://www.thiswasleicestershire.co.uk/

12.13 Pavement memorial to Engelbert Humperdinck, part of Leicester's 'Walk of Fame' located in Rutland Street outside the Curve Theatre in the Cultural Quarter. The singer also received an honorary degree from Leicester University (2006) and the Freedom of the City (2009).

Source: Richard Rodger.

Ric Grech came back to Leicester in 1977 and died there in 1990 of a brain haemorrhage, a condition aggravated by alcoholism and prolonged drug use.

The highly contrasting Arnold George 'Gerry' Dorsey was born in Madras in 1936 and moved to Leicester with his family after the Second World War. He sang in pubs and working men's clubs in the city during the 1950s and early 1960s while working in local factories during the daytime. A singer in the crooning tradition, he hit the big time in 1967 when he, somewhat bizarrely, took the name of the nineteenth-century German composer Engelbert Humperdinck and his recording of 'Release Me', a country song written by the American Eddie Miller in 1956, went to number one in the British hit parade. The appropriation of the name 'Humperdinck' was classically 'Sixties' in two senses: the emergent pick-and-mix approach to cultural forms of all kinds, and the emphasis on marketing. Few people would forget the English crooner now arbitrarily given an obviously German surname. Dorsey/Humperdinck typified the changed relationship between the local and the global. Resident largely in the United States, he became the chief global signifier of the city of Leicester, replacing Tommy Steele's pullovers. He assumed the role of local-boy-made-good and the local press, now properly attuned to the importance of celebrity and global profile, rolled out the red carpet. '"THE HUMP" COMES

HOME,' trilled the *Mercury* in the summer of 1968: 'Chaos As Engelbert's Fans Storm Barriers.'[82] The star himself was coming to town for a charity gala that would raise money for medical equipment at the Leicester Royal Infirmary. Leicester, improbably, had become the place where 'Engelbert Humperdinck' came from. His earlier existence as a struggling local singer became one of the principal ways by which his contemporaries organised their own memories. They were his fellow workers, perhaps, at the British United Shoe Machinery factory, or perhaps they almost danced with him one night, and so on.[83] In April 2009, Gerry/Engelbert, now aged 72, was one of three people to receive the freedom of the city of Leicester.

Leicester and 'the Sixties' in the twenty-first century

The Sixties (and the fifties) live on in Leicester life, as memory and as straightforward practice. There are hundreds of people who remember seeing the Beatles or the Stones, or nearly dancing with Gerry Dorsey, or just missing out on booking Jimi Hendrix into their club. People reminded me that Bob Dylan once played De Montfort Hall, a glimpse of which featured in his film *Never Look Back*.[84] And so on. These reminiscences are all of a piece: they talk of days when the global came to, or once lived in, our town. But 'the Sixties' and their antecedents are more than simply a theatre of memory.[85] They are still lived in Leicester (and elsewhere). Christine and Phyl still go jiving once a week. In 2000 the derelict Bakers Arms on Clyde Street, off Humberstone Gate, which dated back to the early 1900s, re-opened as The Musician, a pub/music venue dedicated in large part to the 'roots' music – blues, R & B, country – that was popular in the Sixties. In April 2009, Cliff Bennett and the Rebel Rousers, who had a hit with Lennon and McCartney's 'Got to Get You Into My Life' in 1966, played the Saffron Lane Working Men's Club in Leicester, though by then Cliff Bennett was approaching his 69th birthday. A month previously, The Hollies, whose first single was released in 1963, came to De Montfort Hall as part of their latest national tour, and in June 1963, The Searchers, whose first single, 'Sweets For My Sweet' also made no. 1, showed up to play a benefit at the Scraptoft Valley Working Men's Club in Leicester's Hamilton district. The band, incorporating one original member and one veteran who had joined in 1964, had been augmented by considerably younger musicians, and their repertoire, recalling the teenage years of most of the audience, was from the 1960s. Around the auditorium lips mouthed the exact words of every song. Also in 2009, the Bootleg Beatles played the same venue in December and two things were reasonably certain: they would sell out and the audience would have a better chance of hearing the songs than they did in 1963.

13

Semi-detached Leicester: social and cultural connections in suburban Leicester

> The debt which we owe to [the Leicestershire Archaeological and Historical Society] through the publication of its Transactions, which first appeared in 1866 and have been continued unbroken until today is quite beyond measure. Nearly all we know about most of our treasured ruins and the social way of life in centuries past has been recorded through the work of the Society.[1]

I N A LETTER to its readership in 1951, the *Leicester Mercury* wrote of the outstanding contribution of the Leicestershire Archaeological and Historical Society to the social and cultural heritage of the city of Leicester. Publicly acknowledging the influence of the organisation on the cultural fabric of the city, the newspaper highlighted an associational world that was often secluded from public view by the 1950s. Despite the society's influence on urban governance as the century progressed, in particular on issues of slum clearance and urban regeneration, questions have been raised more generally regarding the extent of middle-class interest in the twentieth-century city. Were the middle classes as engaged with urban centres as they had been with the Victorian city, when powerful networks of middle-class organisations represented a 'golden era' of associational activity and local engagement? Had Leicester's middle class become disinterested and disengaged in the conduct of public affairs in the city they inhabited? Did the semi-detached house, private cars, and in-home entertainment offered by the TV, DVD and Play Station undermine their engagement in voluntary societies and local government?

13.1
Leicestershire
Archaeological
and Historical
Society logo.
Source: LAHS.

Rather than outward-looking and public-spirited, it has been noted by some that the self-reliant and inward-looking nature of late twentieth-century society damaged social cohesion in local neighbourhoods, fracturing urban communities. Such trends were captured by the image of 'bowling alone' in North America where the camaraderie of ten-pin bowling rinks was replaced by the activity of a lone bowler, offering an explanation for the declining membership of sports clubs and voluntary organisations.[2] The social capital of the American city, it was claimed, was diminished by the introspective middle class of the late twentieth century.

Yet recent research into both the impact of suburbanisation and the role of the urban middle classes in the twentieth-century city, suggest a complex relationship between urban centres and middle-class associational activity.[3] Indeed, as the *Leicester Mercury* article shows, by 1951 organisations like the Leicestershire Archaeological and Historical Society still had an important role to play. As the city expanded in the wake of post-war urban regeneration, the associational sphere in Leicester often acted as a bridge within and between communities, promoting a sense of collectivism across a range of interests.[4] While the depiction of detachment and disinterest often prevails as the dominant image of middle-class suburban Britain, this chapter seeks to review the depth of associational engagement in Leicester and the degree of middle-class influence in the city between the years 1950 and 2005. By connecting middle-class suburban participation to an active associational world, a 'semi-detached' middle class becomes apparent. Undoubtedly the 'suburbans' chose to live in ever increasing distances from the urban centre after 1950. Yet, their connections with numerous local clubs and societies continued to construct associational networks that not only influenced urban governance but created important social relationships at the heart of the city of Leicester.

Middle-class participation

Once perceived as a nation of 'joiners', modern Britain is no longer regarded as a country dominated by local and national organisations, clubs and societies, boasting an environment of inclusion, participation and tolerance.[5] The London bombings of 2005 highlighted on a global stage the extent to which aspects of community cohesion within multi-cultural Britain had been eroded. However, the popularity of modern forms of social interaction, such as networking sites like Facebook and Twitter, suggest that group participation and communication are still evident, and in some cases more popular than ever. In 2006, the *Guardian* suggested that membership levels had soared in recent years, with the average Briton having a membership of seventeen organisations.[6] Such accounts raise interesting questions regarding the importance of the associational sphere in contemporary Britain and the extent of its authority in urban centres.

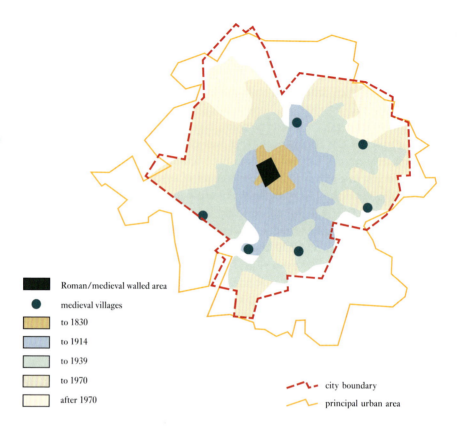

13.2
Leicester's
changing urban
boundaries.
Map based on
that published
in *Local
Development
Framework*,
2010, 16.

Source: Leicester
City Council.

Roman/medieval walled area

medieval villages

to 1830

to 1914

to 1939

to 1970

after 1970

city boundary

principal urban area

On a regional scale, some studies have been quick to note the decline of
voluntary organisations in the twentieth century, attributing their waning
influence to a middle-class exodus from the central districts of cities.[7]
Begley's recent study of Leicester, however, revealed a wealth of associational engagement and middle-class interest in urban affairs between the
years 1870 to 1939.[8] To what extent can this engagement be seen to
continue in the post-war period? Undoubtedly, state programmes of urban
regeneration after the Second World War – particularly the provision of
council housing for the working classes – fuelled suburban development in
Leicester, increasing the geographical separation that allowed the middle
classes to work in the city by day, while retreating to the tranquillity of
leafy suburbia by night. Did such separation, however, constitute an entirely
disconnected attitude to the city among the middle classes? In an era where
the popularity of individual leisure pursuits dominated, did the middle
classes choose to distance themselves not only from the city centre but the
associational life that had traditionally shaped their urban identity and that
of the city?

Residential patterns of club and society members suggest that such
assumptions are inaccurate when considering the Leicester experience.

13.3 Western Park housing development. The rise of suburban housing changed the relationship between individuals, communities and the city centre.

Source: Record Office for Leicester, Leicestershire and Rutland, 0038, Box 31.

Overwhelmingly, middle-class suburban residents, alongside participants residing in satellite villages, continued to make up a significant share of membership in local voluntary organisations during the years 1950 to 2005. The examination of a collection of primary sources, including minute books, transaction papers and membership records taken from clubs and societies in Leicester, revealed an engaged and enthusiastic middle class.[9] In particular, address books and membership databases can be used to show just how many members were drawn from middle-class suburbia. The distances presented in Table 13.1, calculated from the archive collections of nine local clubs and societies in Leicester, show the average distance a member of each society lived from the city centre:[10]

Table 13.1   Average residential distances of club and society memberships

Organisation	Median	Mean
St Martin's Parish Council	1.63	2.00
Women's Luncheon Committee	1.96	2.79
Literary and Philosophical Society	2.05	3.04
Motor Club	3.15	3.72
Oadby Community Association	3.50	3.64
Bradgate Twinning Association	3.85	4.06
Society of Artists	4.05	9.76
Archaeological and Historical Society	4.45	6.29
Bat Group	8.76	9.76
Weighted average		4.45

Sources: see notes 9 and 10.

13.4 Leicester
Society
of Artists
exhibition in
Museum Square,
1950.

Source: Record
Office for Leicester,
Leicestershire and
Rutland, Box 22.

With a suburban area in Leicester calculated to be approximately three miles from the urban core,[11] it is clear that the majority of organisations had members that lived a considerable distance from the city centre. Interestingly, in the majority of organisations, members lived well over three miles away suggesting that the associational sphere drew its membership well beyond the immediate suburban boundary. On average, members of the Leicester Society Artists lived 9.8 miles from the city centre. Seemingly, rather than removing themselves from urban affairs and club activities, members were prepared to travel considerable distances to remain connected to life at the centre of Leicester city.

Through an analysis of individual organisations, it is also possible to identify the types of areas to which associational participants were attracted, and how patterns of dispersal changed as the twentieth century progressed. By comparing the residential dispersal of the Leicestershire Archaeological and Historical Society in 1954 with that of 2004 (13.5; 13.6), it becomes clear that suburban affiliation had not only increased by the turn of the twenty-first century, but social networks continued to be extended farther into county areas. In 1954 approximately 56% of members resided in an outer suburb, surrounding satellite village, or nearby town; by 2004 this number had grown to 72% of the membership.

Interestingly, as figures 13.5–13.6 show, not only did the number of 'suburban' participants increase between the years 1954 and 2004, but the majority resided in south-eastern locations. This is particularly significant when we compare these findings with the 2001 census which indicates that areas towards the south-east of the city were least inhabited by the unemployed and significantly populated by senior officials or those of a managerial profession. Additionally they were the locus of the most educated element of the city, often a useful indicator in terms of middle-class status.

The distribution of membership addresses (13.5 and 13.6) therefore

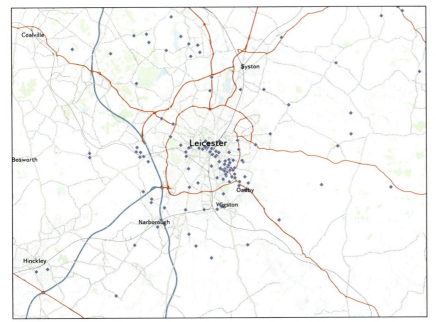

13.5 Residential distribution of members of the Leicestershire Archaeological and Historical Society, 1954.

Source: Data obtained from records of the Leicestershire Archaeological and Historical Society (Record Office for Leicester, Leicestershire and Rutland).

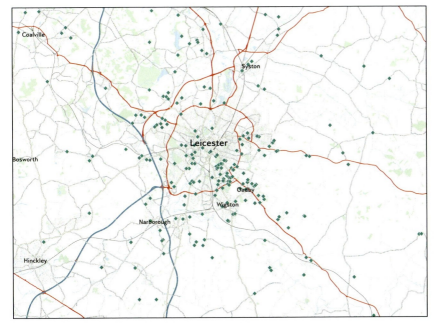

13.6 Residential distribution of members of the Leicestershire Archaeological and Historical Society, 2004.

Source: as for 13.5.

shows both the connection between the middle classes and the associational sphere, and the increasing popularity of middle-class suburban living post-1950. As each decade passed, members increasingly relocated to leafy suburbia and the tranquillity of the urban periphery. An area that was particularly appealing to associational members in Leicester was the suburban location of Oadby. According to Boynton, Oadby is characterised by low-density housing, wide roads and pavements, and a generally 'tranquil ambience' that contrasted heavily with the hustle and bustle of city-centre life.[12] Situated three miles from the city centre, such a distance reinforced the exclusive nature of the suburb, as car ownership enabled only the wealthy to travel to work by car.[13]

The increasing popularity of suburban areas such as Oadby between the years 1950 to 2005 is perhaps unsurprising when we consider the explosion of car ownership during this period. The growth of the suburb itself also owed much to the perceived improvements in the quality of schools, and a reaction to those in Leicester.[14] Yet, the decision of suburban and satellite village residents to remain connected to clubs and societies based in the city showed a deep-rooted commitment by the middle classes to associational activity and group participation. Despite the supposedly inward-looking nature of late twentieth-century society, the 'suburbans' of Leicester did not abandon city-centre membership but, through long-standing social and cultural ties, remained loyal to associational life at the heart of the city.

Nowhere was this more evident than in the residential patterns of the Leicestershire Literary and Philosophical Society (13.7 and 13.8) where middle-class, suburban memberships continued to contribute significantly to the make-up of organisations throughout the latter years of the twentieth century. As the blue markers indicate, in 1954 the percentage of members residing in fringe areas or satellite villages totalled 17%; by 2000 this number had increased dramatically to 47%. Similarly, the geographical spread of members also mirrored the behaviour of the Archaeological and Historical Society with a clustering towards the south-east of the city – particularly Oadby, where residents totalled over 17% during the years 1954 and 2000 – and reaching as far as Hinckley and Melton Mowbray, distances of 15 and 18 miles respectively.

Overall, the chronological analysis of these two organisations indicates that suburban participation in associational life not only flourished during the period 1950 to 2005 but continued to push associational connections farther and farther into county areas. Despite suburban migration and an assumption that the middle classes had withdrawn from public life in the twentieth century, membership records in Leicester reveal a middle class engaged with cultural and creative clubs, contributing significantly to the social capital of the city. Residential patterns confirm a solid commitment by the 'suburbans' to associational life, with members often travelling considerable distances in order to maintain important social connections at the city centre. These networks emphasised a genuine and on-going interest in urban life, contradicting the stereotypical depiction of suburban living as disengaged and isolated. But to what extent did local clubs and societies themselves contribute to social and cultural affairs at the heart of the city? Did voluntary organisations maintain a degree of influence and

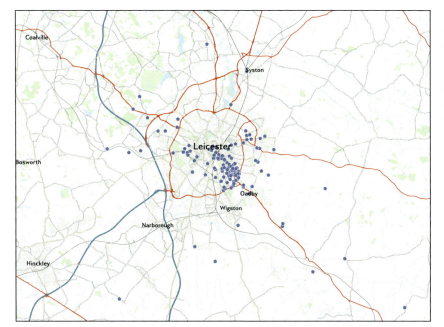

13.7 Residential distribution of members of the Leicester Literary and Philosophical Society, cumulative membership, 1950–2000.

Source: as for 13.5.

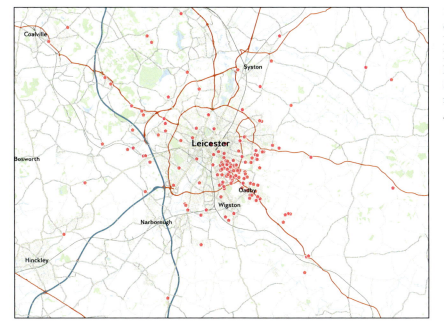

13.8 Residential distribution of Leicestershire Literary and Philosophical Society members, 2000.

Source: as for 13.5.

authority as the twentieth century progressed? Did middle-class organisations, like the Leicestershire Archaeological and Historical and Society, continue to construct cultural and political networks that influenced urban leadership? Furthermore, in an era when the concept of the neighbourhood was arguably in decline, did the middle classes use associational activity in local clubs and societies to stimulate important social relationships, creating 'associational communities' that no longer relied upon the geographical ties of place as a common factor?

Social interaction

Traditionally, social interaction represented a fundamental aspect of associational engagement. At the height of their popularity, local organisations worked to bring together the fractured middle class of the Victorian era, bonding participants through private hobbies and mutual interests. In much the same way, clubs and societies of the twentieth century united like-minded people, creating a wide range of 'associational communities'. These communities no longer relied upon geographical proximity to define their identity; instead they revolved around a growing number of dynamic and engaging leisure activities.

It has been suggested that one of the chief characteristics of twentieth-century leisure has been the extent of its reorganisation around the individual. The popularity of the motor car, the increasing space and comfort afforded

13.9 Road improvements, Welford Road 1975. One of many initiatives to ease traffic congestion and suburban commuting.

Source: Leicester City Council.

Leicester: a modern history

in homes, and technological innovation – for example, televisions and computers – have all contributed to the amount of leisure time individuals spend alone and in the comfort of their own homes.[15] Yet, this did not necessarily negate the need for group participation and the development of important social relationships. As the analysis of local clubs and societies in Leicester suggests, during the period 1950 to 2005, engagement outside the home remained a fundamental part of middle-class, suburban life. Despite the growing attraction of home-based leisure entertainment, social interaction retained its importance. In particular, dinner dances, garden parties and cheese and wine nights were the types of associational events stimulating social cohesion and promoting collegiality among Leicester's middle class.

For the Leicester Asian Business Association, social events not only stimulated sociability among its membership but also provided perfect occasions for different elements of the ethnic minority community to interact. A founding member revealed that:

> Socially what happens is that, whenever we have an event, we either have a dance programme or Indian Bangra, northern Indian folk dancing, or we have had western music, some groups that play after our annual dinner so we have some dancing and so on...we have maximum attendance ... the last gathering we had had 600 people, from various walks of life, a big event.[16]

Events were generally large in scale, providing the ideal opportunity for different ethnic minority groups to interact socially and in the comfort of a relaxed, informal setting. The organisation prided itself on its ability to successfully incorporate men and women, multiple faiths, nationalities, castes and social groups, attributing community integration to the neutral motive of business. This was particularly significant when we consider that minority groups often only engaged within their immediate communities. For example, local studies of Jewish, Irish and Italian immigrants confirm that minority groups are more inclined to settle in close-knit urban communities.[17] Another study concluded:

> Clustering serves not only as a defensive function against racial harassment, but also provides a market for community services ... ethnic food stores and other specialist retailers. It also allows the recreation of dense traditional social networks with all the implications this has for quality of life and transmission of culture.[18]

Yet, Leicester Asian Business Association provides an example of associational activity being used to unite different ethnic minority groups in a social context. Through the organisation of large-scale social events, like

13.10 Asian business on the Golden Mile.

Source: Colin Hyde.

the annual dinner dance, middle-class members gathered together to show a degree of social solidarity. Such occasions were the highlight of the associational calendar and worked to strengthen social relationships that had wider urban implications. Under the neutral motive of business, citizens from different networks of faith and ethnic backgrounds, including immigrants from east Africa, Pakistan, Bangladesh and Sri Lanka all interacted together, strengthening social ties among the minority communities in Leicester.

Not all clubs and societies, however, organised social events attended by 600 people. For the Leicester Society of Artists, organised evenings and events remained an important part of the social calendar throughout the period 1950 to 2005. While a number of events were large in scale, including 'soirees' held during art exhibitions at Leicester Museum and were attended by the Mayor,[19] the majority were more private and for members only, including mid-summer parties and buffet suppers held at the widely dispersed addresses of individual members (13.11).[20]

As the map shows, the majority of members resided at the urban fringe, with the average member living nearly ten miles from the city centre. In a similar way to the Leicester Asian Business Association, social events were used to unite the middle-class membership. Soirees and exhibitions brought the 'suburbans' together in a relaxed social setting, stimulating a sense of community among participants. Indeed, the fact that so many members were prepared to travel considerable distances to attend 'garden parties' and

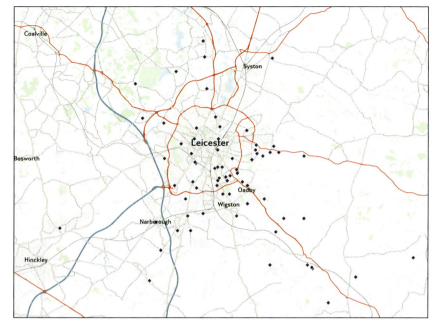

13.11
Residential
distribution of
members of the
Leicester Society
of Artists,
cumulative
membership,
1950–2000.

Source: Data
obtained from
private archive
collection of the
Leicester Society of
Artists.

'buffet suppers' was a testimony to the commitment of the middle classes to contemporary 'associational communities'.

In this respect the very concept of community had become more fluid during the later years of the twentieth century.[21] It has been argued that a modern community is not necessarily anchored by place. The emphasis is no longer on social balance, cohesion and homogeneity, but instead relies increasingly upon social interaction.[22] Seemingly within Leicester during the years 1950 to 2005, organisational activity contributed to the construction of the types of communities identified in this way. Similarly, Clapson suggests in his analysis of post-war working-class suburbia that an alternative form of 'community' developed around associational life, no longer dependent upon the geographical ties of place. For many historians 'community' has been understood as identification with a particular neighbourhood or street, yet Clapson concludes that this was just 'one context which brought people together … groups and associations made social connections around interests which had little to do with local identification.'[23] Such associations created 'communities of interest' or 'associational communities' and supplied an alternative to neighbourhood as a basis for formulating social relationships.

In this context the analysis of associational communities does much to help our understanding of the perception of middle-class withdrawal by the post-war period. For many historians the migration of the middle classes to the suburbs ended not only their engagement in public affairs but also any sense of community or social life.[24] Some authors, however, have alluded to a society whose very patterns of life tended to conceal sociability, which is perhaps more realistic in relation to Leicester's middle class.[25] Previous generations had generally provided public displays of sociability, yet by the post-war era, social activities were often played out behind closed doors, for example, at garden parties and cheese and wine evenings. These events were held in the comfort of members' homes and for the enjoyment of the 'suburbans' only. In many ways the middle classes embraced the twentieth-century culture of home-based leisure entertainment. However, rather than revolving around the individual, the 'suburbans' opened their homes to their fellow associational participants, forging exclusive communities that stimulated strong social relationships. While these communities may have been sheltered from public view, their sense of privacy did not diminish their social significance.

Cultural influence

While the associational sphere in Leicester helped to maintain social relationships, creating a new sense of community that was more in line with the expanding twentieth-century city, associational engagement also stimulated the type of interaction that had wider social and cultural implications. In terms of civic engagement, cultural contributions ranged from active lecturer programmes that enriched and promoted the cultural heritage of the city, to ritualised celebrations which publicly connected voluntary organisations to the local municipality. Celebratory events,

13.12 150th Anniversary Celebrations of the Leicestershire Archaeological and Historical Society. Left to right: Alan McWhirr (former LAHS Secretary); Aubrey Stevenson (Hon LAHS Librarian); HRH The Duke of Gloucester; Councillor Piara Singh Clair (Former Lord Mayor of Leicester); Gerald Rimington (former LAHS Chairman and now a Vice-President).
Source: LAHS.

such as the Queen's coronation in 1953 or the 150th anniversary of the Archaeological and Historical Society in 2005, provided opportunities for collaboration between local organisations and the city and county councils. Public displays of unity helped to construct a sense of civic identity that was reminiscent of the use of pageantry in the nineteenth-century city.

Yet, the relationship between Leicestershire Archaeological and Historical Society and Leicester City Council went much deeper than the organisation of celebratory events. In fact, the extent of their collaborative efforts does much to exemplify the continued influence of voluntary organisations in urban affairs by the mid- to late twentieth century. More than any other, the issue of conservation united the society and the council in a common endeavour: the historical heritage of the city. On a national scale, the slum clearance plans of the 1950s and 1960s did much to change the physical landscape of British towns and cities; it has been claimed that by the late 1950s the rate of houses being demolished reached approximately 50,000 buildings a year.[26] While urban planners often paid little attention to issues of conservation during this period, local organisations took a keen interest in the preservation of important buildings and areas within their immediate communities.[27] Following Leicester's slum clearance plan in the 1950s, the Leicestershire Archaeological and Historical Society became active in the issue of historical conservation, developing a strong relationship with the City and County Council as regards the preservation of specific buildings. The Leicester Guildhall became one of the most iconic buildings in the city to be preserved by the organisation and to the present day houses the society's private library. The Leicestershire Archaeological and Historical Society undoubtedly recognised the need in post-war Britain – particularly during a period of intense housing regeneration – for vigilance regarding conservation. This was an important area in which the organisation, and its middle-class membership, could not only engage with local authorities but also contribute directly to the shaping of urban policy and thus to the physical nature of the city.

In 1964, while referring to their role in conservation issues in the city, the organisation concluded: 'these problems, which can be paralleled in any other county in England, illustrate how the Society can act as guardian.'[28] The use of the term 'guardian' is significant as it shows a deep-rooted interest and connection to the urban environment. It is also important when we consider that the average member of the Society resided nearly seven miles from the city centre during the 1960s, with 62% of members living in a suburban area, satellite village or town.

As the map reflects, suburban participation was a fundamental part of associational life. Through the work of the society in the preservation of historic buildings, the middle classes continued to influence contemporary urban affairs. Post-1950, and in the wake of intense urban regeneration, the 'suburbans' found innovative ways to influence the urban landscape. For

13.13 Leicester Guildhall preserved.
Source: Colin Hyde.

example, the commitment of the Archaeological and Historical Society to conservation issues culminated in their cooperation with Leicestershire County Council in the inauguration of a landmark scheme:

> By the Historic Buildings Act of 1962, local authorities were empowered to make grants to assist the preservation of buildings of historical and archaeological importance. Responsibility for making recommendation lies with the County Records Committee and the City Museums, Libraries and Public Committees. … It was felt that the time had come to utilise to the full all the resources of the society for this important work. … In March it was decided that a Historic Buildings Panel (HBP) should be set up.[29]

In the first year of its foundation, the Archaeological and Historical Society provided the council with a list of 170 buildings and sites recommended for conservation or preservation. By the 1970s the society emphasised the success of the HBP, declaring it to be 'one of the most important aspects of the Society's activities', with the organisation assessing planning applications and providing comprehensive reports for the city, county and urban district councils. During the year 1978–79 the society considered 258 applications for local councils and by 1999 this had increased to 300 applications in one year.[30] For the Archaeological and Historical Society, associational activity was the means through which middle-class participants embraced their urban responsibilities and contributed to the formation of the urban environment. In this respect, not only did organisations contribute to the stock of the city's social capital through a shared sense of historical identity, but they also constructed networks of communication with local government, allowing them to engage with the municipality and influence local decision-making. In an era that arguably produced a middle class devoid of interest in contemporary urban affairs, such actions provide an alternative interpretation to suburban engagement and the role of the middle classes. By simply walking through the streets of Leicester their triumphs become evident. The preservation of historic buildings such as the Guildhall testifies to the continued influence of the associational sphere and its impact on the cultural heritage of the city.

Networks of collaborative action that benefited the cultural sphere in Leicester were also seen in the relationships between the middle classes and important civic institutions, such as New Walk Museum and Art Gallery and also the University of Leicester. For the Leicestershire Literary and Philosophical Society, connections with the city museum were a vital part of the organisation's identity. The society valued their close relationship, recognising the importance of aligning themselves with a prestigious civic institution. In the year 1998–99, the society recorded their joy at having a new president with close relations to the museum:

> That the presidency should reside again this year with an officer of the City Council's museum service, is, for me, a much appreciated mark of recognition of the happy coincidence of restoration of the symbiosis of society and museum with the 150th anniversary of the start of the relationship.[31]

Joint ventures between the organisation and the museum were numerous. In 1970 the Leicester Museum Association and the Literary and Philosophical Society jointly co-ordinated and hosted a meeting of the National Association of Museums, while members of the Museum Association and curators of the museum enjoyed corresponding membership and affiliation with the Literary and Philosophical Society. These types of networks allowed the Literary and Philosophical Society to integrate itself into the cultural life of the city; their activities and membership enriched local engagement while simultaneously providing organisations with different conduits through which to connect with members and new initiatives.

This was equally true of the relationship between the associational sphere and the University of Leicester. For Leicester, the cultural nature of the city was, and remains to the present day, enriched by the presence of the university. Culture and education are closely related, and thus the influence of the university on ambitious associations, specifically the Literary and Philosophical Society and the Archaeological and Historical Society in Leicester, was considerable. In return, the relationship between such associations and the university reflected another aspect of the city's cultural identity upon which local organisations were influential. Guest speakers from the university regularly delivered lectures to society members, and many professors, including W.G. Hoskins and Jack Simmons, enjoyed membership and played significant roles on the executive committees of the associations.[32] In addition, in 1951, the general meeting of the Archaeological and Historical Society took place at the University College, and university lecturers, including Professor Millward, conducted excursions for members of the Literary and Philosophical Society. The university also made grants to the Botany section of the society as an explicit indication of their commitment to and appreciation of the contribution made to the subject by the society.[33] Similarly, close ties between the Geophysics department and the Literary and Philosophical Society continue to the present day. Lecture programmes organised by the society are attended by members of the University of Leicester Geophysical Society, while eminent professors within the department deliver talks specifically for the Literary and Philosophical Society.[34]

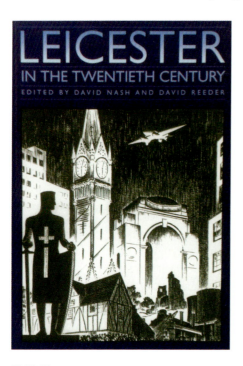

13.15 Front cover of *Leicester in the Twentieth Century* (margin).

Source: author's copy.

Consequently, in Leicester the relationship between associations and the university was significant for the organisations themselves, and also to the cultural foundations of the city. Organisations constructed important networks with the university, broadening their intellectual scope and aligning their activities with an important civic institution. Equally, the university developed projects in conjunction with various associations within Leicester, supplying both funds and support for projects that encouraged greater social cohesion. One such example was the historical research that underpinned the publication of *Leicester in the Twentieth Century*, an earlier City Council project in collaboration with members of the Centre for Urban History at Leicester University and Leicester Polytechnic which involved numerous societies and clubs whose members provided photographs and reminiscences.[35] Thus, the town and gown relationship was mutually beneficial, and for the middle-class 'suburbans' who underpinned organisations with a significant percentage of their membership, such links reflected a continuing influence on the civic identity of a city from which they were far from detached. Instead, they developed important networks that directly influenced the cultural enrichment of Leicester. By supporting institutions that exhibited the finest art work the city had to offer, and encouraging lecture programmes that enriched the historical identity of the city, middle-class voluntary organisations continued to carve out an important place in the urban hierarchy, developing influential networks that benefited the future of the city of Leicester.

This chapter has therefore shown the extent to which the 'suburbans' have often been wrongly stereotyped. The image of a detached and self-centred middle class has generally become the standard rhetoric when considering the twentieth-century middle classes. Yet, the experience of the Leicester 'suburbans' shows that far from removing themselves from urban life, the middle classes continued to use the associational sphere as a conduit to exercise their influence over social, political and cultural issues at the urban core. The semi-detached house, private cars, and in-home entertainment had certainly not undermined their civic commitment by the turn of the twenty-first century. However, much like the on-going revision of suburbanisation in America,[36] there is still scope for further analysis. In order to understand truly the suburban experience in Britain as a whole, more regional analysis is required. While the findings of this chapter have emphasised important connections between suburbia, the middle classes and urban affairs, wider research is needed to provide a more coherent picture of suburban engagement in the years after 1950. As Smith argues in his research of the middle classes during the twentieth century 'it is necessary that there should be much more detailed interactional study on a range of towns and cities which represent as wide a diversity of urban categories as possible.'[37] In this respect a thorough revision of suburban locations throughout the country would allow the contemporary historian to evaluate whether Leicester is the exception or the rule, in the debate over middle-class influence in twentieth-century Britain.

14

Immigration and the emergence of multicultural Leicester

'THE main thrust of Leicester's life as a diverse city has moved from welcoming newcomers, to a recognition that this diversity is Leicester itself and that people of all cultures and races are equally Leicester people.'[1] Taken from Leicester's First Community Plan, this quotation captures the City Council's commitment to multiculturalism. With an ethnic minority population of 36% in 2001, different ethnic groups are not expected to shed their religious, cultural and ethnic identities; rather their diversity is seen as integral to Leicester as a 'city full of surprises'.[2] This diversity has provided exciting selling points for the city. In particular, 'The Golden Mile' in the Belgrave area, home to South Asian shops, Indian restaurants and annual festivals such as Diwali, the largest celebration outside India, is seen as an international tourist attraction, with the potential to develop into an 'Asia Town', akin to London's Chinatown.[3]

The notion that Leicester is a successful melting pot of different cultures has also been incorporated into the narrative of the city's history. Rather than focusing on an exclusive English national identity, such as the medieval Guildhall and country pubs, Leicester City Council claims the arrival of newcomers is part of a long-established process, essential to the city's growth and change and an enduring feature of Leicester:

> It [Leicester] is also a historic meeting place. For centuries people of different races and cultures have gathered in Leicester, creating a rich and unique heritage. This diversity continues today: the city's thriving ethnic minority community accounts for more than a third of Leicester's population and continues to enrich city life.[4]

This move to recognising the historical presence of immigrants can be seen as part of 'reshaping collective memory', designed not only to generate tourism but also to foster inter-ethnic relations, by reminding the public of the benefits of migration to the city.[5]

While other cities, such as Birmingham, also take pride in their cultural diversity and have sought to incorporate migrant histories into the city's history, the multicultural image has a particular resonance for Leicester as its reputation as a tolerant multi-cultural city was given a significant boost following the disturbances in Oldham, Burnley and Bradford in 2001. Due to the absence of ethnic unrest in Leicester, the city was labelled Britain's most ethnically harmonious city and praised as a European model of multi-cultural success.[6] Journalists and scholars contrasted the apparent tolerance and genial character of Leicester with the northern cities and sought to reflect on why Leicester was successful.[7] Here a range of factors were identified, including the absence of poverty compared to other cities; the contribution and efforts of the City Council, police, local faith leaders and local media; the help established migrants have offered to newcomers; as well as the perceived lack of a distinctive identity within the city.[8] Within this, Leicester's transformation has largely been attributed to the development of a self-confident South Asian population who represent the main ethnic minority group in the city and by 2011 made up almost 40% of the city's population.[9] Consequently Leicester is seen as one of Britain's main 'Asian' cities.

Since their arrival, South Asians have established themselves politically and economically within this city.[10] For example, in 1976 councillor Peter Soulsby drew up a Declaration Against Racism that envisaged a multi-cultural future for the city and Leicester City Council along with a number of 'left led' authorities in the Greater London area was seen as one of the 'pioneering' local authorities in response to racism. However, progress was slow and it was not until the 1980s when South Asians established a stronghold within the Labour party that the City Council implemented this vision.[11] By 1983, the City Council included nine Labour South Asian councillors and in 1987 Keith Vaz was elected in Leicester East, the first South Asian MP since 1923. In 1987 Councillor Parmar became Leicester's first South Asian lord mayor. Added to this, South Asians are also seen as revitalising the economy and have established 10,000 businesses in the city.[12] This success is largely attributed to East African Asians who were mainly of an urban, middle-class and Gujarati-speaking background and had developed valuable transferable skills in Africa, including business expertise and familiarity with English lifestyles through the British imperial presence.

This chapter seeks to go beyond this public history of the city, primarily by acknowledging the history of other ethnic groups, who have tended to be overlooked in Leicester's multi-cultural success and are considered marginal to the city's identity. These groups have included European migrants whose white identity and relatively small numbers compared to the city's South Asian population, have contributed to their 'invisibility'.[13] Nevertheless, this

14.1 Main ethnic groups, Leicester, 2001.
Source: http://www.leicester.gov.uk/your-council-services/council-and-democracy/city-statistics/other-statistics/historical-interest/census2001/ethnicity/

14.2 Leicester's first South Asian Lord Mayor, Gordhan Parmar (1987).

Source: Leicester City Council.

should not detract from their significance, particularly as their presence has ensured Leicester's population is one of the most ethnically diverse in the European Union. First, however, it is necessary to establish why Leicester became home for these diverse migrant groups.

Why Leicester?

Leicester's prosperity has been an enduring attraction for immigrants. In the nineteenth century Leicester was an expanding industrial centre; hosiery and footwear manufacture were established as the main local industries and manufacturing developed in the twentieth century with light engineering, printing, clothing made from artificial fibres, adhesive manufacturing and food processing. The city's affluence increased after the Second World War, prompting a shortage of labour, and Leicester's prosperity continued into the 1970s, at a time when other cities were facing decline. Leicester's range of industries provided plentiful employment, at all skill levels and particularly for women, and this encouraged migration from other towns such as Coventry, Birmingham, London, Yorkshire and Blackburn.[14] The opportunities to establish businesses in Leicester has also been cited as a key factor attracting migrants to the city.

Prior to the development of the boot and shoe industry in the nineteenth century, Leicester's economy was dependent on workshop-based industries, leaving a stock of small industrial premises located throughout the city. Other factors included the lack of industrial disputes, the central location

14.3 Imperial Typewriters Factory. This was the location of an intense labour dispute in 1974 when 40 South Asian women were made redundant and all 1,000 remaining South Asian workers walked out (see chapter 8). The area is still home to a large number of Asian businesses.

Source: Colin Hyde.

of Leicester, which facilitated communication between families and businesses throughout Britain, and Leicester's reputation as a safe city, a view promulgated by the local press.[15]

The abundance of cheap housing available for purchase was another major attraction and the Highfields area of the city was an established conduit for immigrants.[16] It was generally deemed unattractive by the white population, following post-war neglect. It contained large Victorian houses and terraced cottages that were inexpensive, albeit deteriorating, and the area was located close to the city centre, the foundries, traditional hosiery mills and new factories, including Imperial Typewriters, John Bull, Metal Box and British Shoe Corporation. Cheap accommodation was also available in the Belgrave area, to the north of the city, due to threats of redevelopment, including the planned demolition of over 1,000 properties to build a motorway.[17] The close proximity of these areas to the city centre ensured that Leicester was, for the newcomers, a compact city, and the availability of affordable accommodation was a key consideration for many Ugandan Asians who had not managed to transfer their savings out of Uganda. Home ownership was particularly important to East African Asians who preferred to have their own property and house an extended family. Finally, migrant networks played a fundamental role in migration to the city as it has long been recognised that migration is essentially a process of network building, that once it has been established, it gathers a momentum of its own as newcomers informed others of the promising prospects in Leicester.[18]

White migrants in Leicester: the 'invisible' minorities

Migration in Britain tends to be associated with the post-war era, beginning with the docking of *Empire Windrush*, the first ship that brought immigrants from Jamaica, to the port of Tilbury in 1948. Yet nineteenth-century Leicester was already accustomed to diversity, including Jewish migrants, comprising small shopkeepers and trades people. By 1875 they established an organised congregation and numbers increased from the 1890s with the arrival of Jews from eastern Europe, fleeing poverty and religious persecution.[19] Despite the prevalence of anti-Jewish sentiment in other parts of Britain, the Jews appeared to have settled into the social, economic, and political life without much difficulty. Most notably, Sir Israel Hart, the leader of Orthodox Jews and a prominent figure at the local and national level, was elected mayor for the city four times. He was a prominent benefactor for the new synagogue built in 1889, and also funded the large fountain for the town hall. Hart's position within the local elite enhanced the prestige and status of the congregation and his success has been cited as evidence of the city's tolerance. As Newman explains, 'It is obviously very important to realise the extent to which nineteenth century Leicester was prepared to admit the stranger, the newcomer, into its midst and give him such opportunities.'[20] However, this apparent acceptance has also been related to the small number of Jews within the city, their desire to anglicise, and their business enterprises which created employment opportunities for the local British-born population.[21]

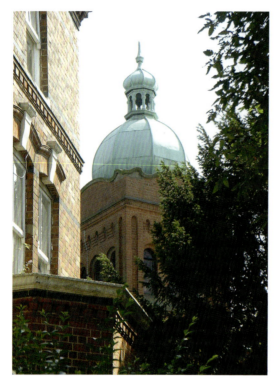

14.4 The Jewish Synagogue in Highfields. The proximity of traditional terraced housing and religious sites was a feature of successive waves of immigrants to Leicester.

Source: Colin Hyde.

While Jewish people represented the bulk of immigration to Leicester in the nineteenth century, they were not the only evidence of ethnic diversity. Irish migration also dates from the early nineteenth century, although numbers were relatively small, with approximately 900 Irish-born in 1851 and fewer than 1,000 in 1901. According to Elliot, the Irish at this time, were very poor and lived in 'centres of poverty, sickness and petty crime'.[22] From the late 1890s a small Italian community developed following the agrarian crisis in southern Italy and, following the trend in other parts of Britain, they turned to catering services such as the ice-cream trade.

In the aftermath of the Second World War Leicester received migrants from eastern Europe and the Soviet Union. The largest group were the Polish but there were also people who originated from twelve other European states.[23] In addition to Displaced Persons and European Voluntary Workers who came to Britain as part of an official policy of forced immigration, many Polish soldiers, sailors and airmen had served under British command during the war and came to Leicester as refugees. By the 1951 census 1,002 people born in Poland were resident in Leicester, and this increased to over 1,500 in 1961 and 1971, when numbers of Polish-born residents in Leicester peaked.[24] In 1961 the Polish represented nearly 14% of the city's foreign-born population, though this dropped to 2.2% in 1981, and by 1991 the number of first-generation Poles had fallen to 833.[25] Despite the relatively small size of the Polish population they exhibited a strong national identity and presence in the city. This included the Polish Saturday school established in Highfields in 1952 which by 1961 taught over 200 pupils, and the Ex-Servicemen's Club which opened in 1956. St Paul's church on Melbourne Road, Highfields and the adjacent club buildings, became the Polish parish church and club in 1965 and the church played a vital role in fostering a shared identity and common values.

However, as research on the Polish population in Leicester revealed, while the church and clubs provided important meeting places, the spatial scale of the community extended beyond this to encompass various reference points which, taken together, formed particular Polish routes through the city. As one Polish woman explained,

> We had this big extended family in Leicester, and the community was like this even bigger extended family. There was a Polish shop on Narborough Road where you could buy Polish sausages and things like that, other Polish people went there as well, so you would see them there sometimes. You would go to a Polish doctor. I think that there was this sense that you were helping somebody out by giving them business, giving them a helping hand. Most of the people you knew were Polish. Our early life was very Polish.[26]

As the population moved away from the city centre the first generation lamented the decline of their vibrant community, yet their experience of displacement provided a basis for enduring networks as their Polish identity was intimately tied to the forced migration process. In particular, their national identity was reinforced through new transnational links, such as TV Polonia, which though not transmitted in Poland linked Polish people from around the world and has ensured that their Polish diasporic identity has not diminished.[27] Membership of the European Union and no-frills airlines such as EasyJet has helped to reinvigorate a Polish identity, as has a new Catholic church located close to the General Hospital.

Alongside the Polish communities, other refugees included Ukrainian soldiers and small groups from Estonia, Lithuania, Latvia and the Ukraine, who were rendered stateless. Italian prisoners of war who had been held in prison camps in rural Leicestershire also moved to the city and this was coupled with the arrival of women from Italy who acquired jobs in private households and local industries. In 1971 there were 660 Italian-born people residing in Leicester, and like the Polish they have also experienced a decline in their population since then, mainly due to return migration.[28] In contrast to the Polish population, however, they have not established the same presence within the city, such as a church or central meeting place for the community or transnational media connections. Though it has been suggested that this was due to the small population, more recent research has identified tensions caused by regional and class differences combined with linguistic differences as undermining the development of stronger community relations.[29] Moreover, the Italians did not share the same history of suffering in terms of forced migration and exile, which served as an important focal point and binding force for the Polish community.

The Irish in Leicester are also an important part of Leicester's multi-cultural history. In common with most other cities in Britain the nineteenth-century presence of the Irish did not go unremarked in Leicester where on the eve of the First World War they represented just under 1% of the population. Their more recent migration to the city began in the 1930s and the population grew in the second half of the twentieth century. In 1951 there were 3,102 Irish-born people in Leicester and in 1971 this reached 4,920, 1.7% of the city's population, and a doubling of the nineteenth-century proportion.[30] However, after 1971 Irish migration had practically ceased and many returned to Ireland due to the downturn in the British economy and the economic boom in Ireland. Nevertheless, prior to this in the 1950s the Irish community was 'vibrant and visible'.[31] Irish newspapers were sold after Mass at the Holy Cross church and weekly Irish dances were held at various venues. This sense of community was assisted by

14.5 The Serbian Orthodox Church in the St George's area. This is an example of the ways in which migrants have re-used religious buildings. St George's was the first Anglican church to be built in the city after the Reformation and became the Serbian Orthodox Church in 1983.

Source: Colin Hyde.

the concentration of the Irish residents in the Highfields area of the city though as the Irish population moved out of the city centre to housing estates on the outskirts, the social visibility of this community declined. When an Irish Centre was proposed in the city in the 1980s, this was met with considerable resistance from wealthier Irish-born residents on the basis that they did not want to highlight their cultural difference from the city's white majority. Nevertheless, a Centre for Irish Studies was formed in the mid-1980s, which included evening classes and Irish dance classes, although this largely catered for the second- and third-generation Irish, rather than the first-generation migrants.[32]

These histories of white European migrants show how different groups have carved their own spaces within the city. Their strength of presence within the city has been influenced by the size of the migrant population, geographical concentration, the circumstances of their migration, the extent of tensions and inner divisions as well as the decision to capitalise on a white identity to align themselves with the local-born population. The new Commonwealth migrants, however, could not share this option. As a very visible ethnic group, they were marked out as an 'other' and had a very different experience of the city.

New Commonwealth migrants

The 1940s and 1950s saw the arrival of the city's African Caribbean population. The earliest settlers were a group of former Royal Air Force officers, mainly from Jamaica, and also nurses working at the General Hospital in response to government recruitment schemes. By 1971 there were nearly 2,920 Caribbean-born people living in Leicester, equivalent to 1% of the city's population, although their numbers decreased thereafter to 2,550 in 1981 and 2,120 in 1991.[33] The largest groups originated from Antigua and then Jamaica, but also included Barbuda, Barbados, Dominica, Grenada, Guyana, Montserrat, St Kitts and Nevis, St Lucia, and Trinidad and Tobago – all islands represented by diverse cultures and histories. Around a half came directly to Leicester on arrival and many had intended to save money and then return to their country of origin.[34]

Migration from the Caribbean was supplemented by that from the Indian sub-continent. The first permanent South Asian settler in Leicester can be traced back to the 1920s and was a Punjab Muslim who was joined by two Punjabis in the 1940s. By 1951 there were some 700 Asians living in Leicester, predominantly Punjabi Sikhs from Jullundur and Houshiarpur, subsequently these were joined by migrants from Pakistan and Gujarat in the 1960s. The main bulk of South Asian immigration was generated after 1968 when Leicester became the main destination for East African Asian refugees who had been expelled at 90 days' notice from Uganda by General Idi Amin; between 1968 and 1978 approximately 20,000 East African Asians arrived in Leicester.[35] This influx had the most dramatic transformation on Leicester's ethnic profile. East African Asians constituted a dominant sub-group within the Asian population, and it is this dimension that made Leicester distinct from other British cities. Prior to their arrival the African Caribbean population was estimated to be twice the size of the South Asian population; by the end of the 1970s, the number of South Asians was six times higher.[36]

In response to this migration, anti-immigration panic developed in Leicester from the second half of the 1960s. Enoch Powell's speech on 20 April 1968 exacerbated racist and anti-racist activities in Leicester, and in September 1972 the city was deemed the most 'unwelcoming' in the country. This was due to a City Council advert that warned potential settlers from Uganda to stay away.[37] Leicester quickly surfaced as a focal point for National Front activity, which exploited the council's failure to deflect the exodus, and the city emerged as a centre for organised racist activity. Leicester's National Front evolved from a coalition of anti-immigration groups and the leaders consisted of middle-class lawyers, led by a solicitor, Anthony Read Herbert, who commanded respect from the political parties and local police. The National Front came close to election victories, most notably in 1976, when they took 29% of the vote in Abbey ward and 18% of the poll throughout the city.[38] The headquarters of the National Front were in Highfields and the city was one of the central National Front strongholds outside London.[39]

14.6 Sign greeting Ugandan Asians at London Road railway station, 1972.

Source: Record Office for Leicester, Leicestershire and Rutland, Box 20, folder 2.

This racism was reinforced in the local press and during the 1970s the *Leicester Mercury* gave considerable coverage to the activities of the National Front, which were presented outside the agenda of racial relations and instead were related to issues of democracy and freedom. News in the *Mercury* consistently focused on incidents of racial conflict and tension and unequivocally depicted minority ethnic groups as a problem.[40] Yet despite this, many local-born white people did not harbour racist views and actively fought against the presence of the National Front. Indeed, the National Front was met with a considerable anti-racist backlash, and it was this combination of both racist and anti-racist tradition that was a defining characteristic of Leicester. Anti-racist organisation took the form of student protest, the Anti-Nazi League and a broad coalition of groups, named the Inter-Racial Solidarity Campaign, who received financial support from Jewish industrialists.[41] The 1970s witnessed a series of confrontations between the National Front, black communities and

South Asians and anti-racist activists, including the Imperial Typewriter strike in 1974 and a National Front demonstration in 1979.[42] The latter was successfully thwarted by anti-racists and signalled the end of the National Front in Leicester.[43]

The experiences of South Asians and African Caribbeans in Leicester echoed those of immigrants to other British cities: in short, they felt disadvantaged in housing, education, and employment.[44] The policies of Leicester City Council simply reflected those of central government, so, for example, the poor housing conditions of these groups was seen as a result of their choices, rather than institutional discrimination within the housing sector. Similarly, experiences of education pre-dated the advent of multi-cultural approaches to education and the approach of Leicestershire Local Education Authority was based on a model of assimilation with the explicit aim of 'Anglicising immigrants'.[45] This not only reduced African Caribbean and South Asian children to the category of 'immigrants' who were defined, collectively, as a problem, but the notion of assimilation was underpinned by the belief that British culture was inherently superior and that ethnic, linguistic and cultural diversity was problematic and should be suppressed.

African Caribbeans and South Asians responded to this hostile environment by creating local sports, religious and cultural activities, in order to cultivate belonging and a positive sense of identity. African Caribbeans played in factory cricket clubs but also formed their own club as early as 1948. This group organised social events, such as dances and film nights, and it became the West Indian Sports and Social Club from 1957 until 1966. Although cricket united those from the Caribbean it also helped foster more positive relations with the white British-born population as it encouraged white players to adopt a more tolerant perspective based on respect towards their fellow cricket players.[46] Football was also a focal point for men from the Caribbean in the 1960s and 1970s. Games were played both on Spinney Hill Park and more formally on Victoria Park, with Antigua versus the Caribbean football matches and in the early 1970s

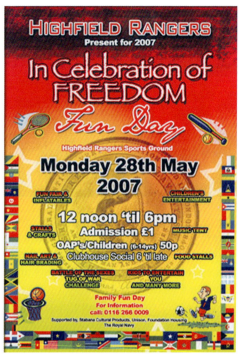

14.9 Slogans still being daubed on the houses of immigrants in Leicester in 1988.
Source: Leicester City Council.

14.10 Highfields Rangers fun day in 2007 demonstrating a message of freedom and solidarity.
Source: Leicester City Council.

Highfield Rangers was formed.[47] This football club was an important focus for a local black identity. As one player explained: 'Highfields in those days was where the black people and them lived. Highfields was recognised for black people. We wanted to be *Highfield* Rangers; well, that's how I felt.'[48]

As African Caribbean's joined local churches, some, such as the Quakers, were more hospitable to them than others. Consequently they began to establish their own church groups, such as the New Testament Church of God, which bought the church on Melbourne Road in 1963. Despite this, some felt that there were limited places for African Caribbean people to meet and this was due not only to the relatively small size of the African Caribbean population, but their lack of funds to rent or purchase buildings. In an attempt to represent the needs to their community, the Leicester United Caribbean Association was formed in the 1970s which was an umbrella organisation for some fifteen African Caribbean groups. However, it was not until after the disturbances erupted in Highfields in July 1981 that inner-city funds were opened up to support ethnic diversity by means of community groups, and as a result African Caribbean cultural expression flourished. The annual Caribbean Carnival, which began in 1984, is seen as a manifestation of this.[49]

While South Asians also organised sports and youth activities, they focused on activities to retain their religious and cultural distinctiveness and in particular the growth of their religious organisation has been striking.

Initially, houses were used for religious meetings; however, the first mosque was established in 1962, the first gurdwara in 1966, and the first Hindu temple in 1969.[50] For many women religious associations were perceived as an opportunity to socialise yet it also enabled them to gain prestige. Sikhism encouraged women to partake in the public sphere of religious life and one woman who came to Britain in 1965 explained how she seized the opportunity to take a leading role within her local gurdwara:

> I started doing a lot of the community work at the gurdwaras. I started filling in forms and so forth and all of a sudden they realised, 'oh God this woman's got talent that we haven't got and we need her', and that's how then you know, I got accepted, but I *really* had to earn it.[51]

Since the 1970s, then, the city witnessed the acceleration in associations and religious organisations and this coincided with the arrival of the East African Asians and with the phase of family reunion.[52] While there were no purpose-built Hindu temples in Leicester, Baptist and Catholic churches, factories and private homes were converted into Hindu places of worship representing a wide range of caste affiliations. This included the conversion of a Baptist church in 1971 to the Shree Sanatan Mandir, Leicester's largest Hindu temple, and the conversion of a Roman Catholic church to the Shree Shati Mandir Hindu Temple in 1975. It was not until the mid-1980s that the City Council actively endorsed the establishment of purpose-built places of worship for minority ethnic groups, and the city's first purpose-built mosque was completed in 1987 in Loughborough Road, Belgrave.[53]

Consequently, the meaning of the landscape was dramatically altered so that it was not an expression of an English identity, but signified the distinctive South Asian character of the city. For example, mosques incorporated architectural traditions such as domes and minarets, as shown in the Masjid Umar mosque on Evington Road. This transformation in the landscape was also evident in the growth of South Asian cinemas. Councillor Subedar arrived in Leicester in 1972 and claimed there were five or six South Asian cinemas in the city.[54] This included the purpose-built Natraj cinema and entertainment complex on Belgrave Road which, opened in 1974 and during the 1970s, showed 25 South Asian films each week and included a ladies' night. According to the cinema's manager, Natraj's audience encompassed 'all Asian communities say Muslims, Gujaratis, Sikhs, everybody with their families' from 'all over the Midlands'.[55] This was part of the development of strong and visible transnational linkages back to India, but it also helped to create a friendly and supportive space for many South Asians living in Leicester. Despite the diversity of affiliations and religious and caste divisions, Leicester became an 'Asian place' where you could do 'Asian things'.[56]

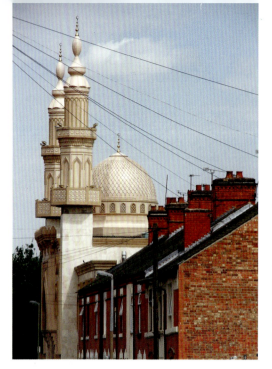

14.12 Asfordby Street Mosque again showing the proximity of places of worship and residences.
Source: Colin Hyde.

14.13 BAPS Shri Swaminarayan Mandir, Hindu Temple, Gypsy Lane.
Source: Colin Hyde.

14.14 Masjid Umar Mosque, Evington Drive Street.
Source: Colin Hyde.

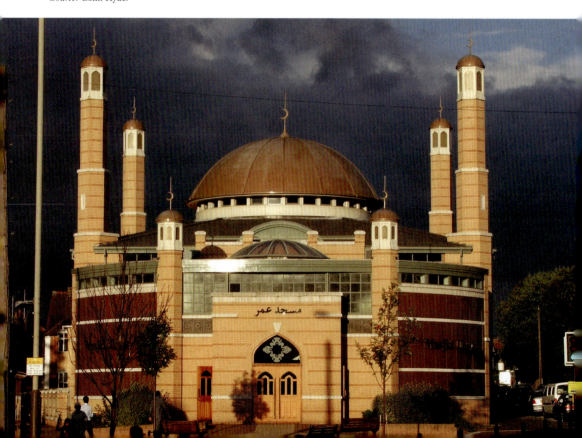

14.15 Multi-
culturalism.
Source: Colin Hyde.

14.16 Diwali.
Source: Colin Hyde.

14.16 Mela.

14.17 Vaisakhi 2006 celebrating the founding of the Sikh community.

Caribbean Carnival.

Feeling at home

This chapter has attempted to trace the many layers of ethnic diversity that have shaped Leicester. It has not been possible here to capture the heterogeneity of these populations or the more negative aspects of living in communities; instead the aim has been to highlight how different groups, including less visible white migrants, have sought to construct communities and a 'home' in the city.[57] In contrast to the earlier European white migrants, both African Caribbeans and South Asians formed their own groups and places to meet within a wider context of racism and hostility. African Caribbeans, for example, encountered rejection from existing churches and, in response, established their own. Despite these shared experiences of hostility, interviews with African Caribbean women have revealed how they perceived themselves as pioneers and felt that their encounters with discrimination had 'paved the way' for subsequent migration. As one woman explained:

> We were the ones, the Caribbean women, the Black women from the Caribbean, we were the ones who paved the way. ... We have blazed the trail here. You know, in England, and because they don't see us with great mansions, great big supermarkets and things like that, they think that we haven't done anything. But we were the ones who put the first stone down, and from that stone now they have mansions, they have supermarkets, and we are quite satisfied with our lot, because we know we have brought our children up, to tell them not to hate, event though we have had that hate.[58]

Whilst South Asians also encountered significant levels of hostility, the quote reveals how African Caribbeans felt like a minority group within an (ethnic) minority in Leicester, particularly as they compared unfavourably with the more economically and politically powerful South Asians.[59] Their feelings qualify Leicester's image of multi-cultural success, as it highlights how only some groups have secured considerable gains in the city.[60] Yet the quote also represents a call for their place as African Caribbean women to be acknowledged within Leicester's history, particularly in a context whereby Leicester's multi-cultural success is largely attributed to the East African Asians.

Finally, while Leicester is currently viewed as a trouble-free city, this chapter has revealed the city's history of both racism and anti-racist organisation. Thus, 'success' follows many years of disputes and conciliation. Moreover, it is important to remember that this anti-immigrant sentiment was most salient in the 1970s and although there is an awareness that Leicester may not be as harmonious as the public image suggests, recent interviews with Ugandan Asians reveal how they have developed strong feelings of pride and belonging with the city, and now view themselves as Leicester people.[61] As Panna claimed, 'So everybody's settled down very well in Leicester, we really like Leicester, because it's like—, we think it's like being in Africa, that's how we feel.'[62] While Nisha explained:

> In fact today if you ask us now, you know, 'can we go back to Uganda?' even if you offered us a million pounds we'd say 'no', because we're settled here now. You know, we've been here the majority of our life now and this is home for us now, so we can't go and this is it, where will we go? We've lost all our trace from that country now, so we are glad we are in Leicester.[63]

15

Contesting Liberty

L EICESTER'S MOTTO, *Semper Eadem*, 'always the same', does not sit easily with the demands of urban change. Demands to renew and improve the urban condition as part of an attempt to secure an urban renaissance are at odds with this motto. Yet the roman Jewry wall is juxtaposed with the 1960s ring road, and the landscape of Victorian, inter-war and post-1945 building is further layered with twenty-first-century architecture, as with the performing arts theatre in the St George's Cultural Quarter. If 'semper eadem' is treated with a little licence, as 'constant', then the view of Leicester as one of *constant* change is more convincing.

Since the 1990s, Leicester has been subjected to various local and national government urban initiatives. These have included a City Challenge scheme, Single Regeneration Budget, and an Urban Regeneration Company implanted in various parts of the inner city in order to stimulate economic and urban development and social regeneration. Each initiative sought to renew Leicester's urban landscape in order that the city could become a competitive force in a post-industrial urban world. Inevitably, tensions were aroused between the blend of new architecture and planning with the historical legacy.

The fifteen-year debate that surrounded the future of the Liberty Building on Eastern Boulevard exposed this tension and revealed the layers of previously latent meaning and memory. The urban landscape and the values that were ascribed to the historic environment by residents and planners were a matter of polar opposites. The decision whether to retain or replace, to adapt or demolish, provides an insight into contemporary urban pressures and how these condition the perception and valuation of the historic environment. What were the interests at stake? Do different agencies or organisations interpret buildings as texts in an urban environment; do threats to the historic environment expose these meanings, memories and values?

The Liberty Building as a site of meaning and memory

The architecturally striking Liberty boot and shoe factory was constructed in 1919 to replace a smaller, outdated factory situated in neighbouring Asylum Street. The Lennard Brothers, a prominent family in Leicester's industrial

15.1 Aerial view (1997) of the Liberty Building (top right) and City Challenge Bede Island site foreground).

Source: Leicester City Council.

15.2 The Liberty Building.

Source: Leicester Mercury, 31 July 2000, 'Shoe Designer Recalls the Pristine Liberty Shoes Factory'.

history, commissioned the factory, and Samuel Lennard eventually became mayor of the city and the first President of the Federation of Boot and Shoe Manufacturers Association. After the First World War, Lennard Brothers Ltd ventured into quality ladies shoes, commissioning a state-of-the-art factory on Eastern Boulevard. The company gained 'national and international success as a result of the shorter hemlines of the period that brought women's shoes into greater prominence as fashion items'.[1] The speciality of the factory was women's high grade welted, McKay sewn and cemented shoes.

A replica Statue of Liberty was added in 1921 following a business trip made by the factory's owners to New York, a move that also saw the company name changed, significantly, from Lennards to Liberty. Until its closure in 1994 the building fulfilled a number of functions: a boot and shoe factory; a bomb shelter during the Second World War; and then a printworks owned first by Lowe and Carr and then by LCV International.

The original building plans indicate that the factory was designed to employ 463 people, of which 250 were men and 213 were women.[2] The factory became a central feature in the local community as their place

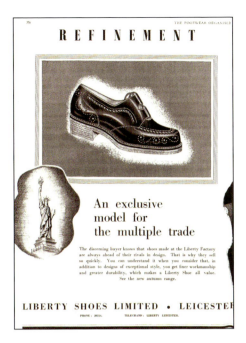

REFINEMENT

An exclusive
model for
the multiple trade

The discerning buyer knows that shoes made at the Liberty Factory
are always ahead of their rivals in design. That is why they sell
so quickly. You can understand it when you consider that, in
addition to designs of exceptional style, you get finer workmanship
and greater durability, which makes a Liberty Shoe all value.
See the new autumn range.

LIBERTY SHOES LIMITED • LEICESTER

PHONE : 26314.   TELEGRAMS : LIBERTY LEICESTER.

15.3 Advertisement for Liberty Shoes

Source: *Footwear Organiser*, 370 (no date), Joan Skinner collection, University of Leicester Special Collections.

15.4 Liberty Shoes

Source: Joan Skinner collection, University of Leicester Special Collections.

of work. Over several generations there was a shared experience not just of production, but the positives of friendships, and of disappointments too. Generations of family members worked in the factory and it became deeply embedded in Leicester's urban landscape, as when it was festooned with garlands for King George V's jubilee in 1935. The building and the Liberty statue were also permanent visual markers that were located in a working-class neighbourhood and gave access to Leicester from the west by commanding one of only three bridges that cross the Grand Union canal. It was part of the everyday life of many Leicester folk. The building was Grade II listed in 1994 as a rare example of a building in the United Kingdom that was built using Hennebique construction methods.[3] Francois Hennebique was an early French pioneer in the use of reinforced concrete in which he devised his own structural system, available only under licence to ensure that strict specifications were observed.

Over the course of eighty years the factory became a locus of conflicting, overlapping layers of meaning and memory. These feelings and reactions are elusive, but a person's memories become explicit through their relationship with the built environment. Indeed every recollection had a spatial and temporal framework. Collective memory 'draws upon spatial images. ... A group's thoughts and movements are ordered by the succession of images from external objects.'[4] In this view memory always unfolded in 'space' and the activity of recollection was based on spatial reconstruction. Thus the Liberty Building, as part of Leicester's urban landscape, had the capacity to be a site of memory. For some, Liberty was a place of work and deeply embedded in their consciousness, as one worker explained: 'both my parents were employed at the factory and I started work there in 1940.'[5] The building was a signifier of the boot and shoe industry, an architectural icon, an orientation point and a landmark: 'everyone in Leicester knows where they are when they see the Liberty Building.'[6] For others it was a blot on the landscape: 'there's not much to conserve, frankly it's an eyesore,'[7] a visual marker and reminder of the decline of the manufacturing sector, a place of suffering, and later a piece of real estate and a development opportunity. The descriptions here are stark and simplistic; in reality there was a mixture of meanings and memories, both positive and negative, and these varied both between individuals or collectives and over time. Significantly, though, Liberty, like so many buildings, was a repository of meaning and memory, often personalised but rarely elucidated.

The controversy surrounding the Liberty Building, however, wakened these reactions and the investment of meaning and ascription of value

Table 15.1 Liberty Building developments since 1919

Date	Event
1919	Liberty Building constructed by Lennard Brothers Limited.
1921	Replica statue of Liberty sculpted by Herbert Morcrom and erected atop the Liberty Building.
1935	Festooned with garlands for King George V's jubilee.
1940s	Used as a bomb shelter during World War II.
1960s	Change in ownership to Lowe and Carr.
1980s	Change in ownership to LCV International.
1991	Planning application to change the use from general industry to student flats and build a four-storey extension given conditional approval.
1992	Planning application to demolish the existing buildings.
1993	Planning application to demolish the existing buildings withdrawn. Liberty comes under the jurisdiction of City Challenge.
1994	Liberty building listed with Grade II status as a result of the spot-listing application researched, prepared and submitted by the Leicester Group of the Victorian Society.
1996	Planning application to convert the factory for retail and residential use. This was submitted by Liberty 21 Limited and given conditional approval.
2002	Planning application to demolish the Grade II listed Liberty building given conditional approval.
2002	Building demolished but statue retained. Planning condition inserted that the statue should be restored, maintained and re-sited on the new building.
2008	Planning application to re-site the statue on a plinth on the junction of Upperton Road and Western Boulevard. Accepted, and statue re-sited in December 2008.

was exposed in three ways. Firstly, through the local historical societies' campaign to list the building; secondly, through the same organisations' desire to maintain Liberty; and, thirdly, through the competing visions and conflicting ideas surrounding the Liberty Building and Statue's role in Leicester's urban regeneration and therefore its contemporary relevance. In this context the Liberty Building was the object of conflicting valuations which were wakened by the threats of demolition, conditioned by planning pressures and the urban agenda, and mediated by the presence of the Statue.

Valuing Liberty: reacting to the threat of demolition

The meanings and memories related to the Liberty Building were exposed under the threat to demolish the building, and any threat to demolish an existing part of the environment can, 'have a deep-seated effect on a community, as it effectively wipes out a significant chapter in the history of a place and erases memories of its heritage for the majority of its present and future inhabitants'.[8]

The threat to demolish Liberty, the fear of losing part of a familiar urban landscape, motivated action and exposed previously hidden feelings towards the building. In the context of neighbourhood protests, as 'long as there is no suggestion of change, no perception of threat' then the meanings invested in a place 'tend to remain implicit and unexpressed'.[9] However, in times of rapid change, such as that envisaged between the Local Plan (1992) through to City Challenge (1993–98), the past has the capacity to be ascribed with a contemporary value as the 'continued existence of familiar surroundings may satisfy a psychological need, which even if irrational, is very real. Nothing gives more tangible assurance of stability than bricks and mortar.'[10] This is commonly seen in wartime as patriots fight to protect their symbolic and historical environment, as with St Paul's Cathedral, the Forth Bridge, Warsaw Castle and the protection given to open cities such as Rome during the Second World War. Furthermore, as with Liberty, the historic significance of a structure may only be discovered when it is threatened.

This threat of demolition was first evident with the planning application of 1992. From this point local historical societies, namely the Leicester Group of the Victorian Society (LGVS), the Leicester Civic Society (LCS) and national organisations such as English Heritage, the Twentieth Century Society and the Ancient Monuments Society co-ordinated an eight year campaign to list, maintain and retain the building. Motivated by a concern that the building would be demolished since it was 'located in the City Challenge area of the city where redevelopment is going on at pace',[11] the various historical societies worked to retain the Liberty Building.

Liberty was spot listed and given Grade II status in 1994 after the Leicester Group of the Victorian Society (LGVS) comprehensively researched the history of the building.[12] Liberty had previously been on Leicester City

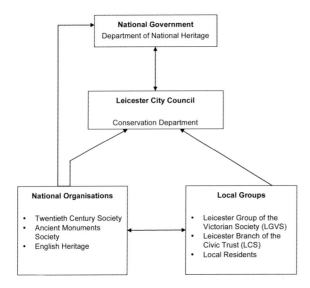

National Government
Department of National Heritage

Leicester City Council
Conservation Department

National Organisations

- Twentieth Century Society
- Ancient Monuments Society
- English Heritage

Local Groups

- Leicester Group of the Victorian Society (LGVS)
- Leicester Branch of the Civic Trust (LCS)
- Local Residents

15.5 Actors involved in securing listed status for Liberty and in campaigning for adequate maintenance.

Council's 'buildings of special interest' list, but this did not afford the building any statutory protection. Furthermore, English Heritage (now Historic England) had not listed the building during their periodic listing surveys. However, research carried out by Joan Skinner included correspondence with the building's constructors, while archival data and architectural examinations revealed that Liberty was a rare example of the Hennebique method of construction. Ironically, it was this method of construction that ultimately caused Liberty's downfall as years of lying redundant saw the building suffer from concrete cancer and in need of regular cathodic protection.

LGVS were not content just to list the Liberty Building. They lobbied the City Council to request adequate maintenance of the former factory, while discussions over a viable use for the building was begun. LGVS were in regular contact with Leicester City Council to ensure that the building was maintained adequately. In 1995 the City Council's Building Conservation Officer informed the LGVS that 'Liberty Works has recently been the subject of a notice under the Public Health Act requiring the owner to make the building secure against intruders'.[13] However, the continuing deterioration of the building led the LGVS to campaign for its further protection from vandals in 1996 stating that:

> Liberty has for many weeks now been open to anyone to walk in and there has been much vandalism. We believe that the owners should be required to board it up properly so that it is impossible for intruders to get inside. The current neglect will simply make it more expensive to rehabilitate.[14]

By 1998 the building was adjudged to have fallen into such disrepair that the Chairman of the Leicester Group of the Victorian Society felt compelled to write to Leicester City Council's Chief Executive asking if it was possible to 'effect a repairs notice on the owners as to allow such a building to decay would bring derision on the whole concept of listing and

15.6 The
Liberty Building
in a state of
decay during the
1990s.

Source: Joan
Skinner Collection,
University of
Leicester Special
Collections.

opprobrium on those who allowed such decay to happen'.[15] This process was repeated in 2001 when the LGVS 'requested the immediate imposition of an urgent works notice to have the building made wind and weatherproof until an enterprising buyer is willing to refurbish it in the way it deserves'.[16] The LGVS, therefore, consistently pressed the City Council to try to ensure that Liberty was maintained.

In addition to listing and lobbying, LGVS brought other organisations into the campaign. Indeed, they wrote to the Twentieth Century Society, the *Leicester Mercury*, and the City Council firmly opposing demolition'.[17] This had tangible outcomes as the *Mercury* followed the debate closely and reported the polarisation of opinion between the major actors. The *Mercury* reported the different opinions of local people as well as the urban agencies. Some local residents were in favour of demolition as they viewed the building as an eyesore, while others wanted to see the building retained. Residents were also concerned over the potential new use of the site as student accommodation. Concerns were expressed by residents about traffic and noise pollution from an increase in cars and bars to cater for the student market. Headlines such as 'Don't take a Liberty with the Future of our Landmark', 'I Say, What a Liberty' and 'Liberty Plan will lead to Bedlam' and 'Pull down Liberty Works Eyesore'[18] reflected different aspects of this debate. Furthermore, both the Twentieth Century and Ancient Monuments societies lodged official objection letters to the application in 2001 to demolish Liberty. These were both based on an examination of

Contesting Liberty | 353

the various structural and engineering assessments of the Liberty Building. These assessments were an integral part of marketing and finding a new use for Liberty and were the subject of much contention.

Three separate surveys were carried out between 1990 and 2001 which each found that the Liberty Building was decaying continually. In 1990 the cost of rehabilitating the building was placed at £0.31 million. There were various cracks in the reinforced concrete floors but the consulting engineers 'formed the opinion that these various cracks were not indicative of any serious structural defects'.[19] By 2000 the next structural survey, commissioned by the building's developers on behalf of the owner to determine 'as far as possible the condition of the reinforced concrete structure',[20] estimated that '15 per cent of the structure was defective'.[21] This proved to be the main point of contention between the developers/owners and English Heritage and the historical societies. The same survey revealed that 15% was a high proportion of degradation and if 'not addressed at this stage [November 2000], further deterioration of the damage will occur, which in the long term, could impair structural stability'.[22] The structural report stated 'in its present condition, the building will not satisfy present day regulations in having to produce guarantees, insurance etc. for potential owners/end users and financial institutions'.[23] By 2000 the costs of rehabilitating Liberty ensured that the proposed residential projects would have seen a shortfall of between £2.5 million and £3.8 million, dependent on the type of re-use. However, these findings and the plans to demolish and replace the Liberty Building were condemned by the national and local historical societies.

The Twentieth Century Society was 'concerned at the lack of understanding of the existing structure given in the structural report'.[24] From this basis the Twentieth Century Society concluded that 'that not all avenues have been explored, hence the proposal to demolish the Liberty Building is not justified'.[25] English Heritage added to the contention surrounding the assessments of the Liberty Building by stating that 'repairs to the reinforced concrete framed structure would be technically possible',[26] while Leicester Civic Society believed that that the 'structural survey has created a deliberately gloomy outlook for the Liberty Works'.[27] Ultimately the demolition of the Liberty Building hinged on the fact that retention was not a commercially viable option and thus historic significance identified by LGVS could not be translated into a contemporary value.

Valuing Liberty: urban planning pressures

Any contemporary valuation of Liberty was based on its capacity to contribute to the on-going regeneration of the Bede Island and West End areas of Leicester. Contained within this 370 hectare area was a quarter of Leicester's derelict land. Unemployment in this area reached 13.6%; two fifths of households were on benefits, and the prevailing condition of the physical environment was one of decay and dilapidation.[28] The area surrounding the Liberty factory had gone from being one of Leicester's thriving industrial heartbeats to a decaying, derelict district of distress. Neither historic significance in the form of listed building status nor local affection was enough to give the building a contemporary relevance under an urgent need to stimulate urban and economic development. This was the context between 1987 and 2002 in which the Liberty building was the subject of seven different planning applications. These applications ranged from a mixed-use scheme comprising a casino, restaurant, betting shop and snooker hall (1987) which the Council refused on the grounds that this particular re-use was 'detrimental to the amenity of nearby residents'[29] to offices and student accommodation. Following the first application to demolish Liberty in 1992 the building came into sharper focus under the jurisdictions of both the Local Plan (1992) and City Challenge (1993–98).

Table 15.2   Planning applications for potential re-use[30]

Date	Application	Outcome
1987	Change of use of factory to entertainment centre to include snooker squash restaurant casino and betting shop.	Refused
1988	Change of use of factory (class b2) to offices (class b1) and provision of enlarged parking area.	Conditional approval
1991	Change of use from general industry (class b2) to 36 student flats (class c3); four storey extension on Walnut street.	Conditional approval
1992	Application to demolish.	Withdrawn
1995	Blocking up lower floor windows to a Grade II listed building.	Withdrawn
1997	Conversion of factory, (a grade ii listed building,) (class b2) to ground floor retail (class a1); floors 1, 2, 3 and additional fourth floor converted to 44 cluster flats (class c3); external alterations.	Conditional approval
2001	Demolition of grade 2 listed building.	Conditional approval Planning condition for re-erection of statue on new building.

In cities across Britain, from Nottingham's Lace Market to Plymouth's naval dockyards, the historic environment increasingly became an integral part of the urban redevelopment jigsaw during the 1990s. This decade saw an increase in the adaptive re-use of the industrial historic environment as urban actors – local planning authorities, entrepreneurs, the private sector and single-issue agencies such as development corporations – started to reassess the ways in which they could regenerate urban centres. Owing to land pressures due to the over-development of suburbia and the comparative neglect of the inner city, the economic recession, environmental awareness, and a changing attitude towards the historic environment as illustrated by increasing tourist visits to historic industrial sites such as Ironbridge Gorge, Wigan Pier and later Birmingham's Jewellery Quarter, derelict factories and warehouses started to be viewed as positive assets that could contribute to urban regeneration through conversion schemes for offices, apartments and tourism.

This was reflected in the Leicester Local Plan (1992) which nominated ten objectives for the improvement of the city centre. One of these objectives related to Leicester's status as Britain's first Environment City and thus the 'protection of historic buildings and areas which add so much to the quality of the city' was an important component of the Local Plan.[31] Accordingly, the plan listed successful schemes to re-use buildings such as the conversions of Midland House on Charles Street into offices and St John the Divine church on South Albion Street into flats, and proposed that the 'current availability of City Grants should encourage developers to

15.7 Pex Sock factory, built in the 1840s.

15.8 The adaptive re-use of the Pex Sock factory. These images show the factory before and after the City Challenge works, and contrast with the medieval structures of Trinity Almshouses (top right) and St Mary's de Castro Church (top left) across the 'Mile Straight' Canal.

Source: Record Office for Leicester, Leicestershire and Rutland, Box 31, and Leicester City Council 1997.

Leicester: a modern history

participate further in similar redevelopment and conversion schemes'.[32] City Challenge which was created in 1993 to:

> achieve by March 1998, sustainable improvement in the physical, economic, social and environment of the City Challenge and linked areas ... thereby improving the quality of life for the people who live in, work in and visit the area ... and creating a model for future regeneration.[33]

adopted a similar stance which saw the £10 million conversion of the Pex Sock factory into the Land Registry and apartments become one of their flagship schemes.

In this context Liberty was proposed as part of a potential solution to housing, commercial, leisure and business problems in Leicester. However, due to on-going and ultimately irreversible structural problems and a changing urban-economic context, Liberty became a vocal point, rather than a focal point, of Leicester's urban regeneration. Only one planning application was submitted (November 1996) during the City Challenge era, but this masked the on-going debate and tension that surrounded the future of the building. Liberty was initially considered by City Challenge to be a 'prime asset for facilitating the regeneration of the Bede Island area',[34] but this sentiment was not supported with viable ideas for a new use. Tentative plans were rebutted at every stage, ideas were proposed from various leisure, community and residential agencies in the city but for various reasons

Figures 15.9, 15.10 The site of the former Cattle Market at Freeman's Common. This became a key strategic site for regeneration during City Challenge.

Source: Record Office for Leicester, Leicestershire and Rutland, 8724 and 0010, Box 30 (Folder 1) and Box 7.

including a changing economic climate, ownership and fluctuating urban priorities these ideas never formalised into feasible projects.

Despite the best efforts of the LGVS and other local historical societies, Liberty's unresolved future saw it lie vacant and unmaintained. Predictably it fell into further decay. By 2001 the Liberty Building required 'grant assistance in excess of £2m'.[35] This money was not forthcoming for several reasons. Firstly, financial support from English Heritage was impossible as the building did not lie in a Conservation Area.[36] Secondly, the City Council did not have any grant money for the project.[37] Thirdly, neither Leicester Regeneration Company nor East Midlands Development Agency nor English Partnerships was able to provide 'grant funding to schemes which are wholly or substantially for residential purposes'.[38] As the planning application for the Liberty Building had been submitted for residential use, and a 1991 application for mixed-use of the site was refused, the stance of the three agencies condemned Liberty. Finally, potential funding from the European Union was only available for deprived wards, and though only a stone's throw away, the Liberty Building stood in Castle ward, not considered to be one of Leicester's most deprived. Thus, another funding avenue was closed.[39] Having satisfied national government Planning Policy Guideline 15 regulations, which ensured that a number of steps have to be taken before a listed building can be demolished, that the building was 'past economic repair',[40] Liberty was demolished one month after the expiry of the 1997 application in March 2002.

Statue: iconic value?

Competing values surrounded the Liberty building. Simplistically, local societies valued the building for its historic significance yet the changing urban context prevented this from being translated into contemporary relevance. Another impediment was the Liberty statue itself, since this assumed a value that appeared to outweigh and be separate from that of the listed building. The replica Statue of Liberty was a powerful component of Leicester's urban landscape – a symbol whose status was arguably unmatched throughout the city and as such was held in high regard by the citizens of Leicester. Indeed, as one resident explained: 'I have always identified the Statue of Liberty as a local landmark.'[41] There were also more personal recollections of the power of the statue on the citizens of Leicester:

> I remember the statue from before the Second World War. I served overseas in the Leicestershire Regiment during the war and the statue has always reminded me of when I came back to Leicester from the Army. We always looked up to the statue and it reminded us of what Leicester was like and what we were fighting for. We've known it as a landmark for many years.[42]

The statue was a source of pride for Leicester and 'adorned the building as a monument to Leicester's once-thriving shoe industry'.[43] The view of some local residents was matched by the official actors involved in Liberty's fate. Leicester City Council considered the statue to be 'a significant feature and some local people have more regard for it than the rest of the building'.[44] This was reflected in *Leicester Mercury* headlines that implored: 'Preserve our Liberty say Statue Admirers'.[45] English Heritage commented that there was 'considerable local attachment to the iconic Statue of Liberty',[46] and the developers also realised 'how important the statue is'.[47] The significance of the statue as a local landmark was, therefore, widely acknowledged by both local citizens and by the public and private sector agencies involved. While there was conflict concerning the contemporary value of the Liberty Building due to its structural problems and unresolved issues concerning a potential new use, there was initially a shared appreciation of the contemporary importance of retaining the historic and symbolic statue.

This affectionate valuation of the replica Statue of Liberty was reflected during the debate over the building's future. The developers decision to apply for permission to demolish the Liberty Building in February 2001 sparked outrage from some local residents[48] who 'wanted to see the building – or, at the very least, its Statue of Liberty preserved'.[49] Indeed the *Leicester Mercury* reported that 'Leicester's West End residents today urged developers to spare the statue if the Grade II listed Liberty Building is bulldozed'.[50] 'Many readers stated that they would like to see the statue saved,' and indeed a public meeting was held at the nearby football stadium to discuss both the saving of the statue and the residents' objections to the new use for building as student accommodation.[51] Other readers called for the building to be saved and, that if it cannot be saved, the existing statue should be put on top of a pillar in Bede Island.[52]

Ironically, these campaigns were relatively uncoordinated when compared to the sustained lobbying of Leicester City Council by the historical societies. However, these campaigns seemed to strike a chord with the developers and Leicester City Council's planning department in a way that the historical societies could not. The plans for the new building were based around the Liberty theme, with replica statues seen on the architect's plans and the universal acceptance that the statue must remain was expressed by Leicester City Council who requested that:

... prior to any demolition works commencing, the Liberty statue shall be removed from the building and then repaired, restored, stored whilst redevelopment on the site is in progress, and replaced on the site or some other location in accordance with details previously agreed in writing with the City Council as the local planning authority. The restored statue shall be placed in its agreed new location within one month of the first occupation of any part of an approved redevelopment scheme, retained and maintained to the satisfaction of the City Council as local planning authority.[53]

However, after demolition the perspectives of the agencies changed. Leicester City Council was asked by the architects to confirm in writing that 'you would not insist on the Statue of Liberty being installed at the site' and it was found stored in a car park skip.[54]

However, in December 2008 the statue was re-sited following a planning application submitted by the City Council in June 2008. The council stressed that they were 'mindful of the fact that the statue is cherished by many people who have been pressing for its reinstatement for a number of years'.[55] The statue is now located on a plinth on the Swan Gyratory roundabout following evidence supplied by the developers of the replacement Liberty building that the 'weight of the statue combined with the structural design of the building, coupled with safety concerns' meant 'it could not be sited on the roof'.[56]

The legacy of the Liberty building continued to provoke opinion among citizens, with some writing to the *Mercury* to express either delight or dismay. However, the symbolism of the statue remained, and one reader summed up the meaning of the statue:

15.11 Statue of Liberty in a skip.
Source: Colin Hyde.

15.12 Statue of Liberty re-sited, and displaying the Leicester FC scarf following the team's success in winning the 2015–16 Premier League title.
Source: Richard Rodger.

it has its own important message to convey, which is
that Leicester was at one time world-renowned for its
shoe manufacture – and, that although we are experiencing tough times presently with the whole world in
recession, which could eventually shift the power of
production back to this land of ours, the Liberty statue
holds the lamp aloft to the hope of the future and of
Leicester being once more a famous place for its shoe
manufacturing.[57]

This connection to the former Liberty building and the
boot and shoe industry relies solely on local knowledge
and collective memory. While the statue may be located
in the proximity of where the former factory stood there
is no mention of the history of the statue, nor indeed why
it is located on the plinth on the roundabout. Rather, the commemoratory
plaque uses a quote from Thomas Paine and fails to mention the link to
the manufacturing industry. Once again the statue continued to provoke
reactions and calls into question whether the statue or the building was
the icon. In terms of the listed building status it was the building that was
historically significant; however, as the Liberty saga unravelled the fate of
the statue became increasingly important to the extent that both the local
and planning debates centred on the future of the unlisted statue and not
the listed building.

Conflicting valuations: contesting Liberty

As the Liberty debate illustrated, meanings, memories and values are not
singular, objective or fixed, but are plural, selective and transitory. The
values ascribed by official actors can be, and are, contradicted by local users.
Indeed, 'each person or group views, uses and constructs the same landscape
in different ways; these are neither "right" or "wrong", but rather are part
of the many layers of meaning within one landscape.'[58] The ways in which
different urban actors see the city, perceive and relate to the urban landscape
and react to threatened and real changes to the urban fabric are conditioned
by the 'particular cultural, intellectual, historical and psychological frames
of reference held by the individuals of groups involved'.[59] During the fifteen-
year debate, numerous 'frames of reference' can be identified. On the one
hand the pressures arising from the contemporary urban agenda saw the
on-going saga with Liberty 'detract from regeneration efforts made in the
area in the last few years'.[60] Additionally, without funding the building
was not seen as 'commercially viable',[61] and as such urban and economic
considerations conditioned the perspective of certain urban actors towards
the Liberty building. On the other hand, the Liberty building was seen as

a 'vital historic asset',[62] a local landmark and an integral part of Leicester's urban fabric. The historical importance was not enough to ensure that this was translated into contemporary relevance; indeed, values are not 'inherent in any cultural items or properties received from the past; rather historic buildings, especially in the context of urban regeneration schemes, have to be ascribed with a contemporary as well as an historic value.

Tensions between personalised places in which collective memories were embedded and institutional spaces where visions and new conceptions were envisaged were apparent with the different viewpoints concerning the Liberty building and statue. The Liberty building was contested along several different lines: between the public and the private sector, between the private and voluntary sector, between the public and voluntary sector, and within the public sector. All these tensions were ultimately unresolved as Liberty continued to polarise opinion between urban actors around the balance of historic significance with contemporary relevance. This aligns with various ideas and research into the concept of collective and urban memory. Collective memory only 'retains the elements which continue to live, or are capable of living in the consciousness of the group that keeps the memory alive'.[63] These memories can then adopt a particular form according to a group's or an institution's wishes. In this context the Liberty building was viewed from varying and competing contemporary perspectives that at no point aligned. The stark binary between past and present was never resolved, a situation which led English Heritage to state that they:

> intend to review with Leicester City Council their strategies for conservation-led regeneration, identifying any case where statutory intervention and/or practice planning policy can encourage the repair and re-use of listed and other historic buildings before the deteriorate beyond the point of economic repair.[64]

The failure to find a new use for Liberty can be attributed to issues surrounding funding, ownership, and the urban agenda, but the overriding reason rests with the ways in which individuals and collectives invest meanings and ascribe values to the historic environment and how this is conditioned, regulated and mediated by a series of contemporarily determined factors. In this way although the urban landscape will change, the ways in which urbanites react to the urban fabric will continue to be, 'always the same'.

16

The spirit of the city:
what is Leicester's *genius loci*?[1]

T o ask what comprises the *genius loci* of Leicester, or rather what constitutes the city's spirit or prevailing character or atmosphere, is a difficult question. Leicester's marketing slogan in 2014 was 'One Leicester' but the city cannot be reduced simply to a single iconic image in the way that Paris can with its Eiffel Tower or Edinburgh with its castle. Picture postcards of Leicester often contain the Clock Tower, the Guildhall, and soon will contain images related to the discovery of King Richard III's remains under a car park. However, the external image of Leicester is not easily retrieved either on a national or an international scale.

An elusive single image of the city has meant that writers and commentators have struggled to describe it. Arthur Mee's view that Leicester was 'one of the remarkable cities of the world'[2] was counterbalanced by Ray Gosling's belief that Leicester is 'the most Midland of Midland cities'.[3] Perhaps that great travel writer J.B. Priestley best summed up the external image of Leicester in his travelogue from 1933:

It is hard to believe that anything much has ever happened there [Leicester]. ... The town seems to have no atmosphere of its own. I felt I was quite ready to praise it, but was glad to think I did not live in it. ... There are many worse places I would rather live in. It seemed to me to lack character, to be busy and cheerful and industrial and built of red brick, and to be nothing else. Such was my immediate impression.[4]

Priestley also listed what he saw as the surprising history of the city:

Actually, it is very old and offers you a very rum mixed list of historical associations: for example, King Lear and his daughters lived here, if they ever lived anywhere; it is Simon de Montfort's town; the broken Cardinal Wolsey came here to die, and has now acquired a new immortality by having his name stamped on thousands of bales of stockings and underclothes; John Bunyan saw the siege here during the Civil War; and among its 19th-century citizens was the original

Thomas Cook, who ran his first little excursion out of Leicester station.[5]

Priestley's immediate impression led him to state that 'somehow you do not believe in all these goings on', so that Leicester could not quite be as remarkable as Mee would later state. In fact Leicester has continued to contribute quietly to the history of the twentieth and twenty-first centuries. Leicester folk, as the authors here have shown, have contributed further layers to the complex image of Leicester.

The chapters within this book, in covering the period in which the city both industrialised and deindustrialised, have illustrated that Leicester has remained radical and revolutionary as it sought to create and maintain the conditions that ensured it was once lauded by the League of Nations as the 'most prosperous city in the British Empire and the second most prosperous community in the world'.[6] Moreover, Leicester has remained plural – in its population, economy, cultural provision, religious institutions, built environment, and especially in its image. In fact Leicester's position as the first city outside of London to be seen as 'plural' is due to the fact that no ethnic group is in the majority.[7] However, while this is a key component of its plurality it is by no means the only component.

Economic and social plurality

Leicester's plurality itself ensured that for the nineteenth, twentieth and much of the twenty-first century the city did not have an easily identifiable and thus marketable external image. Often this was revealed, in other cities, by industrial occupations: Manchester is known as 'Cottonopolis', whereas Northampton Town (*Cobblers*), Sheffield United (*Blades*) and West Ham (*Irons*), to name just three, embedded their industrial traditions in their football clubs. Leicester, as this book has demonstrated, is not easily reducible to a nickname based on its occupational history.[8] Whilst the boot and shoe and hosiery industries were important sources of employment they were certainly not the only ones. The town of a 'thousand trades' evoked by the Leicester Song ensured that Leicester's post-industrial decline was not as severe as many other industrial cities but also ensured that plurality characterised the economy of the city.[9]

The Leicester Song

Leicester town where there's dyeing and spinning
Heeling, soiling and cold iron rolling.
Stockings, shirts and good tools too
Electrical machinery and a well made shoe ...

... We like Leicester it's our sort of town
Not too stuck up and far from being down
Leicester's full of people, folks like you and me
This is what makes Leicester such a pleasant place to be[10]

In the twenty-first century Leicester's economy retains its diversity and its traditional independence from any single manufacturing sector or dominant employer. The city has developed a strong profile in logistics and distribution, food and drink, and retailing, with a significant number of independent stores complemented by the large-scale regeneration of the city centre through the Highcross development. However, while private enterprises have been a long-run feature of the city there remains a strong emphasis on public sector employment. Indeed one in four jobs (25.4%) is based in public sector occupations in local government, education and health.[11] Indeed, the presence of two universities and three large hospitals within the city boundaries helps to account for the dependency on public sector employment. This and the retention of a 'very strong and diverse small business community' ensured that the city has not yet developed an easily identifiable external economic profile.[12] Leicester has, however, outlined its 'key potential competitive advantages' which include 'the diversity and enterprising traditions of its many communities, its strong physical and cultural international connectivity ... and its healthy manufacturing base in key sectors'.[13] In an increasingly competitive world in which cities compete for human and capital investment, projecting an image of Leicester as connected, innovative and entrepreneurial across a range of different industries has become central to attracting businesses and delivering sustained economic growth.

16.1 Postcard from Faire Brothers.

Source: Leicester and Leicestershire Record Office.

Economic diversity in twenty-first-century Leicester is an extension of that experienced throughout the nineteenth and twentieth centuries. A glance at the postcards produced by firms such as Faire Brothers shows not just the different industries within Leicester but also the geographical reach of Leicester businesses.

Mee stated in 1937 that 'Men and women tramp the Earth in every part wearing shoes and stockings from Leicester. There is not an article of clothing from head to foot which is not made in Leicester.'[14] Indeed *The Times* stated in 1969 that Leicester still 'clothes the world'.[15]

This sustained economic diversity represents a strong competitive edge for Leicester as it attempts to build international trade relationships to rival those developed in the industrial era. In 2003 Singh found that there were:

> ... over 10,000 registered Asian businesses in the city, including some of the most successful Asian businesses in the UK; and many of these have substantial transnational trading links with Europe, South Asia and North America. Ethnic business success in Leicester is symbolised in the Belgrave Road 'Golden Mile' which has become a retail and commercial centre of international renown.[16]

The potential of these international trade networks was acknowledged in the Economic Action Plan (2012) which stated that 'The city council is particularly keen to build on the opportunities presented by the strong international links and networking many local businesses have in order to attract new investment and private equity into the city and increase trade with Asia and the "BRIC" countries [Brazil, Russia, India and China].'[17] Leicester's long-standing links to cities within the BRIC countries offers further potential economic advantages, and the city's long-standing town twinning relationships with Rajkot in India and Chongqing in China provide a historical legitimacy to the development of more formal trade relations.[18]

Despite the fact that the Leicester lost '20,000 manufacturing jobs in the early twenty-first century',[19] the city still has an above average manufacturing base. Indeed, 14.3% of the workforce are employed in this sector; the comparable figure Britain as a whole is 8.5%. This means that Leicester's export business maintains some of the international connections developed during the industrial era. Furthermore, anecdotal tales of international clothing companies reassigning business to Leicester firms in the face of increased transportation costs and logistical issues with international providers demonstrates the role of Leicester's clothing heritage in re-energising the twenty-first-century local economy.[20]

In addition to the strong manufacturing base in the city, the Leicester and Leicestershire Economic Partnership (LLEP) acknowledged the 'strong entrepreneurial culture' of the multi-cultural urban community within Leicester which now stands at over 40% of the city's population.[21] Some 22% of those who are self-employed in Leicester originate from Pakistan – significantly more than the national average.[22] Furthermore, the diversity of the independent retailers in The Lanes, Silver Arcade, St Martin's, Stoneygate and Belgrave Road visually illustrates to visitors and residents alike the tradition of small businesses throughout the city. In 2013 Leicester had the highest number of small enterprises within the East Midlands and contained a higher percentage of small enterprises (12.3%) and small local units (16.2%) than the Great Britain average.[23]

As noted in chapter 8 the demographic profile within Leicester is significantly different to that of most other UK cities. Leicester is the 'tenth largest city in England' in 2011 with an estimated 333,800 residents.[24] Following the waves of immigration in the late 1960s and 1970s there was a 'relatively static population level until the turn of the millennium, from which point it has grown by 17%, almost double the national rate of population growth'.[25] This population expansion featured a high proportion of working age newcomers and waves of immigrants from a range of countries including India, Pakistan, Poland, Somalia, Bangladesh and eastern European countries. Of the 34% or 111,000 Leicester residents in 2011 who were born outside the UK just under half (53,000) arrived between 2001 and 2011, and was partly due to the expansion of the European Union in 2004.[26] The continued diversity within the population is demonstrated by the 2011 Census, with 51% of people identified as 'white British', and 37% are people from ethnic minority groups, of which the largest group is Indian (28.3%).[27] Alongside the issues outlined in chapters 8 and 14, this breadth and diversity in population continues to influence the socio-economic profile of the city.

This mix in the social and economic fabric of the city is reflected in its built environment and cultural facilities. Leicester's heritage spans 2,000 years and ranges from listed structures such as the Roman Jewry Wall to College Hall in Clarendon Park built in 1960. More recently, iconic structures such as Curve in the Cultural Quarter and the BAPS Shri Swaminarayan Mandir on the corner of Catherine Street and Gypsy Lane have added to the international flavour of architecture within the city boundaries. However, a walk around what is now the Cultural Quarter reveals a tradition of eclectic international influences in the architectural styles of many buildings, most notably The Exchange and the former Pfister & Vogel building on Rutland Street.

To the construction of new buildings further layers have been added to the Leicester's built heritage. Many former industrial buildings have been re-used to meet the varied needs of small and medium businesses and artistic enterprises, as in the rehabilitation of Maker's Yard and the LCB Depot. These demonstrated the continuing value of former industrial buildings. Donisthorpe Mill, purchased by the City Council for £550,000, followed the precedent set by the Pex Sock Factory, re-used for business space, and both are vital elements in the social and economic development of the city.

The long-term impact of demographic pluralism in Leicester is also reflected in the changes to the built environment and land use patterns. A number of new religious buildings including the BAPS Shri Swaminarayan Mandir have been built on former industrial land or have been developed in the redundant warehouses within the city. The close relationship between deindustrialisation and the reclamation of land and buildings to strengthen the cultural identity of Leicester citizens adds yet a further layer to the

16.2 St Martins.
Source: R. Madgin.

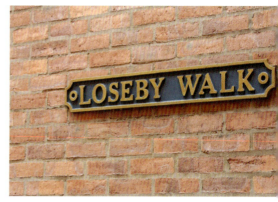

16.3 Belgrave Road.
Source: R. Madgin.

Leicester palimpsest. The diverse cultural offerings within the city are demonstrated by the sheer number of popular festivals such as Diwali, Riverside, Holi, Caribbean Carnival, Vaisakhi Parade and Leicester Pride. The fact that the Queen chose the city as the start of the Diamond Jubilee tour reflected the view that Leicester represents the multi-culturalism of twenty-first-century Britain.

16.4 The Exchange Building. This closely resembles the design of the Flatiron building in New York.

Source: R. Madgin.

16.5 The former Pfister & Vogel Building has connections to Philadelphia.

Source: R. Madgin.

Connecting Leicester

Plurality has been identified throughout this book as a feature of Leicester. In terms of governance, and in relation to economic development, external agencies have also had an influence on the fortunes of the city. Alphabet agencies such as the LLEP (Leicester and Leicestershire Economic Partnership), EMDA (East Midlands Development Agency, 1999), and LRC (Leicester Regeneration Company 2002, later Prospect Leicestershire, 2009), influenced the economic development of the city. A complex web of agencies was involved in delivering urban change within the city boundaries. Organisations such as the Leicester Asian Business Association and the Leicester African–Caribbean Business Association, established in 1995, reflected the variety of interests within the city itself. However, the most profound change to Leicester's governance came with the election in 2011 of a City Mayor, Sir Peter Soulsby, and Leicester joined a small club of fourteen other local authorities who now have elected mayors.[28] Whilst the LLEP and Prospect Leicestershire are still in operation the elected mayor has introduced a series of initiatives designed to draw connections across the many different facets of Leicester's socio-economic development.

Since his election and re-election the City Mayor has instituted a series of urban regeneration initiatives designed to improve the socio–economic position of Leicester. These initiatives are contained within an umbrella scheme, *Connecting Leicester*, on the premise that there is a need to 'raise awareness and understanding of the attractiveness and cosmopolitan nature of Leicester as a place to live, work and visit'.[29] Leicester is not immune to the ultra–competitive world of global cities, and as one of many medium–sized UK cities Leicester is mindful of the importance of inward

16.6 Connecting Leicester.

Source: R. Madgin.

The Connecting Leicester project is transforming the heart of the city, revealing and connecting the city's unique historic buildings, streets and spaces.

The Haymarket Shopping Centre is open as usual.

Connecting Leicester
people and places

leicester.gov.uk/haymarketbusstation   /leicestercitycouncil   @leicester_news

Haymarket SHOPPING   Department for Transport   Leicester City Council investment. City Challenge demonstrated that mid-1990s Leicester could compete with UK cities for investment, yet 'against the backdrop of the current economic climate it is even more important for Leicester do so to improve its attractiveness for investment'.[30] It was imperative that the city developed a strong and 'distinctive identity ... to differentiate it from other UK cities'.[31] However, due to the pluralism so characteristic of Leicester it is very difficult to isolate one industry or feature and use this to market the city.

Soulsby traced both the loss of manufacturing in the 1960s and relegation to the status of a non-metropolitan district in the local government reorganization of 1974 as critical issues undermining the prosperity of Leicester in the later twentieth century. From a position in which industrial Leicester was connected to the world, the political landscape in Leicester was rendered comparatively impotent by its loss of status, and with it the loss to Leicestershire County Council of two powerful departments – education and social services – both capable of contributing to an economic revival. There was, as the *Leicester Economic Action Plan* realised, a need to 'restore the city's pride and self-confidence'. Like Arthur Mee, J.B. Priestley, Ray Gosling and the words contained within the charity single *Well Leicester,* the City Mayor joined the ranks of a number of commentators who acknowledged that Leicester is not only 'a city without a clearly defined identity' but that it is suffering from an inferiority complex. Theme 5 in the Leicester Economic Action Plan 2012–2020 entitled 'Confident City' explicitly recognised this shortcoming and was designed to implement a marketing communications plan that would attract 'inward investment, tourism, businesses and consumers and residents'.[32] It was also felt that 'there is also a need to communicate more effectively the pride in the city felt by its residents and the substantial change that has occurred in the city in recent years resulting from the significant level of investment and regeneration that the city has enjoyed'.[33]

This lack of awareness of the city's proud past was perpetuated both by the economic downturn following the transition from a de-industrial to a post industrial city and by the architectural amnesia caused by the large-scale demolition of the city's built environment from the 1960s onwards. This ensured that twenty-first-century Leicester needed to physically and psychologically reconnect the city and its proud past to its citizens and the outside world. In scope and vision the twenty-first-century re-design of the city is as wide-ranging and ideological as Smigielski's in the 1960s. *Connecting Leicester* has resulted in changes to both the physical and mental landscape of the city. The city's gateways are being improved by the demolition of the Belgrave flyover and works to Humberstone Gate – just two of the many schemes in operation to facilitate the movement of people around and within the city. Furthermore, new public spaces such as Jubilee Square and the re-designed Market Place have been constructed to create

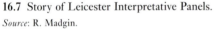

16.7 Story of Leicester Interpretative Panels.
Source: R. Madgin.

new physical connections through the city. These capital improvement works, in easing movement into and through the city, are balanced by a desire to re-connect the city in the mindscape which is a strong, yet less obvious, element of the redevelopment of Leicester.

At the heart of the twenty-first-century plan is a desire to connect Leicester citizens to the past, present and future of their city. The improvement of the existing built fabric is based on both internal and external funding, as in the case of the Heritage Lottery funded Townscape

Heritage Initiative for improvement of the Greyfriars' area of the city, and the approximately £7 million of inward investment levered from European Regional Development funds to improve the Market Place, Donisthorpe Mill, Cathedral Gardens and Makers Yard. These and other schemes have demonstrated the importance of heritage in supporting connections between Leicester citizens and the many layers of the city's history.[34] Added to this is the investment in the *Story of Leicester*, which is both a mechanism to re-connect Leicester citizens psychologically to their proud past and to improve the city's socio-economic position. Accordingly a, 'set of council priorities relate to using Leicester's heritage to maximise economic and social benefits for its modern citizens. These are drawn together in a single Story of Leicester plan. The "One Story" of Leicester's proud history, made up of many, celebrates all the communities that make up the one community of Leicester.'[35]

This *Story*, like so many initiatives within the city, is delivered in partnership. Community groups, the universities, local businesses, religious and youth groups are all part of the decision-making processes within the city. To take one example, the Heritage Partnership, comprises an extraordinary array of interests: local amenity associations (Leicester Civic Society; The Victorian Society (local branch); Leicestershire Industrial History Society; Leicestershire Archaeological and Historical Society; and Stoneygate Conservation Area Society), national organisations (Historic England; Heritage Lottery Fund), and regional organisations (religious interests through Leicester Cathedral and the Diocese of Leicester); architectural interests (Leicestershire and Rutland Society of Architects; OPUN – Architecture and Design Centre for the East Midlands); educational institutions (University of Leicester and DeMontfort University); and City partners (City Council Conservation team, local councillors and the City Mayor). Lessons learned from the successful City Challenge scheme, in which working in partnership working delivered the long-term regeneration of the Bede Island area have been extended to the twenty-first-century renaissance of the city. This ethos of working in partnership has both practical benefits in terms of combining resources and expertise, and moreover has the core advantage of including a range of stakeholders that 'will result in their engagement with the city'.[36] The inclusion of a wide range of stakeholders from across the socio-economic profile is critical in a city where plurality reigns dominant and the single image is hard to locate.

Understanding the history of the city, acknowledging its historical achievements and its role in creating the 'Leicester model' of multi-culturalism during the twentieth and twenty-first century in conjunction with recognising the role of the city and its citizens in creating the Leicester of today is key to developing this distinctive identity. There might be 'one Leicester' and 'One Story' of Leicester in the official rhetoric but in reality the city is still:

... worthy of its great repute, for it is the setting for an admirable group of buildings. It has one of the noblest of all the memorials to the men who never came back from the war. It has bought for its people the great park of Bradgate with Lady Jane Grey's tower still standing, and has a thousand acres of green space. ... It traces its birth back to the Romans, and is proud of the Roman pavements and walls that all may see in its streets. Its great Earl of Leicester was the founder of our first Parliament, and his castle was the scene of one of Parliament's first meetings.[37]

This book has demonstrated that modern Leicester has many elements of which the city and its citizens can be proud. Radical, independent, tolerant, and free Leicester are values associated with a moral, social and economic multi-layered environment that cannot and should not be reduced to a single point in time, a single story or a single event. The discovery of the king in the car park may well provide the external stimulus that the city needs to develop its distinctive identity, but within its boundaries the citizens of this 'no mean city are the hard-working and plain-thinking people of Leicester',[38] and the city is much the richer for its confusing, surprising, plural and diverse layers of past, present and future. The *genius loci* of Leicester is thus plural not singular – the multiple spirits of place have ensured that the city's Latin motto of *Semper Eaden* could sit alongside the more evolutionary '*genii loci*'.[39]

Notes to chapters

Notes to Chapter 1: Understanding Leicester: independent, radical, tolerant

1 J. Storey, *Historical Sketch of Some Principal Works and Undertakings of the Council of the Borough of Leicester* (Leicester, 1895), 143.

2 See J.V. Beckett, *City Status in the British Isles, 1830–2002* (Aldershot, 2005) for further information on the development of city status.

3 J. Simmons, *Leicester Past and Present: vol.1 Ancient Borough* (London 1974), 127–53; A.T. Patterson, *Radical Leicester: A History of Leicester, 1780–1850* (Leicester, 1954), 198–246.

4 N. Pevsner, *The Buildings of England: Leicestershire and Rutland* (Harmondsworth, repr. 1992), 224.

5 Garendon Street (1883), Westcotes (1888) and Belgrave Road (1894) were the first branch libraries.

6 See chapter 6.

7 See chapter 7 on the Abbey Park and the Leicester Pageant.

8 St Margaret's vestry sold 12 acres of land on which Belgrave Road Recreation Ground was laid out, and opened in 1894.

9 The Corporation also moved into electricity supply in 1892 after a period of indecision concerning the lighting of the borough. Brush Electrical Engineering Co. Ltd of London and Loughborough won the contract to supply lighting for the central area.

10 *Victoria County History of Leicester*, vol. IV, 280.

11 M. Elliott, *Victorian Leicester* (Chichester, 1979), 53–73. See also chapter 5.

12 See chapter 5.

13 *The Times*, 11 November 1889, col. 6c.

14 These radial roads included: Evington Lane; Belgrave Road; Churchgate; Narborough, Hinckley and Fosse Roads; London Road; Highfield Street; Mere Road.

15 See chapter 11.

16 City of Leicester, *Published Minutes of Council* (Leicester, 9 November 1892), 505–7. See also chapter 4.

17 J. Storey, *Historical Sketch*, 176.

18 B.R. Mitchell and P. Deane, *Abstract of British Historical Statistics* (Cambridge, 1971), 24–7. Nottingham resumed its numerical superiority from 1881 until overtaken by Leicester in 1981. The population of Derby remained about two-thirds that of its neighbours.

19 N. Pye (ed.), *Leicester and its Region* (Leicester ,1972), 433–7, tables 37 and 29.

20 P.R. Mounfield, 'The footwear industry of the East Midlands, (IV) Leicestershire to 1911', *East Midland Geographer*, 25 (1966), 8–23, and 'The footwear industry of the East Midlands (V): the modern phase', *East Midland Geographer*, 27 (1967), 154–75.

21 Spencer's *New Guide to Leicester*, 1868, 109. See J.D. Martin, 'Elastic web manufacture', *Victoria History of the County of Leicester*, vol. IV (1958), 326–7; P.R. Mounfield, 'The foundations of the modern industrial pattern', in N. Pye, *Leicester and its Region*, 370–3.

22 Vulcanising rubber involved treating it with sulphur, resulting in a product that was resistant to heat and cold, and had several uses to the hosiery industry.

23 J. Simmons, *Leicester Past and Present* vol.1, 154.

24 J. Simmons, *Leicester Past and Present* vol.1, 156.

25 N.J. Wood, 'Debt, credit and the management of business relations 1860–90', Leicester University, Ph.D. thesis, 1999. See also, M. Casson,

'Institutional economics and business history: a way forward?', *Business History*, 39 (1997), 151–71.

26 N.J. Wood, 'Debt, credit', thesis, 178–80. There was a rising scale of charges according to the number of enquiries made.

27 Census of England, 1911. The participation rates were as follows: Leicester 54%; Nottingham 51%; Birmingham 47%; Northampton 45%; England 37%; Coventry 36%; Derby 35%; Sheffield 32%.

28 J. Humphries, 'The working-class family, women's liberation, and class struggle: the case of nineteenth-century British history', *Review of Radical Political Economics*, 9:3 (1977), 25–41.

29 Liz Tacey's information on this point is particularly appreciated. For other studies see D.R. Green, 'Independent women, wealth and wills in nineteenth-century London', in J. Stobart and A. Owens (eds), *Urban Fortunes Property and Inheritance in the Town, 1700–1900* (Aldershot, 2000), 205.

30 M.A. Utton, 'Some features of the early merger movements in British manufacturing industry', *Business History*, 14 (1972), 51–60; L. Hannah, 'Mergers in manufacturing industry, 1880–1919', *Oxford Economic Papers*, 26 (1974), 1–20.

31 D. Smith, *Conflict and Compromise: Class Formation in English Society, 1830–1914. A Comparative Study of Birmingham and Sheffield* (London, 1982).

32 The number of persons per household rose to 6.0 in 1891 and 6.4 in 1901.

33 Leicester & Leicestershire Economic Assessment (Leicester, 2011), chapter 6, Housing.

34 *The Builder*, 29 (1871), 779, quoted in J. Simmons, *Leicester Past and Present: the Modern City* (London, 1974), 14.

35 An earlier attempt at annexation was made in 1886.

36 See www.le.ac.uk/emoha/leicester/wakerley.html for an illustrated trail.

37 *Transactions of the Leicestershire Archaeological Society*, VII (1893), 222, 273; VIII, (1899), 133–4; 205, 375.

38 N. Pevsner, *The Buildings of England: Leicestershire and Rutland* (Harmondsworth, 1992), 43. An exhibition of Gimson's work held in Leicester Museum can be seen at http://gimson.leicester.gov.uk/gimsonpage/gimson-as-a-designer/

39 G. Brandwood and M. Cherry *Men of Property:*

the Goddards and Six Generations of Architecture (Leicester, 1990).

40 M. Stratton, *The Terracotta Revival: Building Innovation and the Image of the Industrial City in Britain and North America* (London 1993), 85.

41 P.N. Jones, 'Politics' in D. Nash, D. Reeder, P. Jones and R. Rodger (eds), *Leicester in the Twentieth Century* (Stroud, 1993), 92.

42 C. Wessel, 'The Club', in J.P. Boyland and C. Wessel (eds), *Exchanging Ideas Dispassionately and without Animosity: the Leicester Literary and Philosophical Society 1835–2010* (Leicester, 2010), 85–96.

43 Mayor Edward Wood left the equivalent in 2011 prices of £7.5 million; Arthur Wakerley £7 million; Sir Israel Hart £15 million.

44 D.H. Aldcroft (ed.), *British Industry and Foreign Competition, 1875–1914: Studies in Industrial Enterprise* (London, 1968).

45 D. McCrone and B. Elliott, *Property and Power in a City: the Sociological Significance of Landordism* (Basingstoke, 1989), 84.

46 D.S. Nash, *Secularism, Art and Freedom* (Leicester, 1992).

47 F.J. Gould, *History of Leicester Secular Society* (Leicester, 1900); F.J. Gould, *The Life-Story of a Humanist* (London, 1923). See also: http://www.leicestersecularsociety.org.uk/history_gould.htm.

48 See chapter 2.

49 J. Simmons, 'A Victorian social worker: Joseph Dare and the Leicester Domestic Mission', *Transactions of the Leicester Archaeological and Historical Society*, 46 (1970–71), 65–80.

50 G.T. Rimmington, 'The Oxford movement in Leicester in the nineteenth and twentieth centuries', *Transactions of the Leicester Archaeological and Historical Society*, 78 (2004), 124–40, discusses the Anglican response to nonconformity.

51 B. Haynes, *Working-class Life in Victorian Leicester: The Joseph Dare Reports* (Leicester, 1991), 10.

52 B. Haynes, *Working-class Life*, Appendix 2. Dare was in post from 1845, and wrote annual reports from 1846 to 1877, when he retired because of ill-health. In 1874 the subscriptions list amounted to £103 from Bankart, Clephan, Fielding Johnson, Gimson, Paget, Rowlett, Stone, Whetstone, and many others. One-third of the subscribers were women. See also S. Aucott, *Women of Courage,*

Vision and Talent: Lives in Leicester 1780 to 1925 (Leicester, 2008).

53 C. Brown, *A Blessing to the Town: 150 years of Vaughan College, Leicester* (Leicester, 2012), 9–23.

54 A. Hardy, *The Epidemic Streets: Infectious Disease and the Rise of Preventive Medicine, 1856–1900* (Oxford, 1993) uses the phrase domestic nurses. See also S. Szreter, 'The importance of social intervention in Britain's mortality decline 1850–1914: a re-interpretation of the role of public health', *Society for the Social History of Medicine*, 1:1 (1988), 1–37.

55 M. Damant, 'District nursing: professional skills and knowledge in domestic settings: linking national and local networks of expertise, 1866–1974', Leicester University, Ph.D. thesis, 2005, 115, provides a chronology. The ITNL was renamed The Leicester District Nursing Association in 1909.

56 'Leicester Corporation Milk Depot', *British Journal of Nursing,* vol. 54 (19 June 1915), 534.

57 Quoted in D. Nash *et al.*, *Leicester in the Twentieth Century*, 131.

58 See chapter 10.

59 For further details see R. Rodger, The built environment', in D. Nash and D. Reeder (eds), *Leicester in the Twentieth Century*, 8–22.

60 Fourteen of Wakerley's Leicester buildings are listed Grade II. These are 8 Bishop Street; 122 London Road; 138 Gwendolen Road/Gedding Road/Margaret Road (Wycliffe Hall, houses, and workshops); Synagogue, Highfield Street; Belgrave Hall Wesleyan Methodist Church (now Community Centre); Asfordby Street (police station); Singer or Coronation Building, 76–88

High Street; council housing designs at 18–20 Linton Street; 17–19 Dore Road; 19–21 Great Arler Road; 59–61 Westcotes.

61 R. Puttnam, *Bowling Alone: The Collapse and Revival of American Community* (New York, 2000), 19.

62 S. Begley, 'Voluntary associations and the civic ideal in Leicester, 1870–1939', Leicester University Ph.D. thesis, 2009, 101–25, for Leicester clubs and societies before 1914.

63 S. Ewen, 'Power and administration in two Midland cities, *c.*1870–1938', Leicester University, Ph.D. thesis, 2004, 130–5. See also chapter 4.

64 G.H. Etherton, 'Employment and organization of committees in local government administration', *Public Administration*, 2 (1924), 390.

65 Leicester was characteristically a city of small family firms, though in the inter-war years new forms of corporate organisation diluted family interests. See Nash and Reeder, *Leicester*, 54, 93–4.

66 B. Burch, *The University of Leicester: A History, 1921–96* (Leicester, 1996).

67 Leicester Education Committee assumed responsibilities of the School Board in 1903. Numeracy and literacy pass rates exceeded 90% in 1882 and attendance rates also rose to 90% by 1890. 'The City of Leicester: schedule of schools', *A History of the County of Leicester: volume 4: The City of Leicester* (1958), 335–7.

68 G.T. Rimmington, 'L.H. Marshall's ministry in Leicester, 1930–1936', *Baptist Quarterly*, 36:8 (1996), 409. See also *The Times*, 15 December 1969, 3d.

69 See Appendix I.

Notes to Chapter 2: Leicester: metropolis of dissent

1 A.H. Thomas, *A History of the Great Meeting, Leicester and its Congregations* (Leicester, 1908), 12–13.

2 A. Temple-Patterson, *Radical Leicester* (Leicester, 1954), 15–17.

3 Temple-Patterson, *Radical Leicester*, 48.

4 R.G. Waddington, *Leicester: The Making of a Modern City* (Leicester, 1932), 147.

5 Arthur Miall, *Life of Edward Miall: Formerly Member of Parliament for Rochdale and Bradford* (London, 1884), 23.

6 A. Miall, *Life of Edward Miall*, 27–8.

7 Joseph Priestley and Harriet Martineau preached at the Bond Street Chapel. See R.G. Waddington, *Leicester: The Making of a Modern City*, 149.

8 B. Haynes, *Working-class Life in Victorian Leicester: The Joseph Dare Reports* (Leicester, 1991).

9 Joseph Dare, *Domestic Mission Report*, 1857, 12.

10 Haynes, *Working-class Life in Victorian Leicester*, 34–5.

11 Waddington, *Leicester: The Making of a Modern City*, 147–8.

12 Haynes, *Working-class Life*, 82–3.

13 Figures aggregated from D.M. Thompson, 'The churches and society in Leicestershire 1851–1881', University of Cambridge, Ph.D thesis, 1969, 66.

14 See Waddington, *Leicester: The Making of a Modern City*, 146.

15 *Victoria County History of Leicester*, IV (1958), 393. Quoted in Bill Lancaster, *Radicalism, Co-operation and Socialism: Leicester Working-class Politics, 1860–1906* (Leicester, 1987), 66.

16 Waddington, *Leicester: The Making of a Modern City*, 149.

17 See Lancaster, *Radicalism, Co-operation and Socialism*, 67–8.

18 C. Rumsey, *The Rise and Fall of British Republican Clubs, 1871–1874* (Oswestry, 2000).

19 Lancaster, *Radicalism, Co-operation and Socialism*, 82–3.

20 See D. Freer 'Business families in Victorian Leicester', University of Leicester, M.Phil. thesis, 1975, ch. 9. Quoted in Lancaster, *Radicalism, Co-operation and Socialism*, 68.

21 See Lancaster, *Radicalism, Co-operation and Socialism*, 74–5.

22 *The Leicester Papers on Questions in Church and State being five papers read at conferences held in Leicester, under the auspices of the Liberation Society, in the winter of 1870–1* (London: The Society for the Liberation of Religion from State Patronage and Control), 1.

23 For a full-length study see D.S. Nash, *Secularism, Art and Freedom* (Leicester. 1992).

24 N. Pevsner, *The Buildings of England: Leicestershire and Rutland* (1960, 2nd edition 1984).

25 *Midland Free Press*, 28 September 1880, 8.

26 The work of Ernest Gimson was showcased in a recent exhibition in Leicester. See http://gimson. leicester.gov.uk/exhibition/

27 See Nash, *Secularism, Art and Freedom*, chs 9 and 10.

28 *Midland Free Press*, March 1906.

29 See D.S. Nash, 'F.J. Gould and the Leicester Secular Society: a positivist commonwealth in Edwardian Politic' *Midland History*, 16 (1991), 126–40.

Notes to Chapter 3: 'Red Leicester': a reputation for radicalism?

1 B. Lancaster, *Radicalism, Co-operation, Socialism* (Leicester 1987); A. Patterson, *Radical Leicester* (Leicester, 1954).

2 For background see J. Moore, *The Transformation of Urban Liberalism* (Aldershot, 2006).

3 F. Gould, *The History of Leicester Secular Society* (Leicester, 1900).

4 The classic accounts of the rise of Labour are H. Pelling, *Origins of the Labour Party, 1880–1900*, second edition (Oxford, 1965); D. Howell, *British Workers and the Independent Labour Party, 1888–1906* (Manchester, 1983); D. Tanner, *Political Change and the Labour Party, 1900–1918* (Cambridge, 1990).

5 *Illustrated Leicester Chronicle* (hereafter *ILC*), 17 November 1935.

6 A. Little, 'Chartism and Liberalism: Popular Politics in Leicestershire', 1842–1874, University of Manchester, Unpublished Ph.D. thesis, 1991, 40–88.

7 Little, 'Chartism and Liberalism', 252–93.

8 For background on Nonconformity and Liberalism see D. Bebbington, *The Nonconformist Conscience: Chapel and Politics, 1870–1914*

(London, 1982).

9 *Leicester Daily Mercury* (hereafter *LDM*), 16 March 1886.

10 *Midland Free Press* (hereafter *MFP*), 30 January 1892.

11 J. Simmons, *Leicester Past and Present Volume II: The Modern City* (London, 1974), 122.

12 Figures from the 1851 religious census suggest Leicester actually had less religious accommodation than comparable towns. Moreover some statistics indicate that Anglicanism enjoyed faster growth than nonconformity in Leicester during the second half of the nineteenth century. See Lancaster, *Radicalism*, 65–7.

13 Little, 'Chartism and Liberalism', 281.

14 Little, 'Chartism and Liberalism', 282–4.

15 M. Elliott, *Victorian Leicester* (London 1979), 165–6.

16 R. Read, *Modern Leicester* (London 1881), 259–62.

17 R.A. McKinley and C.T. Smith 'Parliamentary history since 1835' in R.H. Evans (ed.), *The Victoria History of the County of Leicester*, IV (1958), 224–51.

18 Little, 'Chartism and Liberalism', 284.

19 B. Lancaster, 'Breaking moulds: The Leicester ILP and popular politics' in D. James, T. Jowitt and K. Laybourn (eds), *The Centenary History of the Independent Labour Party* (London, 1993), 78–9.

20 Read, *Modern Leicester*, 261–2; Leicester and Leicestershire Conservative Club, First Annual Meeting, 26 March 1881, Leicestershire Record Office (LRO), DE 1574.

21 Read, *Modern Leicester*, 261–2.

22 *LDM*, 16 March 1884.

23 *LDM*, 26 January 1884.

24 See *LDM*, 27 February 1884; *MFP*, 1 March 1884.

25 *LDM*, 4 March 1884.

26 *LDM*, 27 February 1884; 8 March 1884. Picton was the Independent (Congregational) minister for Cheetham Hill Manchester, and then for Gallowtree Gate Church between 1862 and 1869, and was one of the chief promoters of the so-called Leicester Conference, a meeting for liberal Congregationalists which was held to coincide with the Congregational Union's autumn assembly at Leicester in 1877.

27 *LDM*, 19 March 1884.

28 *LDM*, 25 March 1884.

29 *MFP*, 5 April 1884.

30 *LDM*, 3 April 1884.

31 *LDM*, 9 April 1884; *LDM*, 19 April 1884.

32 Evans, *Victoria History*, IV, 224–31.

33 *Leicester Journal* (hereafter *LJ*), 2 May 1884.

34 *LJ*, 9 May 1884.

35 *LJ*, 4 April 1884.

36 *LDM*, 25 June 1884.

37 *MFP*, 28 June 1884; *MFP*, 5 July 1884.

38 See J. Moore, *The Transformation of Urban Liberalism* (Aldershot, 2006), ch. 2.

39 *LDM*, 7 April 1886.

40 A ruling by the Local Government Board, in response to a request from the Dewsbury Board of Guardians, meant that vaccination officers were expected to obtain the consent of the Guardians before proceeding with prosecutions – effectively giving the guardians the choice of whether to prosecute. *LDM*, 16 March 1886.

41 *LDM*, 5 May 1886.

42 *MFP*, 27 March 1886.

43 *LDM*, 31 March 1886.

44 *MFP*, 17 April 1886.

45 *LDM*, 22 May 1886. *MFP*, 5 June 1886.

46 W. Pike and W. Scarfe, *Leicestershire and Rutland at the Opening of the Twentieth Century* (Leicester, 1900); reprint (Edinburgh, 1985), 170.

47 *LDM*, 1 July 1886, letter, 'Reformer'.

48 *LDM*, 1 July 1886, letter, 'An Old Liberal'.

49 Leicester Liberal Association (hereafter LRA), Executive Committee, 9 October 1896, LRO, 11 D 57/3.

50 Lancaster, *Radicalism*.

51 D. Cox, 'The Labour party in Leicester: a study in branch development', *International Review of Social History*, 6 (1966) 200, 207.

52 D. Howell, *British Workers and the Independent Labour Party* (Manchester, 1983), 278.

53 B. Lancaster, 'Breaking Moulds: The Leicester ILP and Popular Politics', in D. James, T. Jowitt and K. Laybourn (eds), *Centennial History*, 43–62.

54 B. Lancaster, *Radicalism*, 132.

55 *MFP*, 19 October 1895.

56 *Workman's Times* (hereafter *WT*), 19 June 1891.

57 *MFP*, 25 August 1894.

58 *LDM*, 22 August 1894.

59 *LDM*, 22 August 1894.

60 *LDM*, 29 August 1894.

61 *MFP*, 9 February 1895.

62 *Labour Leader* (hereafter *LL*), 1 December 1894.

63 *MFP*, 13 April 1893; *MFP*, 20 April 1893.

64 *MFP*, 20 July 1895.

65 P. Stansky, *Ambitions and Strategies: The Struggle for the Leadership of the Liberal party in the 1890s* (Oxford, 1964).

66 G. Bernstein, 'Liberalism and the Progressive Alliance in the Constituencies, 1900–1914: Three Case Studies', *Historical Journal* 26 (1983) 617–40, esp. 631.

67 Lancaster, *Radicalism*, 165.

68 Bernstein, 'Liberalism', 635–6.

69 R. McKibbin, 'James Ramsay MacDonald and the problem of the independence of the Labour Party, 1910–1914', *Journal of Modern History*, 42 (1970), 216–35.

70 McKibbin, 'James Ramsay MacDonald', esp. 224–9.

71 H. Matthew, R. McKibbin, and J. Kay, 'The franchise factor and the rise of the Labour party', *English Historical Review*, 91 (1976) 723–52.

72 G.R. Searle, *Country Before Party Coalition and the Idea of 'National Government' in Modern Britain, 185–1987* (Harlow, 1995), esp. 117–95.

73 *LDM*, 4 December 1918.

74 Liberal advertisement printed in *LDM*, 5 December 1918.

75 *LDM*, 2 December 1918.

76 *LDM*, 16 November 1922.

77 *LDM*, 24 November 1923.

78 *Leicester Mail* (hereafter *LM*), 7 October 1924.

79 *LM*, 14 October 1924.

80 *LM*, 30 October 1924.

81 *LM*, 30 October 1924.

82 *ILC*, 1 June 1929.

83 *ILC*, 1 June 1929.

84 *LDM*, 31 May 1929.

85 *LDM*, 31 May 1929.

86 See comments of Councillor Easom, *LDM*, 20 October 1931.

87 *LDM*, 21 October 1931.

88 See comments of F.W. Pethick Lawrence, *LDM*, 20 October 1931.

89 *LDM*, 28 October 1931.

90 *Leicester Evening Mail* (hereafter *LEM*), 15 November 1935.

91 For coverage of the results see *ILC*, 28 July 1945, *LDM*, 26 July 1945.

92 *LEM*, 15 November 1935.

93 *LDM*, 20 October 1931.

94 See comments of the Labour candidate, *LEM*, 2 November 1935.

95 This was denied by Nicholson, *LEM*, 2 November 1935. Mosley had also formerly been a Labour MP.

96 B. Doyle, 'Urban Liberalism and the 'Lost Generation': politics and middle-class culture in Norwich, 1900–1935', *Historical Journal*, 38 (1995), 617–34.

Notes to Chapter 4: Watching the town: protecting Leicester from fire and crime, c.1870–1930

1 This chapter is based upon S. Ewen, 'Power and administration in two midland cities, c.1870–1938', University of Leicester Ph.D. thesis, 2004.

2 C. Emsley, 'Policing the English frontier', *H-Urban Book Reviews*, accessed at www.h-net.org/~urban/, 26 March 2003; C. Steedman, *Policing the Victorian Community: The Formation of English Provincial Police Forces, 1856–80* (London, 1984); D. Taylor, *Policing the Victorian Town: The Development of the Police in Middlesbrough c.1840–1914* (Houndmills, 2002); D.S. Wall, *The Chief Constables of England and Wales: The Socio-Legal History of a Criminal Justice Elite* (Aldershot, 1998).

3 C.A. Williams, 'Rotten boroughs: the crisis of urban policing and the decline of municipal independence, 1914–64', in J. Moore and J.B. Smith (eds), *Corruption in Urban Politics and Society: Britain, 1780–1950* (Aldershot, 2007), 155–75; N. Hayes, *Consensus and Controversy: City Politics in Nottingham, 1945–67* (Liverpool, 1996), 135–60.

4 This debate is summarised in S. Ewen, '"Policing" party politics in the midlands, c.1900–1938' in B.M. Doyle (ed.), *Urban Politics and Space in the Nineteenth and Twentieth Centuries: Regional Perspectives* (Newcastle, 2007), 64–79.

5 The other standing committee was the Finance Committee.

6 D. Fraser, *Power and Authority in the Victorian City* (Oxford, 1979), 1–21.

7 T.A. Critchley, *A History of Police in England and Wales* (London, 1967), 197–8; C.A. Williams, 'Police and crime in Sheffield, 1818–1874', University of Sheffield Ph.D. thesis, 1998, 133.

8 H. Finer, 'The police and public safety', in H.J. Laski, W.I. Jennings and W.A. Robson (eds), *A Century of Municipal Progress* (London, 1935), 271–98; K.B. Smellie, *A History of Local Government* (London, 1946), 36–7, 54–5.

9 S. Ewen, 'Chief officers and professional identities: the case of fire services in English municipal government, c.1870–1938', *Historical Research*, 81 (2008), 127–30; S. Ewen, *Fighting Fires: Creating the British Fire Service, 1800–1978* (Basingstoke, 2010), ch. 3.

10 Ewen, 'Chief officers', 131–2, 137.

11 Ewen, 'Power and administration', 70; City of Leicester, *Published Minutes of Council*, Leicester, 9 November 1892, 505–7.

12 Ewen, 'Power and administration', 69–71.

13 G.H. Etherton, 'Employment and organization of committees in local government administration', *Public Administration*, 2 (1924), 390.

14 *Leicester Daily Mercury* (*LDM*), 29 January 1926; *Leicester Mail Yearbook* (Leicester, 1926), 24. The Education Committee alone had 33 sub-committees in 1926.

15 Accounts, Uniform, Emergency, Fire Brigade, and Lighting. The Traffic Sub-Committee also

served for two years on an *ad hoc* basis, and a further seven permanently. The majority were single-issue groups that met once or twice to resolve a technical issue, e.g. those dealing with the detective department, police car, special investigations, policewomen, and police boxes.

16 City of Leicester, *Published Minutes of Council*, Leicester, 9 November 1934, 29–31; Ewen, 'Power and administration', 130–5; Record Office for Leicester, Leicestershire and Rutland (ROLLR), 10/D/58/193, Leicester City Police Annual Report, 1931, 11–12. The growing burden of traffic policing and police control systems are discussed in C.A. Williams, *Police Control Systems in Britain, 1775–1975: From Parish Constable to National Computer* (Manchester, 2014); K. Laybourn and D. Taylor, *The Battle for the Roads: Police, Motorists and the Law, c.1890s–1970s* (Basingstoke, 2015).

17 Ewen, 'Power and administration', 75.

18 *LDM*, 4 February 1926; *LDM*, 6 February 1926.

19 J.A. Chandler, *Explaining Local Government: Local Government in Britain since 1800* (Manchester, 2007), 154.

20 *Leicester Corporation Annual Diary* (Leicester, 1867–1938); D.N. Chester, 'Council and committee meetings in county boroughs', *Public Administration*, 32 (1954), 429–30; Etherton, 'Employment', 396.

21 The average membership of the committee during these respective periods was 23 and 19.

22 Ewen, 'Power and administration', 89–92.

23 Ewen, ''Policing' party politics', 68–70; N. Hayes, 'Things ain't what they used to be! Elites and constructs of consensus and conflict in twentieth-century English municipal politics' in Doyle (ed.), *Urban Politics and Space*, 55–6.

24 Emsley, 'Policing'.

25 Almond, a provision merchant, was chairman of the watch committee from 1883–85; Anderson, a draper, was chairman from 1878–80, while Wheeler, a wholesale grocer, chaired the committee between 1885 and 1888.

26 *Leicester Daily Post*, 27 October 1911.

27 *Leicester Daily Post*, 28 October 1911.

28 Ewen, '"Policing" party politics', 73; Hayes, 'Things ain't what they used to be!', 56–7.

29 *Institute of Fire Engineers Annual Report* (Edinburgh, 1930), 3–4, 26.

30 Ewen, *Fighting Fires*, ch. 5; B.M. Doyle, 'The changing functions of urban government: councillors, officials and pressure groups' in M.J. Daunton (ed.), *The Cambridge Urban History of Britain, Volume III: 1840–1950* (Cambridge, 2000), 287–313; M. Dagenais and P.-Y. Saunier, 'Tales of the periphery: an outline survey of municipal employees and services in the nineteenth and twentieth centuries', in M. Dagenais, I. Maver and P.-Y. Saunier (eds), *Municipal Services and Employees in the Modern City: New Historic Approaches* (Aldershot, 2003), 1–30.

31 B. Keith-Lucas, 'The independence of chief constables', *Public Administration*, 38 (1960), 1.

32 C. Emsley, *The English Police: A Political and Social History*, 2nd edn (London, 1996), 137–8, 163–4; H. Finer, *English Local Government*, 4th edn (London, 1946), 255–73. K. Laybourn and D. Taylor, *Policing in England and Wales, 1918–39: The Fed, Flying Squads and Forensics* (Basingstoke, 2011), 13–48.

33 ROLLR, CM/42/23, Watch Committee Minutes (WCM), 10 February 1913, 316; 1 September 1914, 201.

34 For examples, ROLLR, DE/3831/226, Chief Constable's Special Order Book, 26 September 1892, 76; 12 May 1897, 276; ROLLR, DE/3831/267, Chief Constable's Special Order Book, 30 October 1902, 105.

35 For examples, ROLLR, CM/42/22, WCM, 22 September 1908, 22; 21 September 1909, 218.

36 Wall, *Chief Constables*, 99–104.

37 T.R. Gourvish, 'The rise of the professions' in T.R. Gourvish and A. O'Day (eds), *Later Victorian Britain, 1867–1900* (London, 1988), 16–17.

38 *LDM*, 8 February 1890; *LDM*, 23 February 1895.

39 *Fire & Water*, X (1893), 18.

40 Institute of Fire Engineers (unreferenced), Letter Book, Henry Neal, Chief Officer of Leicester Fire Brigade, to Commander Sladen, Chief Officer of London Fire Brigade, 9 November 1918, 1–5.

41 H. Perkin, *The Rise of Professional Society: England since 1880* (London, 1990), 3; R. Macleod, 'Introduction' to idem (ed.), *Government and Expertise: Specialists, Administrators and Professionals, 1860–1919* (Cambridge, 1988), 3.

42 Critchley, *A History of Police*, 219–20; H. Taylor, 'Forging the job: a crisis of 'modernization' or redundancy for the police in England and Wales,

1900–39', *British Journal of Criminology*, 39 (1999), 113–15.

43 W. Grant, 'Bringing policy communities back in: the case of fire service cover', *British Journal of Politics and International Relations*, 7 (2005), 301–16.

44 Smellie, *History of Local Government*, 99.

45 National Archives HO/158/15, Home Office Circular 200,074, 14 February 1911; ROLLR, DE/5491/285, Leicester Police General Order Book, 6 January 1930, General Order 3; ROLLR, DE/5491/286, Leicester Police General Order Book, 14 June 1935, General Order 620; *LDM*, 11 February 1936.

Notes to Chapter 5: 'The Taming of the Soar': Leicester transforms its river environment

1 *Leicester Chronicle and Leicestershire Mercury*, 17 July 1880, 8, 'Great Floods in Leicestershire'. Leicester has been identified as a typical example of a 'central place' in the sense that the city had a variety of central functions in administration, law and markets that enabled it to expand over many centuries. See P. Hohenberg and L.H. Lees, *The Making of Urban Europe, 1000–1994*, 2nd edn (Cambridge, MA, 1995), 23–7.

2 According to R. Millward, *A History of Leicestershire and Rutland* (Chichester, 1985), 115, the improvement of the Soar was 'the greatest undertaking [of Leicester] during the nineteenth century'.

3 The extensive problems caused by flooding in urban settings were recently demonstrated by the extensive floods in northern England in December 2015. Historical scholarship has developed increasing interest in city–river relations over the last years. See S. Castonguay and M. Evenden (eds), *Urban Rivers: Remaking Rivers, Cities and Space in Europe and North America* (Pittsburgh, 2012); M. Knott, U Lübken and D. Schott (eds), *Rivers Lost, Rivers Regained: Rethinking City–River Relations* (Pittsburgh, 2016).

4 N. Pye, 'The regional setting', in N. Pye (ed.), *Leicester and its Region* (Leicester, 1972), 3–15; D. Wix, *River Soar in Old Photographs* (Stroud, 1992), 6–7.

5 Pye, 'The regional setting', 4–5.

6 Millward, *History of Leicestershire*, 79.

7 In spite of the railway, canal shipping for commercial purposes remained viable for some goods until the second half of the twentieth century. See Wix, *River Soar*, 45.

8 Wix, *River Soar*, 46.

9 Regular and controlled flooding during winter obviously increased the fertility and productivity of river meadows significantly, as long as the water did not remain on the land for too long.

10 S. Watts, *A Walk Through Leicester*, (first published 1804; repr. Leicester, 1967), 54; H. Boynton, *The History of Victoria Park, Leicester* (Leicester, 2000), 7.

11 In addition to the hazard of flooding hazard the fact that land on the west bank of the Soar belonged to two large estates, Westcotes and Dannet's Hall, prevented development. The sale of these estates in the 1860s opened up the west bank of the Soar for development, Millward, *History*, 114.

12 These issues become very evident from a representation made by landowners from Leicestershire to the President of the Local Government Board, Mr Dodson, on 11 December, 1880. See *Leicester Chronicle*, 18 December 1880, supplement, 4.

13 William Cobbett, *Rural Rides* (1830), quoted from Millward, *History*, 112.

14 Millward, *History*, 113.

15 On factories and the river, see Millward, *History*, 113.

16 J.S. Phipps, *Leicester in Parliament* (Leicester, 1988), 78–85; J. Storey, *Historical Sketch of some of the principal works and undertakings of the Council of the Borough of Leicester* (Leicester, 1895), 77–81. By 1853 the Corporation had already commissioned a report on flood prevention, which was reprinted several times when new floods brought greater urgency to the matter. See J.S. Crossley and G. Foxton, *Report on the Condition of the River Soar and the remedies to be adopted for preventing the recurrence of floods at the westward parts of the town* (Leicester, 1853); J. Gordon, *Report on the Parliamentary Scheme of 1881, and a proposed deviation therefrom, for carrying the river Soar to the lower level below Evans' Weir* (Leicester, 1882) 2.

17 Storey: *Historical Sketch*, 77–81.

18 F. Griffith, *Report on the July Floods and the proposed Extension of the Flood Scheme* (presented 23 August 1880 to the Engineering Works Committee), ROLLR, Pamphlet Vol. 82.

19 *Leicester Chronicle and Leicestershire Mercury*, 18 December 1880, Public Meeting.

20 *Leicester Journal*, 17 December 1880, report on meeting 'of the owners and ratepayers of the Borough' where Mayor Bennett underscored these points and Alderman Stretton estimated, that municipal land would rise fivefold in value due to the measures.

21 In fact authorities for control of flooding were only set up on the basis of watersheds as a result of the Land Drainage Act, 1930. See J. Sheail, 'Water management systems: drainage and conservation' in H. Cook and T. Williamson (eds), *Water Management in the English Landscape. Field, Marsh and Meadow* (Edinburgh, 1999), 227–43.

22 Storey, *Sketch*, 83.

23 *Leicester Journal*, 3 December 1880, 'The Leicestershire Floods'.

24 *Leicester Journal*, 17 December 1880, 'The Prevention of Floods', report on meeting of a deputation of Leicestershire landowners with Mr Dodson, 11 December 1880. The views of the Leicestershire representatives was most probably based on a comprehensive report to the Soar Valley Flood Committee, delivered by a drainage engineer Brundell in January 1881. Although the meeting predates the publication of this report, it is likely that Brundell had already presented an oral or preliminary report to the committee in which special emphasis is placed on badly constructed or maintained weirs and other obstructions that tended to keep the water-level unnecessarily high and thus prevented drainage of low lands after flooding. ROLLR, DE 721/1 Report on the Prevention of Floods in the Soar Valley by Mr B.S. Brundell, Doncaster, 1881.

25 Storey, *Sketch*, 91; Millward, *History*, 115.

26 E.J. Emery, *The History of Abbey Park* (Leicester, 1982), 8.

27 Borough of Leicester, *Opening of the Abbey Park by their Royal Highness the Prince and Princess of Wales on Whit-Monday, the 29 May, 1882* (Leicester, 1882), 20.

28 Emery, *Abbey Park*, 19–21, on popular use before the First World War.

29 Storey, *Sketch*, 154.

30 Storey, *Sketch*, 19.

31 Leicester was not alone in seriously polluting its river. The practice of using rivers as 'sinks' for all kinds of wastes was common in British cities in the late nineteenth century, particularly when sewage systems were introduced. See L.E. Breeze, *The British Experience with River Pollution, 1865–1876* (New York, 1993). In an epilogue covering the post-1876 period Breeze emphasizes (195–7) the roles of local authorities as major polluters and the fierce resistance of vested interests, including town councils, towards tougher environmental legislation in the 1880s. See also I.C. Simmons, *An Environmental History of Great Britain* (Edinburgh, 2001), 161, who notes, 'Attempts to clean up rivers have been particularly slow in Great Britain'.

32 J. Sheail, 'Town wastes, agricultural sustainability and Victorian sewage', *Urban History*, 23 (1996), 189–210.

33 Storey, *Sketch*, 15–16.

34 Storey, *Sketch*, 16–18.

35 Storey, *Sketch*, 27–8.

36 ROLLR, CC/4/1, Minutes from Committees of Leicestershire County Council, River Pollution Committee. At a meeting of 5 June 1890 it was announced that Beaumont Leys would be in full operation with all engines in working order in September 1890. The River Pollution Committee was established in December 1889 and met fairly regularly until 1894. It employed analysts to regularly analyse water samples for quality. At times the Committee threatened to open proceedings against Leicester Corporation under the River Pollutions Act; at other times the experts suspended such proceedings when the water quality was acceptable. Moreover, pollution also arose from other emissions such as from factories in Birstall. After May 1896 there are no more entries in the Minutes Book, which might be read as an indicator for normalisation.

37 Storey, *Sketch*, 161.

38 T. Wright, E. Wood, J. Storey, *Leicester Extension Act, 1891*. Report of the Parliamentary Sub-committee and the Town Clerk on details connected with the promotion of the bill. ROLLR, Pamphlet Vol. 80.

39 Areas mentioned include Washbrook/ Saffron Brook, Aylestone Road, Saffron Lane, Knighton

Church, Evington Brook (golf course), Highway Road, Broadway Road, Willow Brook, Melton Brook, Braunstone Brook; ROLLR, L 628.2, October 1983; City of Leicester, The Flooding (Special) Committee, appointed by the City Council on 30 July 1968.

40 City of Leicester, The Flooding (Special) Committee, 31.

41 City of Leicester, The Flooding (Special) Committee, 41.

42 ROLLR, L 386, Leicester City Council/ City Planning Department, *Leicester's Riverside: The River Soar and Grand Union Canal: A New Lease of Life* (March 1978), 1.

43 *Leicester's Riverside*, 2.

44 Leicester City Council: Discover Leicester's Riverside Park.

Notes to Chapter 6: Radical departures? Changing landscapes of death in Leicester

1 *Leicester Chronicle* (subsequently *LC*), 27 September 1845.

2 J. Rugg, 'The emergence of cemetery companies in Britain, 1819–52', unpublished Ph.D. thesis, University of Stirling (1992), Appendix 1. See also M. Cox, *Grave Concerns: Death and Burial in England, 1700–1850* (York, 1998).

3 H. Macleod, *The Theory and Practice of Banking* (London, 1855), 243.

4 *Prospectus of the Portsea Island Cemetery Company* (1830). Sanderson Collection, Local History Library, Portsmouth.

5 G. Collison, *Cemetery Interment* (London, 1840), 183.

6 See, for example, K. Grady, 'Profit, property interests and public spirit: the provision of markets and commercial amenities in Leeds 1822–29', *Publications of the Thoresby Society*, 54 (1979), 165–95.

7 *LC*, 21 September 1844.

8 *LC*, 27 September 1845.

9 Collison, *Cemetery Interment*, 182.

10 Collison, *Cemetery Interment*, 182.

11 *LC*, 6 February 1847.

12 W. Ranger, *Report to the General Board of Health on Burial Grounds and the New Cemetery at Leicester* (London, 1851) 10.

13 Ranger, *Report to the General Board of Health*, 12.

14 *LC*, 23 January 1847.

15 Ranger, *Report to the General Board of Health*, 13.

16 *Leicester Mercury* (subsequently *LM*), 23 June 1849.

17 P.C. Jupp, *From Dust to Ashes: Cremation and the British Way of Death* (Palgrave, 2006); B. Parsons, *Committed to the Cleansing Flame: The Development of Cremation in Nineteenth-century England* (Spire, 2005).

18 Parsons, *Committed to the Cleansing Flame*.

19 Sir Henry Thompson, 'The treatment of the body after death', *Contemporary Review*, January 1874, quoted in Jupp, *From Dust to Ashes*, 47.

20 *Leicester Daily Post*, 1 May 1885.

21 *Leicester Daily Post*, 12 April 1886.

22 Page Hopps was the author of the undated *Cremation, Some Reasons for Preferring it to Burial*, as noted in A. Wilson and H. Levy, *Burial Reform and Funeral Costs* (Oxford, 1938), 42.

23 CM9/2 Cemetery Committee Minutes, 21 November 1889. Note that these and all following minutes are held by the Record Office for Leicester, Leicestershire and Rutland (ROLLR).

24 ROLLR, CM1/32 Notes of Council Meetings, 26 September 1899.

25 ROLLR, CM1/32 Notes of Council Meetings, 18 December 1901.

26 *Leicester Daily Post*, 22 August 1902.

27 *Transactions of the Cremation Society* (1935), 25.

28 ROLLR, CM12/15 Minutes, Estates &c. Committee, 12 December 1923; 28 September 1927.

29 ROLLR, CM12/14 Estates and Burial Grounds Sub-Committee, 9 January 1924; 13 February 1924; CM12/15 Minutes, Estates and &c Committee, 27 October 1927.

30 Although note J. Rugg, 'Lawn cemeteries: the emergence of a new landscape of death', *Urban History*, 33, 2 (2006), 213–33.

31 *LM*, 21 October 1931.

32 Observation from author's ESRC project, 'Burial policy and the management of death in England, 1939–79', grant number RES–000–22–003

33 J.D. Robertson, in *National Association of Superintendents Yearbook, 1921* (London, 1921), 23.

34 E. Prentice Mawson, 'Garden cemeteries', *Landscape and Garden*, Autumn 1935, 125.

35 F. Stirling, 'Grave re-use: a feasibility study', University of Sheffield, unpublished Ph.D. thesis, 2009.

36 For example, C. Brooks, B. Elliot, J. Litten, E. Robinson, R. Robinson and P. Temple, *Mortal Remains* (Exeter, 1989).

37 J.-M. Strange, *Death, Grief and Poverty in Britain, 1870–1914* (Oxford, 2005); A. Herman, 'Death has a touch of class: society and space in Brookwood Cemetery, 1853–1903', *Journal of Historical Geography,* 36, 3 (2010), 305–14.

38 *LM*, 30 November 1889.

39 Strange, *Death, Grief and Poverty.*

40 S. Barnard, *To Prove I'm Not Forgot* (Manchester, 1990).

41 J. Rugg, 'Constructing the grave: competing burial ideals in nineteenth-century England', *Social History,* 38, 3 (2013), 328–45.

42 ROLLR, CM12/15 Minutes, Estates &c Committee, 12 May 1927.

43 ROLLR, CM12/15 Minutes, Estates &c Committee, 26 July 1927.

44 ROLLR, CM12/16 Minutes, Estates &c Committee, 14 May 1930.

45 ROLLR, CM12/16 Minutes, Estates &c Committee, 17 June 1931.

46 Mawson, 'Garden cemeteries', 127.

47 E.H. Marsh, 'Leicester City Cemeteries and Crematorium' *Journal of the Institute of Burial and Cremation Administration,* August 1950, 49.

48 J. Rugg, *Churchyard and Cemetery: Tradition and Modernity in Rural North Yorkshire* (Manchester, 2013).

49 See http://www.mbcol.org.uk/Home/MBCOL/tabid/55/language/en-GB/Default.aspx

Notes to Chapter 7: Representing the city: the opening of Abbey Park (1882) and the Leicester Pageant (1932)

1 D. Cannadine, 'The transformation of civic ritual in modern Britain: the Colchester Oyster Feast' *Past and Present*, 94 (1982), 107–30. In Cannadine's account of civic ritual in Colchester, the heyday of civic ritual was between the 1880s and the First World War. From 1919 to 1938 'the ceremonial elaborated in this earlier period was perpetuated, consolidated and extended', 108. See also S. Gunn, *The Public Culture of the Victorian Middle Classes: Ritual and Authority in the English Industrial City, 1840–1914* (Manchester, 2000). Gunn's research focuses on Manchester, Leeds and Birmingham. He argues that the importance of civic ritual was in decline from the 1880s onwards and in 'freefall' after 1918. However, a study by Dickie describes a three-day pageant held in Northampton in 1925 and shows that in the inter-war years local enthusiasm for civic ceremony was still fresh. M. Dickie, 'Town patriotism in Northampton, 1918–1938: an invented tradition', *Midland History*, XVVII (1992), 109–17.

2 The descriptions of the opening of Abbey Park Ceremony in Leicester are made with reference to the *Leicester Daily Mercury*, (*LDM*) 1882 and the *Leicester Daily Post* (*LDP*), 1882. The descriptions of the Leicester Pageant and related celebrations are made with reference to the *Leicester Evening Mail* (*LEM*), 1931 and 1932.

3 The population had more doubled from 60,642 in 1851 to 122,376 in 1881. See J. Simmons, *Leicester Past and Present Volume Two: Modern City* (London, 1974), 150. Simmons refers to the published returns of census figures.

4 Simmons, *Leicester Past and Present*, 48–9.

5 Borough of Leicester, *The Opening of Abbey Park* (Leicester, 1882), 9; *LDP*, 9 January 1882.

6 For accounts of royal visits to Leeds in 1858 and Manchester in 1851 see A. Briggs, *Victorian Cities*, 139–84; S. Gunn, 'Ritual and civic culture in the English industrial city, *c.*1835–1914', in R.J. Morris and R.H. Trainor (eds), *Urban Governance in Britain and Beyond since 1750* (Aldershot, 2000), 227–39, and S. Gunn, 'Public Culture', 163–85.

7 Borough of Leicester, *The Opening of Abbey Park* (Leicester, 1882), 37–41, gives the list of subscribers.

8 *Leicester Evening Mail* (*LEM*), 25 June 1932.

9 There was no equivalent to the 1932 Pageant Master in 1882.

10 *LEM*, 16 June 1932–30 June 1932. See also F. Shakespeare Herne (ed.), *The Historical Pageant of Leicestershire: Official Souvenir* (Leicester, 1932).

11 *LEM*, 17 June 1932.

12 *LEM*, 17 June 1932.

13 *LEM*. The Mayor had been granted a £500 hospitality grant for the Pageant. See *LEM*, 19 January 1932.

14 *LEM*, 21 June 1932.

15 *LEM*, 17 June 1932 and 24 June 1932.

16 *LEM*, 24–30 June 1932.

17 *LEM*, 30 June 1932.

18 E.J. Hobsbawn, 'Introduction: inventing traditions' in E. Hobsbawn and T. Ranger (eds), *The Invention of Tradition* (Cambridge, 1983), 1–14

19 Dickie, 'Town patriotism in Northampton', 109–17.

20 J. Harris, *Private Lives Public Spirit: Britain 1870–1914* (Oxford, 1993), 1–38.

21 D.N. Cannadine, 'The context, performance and meaning of ritual: the British monarchy and the invention of tradition *c.*1820–1977' in E. Hobsbawn and T. Ranger (eds), *The Invention of Tradition*, 101–64.

22 *LDP*, 30 May 1882.

23 *LDP*, 30 May 1882.

24 *LEM*, 16–30 June 1882.

25 J. Davis, 'Central government and the towns' in M.J. Daunton, (ed.), *The Cambridge Urban History of Britain*, vol. 3, *1840–1950* (Cambridge, 2000), 261–86.

26 *LEM*, 21 June 1932.

27 *LEM*, 21 June 1932.

28 *LEM*, 4 May 1932.

29 *LEM*, 17 June 1932.

30 *LEM*, 17 June 1932.

31 *LEM*, 21 June 1932.

32 W. Kelly, *Royal Progresses and Visits to Leicester* (London, 1884), 600.

33 J. Simmons, *Leicester Past and Present, Volume One: Ancient Borough* (London, 1974), 150.

34 Information given by the Lord Mayor's Office, Leicester. The date 1867 is engraved on the back of the chain.

35 *LEM*, 15 December 1931.

36 *LEM*, 19 January 1932.

37 *LEM*, 25 April 1932.

38 *LEM*, 11 April 1932.

39 This list is based on a series of features in the *LEM* entitled 'the men and women behind the Pageant' published between February 1932 and May 1932.

40 *LEM*, 15 April 1932.

41 For example, *LEM*, 19 January 1932 and 11 April 1932.

42 *LEM*, 9 April 1932 in an article entitled 'Helping on the Pageant', the journalist observed that there were very many organisations in the city with dramatic societies and that there might not be enough principal parts to go round. Readers were urged to remember that 'a minor character in a crowd' could be just as important as a principal character.

43 *LEM*, 21 June 1932. These words were actually used by the Lord Mayor at the opening of Charles Street. However, the theme was a recurrent one.

44 Frank Lascelles' (1875–1934) pageants earned him the epithet 'the man who staged the empire'. They included: Carlisle (1928), Stoke-on-Trent (Wedgwood Bicentenary Celebrations) (1930), Rochester (1931), Bradford (1931), Barking (1931), Leicester (1932), Essex (1932), and Kent (1932). See *Oxford Dictionary of National Biography*.

45 *LEM*, 11 February 1932 and *The Surrey Advertiser* 24 June 2005. The article in *The Surrey Advertiser*, was in response to a recent exhibition in Guildford about the careers of professional pageant masters in the early decades of the twentieth century.

46 Hobsbawn, 'Introduction: Inventing Traditions', 1–14.

47 S. Gunn, *Public Culture*, 191.

48 *LEM*, 18 June 1932.

49 *LEM*, 4 April 1932.

50 *LEM*, 15 December 1931.

51 *LEM*, 15 December1931.

52 *LEM*, 27 January 1932.

53 Source: ROLLR, L 394 5, Letter from Laurie Pears to Mr Stevenson L 394 5.

54 *LEM*, June 18–30. This was general feature of the *LEM* during this period.

55 F.S. Herne, *The Historical Pageant of Leicestershire*, 46–7, and *LEM*, 17 June and 24 June 1932.

56 Herne, *Historical Pageant*, 46–7 and *LEM*, 20 June 1932.

57 Herne, *Historical Pageant*, 46–7 and see *LEM*, 17 June 1932 and 24 June 1932.

58 *The Times*, 16 June 1932. See also *The Times*, 22 June 1932 where there is also a favourable report of the Lord Mayor of London's visit to Leicester on Civic Day.

59 D.Reeder, 'The local economy' in D. Nash and D. Reeder (eds), *Leicester in the Twentieth Century* (Leicester, 1993), 54.

60 *LEM,* 4 May 1932 the suggestion here that Lloyd George would attend seemed to 'fizzle out'.
61 *LEM,* 19 January 1932.
62 *LEM,* 20 May 1932.
63 *LEM,* 24 June 1932.
64 *LEM,* 20 June 1932.
65 *LEM,* 20 June 1932.
66 *LEM,* 30 June 1932.

Notes to Chapter 8: Reinventing the city after 1945

1 http://www.britishpathe.com/video/king-and-queen-visit-leicester; http://freemp3x.com/king-george-vi-visits-leicester-england-april–30–1946-kings-speech-silent-mp3-download.html
2 *The Guardian,* 31 October 1946, 4c.
3 http://www.leicesterchronicler.com/war.htm
4 P.J. Larkham and K.D. Lilley, *Planning the City of Tomorrow: British Reconstruction Planning* (Pickering, 2001).
5 B. Beazley, *Post War Leicester* (Stroud, 2006), 32.
6 Konrad Smigielski was previously senior planning officer in Cracow before serving with the Polish forces during the war. *The Times,* 7 March 1962, 9g.
7 *The Times,* 13 Apr 1960, 7e. Brackets added.
8 *The Times,* 28 Oct 1966, 10a.
9 G. Ortolano, 'Planning the urban future in 1960s Britain', *The Historical Journal,* 54: 2 (2011), 491–2. http://youtu.be/GHjrFv4FMoM and http://liberalengland.blogspot.co.uk/2012/01/konrad-smigielski-and-destruction-of.html
10 British Railways Board, *The Reshaping of British Railways* (HMSO, London, 1963) and *The Development of the Major Railway Trunk Routes* (HMSO, London, 1965).
11 W.K. Smigielski, *Leicester Traffic Plan: Report on Traffic and Urban Policy* (Leicester, 1964).
12 *The Telegraph,* 10 December 2001, obituary Professor Sir Colin Buchanan. See also *The Times,* 5 November 1964, 5de, 'Traffic Plan for Leicester has national importance.'
13 *The Times,* 15 December 1969, 3a–f, 'Park 'n Ride' motto for Leicester.
14 *The Times,* 15 December 1969, 3hi.
15 *The Times,* 24 May 1971, 3a–c.
16 W.K. Smigielski. 'The planning of the Leicester of the future', in N. Pye (ed.), *Leicester and its Region,* 590–603, provides in his own words a vision for the future of Leicester.
17 For further information on the greening of Leicester see R. Rodger, 'The built environment', in D. Nash and D. Reeder (eds), *Leicester in the Twentieth Century,* 36–9.
18 *The Times,* 24 May 1971, 2c.
19 N. Pevsner, *The Buildings of England,* 47. The original plan in 1956 was to relocate the council offices to Victoria Park. The *Leicester Mercury* spearheaded a vigorous campaign against the proposal.
20 For comments in 1968 see the ATV documentary on Konrad Smigielski's market plans: http://www.macearchive.org/Archive/Title/meet-the-mayor–08121968-leicester/MediaEntry/1564.html
21 B. Beazley, *Postwar Leicester,* 75.
22 Census of England, 1881, Leicestershire. A number of those in North America and the empire were British citizens registered as born abroad and so inflate the numbers to some extent.
23 Hywel Maslen's comments on this point are gratefully acknowledged.
24 *Socialist Worker,* 18 July 1981.
25 It was the National Union of Hosiery and Knitwear Workers that failed to support the workforce in the Loughborough dispute. See *The Times,* 17 October 1974, 2
26 *Leicester Mercury,* 'Imperial: 9 Held in Battle with Police', 16 and 30 May 1974.
27 *Leicester Mercury,* 6 May 1974. The management of Imperial Typewriters mounted a vigorous statistical case to demonstrate non-white promoted staff was consistent with the overall racial balance of the workforce. See *Leicester Mercury,* 15 May 1974.
28 J. Herbert, *Negotiating Boundaries in the City: Migration, Ethnicity, and Gender in Britain* (Aldershot, 2008), 27.
29 J. Herbert, *Negotiating Boundaries,* 15, and personal correspondence, for which I am grateful.
30 Leicester Council of Faith, *Places of Worship in Leicester* (Leicester, 2004, updated).
31 J.P. Dunleavy, *The Politics of Mass Housing in Britain 1945–1975: A Study of Corporate Power, and Professional Influence in the Welfare State* (Oxford, 1981), 9–52.
32 The Ministry of Housing and Local Government, *Studies in Conservation* (HMSO London 1968).

See also MHLG, *Historic Towns: Preservation and Change* (London, 1968).

33 Civic Amenities Act 1967, c.69, Section 1. For an overview see D. Smith, 'The Civic Amenities Act: conservation and planning', *Town Planning Review*, 40:2 (1969), 149–62.

34 J. Delafons, *Politics and Preservation: A Policy History of the Built Heritage, 1882–1996* (London, 1997), 93–100.

35 Town and Country Planning Act, 1968, c.72.

36 Housing Act, 1980. The detailed arrangements and discounts have changed several times since they were first introduced.

37 Leicester City Council (subsequently LCC), Cabinet papers, 2004, s4941; Aylestone, Eyres Monsell & Freemen, Area Profile (2002), 10. Overall, council housing stock since 1982 has fallen by 15,000 to 22,000 in 2012, see LCC, Tenancy Strategy, 2012.

38 P. Balchin and M. Rhoden, *Housing Policy: an Introduction*, 3rd edn (London, 2002), 160. The five giants were: Squalor, Want, Disease, Ignorance, and Idleness.

39 *The Guardian*, 22 June 1994, p. 8, 'Trickle-down "of no help to the cities".'

40 The phrase is taken from E.K. Wyly and D.J. Hammel, 'Islands of decay in seas of renewal: housing policy and the resurgence of gentrification', *Housing Policy Debate*. 10:4 (1999), 716–20; M. Parkinson, 'The Thatcher government's urban policy 1979–1989', *Town Planning Review*, 60 (1989), 421–40.

41 *The Guardian*, 5 March 1994, 8. 'Inner city funding faces cut of 40pc'; R. Atkinson and G. Moon, 'The City Challenge initiative: an overview and preliminary assessment', *Regional Studies*, 28 (1994), 95.

42 *The Times*, 1 August 1991, 'Heseltine picks 11 city winners to share £41 million'.

43 LCC, Management Plan for Bede Park (Leicester, 2002), 27.

44 Six historic parks and gardens (Abbey, Belgrave Hall, New Walk, Victoria, and both Saffron Hill and Welford Road Cemeteries) were listed as Grade II status by English Heritage.

45 R. Atkinson and G. Moon, 'The City Challenge initiative', 94–7.

46 LCC, *The Quality of Leicester* (Leicester, 1993).

47 H. O'Brien and C. Tregaskes, *Bioblitz Leicester* (2010). For details of this annual event see http://www.leicester.gov.uk/bioblitz/

48 A. Darlow and L. Newby, 'Partnerships: panacea or pitfall? Experience in Leicester Environment City', *Local Environment: The International Journal of Justice and Sustainability*, 2:1 (1997), 73–81.

49 See http://www.forumforthefuture.org/project/sustainable-cities-index/more/2010-index

50 Danehills and Westcotes Drive were replaced by West End. Some other minor boundary changes were also made after 2003.

51 ONS, Communities and Local Government (2004) used the follow weights to calculate the Index of Multiple Deprivation: Income 22.5%; employment deprivation and disability 22.5%; health and disability 13.5%; education, skills and training 13.5%; barriers to housing and services 9.3%; crime .3%; living environment 9.3%.

52 ONS, Households by Deprivation Dimensions, 2011 (QS119EW).

53 Leicester City Council, *The Diversity of Leicester*: *Summary of Key Facts, 2011* (Leicester 2011). In 2005 'White' boys out-performed only 'Black' boys in examinations.

54 Leicester City Council, *Understanding Leicester: Ethnic Diversity, Young People and Deprivation* (2010).

55 NHS Leicester City, Directorate of Public Health and Health Improvement, 2010; Department for Education and Skills (DfES), 2005; http://www.dfes.gov.uk/rsgateway

56 Office of the Deputy Prime Minister, State of the English Cities, Report, 2006. In a survey of 56 towns and cities Leicester ranked 10th in terms of White/non-White segregation, 13th for White/Asian segregation and 25th for White/Black segregation in 2006. See also the Annual Labour Force Survey 2003.

57 Leicester Economic Survey, *Office Employment and Accommodation* (Leicester, 1984), 62.

58 I. Turok and N. Edge, *The Jobs Gap in Britain's Cities: Employment Loss and Labour Market Consequences* (Bristol, 1999), 7.

59 City Planning Department Industrial Surveys, 1950 and 1964.

60 I. Turok and N. Edge, *The Jobs Gap*, 16.

61 I. Turok and N. Edge, *The Jobs Gap*, 43. The net figures for 1995–2008 for other towns and cities were: Sunderland (+6%); Wigan (–20%); Stoke (–25%); Cardiff (–32%); Plymouth (–37%);

Coventry (–44%); Nottingham (–45%); Bristol (–53%); Edinburgh (–59%); Office of National Statistics, Annual Business Enquiry Employee Analysis, 2009.

62 S.S.Cohen and J. Zysman, *Manufacturing Matters: the Myth of the Post-Industrial Economy* (New York, 1987).

63 S.S.Cohen and J. Zysman, *Manufacturing Matters*, 14.

64 D. Reeder and R. Rodger, 'Industrialisation and the city economy', in M.J. Daunton (ed.), *Cambridge Urban History of Britain*, vol. 3 (Cambridge, 2000), 553–92.

65 I. Turok and N. Edge, *The Jobs Gap in British Cities*, 7.

66 LCC, http://citymayor.leicester.gov.uk/welcome/connecting-leicester/

Notes to Chapter 9: The transformation of home?

1 R.M. Pritchard, *Housing and the Spatial Structure of the City: Resident Mobility and the Housing Market in an English City Since the Industrial Revolution* (Cambridge, 1976), 3.

2 Joseph Dare, Unitarian missionary, estimated that there were around 1,500 back-to-backs in 1865; M. Elliott, *Victorian Leicester* (London, 1979), 105.

3 D. Nash and D. Reeder (eds), *Leicester in the Twentieth Century* (Stroud, 1993), 2.

4 The 1919 Housing and Town Planning Act ('Addison Act') was the first to provide central government subsidies to local councils.

5 D. Nash and D. Reeder, *Leicester*, 21.

6 B. Dobski, 'Highfields Remembered': http://highfields.dmu.ac.uk

7 George Smith's homepage: http://sgt-george-smith.co.uk/

8 L. Faire, '"A room of happiness and love": the functions and meanings of the working-class kitchen', paper to Urban History Group Annual Conference, March 2007; K.P Ellis, 'Childhood Memories', unpublished typescript, 1976, 6.

9 R. Battison, b. *c*.1928: Record Office for Leicester, Leicestershire and Rutland (ROLLR), interview 01223/01 CD CH/136.

10 L. Faire, 'Making home: working-class perceptions of space, time and material culture in family life, 1900–1955', Leicester University Ph.D. thesis, 1998, 79–83.

11 C. Hyde, *Walnut Street: Past, Present and Future: An Oral History of the Walnut Street Area of Leicester* (Leicester, 1995), 26.

12 J. Freeman, *The Making of the Modern Kitchen: A Cultural History* (Oxford, 2004), 72.

13 L. Faire, 'Making home', 51–2.

14 There was a shift from recording 'family' to 'household' size between 1911 and 1951.

15 These figures do not include those who had to share hot taps which was 2.1% in 1961 and 3.3% in 1971. The national average for those without a hot tap was 6.4% in 1971. *Census 1971, England and Wales County Reports: Leicestershire*, Part III (London, 1973), table 25, 2–3.

16 *Census for England and Wales: Housing Report 1951* (London, 1956), 67, cxi.

17 William Abbot, b.1918: ROLLR interview 0941/01CD LO/296/247.

18 L. Faire, 'Making home', 56–8.

19 Gerald Morris, b.1903: ROLLR interview 951 01CD LO/306/257.

20 Cited in B. Willbond, *A Home of Our Own: 70 Years of Council House Memories in Leicester* (Leicester, 1991), 55.

21 Barbara Cavanagh living in Green Lane Road in the 1920s; cited in B. Willbond, *A Home of Our Own*, 25.

22 C. Hyde, *Walnut Street*, 18.

23 Albert Hall, b.1907, in C. Brown (ed.), *Leicester Voices* (Stroud, 2002), 70; Hyde, *Walnut Street*, 18.

24 P. Orange, *My Recollections* (Oadby, 1974), 11.

25 M. Green, *The Boy Who Shot Down an Airship: The First Part of an Autobiography* [1988] (London, 1989), 20.

26 J. Burnett, *A Social History of Housing*, 2nd edn (London, 1986; repr. 1993), 214.

27 ROLLR, plan 13763, The Oval, New Walk: proposed new room and bathroom for Mr and Mrs Alpin (1880).

28 Eric Tolton, b.1916, 'Highfields Remembered'.

29 Burnett, *A Social History of Housing*, 224.

30 These were the Housing Act, 1923 (Chamberlain) and the Housing Act, 1924 (Wheatley) Acts.

31 Elsie Sutton: ROLLR interview 00752/01CA LO/120/071.

32 Albert Hall cited in Brown, *Voices*, 77.

33 Norman Pilgrim, b.1931: ROLLR interview 00850/01CA LO/214/165.

34 There were baths in Bath Lane and Vestry Street. The former were built in 1879 and the latter around 1892. A 1905 guide for Leicester recorded 32 and 36 slipper baths at the Bath Street and Vestry Street baths respectively: G.C. Nuttall, *Guide to Leicester and Neighbourhood* (Leicester, 1905), 105.

35 Frank Brooks, b.1929: ROLLR interview 00716/01CA, LO/083/035.

36 Sandy Coleman, b.1944: 'Highfields Remembered'.

37 C. Hyde, *Walnut Street*, 25.

38 Brett Pruce, b.1955: 'Highfields Remembered'.

39 C. Hyde, *Walnut Street*, 12.

40 Elsie Sutton: ROLLR interview 00752/01CA LO/120/071.

41 C. Hyde, *Walnut Street*, 17.

42 G.C. Nuttall, *Guide to Leicester*, 101.

43 *The City of Leicester Official Guide* (Leicester, 1937), 40, 12–13.

44 G.C. Nuttall, *Guide to Leicester*, 101.

45 Bel Weldon, b.1923, 'The Way We Were', unpublished typescript: ROLLR 001414/PM SP1008, 3.

46 Gordon Baker, b.1917: ROLLR interview 00607/01 CO CH/103/0184.

47 J. Burnett, *Social History of Housing*, 308.

48 C. Hyde, *Walnut Street*, 18.

49 A. Jackson, *The Diary of Ada Jackson 1883* (Leicester, 1993), 82–3.

50 L. Needleham, 'The demand for domestic appliances', *National Institute Economic Review*, 12 (1960), 27.

51 Winifred Dickens, b.1916: ROLLR interview 929 01CD LO/284/235.

52 Blanche Harrison, b.1917, in Brown, *Leicester Voices*, 71.

53 For a comparative perspective on household routines see L. Faire, 'Making home', ch. 7.

54 L. Faire, 'Making home', 153–4.

55 L. Faire, 'Making home', 155–6, 159–60.

56 Leicester Oral History Archive, 'Mining Memories', Tape 381, LO/001/C1.

57 C. Hyde, *Walnut Street*, 12.

58 Winifred Renshaw, *An Ordinary Life: Memories of a Balby Childhood* (Doncaster, 1984), chapter 18.

59 M. Essinger, *In My Fashion: Starting Work in the Heyday of Leicester's Knitwear Factories* (Wymeswold, 2005), 7.

60 C. Brown, *Voices*, 73–4.

61 Barbara Cavanagh in B. Willbond, *A Home of Our Own*, 24.

62 G.E. Miles, *Fragments from the Tapestry of Life: Short Stories from a Working-class Childhood on the 'Pool* (Leicester, 1995), 12.

63 A. Jackson, *Diary*, 17, 18.

64 J. Bourke, *Husbandry to Housewifery: Women, Economic Change, and Housework in Ireland, 1890–1914* (Oxford, 1993), 212–23.

65 P. Orange, *Recollections*, 12.

66 In 1948 it was estimated that 71.3% of the upper and upper middle classes had vacuum cleaners; 51.2% of the lower middle class; and of the remaining 71% of the population only 18% had one. By 1959 this latter figure had risen to 51.1%: Needleham, 'Domestic appliances', 27.

67 M.G. Skinner, 'Leicester' in C. Black (ed.), *Married Women's Work* [1915] (London, 1983), 222–3, 227.

68 C. Hyde, *Walnut Street*, 50.

69 Gerald Morris, b.1903: ROLLR interview 951 01CD LO/306/257.

70 The 1931 census for the city recorded that 18% of married women were in employment.

71 C. Langhamer, *Women's Leisure in England, 1920–60* (Manchester, 2000), 20.

72 D. Fowler, *The First Teenagers: The Lifestyle of Young Wage-earners in Interwar Britain* (London, 1995).

73 G.E. Miles, *Fragments*, 12.

74 A. Jackson, *Diary*, 20–1.

75 P. Orange, *Recollections*, 18.

76 V. Tedder, *Post War Blues* (Leicester, 1999), 102.

77 K.P. Ellis, 'Childhood memories', 2–3.

78 Cecil Bell: ROLLR interview 00719/01CA LO/087/038.

79 C. Hyde, *Walnut Street*, 26.

80 The guide estimated there were around 73,000 occupied dwellings in Leicester at the time, 40.

81 V. Tedder, *The Pantry Under the Stairs: Childhood Memories of World War II* (Leicester 1994), 85; and Essinger, *In My Fashion*, 7.

82 V. Tedder, *Post-War Blues*, 116; Essinger, *In My Fashion*, 73.

83 J. Needleham, 'Domestic appliances', 27.

84 M. Jancovich and L. Faire, with S. Stubbings, *The Place of the Audience: Cultural Geographies of Film Consumption* (London, 2003), 159.

85 M. Jancovich *et al.*, *Place of the Audience*, 160.

86 S. Bowden and A. Offer have argued convincingly for alternative reasons: S. Bowden, and A. Offer, 'Household appliances and the use of time: The United States and Britain since the 1920s', *Economic History Review* 47, 4 (1994), 725–48.

87 G.E. Miles, *Fragments*, 12. Majorie Marston, b.1942 in Highfields, also described playing cards and darts: Marjorie Marston, b.1932, 'Highfields Remembered'.

88 L. Faire, 'Making home', 227–9.

89 A. Jackson, *Diary*, 39; P. Orange, *Recollections*, 8.

90 A.H. Halsey, 'Leisure' in A.H. Halsey (ed.), *Trends in British Society Since 1900: A Guide to the Changing Social Structure of Britain*, 2nd edn (London, 1988), 564–5.

91 A survey of Glaswegian teenagers from the 1960s found that 82% of girls and boys interviewed claimed to read a daily newspaper. In answer to the question 'Do you read books?' 50% said yes: P. Jephcott, *Time of One's Own: Leisure and Young* People (Edinburgh, 1967), 162.

92 The house was intended to raise funds for a children's school and hospital; *Mirror Grange: The Book of the 'Daily Mirror's' House for Pip, Squeak and Wilfred* (London, c.1930).

Notes to Chapter 10: Wealthy city, healthy people?

1 For more information on the issues and themes covered in this chapter see J. Welshman, *Municipal Medicine: Public Health in Twentieth-century Britain* (Bern, 2000).

2 E.R. Frizelle and J.D. Martin, *The Leicester Royal Infirmary, 1771–1971* (Leicester, 1971).

3 See, for example, C.K. Millard, 'The influence of hospital isolation in scarlet fever: an appeal to statistics', *Public Health* (1901), 462–503.

4 Leicester Sanitary Committee, (subsequently LSC), *Annual Report of the MOH, 1902* (Leicester, 1903), 58.

5 LSC, *Annual Report of the MOH, 1909* (Leicester, 1910), 24–5.

6 Medical Research Committee, *First Report of the Special Investigation Committee Upon the Incidence of Phthisis in Relation to Occupations* (London, 1915), 2–21.

7 LSC, *Annual Report of the MOH, 1907* (Leicester, 1908), 42–5.

8 LSC, *Annual Report of the MOH, 1910* (Leicester, 1911), 42–3.

9 LSC, *Annual Report of the MOH, 1912* (Leicester, 1913), 35–8.

10 N. Williams and G. Mooney, 'Infant mortality in an "Age of Great Cities": London and the English provincial cities compared, c.1840–1910', *Continuity and Change*, 9:2 (1994), 185–212.

11 Record Office for Leicester, Leicestershire and Rutland (hereafter ROLLR): minutes of the Medical Services Special sub-committee, 20 February 1923, letter from A.H. Wood.

12 See, for example, Ministry of Health, *Hospital Survey: The Hospital Services of the Sheffield and East Midlands Area* (London, 1945).

13 J. Welshman, 'Eugenics and public health in Britain, 1900–40: scenes from provincial life', *Urban History*, 24, 1 (1997), 56–75.

14 Leicester Education Committee, *Annual Reports of the SMO, 1910–38* (Leicester, 1911–39).

15 ROLLR: minutes of the Medical Special Services sub-committee, 19 July 1937, SMO, 'Report by the MOH on the future School Medical Service and Child Welfare Clinic Service for the city of Leicester', 19 July 1937.

16 Leicester Education Committee, *Annual Reports of the SMO, 1912–38* (Leicester, 1913–39).

17 See, for example, E.K. Macdonald, 'The NHS Act, 1946, and the public health service', *Medical Officer*, 77 (1947), 251–3.

18 Leicester Health Committee (subsequently LHC), *Annual Report of the MOH, 1947* (Leicester, 1948), 44.

19 LHC, *Annual Report of the MOH, 1929* (Leicester, 1930), 6.

20 LHC, *Annual Report of the MOH, 1936* (Leicester, 1937), 82.

21 ROLLR: minutes of the Isolation Hospital, Dispensary and Venereal Disease sub-committee, 14 December 1938, 49.

22 ROLLR: minutes of the National Health Campaign sub-committee, E.K. Macdonald, 'National health campaign', 14 July 1937.

23 See C. Webster, *The National Health Service: A Political History* (Oxford, 1998; 2nd edn 2002).

24 See, for example, J. Welshman, 'Hospital provision, resource allocation, and the early National Health Service: the Sheffield Regional

Hospital Board, 1947–1974', in M. Pelling and S. Mandelbrote (eds), *The Practice of Reform in Health, Medicine, and Science, 1500–2000: Essays for Charles Webster* (Aldershot, 2005), 279–301.

25 Interview between the author and H. Mallett, Leicester, 13 January 1995.

26 LHC, *Annual Reports of the MOH, 1945–70* (Leicester, 1946–71).

27 J. Welshman, 'Tuberculosis and ethnicity in England and Wales, 1950–70', *Sociology of Health and Illness*, 22:6 (2000), 858–82.

28 LHC, *Annual Report of the MOH, 1953* (Leicester, 1954), 65–70, tables I–IV.

29 LHC, *Annual Report of the MOH, 1971* (Leicester, 1972), 11.

30 Leicester Education Committee, *Annual Reports of the SMO, 1950–70* (Leicester, 1951–71).

31 ROLLR, Health Committee Minutes, 16 October 1963, B.J.L. Moss, 'Report of MOH on proposal to create a post of health visitor with special responsibility for health education'.

32 ROLLR, Minutes of the Mental Health Services sub-committee, B.J.L. Moss, 'Mental Health', March 1960, 1–13.

33 J.B. Walker, 'Field work of a diabetic clinic', *Lancet* (1953), ii, 445–7; J.B. Walker and D. Kerridge, *Diabetes in an English Community:*

A Study of its Incidence and Natural History (Leicester, 1961).

34 Interview between the author and A. Buchan, 23 February 1994.

35 Department of Health and Social Security, *Prevention and Health – Everybody's Business: A Reassessment of Public and Personal Health* (London, 1976).

36 P. Townsend and N. Davidson, *Inequalities in Health: The Black Report* (Harmondsworth, 1982).

37 Parliamentary Papers, 1987–88, *Public Health in England*, 5, 20–1, 75.

38 J. Ashton and H. Seymour, *The New Public Health: The Liverpool Experience* (Milton Keynes, 1988).

39 Department of Health, *Saving Lives: Our Healthier Nation* (Cm 4386) (London, 1999), para 11.49.

40 Leicestershire Health, *Annual Report of the Director of Public Health 1995/96* (Leicester, 1996).

41 See http://www.phleicester.org.uk/.

42 Leicester City Primary Care Trust, *Improving Health in Leicester: Annual Report of the Director of Public Health and Health Improvement 2007* (Leicester, 2008), 56.

Notes to Chapter 11: Between Modernism and Conservation: Konrad Smigielski and the planning of post-war Leicester

I would like to acknowledge the generous assistance of George Wilson, Policy, Planning and Design at Leicester City Council, in providing materials for this chapter as well as sharing personal recollections of Konrad Smigielski. All images are from the City Council collection and are copyright of Leicester City Council.

 1 Cited in W.K.Smigielski, *Leicester Traffic Plan: Report on Traffic and Urban Policy* (Leicester, 1964), 17.

 2 *Leicester Mercury* (hereafter *LM*), 26 April 1972.

 3 For a discussion of Leicester's early planning in this context see P. Hall *et al.*, *The Containment of Urban England*, vol.1 (London, 1973), 551–65.

 4 Leicestershire Regional Town Planning Committee, *Regional Planning Report* (London, 1932).

 5 R. Rodger, 'The built environment' in D. Nash

and D. Reeder (eds), *Leicester in the Twentieth Century* (Stroud, 1993), 13–15.

 6 J.L. Beckett, *City Development Plan: Written Analysis* (Leicester, 1952), 4.

 7 Smigielski, *Traffic Plan*, 1.

 8 W.K. Smigielski, *Leicester Today and Tomorrow* (London, 1972), 41.

 9 Beckett, *City Development Plan*, 41.

10 J. Simmons, *Leicester Past and Present: Vol.2, Modern City, 1960–1974* (London, 1974), 86–7.

11 Record Office for Leicester, Leicestershire and Rutland (ROLLR), Biographical details in Smigielski Papers.

12 *Leicester City Council Minutes*, Report of the Town Planning Committee, 28 November 1961, 319.

13 *Leicester City Council Minutes*, Report of the Town Planning Committee, 27 March 1962, 535.

14 C. Buchanan, *Traffic in Towns: A Study of the*

Long Term Problems of Traffic in Urban Areas (London, 1963).

15 Smigielski, *Traffic Plan*, 3–4, 95.

16 Smigielski, *Leicester Today and Tomorrow*, 47.

17 H. Martin, 'Konrad Smigielski: my tempestuous love affair with Leicester', ROLLR, Smigielski Papers, 16.

18 Smigielski, *Traffic Plan*, 23.

19 'How to keep the cars away', *Observer*, 8 November 1964; 'City on the move', *Economist*, 213 (1964).

20 J. Moran, *Roads: A Hidden History* (London, 2009), 245–6.

21 Martin, 'Konrad Smigielski', 16.

22 Smigielski, *Leicester Today and Tomorrow*, 82ff.

23 For a wider discussion see M. Glendinning and S. Muthesius, *Tower Block* (New Haven, 1994).

24 B. Beazley, *Postwar Leicester* (Stroud, 2006), 53–8.

25 *Leicester City Council Minutes*, Report of Estates and Town Planning Committee, 25 January 1972; Smigielski, *Leicester Today and Tomorrow*, 62-6.

26 W.K. Smigielski, 'Urban form in the motor age', *Proceedings of the Newcastle upon Tyne Conference* (London, 1968), 327.

27 Smigielski, *Leicester Today and Tomorrow*, 69; Leicestershire Regional Town Planning Joint Advisory Committee, *Regional Planning Report*, 14.

28 *Leicester City Council Minutes*, Joint Reports of the Town Planning and Markets Committees, 27 July 1965 and 30 April 1968.

29 Smigielski, *Leicester Today and Tomorrow*, 60.

30 *Leicester City Council Minutes*, Report of the Town Planning Committee, 26 January 1965.

31 *LM*, 5 June 1973.

32 Smigielski, 'Urban form', 328.

33 *Leicester City Council Minutes*, Report of the Town Planning Committee, 25 March 1969.

34 Smigielski, *Leicester Today and Tomorrow*, 77.

35 *Leicester City Council Minutes*, Report of the Town Planning Committee, 25 July, 1967.

36 Recollection of George Wilson, Researcher/ Design Coordinator in Policy, Planning and Design, Leicester City Council.

37 *LM*, 14 August 1970.

38 *LM*, 21 August 1970.

39 Beazley, *Postwar Leicester*, 147.

40 *LM*, 4 August 1970 and 6 April 1972.

41 *LM*, 7 April 1972.

42 *LM*, editorial, 7 April 1972.

43 *LM*, editorial, 28 April 1972.

44 *LM*, 26 April 1972.

45 For a recent discussion of these developments more generally in post-war Britain see I. Boyd-White (ed.), *Man-Made Future* (London, 2007). A standard account is L. Esher, *A Broken Wave: the Rebuilding of England, 1940–1980* (London, 1981), 139–71.

46 J. Pendlebury, 'Alas Smith and Burns? Conservation in Newcastle upon Tyne city centre, 1959–68', *Planning Perspectives*, 16 (2001), 115–41.

47 P. Mandler, 'Old towns for new' in B. Conekin, F. Mort and C. Waters (eds), *Moments of Modernity: Reconstructing Britain, 1945–64* (London, 1999).

48 Martin, 'Konrad Smigielski', 18.

49 City of Leicester Housing Committee, *Clarendon Park General Improvement Area* (Leicester, 1971).

50 For an account of new urbanism see E. Talen, *New Urbanism and American Planning: The Conflict of Cultures* (London, 2005).

51 Interview with BBC Leicester, 'Changing Leicester', December 1971, East Midlands Oral History Archive, 01672.

Notes to Chapter 12: Gonna Rock Around the Clock (Tower) Tonight: Leicester and the Coming of 'the Sixties'

This chapter is dedicated to the memory of Eugene Cooper and the shop he kept in Wards End, Loughborough, in the 1950s and 1960s.

Many thanks to Paul Corrall; Simon Gunn; Richard Rodger; Colin Hyde of the East Midlands Oral History Archive; Laraine Porter; Tony Wadsworth and Stephen Butt at Radio Leicester, both of whom allowed me to broadcast requests for information; Peter Walker at the *Leicester Mercury* who printed a similar appeal and gave me much valuable historical material; Phil Giddings, who gave me access to ledgers recording the lettings of De Montfort Hall between 1944 and 1970; Glyn Essex; Christine Bradley; Dil Porter; John 'Jelly' Nixon; C.P. Lee; Mike Raftery at the Leicestershire County Records Office; Barry Suffolk; Sue Chambers; Beryl Simpson; Karin Patrick; Roland Stokes; Darren at *The*

Musician; the staff of Vaughan College, Leicester; and Pete Bramham who was kind enough to read the first draft of the essay and to make helpful suggestions as to how I might improve it.

1 Engelbert Humperdinck, with Katie Wright, *Engelbert: What's in a Name?* (London, 2004), 29.
2 A. Marwick, *The Sixties: Cultural Revolution in Britain, France, Italy and the United States c.1958–c.1974* (Oxford, 1998), 5
3 J. Stephens, *Anti-Disciplinary Protest: Sixties Radicalism and Postmodernism* (Cambridge, 1998), 10.
4 D. Kynaston, *Austerity Britain, 1945–51* (London, 2008), ix.
5 D. Sandbrook *White Heat: A History of Britain in the Swinging Sixties* (London, 2007), xvii.
6 J. Lahr, *Prick Up Your Ears: The Biography of Joe Orton* (Harmondsworth, 1980), 66.
7 R. Gosling, *Two Town Mad*, BBC television, 1963. Gosling revisited the towns in 2005; see www.bbc.co.uk/insideout/eastmidlands/series7/revisit.shtml (accessed 22 March 2009).
8 Local historian Mike Raftery has compiled books of press cuttings on the Leicester music scene. Reference is made here to these books and to the individual cuttings. The latter did not always have page numbers and might, occasionally, be ambiguous as to the newspaper of origin. 'LM' in biro usually could be taken to mean *Leicester Mercury*. Further information was obtained through appeals put out by BBC Radio Leicester, the *Leicester Mercury* and from personal contacts.
9 P. Willmott and M. Young, *Family and Kinship in East London* (Harmondsworth, 1957); K. Coates and R. Silburn, *Poverty: The Forgotten Englishmen* (Harmondsworth, 1970).
10 S. England *et al.*, *Leicester in the Fifties* (Runcorn, 1989), 18, 22–3, 27.
11 C. Brown, *Wharf Street Revisited: A History of the Wharf Street Area of Leicester*, Leicester, 1995), 7, 11, 111–15.
12 C. Hyde, *Walnut Street: Past, Present and Future* (Leicester, 1996), 5.
13 C. Hyde, *Walnut Street*, 23–4.
14 C. Hyde, *Walnut Street*, 31–51.
15 S. England, 59.
16 C. Hyde, *Walnut Street*, 33.
17 S. England, 58–60.

18 M. McIntosh, 'Let's Go Dancing!' *Illustrated Leicester Chronicle*, 17 October 1953, 4.
19 C. Hyde, 'Youth culture in the 1950s and 60s', *Talking History* [newsletter of the East Midlands Oral History Archive] No. 7, May 2003, 5.
20 V.A. Tedder, *Post War Blues* (Leicester, 1999), 55.
21 D. Bell, *Those Were the Days: Leicestershire in the Forties, Fifties and Sixties* (Newbury, 2001), 29.
22 I. Chambers, *Urban Rhythms: Pop Music and Popular Culture* (Basingstoke, 1985), 38.
23 D. Bell, *Those Were The Days*, 84.
24 A. Forrest, *Champions of Your Century, 1900–1999* (Newtown Linford, 1999), 97.
25 P. Morley, *Talk of the Town: Leicester in the 1950s and 60s* (Leicester, 1995).
26 *Illustrated Leicester Chronicle*, 8 September 1956, 1.
27 The concept of the moral panic was developed by Stanley Cohen, *Folk Devils and Moral Panics* (London, 1972).
28 N. Johnstone, *A Brief History of Rock 'n' Roll* (London, 2007). The term rock 'n' roll dates back, musically, to the 1940s and originated as a black American term for sex.
29 Interview with author, 27 March 2009.
30 For some recollection of this see www.wartimeleicestershire.com/pages/memoirs.htm: accessed 28 March 2009
31 *Leicester Evening Mail*, 4 February 1954, 13; M. Raftery (compiler), *Scrapbook of Leicestershire Popular Music (Vol. 1), 1950–1959* (Wigston, 1990), 3.
32 *Illustrated Leicester Chronicle*, 10 October 1954, 5; M. Raftery, *1950–1959*, 5–6.
33 *Leicester Evening Mail*, 21 June 1955; M. Raftery, *1950–1959*, 33.
34 *Leicester Evening Mail*, 19 July 1954; M. Raftery, *1950–1959*, 22.
35 *Leicester Evening Mail*, 9 May 1956; M. Raftery, *1950–1959*, 35–9.
36 M. Raftery, *1950–1959*, 9.
37 P. Bailey, 'Jazz at the Spirella: coming of age in Coventry in the 1950s', in B. Conekin, F. Mort and C. Waters (eds), *Moments of Modernity: Reconstructing Britain, 1945–1964* (London, 1999), 22–40.
38 M. Berger-Hamerschlag, quoted in M. Wright, *Beyond the Jiving: Margareta Berger-Hamerschlag, 1902–1958* (London, 2008), 11.
39 *Leicester Evening Mail*, 29 December 1956; M.

Raftery, *1950–1959*, 52.

40 C. McDevitt, *Skiffle: The Definitive Inside Story* (London, 1997) and M. Dewe, *The Skiffle Craze* (Aberystwyth, 1998).

41 Dewe, *The Skiffle Craze*, 19.

42 See D. Sandbrook, *Never Had It So Good: A History of Britain From Suez to the Beatles* (London, 2006), 469.

43 Dewe, *The Skiffle Craze*, 157.

44 *Leicester Evening Mail*, 9 September 1957; M. Raftery, *1950–1959*, 60. National Service in Britain lasted from 1945 to 1963.

45 *Leicester Evening Mail*, 4 November 1957, M. Raftery, *1950–1959*, 55.

46 Letter to author, 20 December 2008.

47 Sandbrook, *Never Had It So Good*, 472.

48 *The Illustrated [Leicester] Chronicle*, 2 February 1957, 3.

49 Unspecified Leicester evening paper, 15 November 1957; M. Raftery, *1950–1959*, 69.

50 Statement on German TV in 1990. See L. Cole, *Dusty Springfield: In the Middle of Nowhere* (London, 2008), 11.

51 Tommy Steele, *Bermondsey Boy* (London, 2006), 187–8.

52 E-mail to author, 22 December 2008.

53 *Leicester Mercury*, undated, July 1957, M. Raftery, *1950–1959*, 70.

54 *Illustrated Leicester Chronicle*, 7 February 1959; M. Raftery, *1950–1959*, 78.

55 *Leicester Mercury*, 9 March 1960, 9.

56 *Leicester Evening Mail*, 20 December 1962, 7; M. Raftery, *Scrapbook of Leicestershire Popular Music*, vol. 2, *1960–1969*, 14.

57 *Illustrated Leicester Chronicle*, 10 April 1964; M. Raftery, *Scrapbook, 1960–1969*, 32.

58 C. Hyde, *Talking History*, 5–6.

59 *Leicester Topic*, October 1964; M. Raftery, *Scrapbook, 1960–1969*, 40–1.

60 Interview with author, 12 January 2009.

61 Lewis' was a prestigious department store on Humberstone Gate, one of a chain that went into liquidation in 1990.

62 Interview with author, 31 March 2009.

63 Letter to author, 18 December 2008.

64 P. Morley, *Talk of the Town*.

65 I. Macdonald, *Revolution in the Head: The Beatles' Records and the Sixties* (London, 1998), 8.

66 B. Rushin, *Memories of a Leicester Drummer* (Loughborough, 2008).

67 M. Raftery, *Scrapbook, 1960–1969*, 27.

68 Interview with author, 6 January 2009.

69 P. Norman, *The Stones* (London, 1985), 48.

70 R. Bainton, *The Story of the Blues Band* Poole (Dorset, 1994), 27.

71 In an interview in 2004, quoted in *Independent on Sunday*, 9 April 2009, 51.

72 C. Turnell, '"Mr Showbiz"! The man who made Leicester a magnet for the world's top stars', *Leicestershire Chronicle*, 19 September 2007, 4–5.

73 *The Illustrated Leicester Chronicle*, 23 March 1961, 7.

74 Quoted in C. Harper, *Dazzling Stranger: Bert Jansch and the British Folk and Blues Revival* (London, 2006), 174.

75 B. Ward, *Just My Soul Responding: Rhythm and Blues, Black Consciousness and Race Relations* (London, 1998), 223.

76 D.N. Meyer, *Twenty Thousand Roads: The Ballad of Gram Parsons and His Cosmic American Music* (London, 2007), 366.

77 The Beatles largely defined 'The Mersey Sound' – not *vice versa*.

78 Forrest, *Champions of Your Century*, 32.

79 *Leicester Mercury*, 2 December 1963, 1

80 D.N. Meyer, *Twenty Thousand Roads*, 359–68.

81 *Leicester Chronicle*, 18 July 1969, 24.

82 *Leicester Mercury*, 23 August 1968, 1.

83 D. Bell, *Those Were the Days*, 80–1.

84 Dylan played De Montfort Hall in 1966. As at other venues on that tour, and despite having by then released three albums featuring electric instruments, Dylan was booed by some of the De Montfort audience when he brought out a band to play these instruments. Ten years on from Bill Haley, and beneath the headline 'Dylan Booed – but Stays Ahead on (Electric Points)', the *Illustrated Chronicle* welcomed this 'shouting electric poet and his all-steam rave band' and applauded an apparent move away from 'the moaning, protesting whining songs he was responsible for last year.' See J. Bauldie, *The Ghost of Electricity: Bob Dylan's 1966 World Tour* (1988), 158.

85 A phrase coined by Raphael Samuel in *Theatres of Memory, Vol. 1: Past and Present in Contemporary Culture* (London, 1994).

Notes to Chapter 13: Semi-detached Leicester: Social and cultural connections in suburban Leicester

1 *Leicester Mercury (LM)*, 24 January 1951.

2 Robert Putnam explores the changing nature of voluntary activity in America and its influence on social capital in his book *Bowling Alone: the Collapse and Revival of American Community* (London, 2000).

3 The *Journal of Urban History*, 27 (2001), 259–377, published a special issue on suburbanisation in America and acts as an excellent introduction to the complexities of twentieth-century suburbia. In Britain, Barry Doyle in 'The structure of elite power in the early twentieth-century city: Norwich 1900–35', *Urban History*, 24 (1997), 179–99 challenged the assumption of middle-class withdrawal in the city of Norwich during the years 1900–35, arguing increasing interest and civic participation in the pre-war period.

4 D. Nash and D. Reeder (eds), *Leicester in the Twentieth Century* (Leicester, 1993), 158.

5 R.J. Morris, 'Introduction: civil society, association and urban places: class, nation and culture in nineteenth-century Europe' in B. de Vries, R. J. Morris, and G. Morton (eds), *Civil Society, Association and Urban Places: Class, Nation and Culture in Nineteenth Century Europe* (Aldershot, 2006), 1–16, provides an overview of the emphasis often placed on Britain as a country deeply connected to associational affiliation as a means of constructing civil society. R.J. Morris, 'Clubs, societies and associations' in F.M.L. Thompson (ed.), *The Cambridge Social History of Britain, 1750–1950, Volume III* (Cambridge, 1990), 405–17.

6 *The Guardian*, 7 November 2006. When reading this article it is important to understand the different types of organisations that are included within the study. For instance, the survey made no distinction between free and paid-for memberships. The survey also included groups connected to retail organisations, i.e. Tesco club card. There is an important distinction to be made here between organisations people are members of and organisations that promote citizen engagement and contribute to the stock of social capital in towns and cities.

7 As early as 1909 C.F.G Masterman suggested in *The Condition of England* (London, 1960) that the urban middle classes had completely withdrawn from city life to privatised enclaves in the county and outer suburbs. Historians such as Morris, Savage and Thompson have similarly argued that during the twentieth century the urban middle class were unable to take on leading roles in urban life, as their identity was no longer associated with the urban but rather the suburban. For examples see R.J. Morris, 'Structure, culture and society in British towns' in M.J. Daunton (ed.), *The Cambridge Urban History of Britain, 1840–1950*, Volume III (Cambridge, 2001), 395–426; R.J. Morris and R. Rodger (eds), *The Victorian City: A Reader in British Urban History, 1820–1914* (London, 1983), 395–426; M. Savage, *Social Change and the Middle Classes* (London, 1995); F.M.L. Thompson, *The Rise of Suburbia* (Leicester, 1982).

8 S. Begley, 'Voluntary associations and the civic ideal in Leicester, 1870–1939', University of Leicester Ph.D. thesis, 2009.

9 A wide range of local clubs, societies and voluntary organisations were examined for this study, including: Bradgate Twinning Association, Leicester Asian Business Association, Leicester Amateur Operatic Society, Leicester Lawn Tennis Club, Leicester Philatelic Society, Leicester Photographic Society, Leicester Racial Equality Council, Leicester Society of Artists, Leicester Women's Luncheon Committee, Leicestershire Archaeological and Historical Society, Leicestershire Literary and Philosophical Society, Leicestershire Motor Car Club, Leicestershire Twinning Association, Leicestershire and Rutland Bat Group, Leicestershire and Rutland Rural Community Council, National Women's Register (Leicester Branch), Oadby Community Association and St. Martin's Parish Council Social Committee.

10 Distances between individual members' addresses and a common central point were measured and mapped using a batch geo-coder. In Table 13.1 the geo-coded results have been divided into two categories: the mean and median distance for each organisation. The mean distance has also been calculated omitting memberships 50 miles distant from Leicester. This is to prevent undue

distortion resulting from a few long-distance members, for example, where a member has relocated to Australia or where from a distance of over 50 miles from Leicester a member cannot reasonably be expected to be an active participant in monthly meetings or social gatherings. See L. Balderstone, 'Semi-detached Britain? Reviewing suburban engagement in twentieth-century society', *Urban History*, 41:1 (2014), 141–60.

11 In this context a suburb is defined as an area located at the edge of the urban core, a semi-rural location that remains a commutable distance from the urban core and is predominantly inhabited by middle-class residents. Taking into consideration the distance between the core and the edge of the city at north, east, south and westerly points, the average distance of an outer suburb of Leicester is approximately 3 miles.

12 H. Boynton, *A Prospect of Oadby, the Story of its Northern Development from 1902 to 1992* (Leicester, 1993), 53.

13 S.A. Royle, 'The development of small town Britain' in M.J. Daunton (ed.), *The Cambridge Urban History of Britain, Volume III*, 143.

14 In terms of changes in education during this period see D. Rubinstein and B. Simon, *The Evolution of the Comprehensive School* (London, 1969).

15 H. Cunningham, 'Leisure and culture', in F.M.L. Thompson (ed.), *The Cambridge Social History of Britain, 1750–1950, Volume II* (Cambridge, 1990), 317.

16 Interview with Jaffer Kapasee, founding member of the Leicester Asian Business Association, June 2007.

17 M. Farrar draws upon the residential distribution of the Jewish community in Leeds in his article 'The zone of the other: imposing and resisting alien identities in Chapel town, Leeds during the twentieth century' in S. Gunn and R.J. Morris (eds), *Identities in Space: Contested Terrains in the Western City since 1850* (London, 2001), 124.

18 C. Peach, *et al.*, 'Immigration and ethnicity' in A.H. Halsey (ed.), *British Social Trends since 1900: A Guide to the Changing Social Structure of Britain* (London, 1988), 592.

19 Private collection of minute books, Leicester Society of Artists, 6 October 1962.

20 These types of events are recorded throughout the minute books of the Leicester Society of Artists, specific examples can be found in the 1978 annual report and 6 June 1982.

21 N.J. Barnett and D.E.A. Crowther, 'Community identity in the twenty-first century: a postmodernist evaluation of local government structure', *International Journal of Public Sector Management*, 11 (1998), 429.

22 Scherer's argument relating to community and the importance of social exchange as a unifying agent is taken from in N.J. Barnett and D.E.A. Crowther, 'Community identity in the twenty-first century', 430.

23 M. Clapson, *Invincible Green Suburbs, Brave New Towns: Social Change and Urban Dispersal in Post War England* (Manchester, 1998), 156.

24 See Masterman, *The Condition of England*; Thompson, *The Rise of Suburbia*.

25 R. McKibbin, *Classes and Cultures. England, 1918–1951* (Oxford, 1998), 85.

26 B. Wood, 'Urbanisation and local government' in Halsey (ed.), *British Social Trends: A Guide to the Changing Social Structure of Britain*, 322–56.

27 H. Meller, *Towns, Plans and Society in Modern Britain* (Cambridge, 1997), 82.

28 *Transactions of the Leicestershire Archaeological and Historical Society* (TLAHS), 1963–64.

29 TLAHS, 1964–65.

30 TLAHS, 1964–65 1970–71; 1978–79; 1999–2000.

31 *Transaction Papers of the Leicestershire Literary and Philosophical Society* (TPLPS), 1998–99.

32 References to Society lectures can be found throughout the *TLAHS*, 1950–65 and their private archive collection 1950–2005.

33 *TLLPS*, 1950–51.

34 Private conversation with Vice-President of the University of Leicester Geophysical Society, Samuel Cheyney.

35 D.S. Nash, D. Reeder, P. Jones and R. Rodger (eds), *Leicester in the Twentieth Century* (Leicester, 1993).

36 See the special edition of the *Journal of Urban History*, 27 (2001), 259–377.

37 J.B. Smith, 'Urban elites *c*.1830–1930 and urban history', *Urban History*, 27 (2000), 275.

Notes to Chapter 14: Immigration and the emergence of multicultural Leicester

The research for this chapter was funded by the Leverhulme Trust.

1 The plan was drawn up in 2000. See R. Bonney and W. Le Goff, 'Leicester's cultural diversity in the context of the British debate on multiculturalism', *International Journal of Diversity in Organisations, Communities and Nations*, 6 (2007), 46.

2 Office for National Statistics, *Census 2001. Key Statistics for Local Authorities in England and Wales* (London, 2003), 89.

3 'Creating golden smiles out of the Golden Mile', *Leicester Mercury*, 13 April 2001.

4 Leicester City Council website, 'About Leicester', http://www.leicester.gov.uk/about-leicester accessed 13 May 2008.

5 K. Myers, 'Historical practice in the age of pluralism: educating and celebrating identities', in K. Burrell, and P. Panayi (eds), *Histories and Memories: Migrants and their Histories in Britain* (London, 2006), 40. The importance of acknowledging the value of different cultural identities is also a prominent theme in the City Council's cultural strategy for the city. See Leicester City Council. *Leicester: A Culturally Diverse City. Cultural Strategy Action Plan, 2006–2008* (Leicester, 2004).

6 T. Cantle, *Community Cohesion, A Report of the Independent Review Team* (London, 2002).

7 'Side by side', *The Guardian*, 1 January 2001; N. Loney, 'Oldham should match Leicester' (lessons from Leicester's race relations experience), *Regeneration and Renewal*, 22 June 2001, 12, 'A British city finds that tolerance is good business', *The New York Times International*, 8 February 2001.

8 C. Brown, 'Moving on: reflections on oral history and migrant communities in Britain, *Oral History*, 34, 1 (2006), 69–80; G. Singh, 'Multiculturalism in contemporary Britain: reflections on the "Leicester model"', *International Journal on Multicultural Societies*, 5, 1 (2003), 41–54, R. Bonney and W. Le Goff, 'Leicester's cultural diversity', 45–58; A. Amin, 'Ethnicity and the multicultural city: living with diversity', *Environment and Planning A*, 3: 4 (2002), 959–80.

9 The Indian population numbered 72,033 in 2001 and comprised 25.7% of Leicester's population. Office for National Statistics, *Census 2001.* 89.

10 J. Martin and G. Singh, *Asian Leicester* (Stroud, 2002), 9, and Singh, 'Multi-culturalism in contemporary Britain', 42.

11 This included a policy of employing minority staff, celebrating diversity as well as using inner city development funds to create new minority ethnic leadership within the city.

12 J. Martin and G. Singh, *Asian Leicester,* 13.

13 Hence H. O'Connor's title, 'The Irish in Leicester: an invisible community', in N. Jewson (ed.), *Migration Processes and Ethnic Divisions* (Leicester, 1995), 47–65.

14 S. Narain, 'Sikhs in Leicester', in N. Jewson, *Migration Processes and Ethnic Divisions*, 90–1; L. Chessum, *From Migrants to Ethnic Minority: Making Black Community in Britain* (Aldershot, 2000), 62.

15 See *Leicester Mercury*, 28 August 1958, which contrasted the racial violence in Nottingham to the tolerance of Leicester. See also Brown, 'Immigrant communities in Leicester', 9; African Caribbean Support Group Research Project; J. Benyon, B. Dauda, J. Garland and S. Lyle, *African Caribbean People in Leicestershire* (Leicester, 1996), 36.

16 The area encompassed the Wycliffe, Spinney Hill and Charnwood wards of the city.

17 Belgrave included the wards of Belgrave and parts of Abbey and Latimer.

18 J. Herbert, *Negotiating Boundaries in the City: Migration, Ethnicity and Gender in Britain,* (Aldershot, 2008), 20–1; Burrell, *Moving Lives,* 34–40; L. Chessum, *From Migrants to Ethnic Minority,* 33.

19 D. Nash and R. Reeder (eds), *Leicester in the Twentieth Century* (Stroud, 1993), 184.

20 A. Newman, 'Sir Israel Hart', *Transactions of the Leicestershire Archaeological and Historical Society,* 49 (1973–74), 56.

21 R. Ash, 'Jewish migration and community development in nineteenth-century Leicester', in Jewson, *Migration Processes and Ethnic Divisions,* 41–2. Hart and Levy was the main Jewish tailoring firm which employed many hundreds of people.

22 For the Irish see M. Elliot, *Victorian Leicester*

(London, 1979), 118–21.

23 L. Chessum, *From Migrants to Ethnic Minority*, 58.

24 This, however, was numerically small compared to other parts of Britain. For example, in 1981 Greater London had 33,500 Poles, Lancashire 14,500 and West Yorkshire 13,500. Leicestershire had 3,200. See K. Burrell, 'Migrant memories, migrant lives: Polish national identity in Leicester since 1945', *Transactions of the Leicestershire Archaeological and Historical Society*, 76 (2002), 60.

25 K. Burrell, *Moving Lives*, 13–14.

26 Interview with second generation Polish woman, 9 February, 2001; K. Burrell, 'Migrant memories, migrant lives', 73.

27 K. Burrell, *Moving Lives*.

28 In 1981 they numbered 528 just 1% of the foreign born population. K. Burrell, *Moving Lives*, 14.

29 The small size of the community is referred to in D. Nash and D. Reeder, *Leicester in the Twentieth Century*, 186. This is not to suggest that Italian community activities did not exist: Sunday mass was held in a house on Fosse Road South, and another Italian mass on Hinckley road, monthly, K. Burrell, *Moving Lives*, 144, 155.

30 H. O'Connor, *The Spatial Distribution of Ethnic Minority Communities in Leicester, 1971, 1981, 1991: Analysis and Interpretation* (Leicester, 1995), 8.

31 H. O'Connor, 'The Irish in Leicester', 47.

32 See The Emerald Centre, http://www.irishinleicester.org.uk/

33 H. O'Connor, *The Spatial Distribution of Ethnic Minority Communities in Leicester*, 25. However, the census has underestimated the Caribbean-born population and in 1961 the population was more likely to be 2,694. See L. Chessum, *From Migrants to Ethnic Minority*, 49. For problems with the census data see L. Chessum, *From Migrants to Ethnic Minority*, 5–8.

34 L. Chessum, *From Migrants to Ethnic Minority*, 42; J. Benyon *et al.*, *African Caribbean People*, 36.

35 D. Phillips, 'The social and spatial segregation of Asians in Leicester', in P. Jackson and S. Smith (eds), *Social Interaction and Ethnic Segregation* (London, 1981), 108. They migrated from Uganda, Kenya, Tanzania and Malawi.

36 L. Chessum, *From Migrants to Ethnic Minority*, 59.

37 V. Marett, *Immigrants Settling in the City* (Leicester, 1989), 39.

38 D. Nash and D. Reeder, *Leicester in the Twentieth Century*, 107–8,

39 B. Troyna and R. Ward, 'Racial antipathy and local opinion leaders: a tale of two cities', *New Community*, IX, 3 (1982), 454.

40 B. Troyna, *Public Awareness and the Media: A Study of Reporting on Race* (London, 1981).

41 See EMOHA, CHC, CH/095/0104, P. Winstone.

42 The Imperial Typewriter strike is seen as a pivotal event in South Asian resistance against racism. See R. Moore, *Racism and Black Resistance in Britain* (London, 1975), ch. 5. See also chapter 8 on Bedaux system and the Imperial Typewriter dispute.

43 In particular, according to Marett the demise of the National Front was due to the efforts of the Inter Racial Solidarity campaign and the increase in South Asian councillors within the Labour party. V. Marett, *Immigrants Settling in the City*, 59.

44 For example in employment the majority of South Asians and African Caribbeans were concentrated in unskilled manual work, particularly in traditional industries. This work was characterised by low pay, job insecurity, unsociable hours and health risks For the national level see D.J. Smith, *The Facts of Racial Disadvantage: A National Survey* (London, 1976), C. Brown, *Black and White Britain: The Third PSI Survey* (London, 1984).

45 'Immigration and education. The view from the blackboard', *Leicester Mercury*, 16 December 1968. See also 'Teaching the new Britons', *Leicester Mercury*, 15 February 1964.

46 L. Chessum, *From Migrants to Ethnic Minority*, 236.

47 Highfield Rangers Oral History Group, *Highfield Rangers. An Oral History* (Leicester, 1993).

48 J. Williams, 'The story of Highfield Rangers: a 'black voluntary oral history project', *Oral History*, 22:1, (1994), 76. Although they met considerable racism from other teams, Highfield Rangers developed into a successful senior football club.

49 Riots involved black and white youths and occurred in other parts of Britain, such as Brixton and Toxteth.

50 S. Vertovec, 'Multicultural, multi-Asian, multi-Muslim Leicester: dimensions of social

complexity, ethnic organisation and local government interface', *Innovation,* 7:3 (1994), 270.

51 Interview with Mandy, 28 May 2002.

52 S. Vertovec, 'Multicultural, multi-Asian, multi-Muslim Leicester', 270.

53 R.T. Gale, 'Pride of place and places. South Asian religious groups and the city planning authority in Leicester', paper in *Planning Research,* 172 (Cardiff, 1999), 10. By 2002, there were twenty mosques, six gurdwaras, at least eighteen Hindu temples and one Jain temple in Leicester. See R. Bonney, 'Understanding and celebrating religious diversity: the growth of diversity in Leicester's places of religious worship since 1970', *Studies in the History of Religious and Cultural Diversity,* Academic Papers (Leicester, 2003), 30.

54 Highfields Library (HL), Leicestershire Multicultural Archive Project, Highfields Remembered Archive (HRA), Councillor F. Subedar.

55 The British Library National Sound Archive (BLNSA), Millennium Memory Bank collection. (MMB), C900/00006, J. Musa was the cinema manager of the Natraj. He claimed that cinema audiences declined in the late 1970s and 1980s with the growth of videos, thus the Natraj closed.

56 BL, NSA, C900/00011 R. Saujani.

57 For more in-depth analysis, such as the experiences of women within these communities see K. Burrell, *Moving Lives* and J. Herbert, *Negotiating Boundaries in the City.*

58 C. Brown, 'Moving on: reflections on oral history

and migrant communities in Britain', *Oral History,* 34:1 (2006), 75.

59 L. Chessum, *From Migrants to Ethnic Minority.*

60 A survey in 1996 revealed that nearly half of respondents did not believe that African Caribbean people have an effective political voice compared to other groups in Leicester. Although a number of African Caribbean associations exist, 57% of respondents had no knowledge of these groups. See J. Benyon *et al., African Caribbean People,* 136. Within South Asian communities there are also important differences and a survey of Leicester revealed that Pakistanis and Bengalis alongside the African Caribbeans felt they had been unsuccessful in obtaining resources regarding regeneration and voluntary sector funding. See A. Ali, C. Dallison, D. Kaur, H. Joshua and S. White, *Taking Forward Community Cohesion in Leicester* (Leicester, 2002).

61 For Islamophobia following 9/11 see J. Herbert and R. Rodger, 'Narratives of South Asian Muslim women, 1964–2004', *Oral History,* 36:2 (2008), 554–63. There were also attacks on Hindu businesses and temples following the destruction of a mosque in Ayodhya in 1992 by Hindu nationalists. For the growth of Hindu Nationalism see P. Mukta, 'Hindutva in the West: mapping the antinomies of diaspora nationalism', *Ethnic and Racial Studies,* 23:3 (2000), 407–41. For tensions between Sikhs and Hindus see Narain, 'Sikhs in Leicester'.

62 Interview with Panna, 25 February 2008.

63 Interview with Nisha, 27 February 2008.

Notes to Chapter 15: Contesting Liberty

1 Leicester Group of the Victorian Society (subsequently LGVS) Buildings Sub-Committee Report, 5 May 2001. Held in the LCC Planning Archives, File Number: UPRN LPG 5868.

2 Building Plans, 1919, Number 23685, Held in Record Office for Leicester, Leicestershire and Rutland Record Office (ROLLR).

3 National Monuments Record Office, Swindon, Listed Building Description of the Liberty Building, SK 5803–5903.

4 M.J. Miller, *The Representation of Place, Urban Planning and Protest in France and Great Britain, 1950–1980* (Aldershot, 2003), 17.

5 *Leicester Mercury* (subsequently *LM),* 8 August

1998, 8.

6 *LM,* 2 May 2001, 4.

7 *LM,* 14 December 2001, 3.

8 P. Hubbard, 'The value of conservation: a critical review of behavioural research, *Town Planning Review,* 64:4 (1993), 359–74, especially 366.

9 Miller, *Representation of Place,* 29.

10 Hubbard, *Town Planning Review,* 64:4 (1993), 363.

11 Letter, LGVS to the Department of National Heritage, 1 December 1993. Private File of the Secretary of the Leicester Group of the Victorian Society.

12 Grade II status in England applies to buildings of 'special interest' and is the third category behind

Grade I buildings which are of 'exceptional interest' and Grade II* which are considered to be of more than special interest.

13 Letter from LCC Conservation Department to LGVS, 20 October 1995.

14 Letter LGVS to Director of Environment and Development LCC, 7 October 1995.

15 Letter from the Victorian Society Chairman to LCC's Chief Executive, 10 May 1998.

16 Letter, Victorian Society Chairman to LCC Chief Executive, 10 May 1998.

17 Leicester Group of the Victorian Society Buildings Sub-Committee Report, 5 May 2001. Held in the LCC Planning Archives, File Number: UPRN LPG 5868.

18 *LM* headlines, 2 May 2001, 13 April 2002, 26 April 2002, 14 December 2001.

19 Structural Survey of Liberty Works, 24 September 1990, 3. Held in the LCC Planning Archives, File Number: UPRN LPG 5868.

20 Structural Survey carried out in November 2000, point 1.2.

21 Structural Survey point 5.0.

22 Structural Survey point 5.1.

23 Structural Survey Report, January 2001.

24 Structural Survey Report, January 2001.

25 Structural Survey Report, January 2001

26 English Heritage Conservation Engineering Team, Internal Memorandum, 28 June 2001. English Heritage Regional Office, Northampton, Liberty File.

27 e mail from the Leicester Civic Society to Leicester City Council (subsequently LCC), 7 May 2001. Held in the LCC Planning Archives, File Number: UPRN LPG 5868.

28 City Challenge, *Leicester City Challenge Bid* (Leicester, 1992), 8.

29 Planning Refusal Number 87/1958/5, 19 November 1987. The casino was seen as a particularly inappropriate use for the building. Interview with Planning Officer, LCC, December 2005.

30 See LCC Planning Applications for Site Ref (UPRN) LPG5868.

31 LCC, *Leicester Local Plan* (Leicester, 1992) 6.

32 *Leicester Local Plan,* 47.

33 Mission Statement of City Challenge found in City Challenge, *Annual Report 1994–95*, (Leicester: City Challenge, 1995), 2.

34 Interview with City Challenge Officer, January 2007.

35 Letter from the developers to LCC, 7 December 2001.

36 LCC, Development Control Sub-Committee Report, December 2001, 26.

37 LCC, Development Control Sub-Committee Report, December 2001, 26.

38 Letter from Leicester Regeneration Company to the developers, 3 September 2001.

39 LCC, Development Control Sub-Committee Report, December, 2001, 26.

40 English Heritage, Memorandum, 12 February 2002. English Heritage Regional Office, Northampton, Liberty File.

41 Objection letter from Resident A, 3 May 2001. Held in the LCC Planning Archives, File Number: UPRN LPG 5868.

42 *LM*, 28 October 2003, 17.

43 *LM*, 26 April 2002, 4.

44 LCC, Development Control Sub-Committee Report, 18 December 2001, 29. Held in the LCC Planning Archives, File Number: UPRN LPG 5868.

45 *LM*, 19 April 2001, 3.

46 English Heritage, Memorandum, 12 February 2002, point 1.1. English Heritage Regional Office, Northampton, Liberty File.

47 *LM*, 9 October 2002, 15.

48 Not all residents wanted to see the building retained, indeed some viewed it as an eye-sore but they were displeased with the projected plans for student accommodation. This was substantiated by the recently converted Benjamin Russell building which had caused noise pollution, traffic congestion and car parking problems in the area.

49 *LM*, 21 April 2001, 7.

50 *LM*, 21 April 2001, 3.

51 *LM*, 2 May 2001, 4.

52 *LM*, 28 April 2001, 16.

53 Listed Building Consent, Application Number 20010590, 14 February 2002, p. 2. Held in the LCC Planning Archives, File Number: UPRN LPG 5868.

54 Letter from OEA Architects to LCC, 12 May 2003.

55 Planning Application, Case Number 20081115, 26 June 2008, 3. Accessed on http://fdweb.leicester.gov.uk/planning/fdweb/Image.aspx?pbfc=962 14 February 2009.

56 Planning Application, Case Number 20081115, 26 June 2008, 2.

57 *LM,* 'Our Symbol of Hope', Letters Page, 16 January 2009.

58 H.P.M. Winchester, 'The construction and destruction of women's roles in the urban landscape', 140 in N. Moore and Y. Whelan (eds), *Heritage, Memory and the Politics of Identity, New Perspectives on the Cultural Landscape* (Aldershot, 2007), 97.

59 W.D. Lipe, 'Value and meaning in cultural resources' in H.F. Cleere (ed.), *Approaches to the Archaeological Heritages* (Cambridge, 1984), 2.

60 Fax between LCC officers, 14 May 2001. Held in the LCC Planning Archives, File Number: UPRN LPG 5868.

61 Assessment of the Redevelopment of the Liberty Building, Leicester, September 2001.

62 *LM,* 'Causing concern: an artist's impression of the controversial development which could result if the Liberty Building is demolished', 27 April 2001, 3.

63 Miller, *The Representation of Place,* 16.

64 English Heritage, Memorandum, 12 February 2002, point 4.6. English Heritage Regional Office, Northampton, Liberty File.

Notes to Chapter 16: The spirit of the city: what is Leicester's *genius loci*?

1 *Genius loci* refers to the distinctive atmosphere or pervading spirit of a place.

2 A. Mee, *Leicestershire and Rutland* (Rotherham, 1997), 5.

3 R. Gosling, 'Two Town Mad' (BBC Documentary, 1963).

4 J.B. Priestley, *English Journey* (London, 1934), 118.

5 J.B. Priestley, *English Journey,* 118.

6 A. Mee, *Leicestershire,* 5.

7 'Does Britain have plural cities?': http://www.manchester.ac.uk/discover/news/article/?id=9329

8 Leicester Foxes, the nickname of Leicester City was said to originate from the tradition of foxhunting in Leicestershire and thus was not related to an industrial occupation but rather a leisure pursuit.

9 For a comparison on the rate of deindustrial decline in British cities see the report by I. Turok and N. Edge, *The Jobs Gap in Britain's Cities: Employment Loss and Labour Market Consequences* (Bristol, 1999).

10 'The Leicester Song', Words by Dominic Le Foe, music by Peter Greenwell, Expo Leicester '72 Ltd Archive.

11 Leicester and Leicestershire Economic Partnership (LLEP), *Leicester & Leicestershire Economic Assessment* (Leicester, 2011) ch. 3, p. 7.

12 Leicester City Council (LCC), *Leicester Economic Action Plan: A Plan for Jobs and Growth: 2012 to 2020* Confident City, theme five.

13 LCC, *Economic Action Plan,* 13.

14 A. Mee, *Leicestershire and Rutland,* 6.

15 'Leicester article', *The Times,* 15 December 1969, 2.

16 G. Singh, 'Multiculturalism in contemporary Britain: reflections on the "Leicester Model"', *International Journal on Multicultural Societies* (IJMS), 5:1, 2003, 45.

17 LCC, *Economic Action Plan,* 32.

18 For more on the relationship between Leicester and Rajkot please see http://www.leicester-rajkot.co.uk

19 LLEP, *Leicester and Leicestershire Economic Assessment* (Leicester, May 2010), 12.

20 See *Leicester Mercury*: http://www.leicestermercury.co.uk/City-spotlight-textile-boost/story–12041696-detail/story.html and http://www.leicestermercury.co.uk/Far-Eastern-costs-boost-textile-firm/story–12038789-detail/story.html

21 LLEP, *Leicester and Leicestershire Structural and Investment Funds Strategy 2014–20,* (Leicester, 2014), 11.

22 M. Lalani *et al., How Place Influences Employment Outcomes For Ethnic Minorities,* Joseph Rowntree Foundation, May 2014, 23.

23 UK Business Counts 2014 from NOMIS: https://www.nomisweb.co.uk/reports/lmp/la/1946157130/report.aspx?town=leicester

24 Lalani, *How Place Influences,,* 12; NOMIS: https://www.nomisweb.co.uk/reports/lmp/la/1946157130/report.aspx?town=leicester

25 LLEP, *Structural and Investment Funds,* 10.

26 LCC, *Diversity and Migration,* (Leicester, December 2012) (draft version), 1.

27 LCC, *Diversity and Migration,* 2.

28 See House of Commons Research Briefing: *Directly-Elected Mayors,* 22 October 2014 for more details of the local authorities with elected

mayors and of the cities who voted against elected mayors. http://www.parliament.uk/business/ publications/research/briefing-papers/SN05000/ directlyelected-mayors

29 LCC, *Economic Action Plan*, 29.

30 LCC, *Economic Action Plan*, 30.

31 LCC, *Economic Action Plan*, 31.

32 LCC, *Economic Action Plan*, 31.

33 LCC, *Economic Action Plan*, 29.

34 Since 2012 Leicester has secured £22 million of European funding for projects within the city. LCC, *City Mayor's Delivery Plan 2014–15* (Leicester, 2014), 6.

35 LCC, *Story of Leicester Plan* (Leicester, November 2013), 1.

36 LCC, *Economic Action Plan*, 30.

37 A. Mee, *Leicestershire*, 5.

38 A. Mee, *Leicestershire*, 5.

39 *Genius loci* refers to the distinctive atmosphere or pervading spirit of a place whereas the plural form *genii loci* is used for multiple spirits of a single place.

Index

Note: * indicates an illustration

Index of streets and districts

Note * indicates an illustration

Duxbury Road 253

East Bond Street 54*
East Hamilton 200
East Park Road 10, 196
Evington 27, 43*, 47, 133, 189*, 209, 222*, 224, 236, 250, 302, 307, 341
Eyres Monsell 179, 180*, 197, 200, 205, 209, 257, 266, 273, 294

Filbert Street 5, 10
Fleet Street Terrace 227
Fosse Road 10, 27
Freake's Ground 5, 133
Freemen's Common 5
Friar Lane 54, 61

Gallowtree 10
Gallowtree Gate 9
Gilroes 144–9, 146*, 149*, 154*
Glenfrith Way 149
Granby Street 10, 23, 26, 157
Granville Street 10
Grasmere Street 10
Great Central Street 38*, 184
Great Central Way 202
Grey Friars Street 10
Groby Road 247
Gypsy Lane 5, 47, 300, 367

Haddenham Road 253
Halford Street 301
Harvey Lane 54, 56, 61
Havelock Street 294*, 295
Haymarket Centre 286
Hazel Street 10
High Street 10, 41*, 186, 193, 239, 240*, 269*, 288
Highcross Street 15, 217
Highfields 26, 190, 194–5, 220, 273
Highfield Street 43*
Hinckley Road 10
Holy Bones 10
Horsefair Street 10, 289
Humberstone 27, 200, 205, 254
Humberstone Road 10, 62, 115, 268*, 297*, 306, 371
Humberstone Garden Suburb 29*
Humberstone Gate 37, 45, 67*, 68–9, 133, 177*, 296, 311, 371
Humberstone Park 202

Jarrom Street 10, 62*
Jubilee Square 371

Keyham Lane 29*
King Street 128, 133
King Richard III Road 19, 47, 62, 214, 363
Kirkby Road 63*
Knighton 27, 81, 119*, 133, 140, 202, 205, 208, 209
Knighton Fields 32
Knighton Park 205

Lancaster Road 10, 113
Lansdowne 26
London Road 17, 25–7, 31*, 223*, 269*, 271, 288, 307, 338, 377*, 338
Loseby Lane 10
Loughborough Road 223*

Mandela Park 5
Manor Road 26
Market Place xiii, 10, 40*, 103*, 159*, 189*, 190, 276*, 283*, 284–8, 291, 371, 373
Market Street 26
Martin Street 115
Melbourne Road 335, 340, 341
Melton Road 158*, 270*, 298*, 299
Mere Road 10
Mowmacre Hill 266, 294
Museum Square 286, 316*

Napier Street 10
Narborough 245
Narborough Road 27, 32, 335
Netherhall Road 262
Newfoundpool 27, 28*, 47, 133, 236
New Bond Street 306
New Street 18, 20
New Walk xiii, 3, 4*, 5, 129, 187, 189*, 199, 222, 227, 279, 285, 286*, 287, 291, 327
New Parks 178, 179*, 189*, 208–9, 221, 252, 294
Newarke Street 10, 183, 184*
Northampton Street 10, 111*
Northgate Street 10
North Evington 47
North Gate 181*
Nottingham Road 296

Oadby 186, 315, 318
Oxford Street 92*, 295*